D0514872

HIGH SCHOOL
@HOME

YOU CAN DO IT!

DIANA JOHNSON

B&H
PUBLISHING GROUP

ISBN: 978-0-8054-4545-9

Published by B&H Publishing Group,
Nashville, Tennessee

Dewey Decimal Classification: 371.042
Subject Heading: HOME SCHOOLING \ HIGH SCHOOLS

1 2 3 4 5 6 7 8   10 09 08 07

CONTENTS

ACKNOWLEDGMENTS

With special thanks to:

My heavenly Father, Who leads me down paths that continually surprise me.

My husband, John, who encouraged us to try homeschooling in the first place. Of all the projects we've undertaken together, homeschooling has certainly been the biggest!

My children, Brian, Cara, John Aaron, Grace, and Hannah, the true guinea pigs of our schooling adventure. Thank you for never once begging me to put you in "regular" school! I'm proud of each one of you.

David, my manager at The Scroll Christian Bookstore. Your untiring help made the first edition of this book happen. I fully appreciate that this expanded edition wouldn't exist without having had your earlier help.

Dana, who has read what I have written and offered suggestions in her usual encouraging and enthusiastic style. Your help was always carefully crafted despite the busyness of your life. You are amazing!

Bamma, my coworker and dear friend. Your wisdom and tender heart have blessed the ministry of The Scroll's homeschool department and me. Your thoughts have helped form mine.

The customers at The Scroll Christian Bookstore who have freely shared their homeschool triumphs and struggles with me. This book has greatly benefited from your knowledge and in-the-trenches experiences.

The folks at B&H Publishing Group, who were willing to work with a little-known homeschool mom and pastor's wife from East Texas. Thank you!

A NOTE FROM THE AUTHOR

This guide was originally written as a service to our homeschool customers at The Scroll Christian Bookstore where, over the last fourteen years, I have worked part-time developing and managing a homeschool department. Since writing this guide, I have had the opportunity to revise it a number of times, improving and expanding it as I learned from my own homeschool successes and failures and those of my customers.

This latest edition, published by B&H Publishing Group, is significantly expanded and retains the distinct goals that drive my writing style and the information presented.

Because homeschool moms are busy people, I desired:
>   to make the guide as user-friendly as possible.
>   to present the information in a simple, step-by-step format.
>   to keep record keeping to a minimum.

Because each homeschool family is unique, I desired:
>   to make the method adaptable to different approaches to learning.
>   to provide sample courses but encourage personal creativity.

Because our lives are not our own, I desired:
>   to encourage each homeschool to excel for the good of all homeschoolers.
>   to encourage excellence to bring glory to God.

INTRODUCTION

A home-designed education is personally planned by the parents with their student to best meet the needs of their schooling situation. Each homeschool looks and operates differently. Plans change significantly from one student to another. Yet guidelines are needed that encourage academic excellence and purposeful life preparation without unnecessarily hampering the wonderful flexibility and freedom of homeschooling. I hope this book will offer a reasonable structure where creativity and individualized education can flourish.

As you consider the suggested guidelines, realize that they do not represent absolutes. Some of my ideas may not work for you. I do not have your wisdom and insight into the needs of your family and individual students. I have different state regulations from yours. I encourage you to interact with my thoughts, adapt them freely, and plan the program that seems best for you.

Since we began our homeschool adventure in 1985, I have felt both the excitement and fulfillment that comes with success and the frustration and failure when a job is poorly done, sometimes because of me. High school is an especially scary time: will our students be prepared for their life's journey? I have faced that question three times as my older students completed their homeschool program. I will soon face it a fourth time with my present high schooler. I expect the question will still receive the respect it deserves when I face it yet again with my youngest child.

As a pastor's wife, homeschooling mother, and the part-time manager of the homeschool department at a Christian bookstore, I usually live a too-busy life. The suggestions contained in this book grow out of a lifestyle that required simplicity in high school planning and record keeping, or they wouldn't get done. (It's still a struggle!) If your moments of relaxation are limited to the last few minutes before the lights go out at night, then I hope this book's straightforward presentation of information will be just what you are looking for.

Since we began our homeschooling journey, our reasons for homeschooling have grown both in number and eternal significance. Undoubtedly, the greatest blessing and responsibility of homeschooling is guiding our children to both a heart- and a mind-engaged faith in Christ. What an incredible opportunity to impact future generations! That knowledge should create a response of awe and wonder in all of our hearts and a reliance on God to be sufficient in our insufficiencies.

The stakes are high; our children's futures deserve our best efforts. Thankfully, God is there for each part of the journey! May He bless us as we walk the road together.

The Homeschool Choice

Beginning the Homeschool Journey

Should we homeschool? It has been over twenty years since my husband and I first asked ourselves that question. All pumped up from a visit to friends who had chosen this option, my husband's response was a resounding, "Yes!" As a former second-grade teacher, my answer fell more along the lines of, "You've got to be kidding! Let the professionals do their job!"

Yet I knew something had to change. Our oldest son was born with a significant hearing loss, putting him at a disadvantage in large-group settings including the classroom. Private school was not in our budget. As my academic concerns for my son grew, so did my research into homeschooling. Within six months we were withdrawing him from his kindergarten class to start the homeschool adventure.

As expected, the people around us had mixed reactions to our choice. Some people were interested, some were curious, and some were downright hostile. Fortunately, we were blessed to find a few other families also attempting this educational experiment. They became our safe place and sounding board as we worked together toward our mutual success.

Many years have passed since those early tenuous years. The academic choice that seemed right for our first child has seemed right for our other four children. It has also seemed right to thousands of other families. Although experts may disagree on how many homeschool students there are nationally, they all seem to agree on one point: homeschooling is a steadily growing educational alternative. And the future for homeschooling looks bright. Colleges and universities are increasingly smoothing the application process for these nontraditional students. They recognize the tremendous addition these students make to their campuses.

Our three oldest children completed their homeschooling a while ago. One has completed college and is in the workforce. By the time you read these words, our next two will have completed their college graduation requirements with one heading on to graduate school. Over the past few years I have sometimes asked my three oldest, "Has homeschooling prepared you for college and for life?" Their matter-of-fact, affirmative answers have laid my concerns to rest.

We are not a sterling example of the perfect homeschool family, whatever that may be. Our children have been known to bicker on rare occasions (OK, maybe not that rare). I am not a virtuous example of endless patience. We do not bake our own bread. My children were not National Merit Finalists. We have even used workbooks from time to time. Despite our shortcomings, we did, however, learn two significant ingredients for successful homeschooling.

1. *The strength of parental love.* No one loves your student as you do. Your zeal for his or her success in life far surpasses the zeal of any classroom teacher. It is true that a classroom teacher may have the advantage over you in his command of the subject matter. This advantage can be countered by parental education, careful choice of curriculum, selective use of outside resources, and other homeschool tricks. Your advantage, however, is the commitment and sacrificial giving that embodies dedicated parenting. The most successful classroom teacher can only approximate it. Recognize this qualification as uniquely yours. It can provide a helpful anchor in both sunny and stormy homeschool weather.

2. *The necessity of daily plodding.* Success in homeschooling is measured by an ability to stay on task. Day in and day out, for better or for worse, for over twenty years we have opened our books and schooled. And it worked.

So should you homeschool? Perhaps, like my husband, you have a quick, intuitive feeling that it is the right academic choice for your family. Or you may be like I was, requiring six months of thinking, studying, praying, and rethinking before the way seems clear. Either way, with research, determination, parental love, and a reliance on the blessings of God, a successful homeschool adventure can be yours.

BENEFITS OF HOMESCHOOLING

Better Academics

Since the early skepticism of the homeschooling movement, public opinion has changed drastically. This is due in large part to the success of homeschooling students, that has often been reported in both newspapers and magazines. Homeschoolers have taken high honors in national spelling and geography bees. The results of their standardized achievement and college entrance tests have been impressive. These occurrences are not accidental. Conscientious homeschooling sets a student up for success.

Individualized Attention

It is hard to beat the tutorial situation created by homeschooling. A homeschool parent/teacher is more in tune with the needs of a student than a classroom teacher who has twenty or more students to manage. Whether your student is gifted or struggling, you can adapt the program to meet individual needs. Individualized education was our initial catalyst to consider homeschooling.

Family Unity

Homeschooling is not just an academic choice; it is a lifestyle change. Home is no longer a commuter location where our children eat, do homework, sleep, and regroup before setting off for their next school day. Home has regained its rightful place as the hub of family life. Expect both blessings and friction as you find yourself in constant contact with your children. It's a growing time for everyone!

Consistent Religious and Moral Instruction

Many educational establishments question the right of parents to instill their values in their children. Under a banner of freedom, they encourage students to think their own thoughts, free from the moral boundaries of their parents. This has led to a preponderance of questionable learning situations in today's classrooms. Homeschooling replaces these voices with the faith and values of the family. Moral and religious instruction returns to the people to whom God has entrusted it: the parents.

A Solid Future

We cannot predict the future or ensure that all students will use the gifts given them to best advantage. Yet, as a group, homeschoolers have used the benefits of their education well. In a study conducted by Dr. Brian Ray of the

National Home Education Research Institute, homeschoolers in large numbers were found to continue into post-secondary education. They were also active in their churches and communities and satisfied with careers, finances, and the quality of their life. What more could we ask?

BENEFITS SPECIFIC TO HIGH SCHOOL

Increased Parental Influence

Although parental influence increases when homeschooling any age student, it is especially beneficial during the high school years. Teens stand on the threshold of their future. Major decisions await them. Poor choices often change the entire course of a teen's life and can literally have life-and-death consequences. A home-educated teen with more adult influence has a distinct opportunity to make wiser decisions for life.

Homeschooling parents also appreciate the opportunity to know their teen's friends and sometimes a friend's entire family. This is a welcome contrast to a teen developing school friendships, for good or ill, without parental awareness.

Reduced Peer Dependence

A close companion to increased parental influence is a reduction in excessive peer dependence. Parents can significantly reduce negative pressure to indulge in bad attitudes, drug use, or promiscuity until the teen has the ability to handle these issues maturely. Without the overwhelming pull of peers, teens can broaden their horizons beyond their opinions and values. This places an emphasis on life preparation rather than the self-indulgent, me-focused lifestyle common among teenagers. A reduction in peer dependency increases opportunities for strong parent-teen relationships.

Socialization

A person who objects to homeschooling is more apt to bring up the horrible dangers of inadequate socialization rather than the insufficiency of the education. As a longtime homeschooler, I know these comments are spoken with no understanding of homeschooling. Like most parents I continually struggle to keep my children's overactive social lives under control. Between lessons, co-op classes, church activities, and the social opportunities of a well-run homeschool support group, we do not lack socialization. The challenge is to avoid spending too much time in the car!

Although similar in the quantity of activities, the quality of homeschool socialization is different from classroom peer interaction. Homeschoolers spend time with their peers, but they are just as likely to interact with all age groups. This provides experiences that more closely match and prepare them for adult life.

Early Work Opportunities

The flexibility of homeschool scheduling easily accommodates work, volunteer, and apprenticeship opportunities. There are benefits to this early entrance into the workforce. First, many teens feel they sit in a holding pattern waiting for life to begin. A personalized schooling program combined with work or volunteer opportunities in the area of career interest provides direction for a teen. This early direction can foster leadership, independence, and a good work ethic. In addition, the adult interaction it provides helps a teen develop into a mature, responsible adult, able to communicate in the workplace. Be wise; however, some teens lack the farsighted vision to continue their education once they feel some financial independence. Don't allow work outside the home if it tempts a teen to drop his high-school program. Encourage work as a stepping-stone to future goals, not as an academic replacement.

A Word of Caution

I am a homeschooling fan. It has worked admirably for our family. However, I would be remiss to present the benefits of homeschooling without issuing a few cautions.

Homeschooling your high schooler is a serious decision. It is time and work intensive for both the parent and the student. It is a call to a high standard of excellence. Whether a teen receives a quality education and is equipped for the future will rest entirely on the parents' and teen's shoulders.

In addition, homeschooling should never provide a cover for truancy. It should not be a vent for anger toward public-school personnel. Resentment will not sustain you for the difficult task ahead. A reactive homeschooling decision rarely succeeds.

Sometimes, due to a school crisis, a move to homeschooling is thrust upon you. If this is your situation, I applaud you for stepping into unknown waters out of love for your child. I encourage you to get beyond your anger and frustration. Your endurance for the task will come from a growing awareness that homeschooling is the right educational choice for your student. Such positive motivation will sustain you.

Can we return to public high school if homeschooling is not working for us?

The answers to this question will vary widely depending on either your state regulations or your school district's policy. In our area, public schools are reluctant to credit high school work completed at home unless it is completed through a state-recognized school. (Accreditation does not automatically mean the school is recognized by the state's education agency.) Often homeschool students returning to public high school receive no credit for work completed at home or must take an excessive number of tests to validate their work. Check your information carefully before planning a combination homeschool-public high-school experience and bear in mind that a local policy or the word of a counselor is subject to change, particularly if you have reached an oral agreement only. Your local and state homeschool support groups are good places to begin collecting the information you need.

For More Information

Ray, Dr. Brian D. *Homeschooling Grows Up.* Purcellville, Vir.: HSLDA, 2003. Dr. Ray, president of the National Home Education Research Institute, gathered and analyzed research on the lives of adults who were educated at home. The results are encouraging. This booklet summarizes his findings and is available through HSLDA.

Rudner, Dr. Lawrence M., and Dr. Brian Ray. *Home Schooling Achievement.* Purcellville, Vir.: HSLDA, 2001. Highlights and summarizes findings from the two largest research studies to date on homeschooling. Available through HSLDA.

Homeschooling Legalities

The year 1985 seems like distant history. Ronald Reagan was beginning his second term. Mikhail Gorbachev became the general secretary of the Soviet Communist Party. Although the fall of the Berlin Wall was still several years away, hints of political change were in the air. On July 19, with much national fanfare, Vice President George H. W. Bush announced Christa McAuliffe as the first teacher who would go into space. The *Challenger* departure was set for January 28, 1986—a day that would rapidly change from joyful excitement to disbelieving tragedy. A joint French-American expedition found the *Titanic* in its watery grave 12,500 feet below the surface of the Atlantic. A postage stamp was a bargain at twenty cents. And our family, along with many others like us, began homeschooling.

What a challenging time it was for homeschoolers! The legality of homeschooling was a matter of much debate, and aggressive school districts routinely took homeschool families to court. A few parents even served jail time. Curriculum providers, accustomed to serving the public and private school sectors, were reluctant to meet the needs of this unusual breed of educators. Few homeschool parents risked taking their ducklings outside the nest before the big yellow school bus started its afternoon deliveries.

Much has changed since those early days. A parent making the homeschool decision today faces an entirely different world. Laws debated in earlier days have been clarified through legal challenges or changed. New laws have been written. Today's homeschoolers enjoy a legacy of homeschooling freedom arduously won by the ordinary but tenacious homeschool parents who preceded them.

THE HISTORY OF HOMESCHOOLING

Homeschooling, however, was not invented in the 1980s. Parent-taught education was an especially rich Hebrew tradition. A much quoted Bible passage among homeschoolers is Deuteronomy 6:6–7, which instructed the Israelites diligently to instruct their children in the faith of their fathers: "And these words which I command you today shall be in your heart; you shall teach them diligently to your children, and shall talk of them when you sit in your house, when you walk by the way, when you lie down, and when you rise up" (Deut. 6:6–7).

The Judeo-Christian heritage of America's Puritan settlers brought this ancient mandate to the New World. They viewed education as a family responsibility. In colonial New England most students were taught at home. In addition, young children and girls were sometimes taught at a dame school. Parents would employ a neighborhood woman (a dame) to teach their children reading, writing, arithmetic, prayers, and sometimes domestic skills. Boys who aspired to the ministry were educated at grammar schools if parents could spare them from family labors. As the population grew, township schools were formed to meet the Puritan concern for a high level of general literacy. This concern was driven by their belief that a responsible citizenry could only be built on solid biblical knowledge. Therefore, early educational tools, such as the hornbook and the *New England Primer*, which combined reading skills with religious instruction, provided academic instruction. Whether their children were educated at home or in a dame or grammar school, parents retained authority over their children's education.

Education in other colonies was not as well organized or as widespread. The diverse makeup of the middle colonies led to education developed along both ethnic and religious lines. In the Southern colonies education occurred at home, with well-to-do plantation families often hiring private tutors for their children.

As our country expanded westward, the centrality of the family continued. Survival was paramount. Parents provided book learning when the lessons of life weren't taking precedence. Community schooling, when available, served family needs, avoiding interference with planting and harvesting seasons.

Despite the differences in early American education, one constant remains: the right of parents to direct their children's education. Educational decisions were the parents' domain, with varied levels of church and community support. In 1852 Massachusetts enacted the first compulsory education law. A number of public school exemptions were given, including the exclusion of children who received their education elsewhere. Other early compulsory education laws, such as New York's law of 1874, made clear that responsible parents retained the right to make educational choices for their children. The concern was that the child be educated, not that it take place in state or locally funded schools. However, as time passed, these laws took on a more coercive stance. A number of social concerns and interests fostered movement toward standardized, compulsory, government-controlled education: a desire to Americanize the burgeoning immigration population, increased illiteracy, concern over child labor, and an admiration of the German-regimented system of centralized education. By 1918 all existing states had enacted compulsory education laws. Step-by-step, parental rights were being eroded.

These educational changes brought court challenges. Two cases in particular are often cited by proponents of homeschooling. In 1922 an Oregon referendum removed the compulsory education exemption that had previously allowed students to attend private schools. In the resulting court case, *Pierce v. Society of Sisters of the Holy Names of Jesus and Mary*, the court ruled in favor of academic freedom when it determined that there was not "any general power of the State to standardize its children by forcing them to accept instruction from public teachers only. The child is not the mere creature of the state . . ." The 1972 case *Wisconsin v. Yoder* upheld parental rights when it exempted Amish students from compulsory education after the eighth grade because it violated their right to freedom of religion.

Into this historical framework the homeschooling movement was born. To a populace that was now used to compulsory education, homeschooling appeared new and radical. In actuality, government schooling was "the new kid on the block." Parent-directed education was, and remains, the deeply rooted educational tradition of our country. A choice to homeschool simply returns education to its rightful place, the family.

The modern return to parent-directed education did not come without challenges. State by state, legal battles were fought and won. In addition to the judicial and legislative efforts, another hard-fought battle was occurring simultaneously: the fight to win the approval of the American public. Media commentary on homeschooling ranged from absurd allegations to thoughtful analysis. Educational experts were quick to attack parental ability to deliver quality education and issued dire warnings about removing children from the socialization of the public school system. More open-minded reporters highlighted the accomplishments of a homeschool student brought to their attention.

The dust of battle has slowly cleared. Today homeschooling is unquestionably legal in all fifty states. Although many elementary and secondary educators continue to disapprove, colleges have, in increasing numbers, recognized homeschooling as a legitimate educational choice, with some institutions actively wooing the homeschooled student.

HOMESCHOOL REGULATIONS

Despite the homeschooling victories that have secured our educational freedom, additional battles remain to be won. Homeschool laws differ significantly from state to state, with some states offering great parental freedom and others a more complex system of checks and balances. Sometimes school personnel encroach, ignoring established law. Attempts at new federal and state homeschool regulations sometimes threaten our hard-won freedoms, making vigilance and political awareness continually necessary within the homeschooling community.

While we hope and work toward even greater educational freedom, it remains the obligation of every homeschooling family to understand and abide by the regulations in their state. Compliance with these regulations should always supersede any advice given in this or any other homeschooling book. A book of this nature cannot adequately address individual state homeschool laws; that requires a book of its own! A number of excellent resources can provide the information you need to comply with the regulations in your state. A visit to Home School Legal Defense Association's helpful Web site, www.hslda.org, provides information on the homeschool statutes in each state. In addition, seek out advice from your state and local support groups, where members have had personal experience complying with your state homeschool laws.

THE FUTURE OF HOMESCHOOLING

Where is homeschooling headed? Although unable to answer that question definitively, I believe certain directions seem likely.

Homeschooling will continue to grow. In recent years parents have become increasingly concerned about the academic quality, the moral value system, negative peer influences, and the safety of the public school system. With the legality of homeschooling now widely recognized, more and more parents will investigate this option for their family.

More minorities will choose to homeschool. In my work managing the homeschool department at a Christian bookstore, I have seen a slow growth in minorities educating their children at home. A homeschool education offers opportunity to any family who is committed to a consistent, diligent pursuit of educational excellence.

The attacks on homeschooling's credibility will continue. Homeschooling's growing acceptance as a viable, mainstream educational choice threatens the public school system. Private schools draw some families away from government-funded education, but tuition costs prevent many from following their example. Homeschooling, while not cost-free, is more economically feasible for families of school-age children. This increases its potential to draw students away from public education. As school coffers feel the pinch of students leaving their system to homeschool, additional opposition is to be expected. Alternatively, more enterprising and less threatened school systems may choose to incorporate homeschool students into their system, plumping attendance numbers and subsequent school funding.

Homeschooling resources will continually expand. The American entrepreneurial spirit has risen and will continue to rise to the challenge. More books and materials will be designed specifically for the homeschool family. Courses offered via local private schools, colleges, or Internet will expand the educational opportunities for homeschool students in both quantity and quality.

YOUR ROLE IN PRESERVING HOMESCHOOL FREEDOMS

We cannot take lightly or for granted the homeschool freedoms we enjoy today. The preservation of homeschool freedom requires awareness of the political climate at local, state, and federal levels, and a willingness to become involved when necessary.

Follow your homeschool laws. Responsible homeschooling requires an awareness and adherence to existing homeschool laws. With great freedom comes great responsibility, and when freedoms are abused they are often lost.

Embrace your right to educate your child. Parents entering the homeschool community after years of public education are often startled by the amount of freedom they have to control their student's education. Having left educational decisions to the professionals in the past, they are amazed to find that they are now "the pros." At times this can be a difficult adjustment. While you may have chosen to delegate responsibility for your student's schooling in the past, you are not obligated to continue that delegation. Embracing your right to direct your child's education gives you greater ownership of the process.

Be conscientious in your homeschooling. Research, question, and learn. Homeschool with diligence. While critics will always exist, it is wonderful to silence at least some voices with success. However, it is even better one day to hear, "Well done, thou good and faithful servant," from our gracious God who honored us by entrusting His precious children to us.

Be active in local elections. Know the qualifications of local officials and school board candidates. Educational situations not governed by state law will be determined by local policies. These stances can affect your ability to homeschool in peace. Because voter turnout for local elections is often low, a well-educated homeschool group, through intelligent voting, can significantly influence an election and the resultant homeschool climate of their community. Consider giving time or financial support to a candidate who is supportive of a parent's right to homeschool. Be an active member of your local homeschool support group.

Follow the deliberations of your state legislative bodies. The state largely determines education laws. This means legislation that comes out of your state capital can have a tremendous effect on your homeschooling. Join your state homeschool support group. These organizations offer an accurate understanding of your state homeschool laws and other pertinent homeschool information, and often establish and maintain ongoing ties with elected state officials. Such advocacy can be of great benefit in preserving your homeschool freedom. (Also, some state homeschool groups offer additional services. Pennsylvania Homeschoolers, for example, founded an accrediting agency that provides state-recognized diplomas to the homeschooling community. Texas Home School Coalition provides legal assistance when necessary to member families. A number of state groups sponsor book fairs or conventions where homeschoolers can shop for curriculum and attend educational seminars.)

Watch federal legislation. Although education laws are determined by each state, the federal government controls public schools by offering financial incentives to states that adopt federal education programs. This means the federal government must also be monitored for legislation and programming that aversely affects family or homeschooling freedom. A number of organizations, mentioned below, provide this beneficial service.

Join homeschool and pro-family support groups. Be they local, state, or national, a number of organizations watch out for homeschool and family interests. Pro-family organizations, such as Focus on the Family, rally those interested in protecting conservative family values. Your local homeschool group will provide fellowship with like-minded people and, depending on the size of the group, an interesting mix of classes and social events. State groups offer the many services already mentioned above. Home School Legal Defense Association, with a national membership, serves as a political watchdog on both federal and state levels. HSLDA also provides legal help to member families when their homeschooling rights are threatened. Their Web site, www.hslda.org, is a great source for homeschool information. While the purposes of various homeschool groups may sometimes overlap, some roles are unique to each, making membership in each worthwhile. Be as generous as possible in your financial support. In addition, be willing to make phone calls and write letters or e-mails to elected officials when requested.

FOR MORE INFORMATION

Information on the history of American colonial education is widely available from numerous sources, including most American history textbooks. Visit www.en.wikipedia.org for short, easily understood entries on the *Pierce v. Society of Sisters* and *Wisconsin v. Yoder* court cases.

I also found the following two articles on compulsory education helpful:

"Compulsory Education Laws: the Dialogue Reopens." This was the cover article of the September/October 2000 *Home School Court Report* and is available online at www.hslda.org in the Court Report Archives.

Novello, Ed.D., Mary K. "A Case against Compulsion," published March 1998. This article is available online at www.washingtonpolicy.org in the publications section.

Both were available online in May 2007.

The following resource provides more information on homeschool history and success:

Klicka, Chris. *Home School Heroes: The Struggle and Triumph of Homeschooling in America*. Nashville: Broadman & Holman, 2006. (Chris Klicka chronicles the early battles to win our present-day homeschool freedoms. Mr. Klicka is senior counsel and director of state and international relations for HSLDA and a longtime homeschool father of seven.

Defining Your Philosophy of Education

Building a Christian Philosophy of Education

A decision to homeschool changes life for the entire family. Most parents would not even consider such a major move if they weren't anxious for significant changes in their student's education. They often desire to create an environment and study plan that welcomes their Christian faith rather than isolating it to an hour or two each Sunday morning. Many parents are public school products and don't have any idea how to effect such a change. How do they build a homeschool program that reflects their Christian beliefs?

Unfortunately, it is not as simple as using textbooks that put a Bible verse on the bottom of each page. Teaching sentence diagramming and math concepts with examples from the Bible will not get the job done. Such resources are certainly fine, but they do not define Christian education. What does?

True Christian education nurtures a godly condition of the heart. It teaches us to live our lives with a constant awareness that "we are not our own, that we have been bought with a price" (see 1 Cor. 6:19–20). The first question of the Westminster Shorter Catechism asks, "What is the chief end of man?" The answer, "Man's chief end is to glorify God and enjoy Him forever," reflects the attitude to nurture and grow in homeschool students. A homeschool program pursued with the goal of glorifying God is a sacred offering to Him and bears fruit for His kingdom. Each subject studied will progressively reveal God's power and control over His universe. With God's grace this growing awareness will tune a student's heart to Him and result in an obedient Christian walk.

Building a homeschool program that encourages such Christian growth starts with examining our worldview and developing a Christian philosophy of education. This Christian philosophy will then serve as a guide to help choose the methods and materials to use. Hopefully, each choice will enhance a student's walk with God.

WORLDVIEWS

Before parents can develop a Christian philosophy of education, they need to understand a little about worldviews. A worldview is a lens or filter through which one interprets life. It is the presuppositions used to evaluate the experiences of one's life. Sometimes people just fall into a worldview unknowingly by adopting the viewpoints of their parents or a college professor who captivated their attention. One worldview can clash harshly with another. For example, a Christian worldview sees God as the Creator and final authority in life. A humanistic worldview sees man as the captain of his own fate and supreme. There's not much common ground there!

Christian homeschoolers want to promote a worldview in their home and through their lifestyle that encourages students to accept the same Christian worldview their parents embrace. However, many parents don't have the slightest idea how to impact their homeschool with their Christian worldview. There will be no comfortable "falling" into a position. Not having been homeschooled themselves, parents are stumbling into a schooling world totally alien to them. It's time to develop a philosophy of education to guide them safely to their goals.

A CHRISTIAN PHILOSOPHY OF EDUCATION

What is a Christian philosophy of education? I'm sure there are many definitions to be found, but I would summarize it as *a conscious application of your Christian worldview to education*. Another possible definition could be derived from the word *philosophy*. *Philosophy* literally means "friend or lover of wisdom." So a Christian homeschool mom is a "friend of wisdom who blazes an educational path to truth for her children." What truth? Here are just a few pieces of truth that greatly impact the way we homeschool:

1. *God is sovereign.* His rule extends over all of His creation. "All the inhabitants of the earth are reputed as nothing; He does according to His will in the army of heaven and among the inhabitants of the earth. No one can restrain His hand or say to Him, 'What have You done?'" (Dan. 4:35). Since Satan, in the form of the serpent, enticed Eve with his words in Genesis 3:5, "You will be like God, knowing good and evil," man has struggled to exalt himself and claim autonomy.

2. *Absolute truth exists and is resident in the triune God and in His Word.* Other claims to truth are counterfeit. We see God's truth revealed in the Scriptures. "The law of the LORD is perfect, converting the soul" (Ps. 19:7). We also see it revealed in His Son, Jesus Christ. "I am the way, the truth, and the life" (John 14:6). This is different from the world's perspective, which questions whether absolute truth really exists and certainly would not believe it resides in the Bible or in Christ.

3. *God's Word is not only true; it is also the ultimate authority.* Isaiah 8:20 reminds us that if men do not speak in accordance with God's law and testimony, "there is no light in them." God's Word provides the only clear guidance for the moral and ethical struggles of life. This is not to imply that there are never difficult issues but rather that God in His mercy has not left us in darkness. In contrast, the world, in its failure to recognize the authority of God's Word, can offer no definitive answers for the dilemmas of this life.

4. *The whole world and man himself bear the stamp of the Creator and of His character.* God has created and actively sustains His creation. "All things were made through Him, and without Him nothing was made that was made" (John 1:3). Evidences of God's wisdom, power, and majesty can be clearly seen from His creation. Indeed, "the earth is the Lord's and all its fullness, the world and those who dwell therein" (Ps. 24:1). We happily acknowledge that "for of Him and through Him and to Him are all things, to whom be glory forever. Amen" (Rom. 11:36 NKJV), and that "in Him we live and move and have our being" (Acts 17:28).

5. *Man is the crown of God's creation.* We were created to be His image-bearers and, as such, to rule over the rest of creation in His name and for His glory. "Let Us make man in Our image, according to Our likeness; let them have dominion over the fish of the sea, over the birds of the air, and over the cattle, over all the earth and over every creeping thing that creeps on the earth" (Gen. 1:26). As beings made in God's image, we have capacities to create, reason, feel, act, and communicate in ways that animals do not possess. Although sin has marred God's image in us, to the best of our ability we must still use these God-given capabilities to rule the earth as His representatives. Our lives should reflect the character of God in our personal morality, our choices, relationships with others, pursuit of knowledge, dedication to our vocation, and in the wisdom we bring to all areas of life.

6. *God has a plan for man which He actively works out in history—past, present, and future.* In God's divine providence, man fell into sin. Sin brought harshness to life and physical and spiritual death. In mercy God provided redemption in Christ, creating a means eternally to restore His wayward children to Himself. "For God so loved the world that He gave His only begotten Son, that whoever believes in Him should not perish but have everlasting life" (John 3:16).

7. *Man actively participates in God's plan in history.* We experience the struggle of living in this fallen world but rejoice in knowing that this life is temporary and serves as preparation for our complete restoration and perfection in eternity. In the meantime Micah 6:8 encourages us, with God's help, to do justly, love mercy, and walk humbly with our God.

8. *This joyful service should encompass our whole being.* Mark 12:30 reminds us to "love the LORD your God with all your heart, with all your soul, with all your mind, and with all your strength." Most Christians understand the need to have a heart and soul dedicated to God. It is just as important to engage our mind in our faith. A mind that loves the Lord immerses itself in deep study of God's Word. Loving God with all of our strength is also deemed important. We should be quick to expend both our mental and physical energies for Him. God's Word admonishes us in 1 Corinthian 10:31, "Therefore, whether you eat or drink, or whatever you do, do all to the glory of God." All of life is important to Him.

9. *This joyful service should be performed with excellence.* This means developing the gifts and talents God has given us with a conscientiously thankful spirit and exercising them with a recognition of their origin in Him. "Every good gift and every perfect gift is from above" (James 1:17). As God's image bearers we should reflect His character by being a consistent light to mankind in all that we do.

10. *Men's lives either promote glory to God or glory to man.* It is the mind-set a person brings to an action that determines whom the action glorifies. Proverbs 21:4 reminds us that even "the plowing of the wicked {is} sin" because actions that are performed with no desire to please God do not honor Him.

APPLYING A CHRISTIAN PHILOSOPHY TO VARIOUS SUBJECTS

The truths presented can find free expression in Christian homeschools. The list could be beneficially expanded by a careful examination of the whole counsel of God, revealed through His written Word. I encourage you to search Scripture for additional truths you would like to impart to your children. However, a list of truths does not explain how to work these truths into homeschool subjects on a day-to-day basis. Let's look at some subjects and how to apply basic Christian truths to them.

School subjects can be roughly divided into three different kinds:

Subjects That Relate to Man. These include Bible, English, history, cultural geography, and many college disciplines such as psychology, sociology, and anthropology. Whenever we study man or man's accomplishments, we should include the centrality of God's relationship to man in the discussion. This position stands in sharp contrast to a non-Christian worldview that studies man with no reference to the existence of God.

Subjects That Relate to Creation. These include all science fields, mathematics, and physical geography. God's handiwork should be given the praise it inspires. As Psalm 19:1 reminds us, "The heavens declare the glory of God; and the firmament shows His handiwork."

Subjects That Are Skill Building. These classes, while using students' intellect, focus more directly on building their skills. Home economics, auto mechanics, computer literacy, music lessons, and sports are all examples.

(Note: A discussion or application of godly values and principles can be woven into any subject. Schoolwork becomes character building when it is done faithfully and cheerfully unto the Lord. In contrast, any subject, including Bible reading, can become an unholy offering to God when accompanied by a grumbling spirit. Building a Christian philosophy of education into homeschooling is not a magic pill. In faithfulness we plow the ground, plant the seed, and nourish it, but God brings the increase.)

SUBJECTS THAT RELATE TO MAN

Bible

Bible study has a legitimate and pivotal place in the Christian homeschool. A study of the character of God and His Word builds wisdom in students. This study should be both heart-and-mind engaged.

Heart-engaged study builds a devotion to God as He reveals Himself in Scripture. It encourages students to develop a personal relationship with God through meditation on God's Word, the reading of devotional literature, and the development of an active prayer life. Journals can record lessons learned, verses memorized, and prayers offered and answered. All of these activities build awareness that God is personally involved in our lives and in His world.

Mind-engaged study involves a systematic study of God's Word. The use of commentaries, handbooks, and other resources can deepen our understanding of the Bible's content and the history and culture of biblical times. Doctrinal studies provide a systematic presentation of God's character and actions, helping the student understand Scripture as a whole. Highly motivated students will find that a study of Hebrew or Greek greatly enlightens biblical understanding. Mind-engaged study also protects us from error. A lack of study and understanding can find us worshipping a god of our own creation. A thorough knowledge of Scripture will protect us from the philosophies of the world and the errors that sometimes infect the church.

English

God holds language in high esteem. With the entire universe at His disposal, He chose the printed word as the primary means of communicating with man. We need to share His exalted view. How do we do that?

Study God's Word for redemption, instruction, and inspiration. It holds the keys to life for this world and the next. This study can be greatly enhanced by understanding the literary forms contained within the Bible. Historical narrative, poetry, proverbs, parables, and letters are some of the genres represented. Literary devices, such as metaphor and parallelism, are often used in biblical poetry. The understanding of a passage can be deepened significantly by interpreting the truth in its literary context.

Encourage reading. The entertainments and communications of our age via television, movies, video games, e-mail, and the Internet are rapidly displacing the quieter, more contemplative habits of reading. It is difficult to hear the still, small voice of God if the volume of our world is always on high.

Choose literature of lasting distinction and skillful craftsmanship. Look for the beauty or cleverness in a well-worded phrase or carefully developed plot. Since a story can't develop without a conflict, discuss the situations presented and choices made for good or ill. Analyze characters. What truths are they embracing or rejecting? Even pagan literature is profitable, offering many opportunities to discuss the futility of a lifestyle that rejects God's truth.

Work on developing excellent writing skills. Reading excellent literature is the first step to excellent writing. Students can't model what they don't even recognize. Skill in spelling, grammar, language mechanics, paragraph and report formats, and careful research procedures are necessary before one can communicate effectively. Well-honed writing entertains, teaches, inspires, and communicates truth. God created language. It shows us His character—one that communicates, one of order. Write well to bear God's image well.

History

History is the study of the purposes of God and the actions of man intersecting in time. The center of history, initiated before time began and completed after time ceases, is God's plan of redemption for fallen man. This, in a nutshell, is a Christian view of history.

Non-Christian man, however, has a different viewpoint. With the truth of God discarded, history has no solid basis on which to base interpretations. Instead, history becomes a study of opinions.

Historians, Christian or non-Christian, whether writing today or hundreds of years ago, build their thoughts upon their presuppositions. The accuracy of a historian's observations will be directly related to the accuracy of his worldview. He will interpret events in a manner supporting his viewpoints. He may fail even to mention evidence that would contradict his basic ideas.

A historian's view of God is a presupposition that will strongly affect his interpretation of history. When a historian has a high view of God's sovereignty, all of history becomes an unfolding of God's purposes in time. Earthly woes become a part of the cosmic war waged against God's purposes.

The Christian historian recognizes that this world's history is on a horizontal time line with a beginning in creation and a glorious eternal culmination. He acknowledges God's active involvement with His world, that "the king's heart is in the hand of the Lord, like the rivers of water; He turns it wherever He wishes" (Prov. 21:1). The Christian historian also recognizes that he, as a mortal, is unable to delve into the depths of God's intentions, understanding the truth of Romans 11:34, "for who has known the mind of the Lord? Or who has become His counselor?"

In contrast humanistic historians leave God's overarching plan out of the unfolding historical drama. History then becomes a meaningless cycle of events or a march of random occurrences driven by no power higher than man himself.

A second pertinent presupposition is the historian's view of man. The Christian historian realizes that man is a fallen creature and that history is a tale of that depravity in action. Gloriously, it is also a record of God's responding to that depravity with mercy, preserving a people unto Himself. That record is best discovered by reading the Christian's first historical document, the Bible. The continuation of that story is found in the centuries-long and still unfolding drama of church history.

The humanistic historian sees man as whole and valuable without God. Man is his own master, capable of choosing and doing good without any aid from a god who may not exist anyway. History becomes a record of man's achievements. Although remarkable achievements exist, one also sees cruel grasps at power with little concern for the common man. When such a historian views man sunk deep in barbarity toward his fellowman, he has no good explanation for these actions. How can such a view lead to anything but pessimism?

Read history thoughtfully and cautiously. Read to determine the historian's basic beliefs. When you have discovered them, evaluate his message and judge his accuracy in the light of Scripture.

Subjects That Study God's Creation

Science

Science is the study of God's creation, its truths discernable and verifiable by observation and experimentation. Today's world tends to see science and the Bible as contradictory, the first advanced by rational thought, the latter by faith or superstition. This was not the view of early scientists.

Many of our early scientists were devout Christians, their interest in God's world a result of their devotion to its Creator. Even scientists without a personal faith made their discoveries and observations while living in a world that accepted and operated under a Christian worldview. God was recognized as the Creator and Lawgiver, His character and attributes forming and sustaining the workings of the universe. Because God was viewed as orderly, rational, and constant, the universe was believed to operate under orderly and rational laws that could be predictably observed and studied.

Today's scientists, more often than not, do not begin with these underlying presuppositions. Their rejection of a rational, law-giving God leaves them floundering to explain the intricately synchronized workings of the universe. Thus are born branches of science such as evolution, which cannot be studied by observation but must be accepted by faith, a far greater faith than required by a belief in a personal Creator God. Usually muddy, evolutionary thought is only clear in its elevation of man and its rejection of any higher authority. In recent days the intellectual integrity of some scientists has led to a belief in an intelligently designed universe rather than random occurrences. Although a step in the right direction, it does not return to the harmony between theology and science accepted by our earlier scientists.

It is appropriate to direct students in their study of science to read biographies of scientists such as Sir Francis Bacon, Blaise Pascal, and Sir Isaac Newton. It helps us and frees us to realize that scientific discovery can be pursued with integrity while trusting that the heavens declare the glory of God. There is neither contradiction nor compromise in this position. Rather, acknowledging the designer of our physical world is a position of strength.

Math

The Bible is not a mathematical textbook, yet we can learn about God when we study mathematics. Its logical consistencies point to the wise, unchanging character of its Creator. Math works consistently in so far as it reflects this immutability of the Creator God. Made in God's image, we can glean some understanding, albeit limited, of the divine mind when we study the mathematical laws by which He governs and sustains His universe.

Our triune God placed value in a number system. He numbered the days of creation. The animals entered the ark by twos and sevens. He carefully specified the dimensions of the tabernacle and all of its furnishings. The Israelites were counted as they began their journey to the promised land. The disciples counted a small boy's loaves and fishes and noted how many basketfuls were left after the thousands had eaten.

Biblical examples, such as these, can be used to teach mathematical concepts, but are by no means necessary. Whether counting with a preschooler, drilling multiplication tables with a third grader, or learning the logic of geometric proofs with a teen, our eyes and heart can be drawn to the wisdom of God. We are glorifying Him as we master this gift from His hand.

In learning to use mathematical concepts, we can be thankful for a God-given intellect that can be profitably applied to this aspect of God's creation. We can honor God for the truths about Himself that mathematics reveals. Should our studies lead us into career fields that require strong math skills, we can recognize that we are loving both God and our neighbor when we use our skills to govern His creation and to benefit the lives of those around us.

Geography

Geography is a multifaceted study with two main directions: physical and cultural. Physical geography concentrates on God's creation. Cultural geography concentrates on man's interdependence with that creation. Let's look briefly at each.

Physical geography is a study of the Earth's surface and its features. Bodies of water (oceans, lakes, and rivers), landforms (continents and mountains), ecosystems (deserts and jungles) and the animals that inhabit them, climate, and the atmosphere are just some of the topics available for study. All reveal the hand of God. Environmental topics provide opportunities to discuss appropriate ways for man to manage, or, in Genesis's words, "take dominion" over creation. They also provide opportunities to discuss man's failure to use God's gifts appropriately.

Human or cultural geography concentrates on the people and their interaction with the environment. Topographical and climate features (landlocked versus coastal, high rainfall versus low rainfall) can greatly affect the prosperity of a geographic region. Customs, religion, language, food, dress, and political divisions are all examined when studying a people's culture.

Today's emphasis on multiculturalism promotes a viewpoint that all cultures and cultural traditions are equally valuable. As Christians, we must evaluate cultures in the light of God's Word. Do the cultures studied worship God as revealed in the Bible? Do they protect the rights of the individual? Are women and children valued, or are they viewed as property? These and many other questions can thoughtfully integrate cultural studies with biblical truth.

SUBJECTS THAT EMPHASIZE SKILL TRAINING

Fine Arts

In music, art, and dance God has provided a means for man to worship God with his whole being: heart, mind, soul, and strength. God's character is beauty beyond human definition, and His creation clearly reflects this attribute of His being. We are reflecting our kinship to Him when we create works of art with an intricate order and discipline or soaring, swelling beauty.

Because we reflect God's image, we need creativity and beauty in our lives. Even in the most desperate of situations, the need to create beauty still draws our spirits. The vocal orchestra of Sumatra's Palembang women's internment camp of World War II is just such an example. Presbyterian missionary, Margaret Dryburgh combined her phenomenal musical memory with the skills of Norah Chambers, a graduate of the Royal Academy of Music in London. Together they wrote orchestral musical scores in four parts, designed to be "hummed" by women's voices. In her memoirs, *Song of Survival*, Helen Colijn recalls what it was like to hear such beauty among the squalor and deprivation of the internment camp: "Each time we heard the music we marveled again at the beautiful and often familiar melodies, at the purity of sound, at this miracle that was happening to us amid the cockroaches, the rats, the bedbugs, and the stink of the latrines. The music renewed our sense of human dignity." The vocal orchestra continued through 1944 and part of 1945, ending when conditions in the camp had claimed the lives of too many orchestra members for it to continue. Yet for a brief time, two women, image bearers of their Creator, brought moments of rare beauty into darkness.

By God's grace we pray none of us will be called to such desperate situations. But we are called to bring creative beauty to our part of God's creation and to train our students to do the same. I am not a musician, but all five of our children have taken piano lessons for years. The goal was not to develop concert pianists. The goal was for each child to acquire enough musical knowledge and proficiency to feed his spirit and that of his future family for the rest of their lives.

Music is not the only source of beauty God has given us. The two-dimensional graphic arts, such as painting, drawing, printmaking, and the three-dimensional art of sculpting can delight the eyes as much as music can delight the ears. Classic ballet, spirited tap, or intricate folk dances reveal the beauty of the body in motion. All can uplift us from the common, providing glimpses of the divine.

Unfortunately, as is the way of life in a fallen world, all the art forms can be perverted—used to draw us away from the Author of creativity and beauty. Music, art, and dance in pagan hands often reflect the sin, chaos, and confusion of a man-centered world.

Despite the many abuses, it is important that we not reject the arts. Rather, homeschool parents can encourage their students in both the enjoyment and personal development of artistic styles and expressions that glorify God. Following J. S. Bach's example, who signed all of his musical compositions with the inscription "Soli Deo Gloria," our students can proclaim "to God only be glory" with all of their creations.

Life Skills

Life skills courses are both diverse and many: home economics, woodworking, auto mechanics, computer skills, agriculture, and many more. Courses of this nature are studies in *practical creativity*, offering our students opportunities to bring order, resourcefulness, and beauty to the ordinary activities of life. For example:

Home economics—whether meal preparation, garment construction, or interior design—can be done "just to get it done" or to add grace and beauty to the activity. We all know the special ambience that china, fine linen, and candlelight bring to a holiday meal. A garment can be decent and appropriate, or it can be styled in lines and colors that delight the eye. A home can be designed with sterility or with warmth that provides a haven for the family.

The same is true of woodworking. A bookcase can be made with boards and bricks—utilitarian and fit for its task, satisfying the need to create order. It can also be made from a fine-grained wood with glass doors, pleasing the spirit while performing its utilitarian function.

Sometimes there is only time or ability to create order or functionality. This does not detract from the benefit of developing a skill. After all, we can't always get out the fine china; sometimes a paper plate suits the situation just fine. At other times, however, it is also possible to create beauty. This adds an extra, pleasing dimension to the task.

Skill-building courses not only train and apply students' abilities to create order and beauty; they can also help the student restore to use what has become unusable. The student is learning to "take dominion" in his little corner of the universe. He is learning to love the Lord his God with all his strength while developing practical ways to serve his family, community, or employer. The goodness and value of simple work done to the glory of God was rediscovered during the Reformation. Homeschool parents can help students discover this truth for themselves.

Applying These Thoughts

Before concluding, let's take a moment to review. We have briefly discussed worldviews and the importance of conscientiously examining and correcting ours as needed to reflect biblical thought. This enables us to blaze an educational path for our children to truth. We looked at a number of these truths that are resident in Scripture. We then turned our attention to practical ways to include biblical thought into our homeschool using some of the commonly taught subjects as examples.

The information presented will only be helpful to you if it finds practical expression in your homeschooling. Perhaps a few closing questions and comments can aid you in applying this chapter's thoughts to your personal homeschool.

Spend some time thinking about your worldview. Ask yourself:

- Are my actions and words shaped by my Christian beliefs?
- Is my worldview on automatic pilot, or does it need some adjustment as it is held to the light of God's truth?

Review the list of truths presented. Ask yourself:

- Do I agree or disagree with them?
- What Bible verses can I find to support my position?
- What truths would I like to add to the list?
- How can I incorporate God's truth into my homeschooling on a day by day, subject by subject basis?

For More Information

I have attempted no great originality in discussing worldviews and a Christian philosophy of education, nor would an attempt at originality have been wise. Far greater minds than mine have contemplated these issues, much to everyone's benefit.

However, the distillation and organization of these thoughts are mine. In clarifying my thoughts, I have found many individuals helpful. First and foremost would be my husband and pastor, John, whose solid biblical teaching has been my steady nourishing food for thirty years of marriage. Different authors have also influenced my thinking on what comprises a Christian philosophy of education: J. Gresham Machen, Cornelius Van Til, Gordon H. Clark, and Rousas Rushdoony. Leland Ryken and Gene Edward Veith have inspired within me a greater appreciation for language and the arts. Some books of interest are included below.

Berkhof, Louis, and Cornelius Van Til. *Foundations of Christian Education.* Phillipsburg, N. J.: P&R Publishing, 1990.

Clark, Gordon H. *A Christian Philosophy of Education.* Unicoi, Tenn.: the Trinity Foundation, 2000.

Machen, J. Gresham. *Education, Christianity, and the State.* Unicoi, Tenn.: The Trinity Foundation. 1995.

Rushdoony, Rousas John. *The Philosophy of the Christian Curriculum.* Vallecito, Calif.: Ross House Books, 2001.

Ryken, Leland. *The Liberated Imagination.* Colorado Springs: Waterbrook Press. 1989.

Schaeffer, Francis A. *How Should We Then Live? The Rise and Decline of Western Thought and Culture.* Wheaton, Ill.: Crossway, 2005.

Veith, Gene Edward. *Reading between the Lines: A Christian Guide to Literature.* Wheaton, Ill.: Crossway Books, 1990.

Veith, Gene Edward. *State of the Arts: From Bezalel to Mapplethorpe.* Wheaton, Ill.: Crossway Books, 1991.

The Student Connection

Everyone has a different idea of how homeschooling should look. Some picture a miniature classroom complete with desks, wall maps, and chalkboard. Others picture children sprawled comfortably across the floor engrossed in the books they are reading. Whatever form your homeschool takes, it should be one that meets the needs of the student.

Most students, to some degree, are lopsided learners. They have areas of strength and areas of weakness. Strengths and talents often give us insight into future career goals. Weaknesses encourage creative efforts at remediation. Strengths and weaknesses show themselves not only in the subject matter studied but also in the manner in which our students learn.

LEARNING MODALITIES

People take in or process information using their senses. Although tasting and smelling won't contribute much to acquiring academic skills, the other three senses or learning modalities—visual, auditory, and kinesthetic (touch)—play a prominent role. Knowing which modalities your student is strongest and weakest in will help you make appropriate choices as you plan his program.

Students who are strong visual learners are most comfortable learning with their school materials in front of them. This was the situation with my two oldest children. In addition to strong visual preferences, both had moderate genetic hearing losses that made me aware of the need to give them strong visual input. We didn't talk about our school subjects without seeing them at the same time. I often combined their classes, but each had his own book. If we were diagramming sentences or conjugating a Latin verb, they wrote it on their individual whiteboards. Spelling was a subject we studied briefly and then moved on; their strong visual skills made review unnecessary. Note taking, flashcards, and the strategic use of highlighters are also effective tools for this type of student. You know you have a visual learner if you regularly hear, "Don't read it to me; let me see it."

Students with strong auditory skills will have different preferences. Hearing is their preferred method of taking in information. Auditory learners enjoy listening to books read aloud. Taped instruction works well with this type of student. They may survive college lecture classes well if they can read the notes they've taken! A textbook that would be comfortable for a visual learner might overwhelm the auditory student. My third child is a fairly strong auditory learner. He is a natural mimic and has a wonderful memory for music. His love for the cadence of language often had him reading literature assignments aloud. However, his visual skills were strong also, which made him an easy student to accommodate.

Kinesthetic students need to be doing. Find ways to satisfy this need for activity. Accommodations are fairly easy on the elementary level. These students enjoy paste and cut activities, art projects, field trips, and the variety offered by unit studies. Meeting the needs of a kinesthetic learner becomes more difficult on the junior high and high school level. Encourage active note-taking to help them stay tuned in to their studies. Include hands-on electives in their studies. Home economics, auto mechanics, woodworking, and music lessons fit the need. Be generous with the lab in the lab sciences. This type of student often welcomes involvement in theater. And don't forget the physical education credits.

Although some students will decisively favor one learning modality over another, it is just as likely that your student will be a mix. A student may not have distinct preferences but may be fairly balanced in all three areas. This makes curriculum selection easier. Many programs will work well for a balanced student.

LEARNING STYLES

In addition to taking in information better through one sense than another, students also have different learning styles. Learning styles go beyond sensory strengths to involve how the brain processes new information. Although talking about learning styles can get lost in the hallways of educational philosophy, the practical outworking of these styles is sometimes easy to see. We can all identify factors that make it harder or easier for us to learn.

Physical Environment. Does your student prefer absolute quiet or music when studying? Is he more comfortable at a desk or slumped on the couch with his feet on the coffee table? Does he like the room warm or chilly? Is natural light or high intensity bulbs the preferred lighting?

People Interaction. Does he learn best in a group or while studying alone? Does he prefer to work with facts or the intricacies of human nature? Are the unpredictabilities of social interaction stimulating or disconcerting? Is your student skilled in reading social signals? Does he prefer discussion to book study?

Perceiving information. Does he prefer subjects that allow information to be neatly pigeonholed, or does he prefer more abstract learning? Would he rather study the periodic table or analyze a poem? Would he rather dissect a frog or write a creative composition?

Ordering information. Is information retained best when it is carefully, sequentially organized; or is a random, less-structured input preferred? Does he like to stay on topic, or does he enjoy an intellectual rabbit trail? Does he prefer a set schedule or a less formal structure?

The best way to accommodate learning styles is not always easy to discern. My second child is a capable student but tended to underperform while homeschooling. Many subjects just did not light her fire. Her college career began unimpressively. Seeking a change, and no doubt adventure, she moved to Colorado to live with a church camp friend. Years of piano had given her impressive dexterity and she had no trouble securing full-time clerical work. During this time she volunteered at a Denver ministry for transient, hotel-raised children. She had finally found her niche. With a renewed interest in education, she moved back to Texas to complete a social work degree. Her grades were sterling. The head of the department complimented her ability to grasp and effectively apply the theories they discussed. Her degree plan included lots of group discussion, problem solving with abstract theories rather than with cold facts, and hands-on internship opportunities. After completion of graduate school, she hopes to work in a faith-based ministry. Working with her learning style rather than against it has had a profound effect.

However, the truth of the transformation lies far deeper than just accommodating my daughter's learning style. God wires each of us, through our learning modalities and styles, precisely the way He deems best. He designs our strengths and weaknesses to help us better serve Him while on this Earth. We find both great delight and a solid sense of accomplishment in the niche for which God has skillfully prepared us. Learning and ministering through our strengths is a satisfying place to be.

My husband and I have also clearly seen God equip our fourth child. Although all of my children are musical, this child is passionately so. Strong auditory skills are certainly a requirement for a career in music. Although genetic hearing loss is a family trait, God, in His providence, gave this child hearing not only unimpaired but better than average. To our eyes, it is evidence of a God who makes each of us fearfully and wonderfully, equipping us for whatever purpose He has planned for us.

ADDING IN THE TEACHER

Once we gain a general understanding of our student, we have another huge variable to consider. That is the learning preferences of the teacher.

The most difficult situation occurs when a student has strong preferences that are dissimilar from the teacher. This has been the case with my music-minded student. Her best learning occurs through auditory and kinesthetic channels. I am strongly visual. She prefers to learn wrapped in a blanket on a comfortable couch. I get my best work done at a table. She enjoys the stimulus of group classes. Give me a book and a quiet corner. I want her to study music history. She wants her vocalizing to be properly placed in her head (figure that one out!). I want her to remember her music and be on time for her lesson. She was born without a fast-forward. Meeting her academic needs in a way that is comfortable for us both has been a challenge!

TYPES OF INTELLIGENCE

In addition to various learning modalities and styles, some educational psychologists say that different types of intelligence exist. Personal examples can usually illustrate this best. I was always a good student but often lacked common sense. This was sometimes a thorn in my mother's flesh. My mother and I enjoyed a close relationship until her death, but her northern upbringing didn't have the subtleties I've grown used to in the more genteel South. In moments of extreme exasperation at yet another display of my careless reasoning, she would sometimes say, "For someone who is so smart, how can you be so stupid?" I like to believe that time, maturity, and the experiences of life have evened me out, at least a little.

The types of intelligences as developed by Howard Gardner include:
Logical/mathematical—Ability to reason logically and use numbers effectively
Verbal/linguistic—Ability to use words and language
Musical/rhythmic—Ability both to create and to appreciate music
Visual/spatial—Ability to form clear mental pictures
Bodily/kinesthetic—Skillful use of fine and large body movements
Interpersonal—Intuitive understanding of people
Intrapersonal—Self-understanding

I find this list pretty self-explanatory with only visual/spatial intelligence requiring more explanation. People with this type of intelligence tend to think in images. They often make great architects, interior designers, and engineers. People who rarely get lost have strong spatial strengths. Those who get lost in hospital corridors do not.

I find the thought of intelligence types a comforting one. The high school years, with their college focus, can find us obsessing over mathematical and verbal intelligence. Students whose intelligence lies in other areas can also excel if the training and career pursued fit the strengths God has given them.

WORKING TOWARD A BALANCE

As we homeschool our students with all their diverse modalities, styles, and intelligences, it is tempting to focus on the strengths and avoid remediating the weaknesses. This would be a mistake. Higher education, the work force, and life in general do not allow the luxury of always operating within our comfort zone.

College classes have an uncanny knack for requiring strength in all modalities. Courses involve mind-boggling reading in twenty-pound books with microscopic print. After a night of studying, the student must then sit through an hour lecture in an echoing hall with two hundred other students. He may then proceed to a brainstorming session with his project group. That's a lot of modality diversity in the space of a short time period!

The workforce is no different. The lab technician must learn to coexist with a grouchy coworker. The psychologist will need to manage the business details of his practice. The artist's checkbook must be balanced. After a full day of adaptations, home life requires similar adjustments.

Dads whose spirits need quiet restoring may arrive home to the noise of boisterous children. Difficult neighbors may require tact. Home repairs will require skill. Free-spirited homeschool moms find they must teach the boring stuff, too.

We will serve our children well if we encourage at least a modest level of efficiency and competency in all learning modalities and styles. An effective approach uses the student's strongest senses and styles for teaching new information whenever possible while remediating areas of weakness, whether academic, sensory, or processing. This is not an effort to pour a student into an uncomfortable mold, but rather to keep weaknesses from jeopardizing the blossoming of strengths. With such a well-rounded plan a student is better prepared for what life has to offer.

ENCOURAGING LEARNING

Now that all the student-teacher variables have been discussed, I'll offer a few practical suggestions for applying the information to the learning environment.

Create an environment that delivers what your student needs. If he needs a quiet, ordered place free from distractions, create it. If he needs stimulation, look for colorful posters for your learning area. If he needs to be moving, let *him* make those colorful posters. Invest in appropriate music if it will soothe an overstimulated child and make it easier for him to think. In our home Mozart has often lifted the mood of a grumpy reactionary student.

Look for ways to capture your student's interest. Choosing materials with his strongest learning mode and style in mind will set you in the right direction. Look for supplements to the curriculum that enhance what you are learning in your schoolbooks. Movies, music of the time period, and historical fiction can draw your student into the subject you are studying. Studying an amortization table can clarify a word problem about principle, interest, and home mortgages. Capturing student interest is the first step to making learning stick.

Connect new information to old. Our minds retain information best when we link it to information that we have already learned and stored. Understanding that multiplication is addition of the same number over and over is one helpful connection. (It won't help the nitty-gritty of memorizing the facts, but it does make multiplication as a concept more easily understood.) Another is studying the literature of a time period while learning its history. The voyage of the *Mayflower* and the political and religious significance of the early colony it began will be easier to remember if it is accompanied by reading well-chosen excerpts from *Of Plymouth Plantation*. Look for teachable moments that reinforce what you are learning in your studies. For example, my student is more likely to remember that Jefferson Davis was the president of the Confederacy if I mention that one of our city streets was named after good ole Jeff. (You won't find that street name in my native Chicago!)

If your student responds well to rewards, use them. An allowance tied to schoolwork can decrease nagging while teaching the responsible use of money. A trip to a historic reenactment can be a reward for a history unit well learned. A warm word of praise is always welcome.

FOR MORE INFORMATION

If this discussion of learning modalities and styles has whetted your appetite for more information, an Internet search can keep you reading. For direct homeschool application, read Cathy Duffy's book, *100 Top Picks for Homeschool Curriculum*. She offers a thorough presentation of learning styles and an effective system for applying this information to curriculum selections. The book is readily obtainable from homeschool catalogs and bookstores with a homeschool department.

Over the last two chapters we have looked at developing a Christian philosophy of education and understanding the learning preferences of both our students and ourselves. In the next chapter we will pull this information together with a look at teaching methods. We will close with some general guidance for choosing homeschool materials.

Methods and Materials

Methodologies, simply put, are the approaches we take to educate our students. Homeschoolers love to discuss them! We are a creative bunch, eager to meet the needs of our students. The many books and lively discussions on the topic provide ample proof of this interest.

METHODS

To help you in your decision making, we will take a brief look at some of the most popular methods employed by homeschoolers today. The list is not exhaustive but will get you started.

The following information was drawn from my booklet for new homeschoolers, *The Starting Point*, printed by Appalachian Distributor's Homeschool Headquarters. Each methodology discussed covers three main topics: (1) curriculum that follows the method or authors that provide more information about it, (2) a brief description of the method, and (3) the types of parents and students who might be most comfortable with the discussed approach. These statements are often a practical application of the information in the previous chapter. Any one of these methods, with appropriate curriculum selection, can be used in harmony with a Christian philosophy of education.

Traditional

(Examples: A Beka, Bob Jones, Rod & Staff)

Traditional textbooks are produced primarily for the classroom setting and present information in a carefully considered sequence and structure. Support materials usually include tests and teacher's manuals. To use this approach successfully the following may be true:

My child has performed well in public or private school.

My child would welcome a rigorous academic schedule.

I feel that textbooks will guard against academic skill gaps.

I like the ease of ready-made tests.

I want the convenience and security of teacher's manuals.

I want extra practice and drill for my student.

Lifepac or Pace

(Examples: Alpha Omega, School of Tomorrow/Accelerated Christian Education [ACE])

The Lifepac or Pace is a self-contained read-the-text and fill-in-the-blank approach. This approach requires less teacher preparation and is easy to grade. To use Lifepacs or Paces successfully the following may be true:

My child is an excellent reader with good comprehension. (If not, consider placing the child according to his reading level rather than his grade level.)

My child is a self-motivated learner and works well independently.

My child doesn't require lots of flash or variety to learn.

My child likes workbooks and well-defined goals.

My preparation and teaching time is limited.

Living Book Approach

(Examples: Beautiful Feet, Learning Language Arts through Literature, Progeny Press, Total Language Plus)

Living books, also called real books, are books that present information in an appealing, interesting fashion and are usually written by one author. Biographies, historical fiction, fine quality literature, and books with attractive pictures or photographs qualify as living books. Living books excite a child's desire to learn.

The nineteenth-century educator, Charlotte Mason, promoted this type of "twaddle-free" education. Today you will find books by Karen Andreola, Sally Clarkson, and Susan Schaeffer Macaulay promoting this type of learning. Sometimes study guides to living books are available. These may provide a rich assortment of activities, thus becoming a combined "living book, unit study" approach. To use a living book approach the following may be true:

The library is a favorite family spot.

My children love to read.

I enjoy reading aloud.

Designing a reading program from different sources sounds fun, not overwhelming.

Combining grade levels, while exploring subjects through reading, appeals to me.

Unit Study Approach

(Examples: Valerie Bendt, AA Bennett Books, Cadron Creek, Konos)

A unit study approach consists of choosing a theme and then teaching your different school subjects as they relate to this theme. For example, a pilgrim theme might include reading aloud from *Of Plymouth Plantation*, each student choosing additional independent reading from the library, report writing from which spelling and vocabulary words are chosen, learning about the medicine of that day for science, cooking a pilgrim meal, or constructing a cardboard model of the *Mayflower*. The choices are up to you!

Upper-level unit studies most often revolve around history. Usually subjects such as math must still be pursued in a systematic textbook. If unit studies sound appealing, the following may be true:

My child has not done well with textbooks.

My child and I like variety in activities.

I am excited about the many creative possibilities unit studies allow.

I'm not overly concerned with presenting skills and ideas in the "normal" textbook order.

I have extra time, energy, and money to spend in planning and accumulating needed books and supplies.

High-Tech Approach

(Examples: Alpha-Omega's Switched on Schoolhouse, Bob Jones' HomeSat, Internet courses)

A high-tech approach is increasingly available as different companies explore the potential of satellite school and computer or Internet courses. As technology expands rapidly, advertisements in home school magazines and the

Internet may provide the best ways to keep up with the latest products and learning opportunities. To pursue this type of schooling, these may be true:

> I am not intimidated by computers.
> My child enjoys using the computer.
> My child can type properly.
> I appreciate having outside instructional help for my child via satellite or Internet, particularly for subjects I struggle with or to free up my time to help another child.
> I am comfortable with my child's spending extended time before a television screen or computer monitor.

Classical Approach

(Examples: books by Jessie Wise and Susan Bauer, Harvey and Laurie Bluedorn, Doug Wilson, Veritas Press, Cornerstone Curriculum)

Reintroduced in an address given by Dorothy Sayers in 1947 at Oxford University, the classical approach relies on medieval educational methodology. Rigorous academics are pursued by matching content to the natural abilities of children at various stages of intellectual development. It stresses reading the classics and original sources, the study of Latin and logic, and perfecting communication skills in writing and public address. Although highly academic, the insight into a child's intellectual development may be interesting to many homeschoolers. Try this approach if:

> You and your child enjoy the intellectual stimulation of a rigorous academic program.
> You are challenged rather than intimidated when helping your student with courses you never studied.
> Reading good literature is encouraged in your home.
> Thoughtful discussions about the ideas that have influenced our world through the centuries sound enticing.
> You plan for your child to attend a competitive college.

Unschooling Approach

(Example: John Holt's books and the newsletter from those continuing his work, *Growing without Schooling*)

Unschooling was popularized by John Holt, a secular educator frustrated with classroom environments that destroy a child's love of learning. He believed children should have more opportunities to pursue their interests, and with adult encouragement this freedom would lead to greater learning. Is this a sound philosophy for the Christian educator? In its failure to recognize our children's (and our) sin natures, it may represent an overly optimistic view of what children will accomplish when left to their own devices. However, in areas where children have strong interests, an unschooling approach may have great possibilities. For example, my son's love of the classics kept him on a rigorous reading schedule I could never have demanded of him. Used with careful guidance, unschooling can be beneficial in wisely decided doses. Unschooling may appeal to you if:

> Your child has a lot of natural curiosity.
> You have a lot of natural curiosity.
> Your child is a self-starter.
> You have an "encourager" personality.
> You are not concerned that your child have a traditional education.

Mixed or Eclectic Approach

A mixed or eclectic approach occurs when teachers use different methods for different subjects. This can create a smoother fit between method and material; some methods just work better with some subjects. A typical homeschool mix might include using a traditional math book, living books for reading and history, hands-on science experiments, and free exploration in an area of high interest. A computer drill program or an Internet or satellite course might be added. Many homeschoolers take advantage of the incredible flexibility homeschooling allows and choose a variety of approaches.

MATERIALS

When I was pursuing my degree in elementary education, one of my favorite courses was called Materials and Methods. It was a hands-on "doing" class. (I know this is *not* the type of course usually appreciated by a strong visual learner, but sometimes we surprise ourselves.) Time was spent learning how to write legibly on the chalkboard or on flip charts in our best penmanship; it's harder than you think! We created bulletin boards and other learning aids designed to capture the attention of our students. A portion of the semester was taken up with learning how to use overhead, movie, and filmstrip projectors, technologies now largely obsolete. Roughly thirty years later, I still find myself wrapping electrical cords around table legs so that lamps, like projectors, cannot be easily pulled off of a table when the remaining cord is tripped over by little feet.

The materials and tools we homeschoolers use often differ from those of classroom teachers. We don't often create bulletin boards. Our best penmanship on a whiteboard is not routinely needed. However, one tool of the trade is the same. We use books and lots of them! We use textbooks, workbooks, picture books, and novels. We use materials that support and enhance the methods we have chosen to use. We choose materials that incorporate a Christian worldview. We also use materials from secular viewpoints so our students gain skill and wisdom in discerning the differences. These materials, when considered collectively, are what form our curriculum. Curriculum choices for the homeschooler vary widely. We are greatly blessed and challenged as we attempt to choose from the many sources available to us. In section 5, "A Comprehensive Homeschool Course Listing," we will spend time looking at the books we can use to build our high school homeschool curriculum.

Choosing appropriate materials is accomplished by making a successful three-way mesh: the teacher/parent's needs and learning preferences, the student's needs and learning preferences, and the approach of the school material. Without careful thought in this area, you can easily have a closetful of ineffective and often expensive material.

Sometimes homeschoolers are too fond of the word *best*. In my work at the bookstore I hear almost daily, "What is the *best* curriculum?" *Best* is a subjective term. The best methods or materials for your homeschool are what you will actually use and can accomplish. If the method or materials chosen overwhelm you, they will not be best for you, even if they work remarkably well for your homeschooling friend.

Before we leave our discussion on materials, I would like to share a few practical questions you can use to choose schoolbooks. These considerations will be shared in the form of questions. Your answers should help you in your decision making.

Questions for the Teacher (That's You!)

What are my academic strengths? What are my weaknesses?
What is my preferred learning modality and style?
What character strengths or flaws do I bring to our homeschooling?
How much time do I have for designing my student's coursework?
What is my energy level?
Am I most comfortable with a known set of expectations as defined in a textbook?
Am I comfortable with a more free-spirited approach where my student and I set expectations ourselves?
How many students and grade levels will I have?

Questions Regarding the Student

What are his academic strengths and weaknesses?
What is his preferred learning modality and style?
What character strengths or flaws does he bring to his homeschooling?
Can he work well independently?
What is his personality?
What are his career goals?

Questions Regarding the School Material

(These thoughts, with some modification, are taken from my little booklet, *The Starting Point*.)

CONTENT OF THE BOOK

Does the book promote moral and religious teachings compatible with our family's beliefs?

Is the book more concerned about accuracy or pursuing a particular agenda?

Does the teaching style compliment my child's abilities and learning style?

Does the difficulty of the book match the abilities of my student?

What is the overall approach of the book? Does it capture attention through storytelling or the interesting presentation of information or does it give a rapid (and boring) shotgun blast of facts?

Is the copyright relatively current? Will I be teaching outdated material?

PHYSICAL QUALITY OF THE BOOK

Binding and cover—Will it self-destruct after one student?

Print—Is it clear and crisp? Will your student need a magnifying glass to read it? (Will you?)

Pictures—Are they updated or circa 1950?

Color—Is there any, and does it matter to you or your student?

ORGANIZATION OF THE BOOK

Table of contents—Is the book well laid out and helpful?

Index—Does it have a thorough index? It makes life easier, especially with junior high/high school.

Glossary—Does it have a glossary of terms? (A good glossary is a tremendous help.)

SUPPORT MATERIALS

Are they easy to use and time-saving?

Are they priced reasonably?

Are they necessary for a satisfactory learning experience?

Tests and quizzes—Are there any? Do they test important facts or minutia? Do they encourage critical thinking?

Teacher's editions—Are the activities workable and helpful in a homeschool setting?

FINAL QUESTIONS

Does this book appeal to my child?

Does this book appeal to me?

Can our household budget absorb the expense?

Does the material fit our chosen method or approach to the subject being taught?

Do the materials require outside instruction to be used effectively?

Can the materials be mastered within our time constraints?

The next section, "Seeing the Big Picture: Kindergarten through College," may seem unusual for a book on teaching high school. However, the foundation laid with even the youngest learners affects students' preparedness for high school, college, and life. Because of this belief and the fact that many readers are teaching multiple grade levels, we will look at elementary school and junior high before rolling up our sleeves and beginning high school planning.

SECTION THREE

Seeing the Big Picture: Kindergarten through College

College Preparation Begins in Kindergarten

Our homeschool journey has been long and full of change. Rocking chairs, picture books, diapers, and sweet bedtime tuck-ins gave way to schoolbooks, piano lessons, sleepovers, and scout camping trips. Then began a relentless and often bewildering progression of history, science, literature, and algebra courses. When graduation caps and gowns, college campuses, and teary good-byes became commonplace, I have often found myself sighing like an elderly grandmother, "Where has the time gone?"

Two young learners remain in our household. Our youngest will soon start high school. The other already has her eyes set on college. My husband John and I treasure their presence, knowing that our two remaining ducklings will soon join the three who have already ventured out from under our wings. It is our job to prepare them for the personal adventure that awaits each of them.

As homeschooling parents, we are privileged to play a large role in molding our children's future. With God's grace, and in accordance with the talents and abilities each child possesses, we are preparing our children to be kingdom builders for Him. Preparation takes two directions. Academically, we prepare our students for high school, learning a trade, college, and future careers. Spiritually, we prepare our students to live this temporal life in a manner that is consistent with their eternal hope. Such training doesn't begin at ninth grade. High school, college, and life preparation begin with the youngest learners.

READING

Hands down, the most important academic skill we give our children is reading. To negotiate life successfully with poor reading skills is a difficult task. Our kindergartners and primary-age children are forging their future when they complete their phonics work sheets and laboriously sound out their first short vowel readers. In addition, when we read excellent books aloud, we encourage our little learners to persevere so that they may enjoy the many delights awaiting them on the printed page.

While reading opens the vast world of ideas to our students, spelling and composition provide the tools that help them contribute thoughts of their own. Spelling comes naturally to many students; their strong visual memory retains each word's image in their mind. Others spell each word phonetically, happily unaware that their letter choices bear no resemblance to accepted spelling patterns. They are also unaware that a future employer may hesitate to hire them if their application is full of misspellings. For such students, work on building visual memory of words, encouraging them to see their spelling words in their minds. Ask them, "Can you see the word? Spell to me what you see." If it is a short word, try some visual gymnastics and see if they can spell it backward. Don't give up, and be thankful for spell-checker!

WRITING

Composition consists of two types of writing: creative and expository. Creative writing is often introduced through journaling. Writing about firsthand experiences helps a reluctant writer unlock ideas and gain confidence in handling words. This provides practice for the expository writing to come. Expository writing consists of book reports, test essay questions, opinion and research papers, etc. For such writing, organization is crucial. Gently introduce brainstorming, idea-webbing, note-taking, and simple outlining before writing compositions. Proofreading from checklists (rubrics) teaches students to examine completed written work with critical care. (e.g., Does every sentence begin with a capital letter? Check. Does every sentence end with punctuation? Oops! That should be a question mark!) Efficient word processing skills make it much easier for students to write and edit their creations. Start before hunt-and-peck habits become ingrained. Friendly familiarity with these organizational, proofreading, and word-processing skills prepares the student for more involved high school papers and the pressurized college environment to come.

If you are unsure how to begin expository writing projects with your student, book reports provide a good introduction. The student has the benefit of working with familiar information (the book he has just read). In addition to the skills already mentioned, book reports provide practice in the clear expression of ideas, orderly summarization, and thoughtful analysis of characters and ideas. For the best results, make these reports student-teacher projects until the student is comfortable working alone. Working together on the computer, with its wonderful cut-and-paste capabilities, can produce a thoughtful final product with minimal pain. Fine-tuning becomes so easy!

ARITHMETIC

Competence in math skills is the next area of major importance. Mastery of facts and an understanding of math concepts paves the way for the math studied in high school. Don't underestimate the value of drill. Students' confidence in understanding mathematical concepts expands if they are not handicapped by a poor grasp of basic facts. Our students who plan to attend college, whatever their majors, will most likely be required to take some math, particularly college algebra. Make sure they are well prepared.

HISTORY AND SCIENCE

No high school preparation is complete without history and science. The information students acquire in elementary school and junior high serves as an introduction to future studies. Mental hooks are created upon which high school and college information can hang, thus making future learning more easily retained. History, in particular, provides enjoyable ways to gain this knowledge. Put your feet up on the coffee table and dive into those biographies and historical fiction books homeschoolers love so much! Elementary science can whet the appetite for future studies by reading colorful, high interest books and performing well-chosen experiments.

DIVERSIFIED LEARNING

In addition to building a strong academic foundation, we must also teach our students to be diversified learners. Children vary in the way they learn best. However, in a college setting students must learn in many different ways, not only in the style most comfortable for them. Help your student gain confidence in his ability to learn auditorily and visually. Most college learning will take place through these channels. Reading aloud from chapter books is an enjoyable way to develop good listening skills. Consider teaching a new math skill using a whiteboard. Present an occasional history lesson lecture style, with note taking encouraged. Varying your teaching approach will provide good preparation for the diversity in professors and classes that awaits your student.

SPIRITUAL TRAINING

Undoubtedly our most important activity during these preparation years is training children spiritually. Students must be grounded in the content of the Bible, the character of God, and a biblical understanding of right and wrong. When temptations come (and they will), a carefully nurtured teen will have a heavenly friend and a moral compass to guide him through the difficult situations of life. We must reinforce our teaching with a personal lifestyle that strives to glorify God. Practice patience, forgiveness, and humility. Not only is our pursuit of godly virtues right, it hopefully encourages our children to work at acquiring the same patience, forgiveness, and humility toward us when necessary!

Finally, we must commit our children and their life preparation to the Lord. We do not know the future, and our best-laid plans, though laid lovingly, are sometimes laid amiss. As we do our imperfect best, we can rest in His faithfulness and kindhearted love toward His children. He will not fail.

Junior High/Middle School

The junior high years are a great time to bring students home to school. Depending on your location and state situation, the crediting considerations of high school may not yet apply. If this is the case, junior high provides a helpful trial run before making what are often "burn-your-bridges" decisions regarding high school homeschooling.

The junior high/middle school years can encompass any grade from sixth through ninth, depending on your state school system. For our purposes we will be thinking primarily of the seventh and eighth grade years when students move out of childhood and into adolescence. These early teen years are a time of change.

Some of the changes are physical. Before our eyes we watch our offspring transform from children into adults. Voices deepen and figures soften. Those grown-up teeth that once looked so huge and out of place are beginning to fit nicely into their smile. Clear, angel-bright complexions give way to ego-bruising blotches. Easy, cheerful wake-up calls are replaced with pleas for more sleep.

Emotional changes are also evident. Many of us have experienced unexpected female tears. When asking for an explanation, it is not unusual to receive a plaintive wail in return. "I don't kn-kn-knoooow!" She probably doesn't. Nor does a young man always understand the agitation that can unexpectedly surface. Teens' emotions often take them by as much surprise as they do us. With this excessive emotion comes introspection and a great need to be accepted by their peers. Junior high is a hard age if you're not a carbon copy of the rest of your age mates.

Intellectual changes are also occurring. Gone are the years of believing in parental infallibility. Black is no longer black, and white is no longer white. There are now shades of gray. Formerly compliant children may become argumentative in the quest to be masters of their own thoughts.

With all these changes comes a broader outlook. Children who were once content to operate within a family and a small group of close friends start looking beyond the comfortable. An awareness of the bigness of the world and its opportunities captures their imagination. They become dreamers of dreams. Anything seems possible. *Maybe I'll go climb Mount Everest . . . except I've got this zit on my nose.* And they crash to Earth again, lost in a sometimes overwhelming self-focus.

Into this maelstrom of unstable hormones and emotions, we try to interject some academics.

MEETING THE JUNIOR HIGH STUDENT'S NEEDS

Scattered among the parents who would like to grant their young teens an extended absence from family life—say, a mission trip to Siberia for two or three years—are parents who see great opportunity in these years of change. No, the chaos has not affected their reasoning power. They have looked behind the stormy exterior to the young adult struggling to peek through. With the right care, prayer, and grace from the Almighty, a future man or woman of God stands before them. The following are some thoughts for capturing the potential of these years.

Physically

Don't leave your child in the dark about the changes going on in his body. Encourage open dialogue. I am a fairly private person and never found these talks easy. The personality of the child is a major factor in his comfort level in these heart-to-hearts. Some children welcome any information you have to offer. Some find it excruciatingly embarrassing. Either way, with consideration for the child's nature, the talk must go on. A visit to your Christian bookstore can usually provide some literature to make the job easier. The Learning about Sex series from Concordia or God's Design for Sex by NavPress are both series that offer age-appropriate information written directly to the child or teen.

Because young teens are so self-focused, they sometimes have health concerns. When I was this age, a young man in my school stepped on the prongs of a rake, sending the handle crashing into his forehead. Unknown to him or his parents, a slow aneurysm developed, which took his life three days later. The death of a schoolmate is a major trauma for the impressionable teen. Class by class we were taken to the funeral home to view his body, and we attended the funeral en masse. I can't speak for my classmates, but for some time afterward every time I bumped my head I would count off three days and wait to see whether I would die. A few well-directed questions on my part or my parents could have prevented several months of unhealthy speculation. Keep the communication lines open.

Encourage your young teens to be physically active. Help them find an activity they enjoy and facilitate participation. Young men often enjoy competitive sports, but family baseball games may also fill the need. A trampoline, used with appropriate safety precautions, can work off a lot of emotional energy. Some of our local homeschoolers are involved in Irish step dance, a demanding physical exercise. Check out your options, and encourage your student to get moving! If the activity chosen takes place outdoors, so much the better. While strengthening their bodies, they will be calming their spirits. Look for ways to be active with your teen. Walking, jogging, and bike riding provide physical activity and an opportunity to talk.

Emotionally

The emotional tornados that sometimes whirl in our young teens can cause tension between parent and child. One five-word sentence contains the best advice I know for the situation. *Don't overreact to their emotions.* This is not as simple as it sounds. Our young teens know us well. They often have an uncanny ability to fan into full flame the annoyance that can smolder within us. When your teen's emotions are rising, consciously try to keep yours in check. Situations are often forgotten, and life will move on if you don't escalate his emotions by adding yours.

It is not uncommon for young teens to overreact to or misread the social signals from their peer groups. The self-focus so prevalent at this age makes every possible slight or vague response a condemnation of personal worth. Help your young teen think outside himself. Help him recognize that much that occurs is not about him, but about whatever is happening in the other person's life. In some ways it is a bit arrogant to assume that other people spend so much time thinking about us! Help your teen understand that loving his neighbors as himself means giving them the benefit of the doubt when he doesn't understand them.

When my children are stung by a comment or a situation, I will often encourage them to keep it "outside their fence" until they have evaluated it. This advice springs from a talk I heard years ago, which likened each individual to a house surrounded by a fence. Many thoughts try to open our gate and enter our yard and home. Rather than allowing everything in that begs admittance, we should keep our emotional gate closed until we evaluate the visitor. When the criticism the visitor brings is just, we should welcome it and correct our error. When the criticism is unjust, we should lock our gate and let it pass on by. Learning to evaluate criticism dispassionately is learned over a lifetime. This is one possible tool to get your teen started on the lesson.

As parents, we will weather our child's early and later teen years gracefully if we can interact with a compassionate calm spirit. At times I am a "quit whining and get over it" mother, which is not the most helpful approach to effective communication. Therefore, it wasn't until my fourth child and second daughter that I understood the wisdom of a gentle hug and the encouraging words: "Go ahead and cry. It'll make you feel better."

Spiritually

When our children were younger, it was natural for them to accept without question the spiritual truths we offered. As children mature and begin to think their own thoughts, we want them to take hold *personally* of the truths they have been taught. Use this time to channel awakening emotions, intellects, and reasoning abilities into spiritual directions.

Encourage your student to read the Bible devotionally for himself. Our desire is for the Word of God to be personally meaningful to our teens. Many young girls enjoy journaling. Turn this enjoyment in a spiritual direction by encouraging your student to jot down prayer requests and meaningful Bible verses accompanied by her own thoughts. Even a young man who dislikes journaling can begin to highlight and memorize verses he finds meaningful.

With reasoning power developing, junior high is also a good time to encourage a systematic study of the Bible. I have especially enjoyed the Studying God's Word series from Christian Liberty Press. By completing Books *E* through *H*, a student can chronologically study the Bible from Genesis through Revelation in a few years. Although designed for grades four through seven, I have found this series can be used for independent study with slightly older students. *The Victor Journey through the Bible* by V. Gilbert Beers would add interesting information to the study.

In addition to encouraging growth in independent devotion and Bible study, we must often address character issues. Sometimes a child views parental instructions as an oppressive attempt to control. Simple requests can be met with stubborn silence, hysterical exaggerations, or belligerent monosyllables depending on the personality of the child. When heart issues are involved, heart issues should be addressed. Paul Tripp's *Age of Opportunity* offers helpful insight into the sin issues that arise during the teen years. Lou Priolo's *The Heart of Anger* and Tripp's *War of Words* may also prove helpful.

Sometimes, however, a situation can be diffused if we show a little more parental wisdom. Young teens, in their tentative movement toward adulthood, are trying to establish some sense of autonomy. Cooperation may be easier to gain if we provide choices rather than issue ultimatums. When you need help in several areas, let your teen choose between options. Let him enjoy a little adult-like dignity as he contributes to the family team.

Academically

Determined state by state, educational laws establish no set national curriculum. This is a boon for homeschool freedom but unhelpful if we really want some direction. Should your state offer clear academic guidelines for the junior high years, it is important to follow them. Otherwise, you best serve junior high students if you follow one of two academic directions: polishing or plunging ahead.

POLISHING OR PLUNGING AHEAD

Some students will make it to the junior high years without mastery of elementary skills. If this is the situation in your homeschool, there's hope! The next few years are a special gift to you and your student.

Most subjects are taught in a spiral fashion, the groundwork laid in elementary grades. In junior high, subjects spiral down to review previously taught skills before spiraling upward with added information. More downward, then upward movements occur in high school and college as subjects are revisited with added depth and breadth. All this repetition is not necessarily wasted time. Students bring more maturity to the subject each time they learn it. In addition most of us need to be exposed to information more than once to retain it.

For the eighth-grade student in particular there is a special benefit to all this spiral motion. Little new information will be introduced. Rather, it is a time for polishing skills before the spiral takes a more aggressive turn upward during the high school years. Careful attention to mastery of reading, writing, and mathematical skills now will help your student begin high school with a greater expectation of success.

What if your eighth-grade student is all spit polished and ready for a new challenge? Don't look to junior high material. If you are sure that all skills are in place, there is no reason to delay high school coursework. Go ahead and plunge in! And brush up on your calculus and trigonometry; you may be teaching these subjects in the years to come!

Still not sure what to teach during the junior high years? The following list provides some suggestions for profitably filling the junior high years. In addition, section 5 offers an extensive course listing with curriculum suggestions for both junior high and high school.

Encourage serious Bible study.

Follow a rigorous Bible memory schedule. (*The Topical Memory System* by NavPress is one possibility.)

Combat the "me" focus with volunteer work.

Encourage contact with all age levels.

Remediate skills to ensure high school success or begin high-school studies.

Teach test-taking skills in preparation for high school.

Study a foreign language (a conversational study like *Rosetta Stone* is a good fit).

Teach principles of logic and debate.

Teach etiquette.

Take a public-speaking course.

Teach life skills, such as cooking, baking, cleaning, needlework, gardening, auto repair, and basic consumer math.

The Need for Postsecondary Education

My father was a hardworking man, often working two jobs to support his growing family. He spent most of his career in middle management, running chemical plants that manufactured detergents. Our frugal household had one luxury: we could take baths with as much bubble bath as we wanted, courtesy of the great discount provided by my dad's workplace. Although my father was competent at his job and reached a moderate level of worldly success, he always regretted not having a college education. Even in an age where a college degree was not the norm, he felt his educational lack had prevented him from making the career advancements he desired.

My parents raised my siblings and me to be independent. We were making adult decisions by the time we graduated from high school. When it came time for me to spread my wings, I spread them widely. I chose a college seven hundred miles from home, a decision that made my mother nervous but was not discouraged by my father. Because of the distance, my parents never visited me at college until the day I graduated. I achieved a goal my dad had never reached, and he wanted to be a part of the triumph.

While getting a college degree may be part of the American dream for many people, it is not necessarily so for many homeschoolers. There is good reason for this caution. After working years to instill a godly character into our children, why would we risk it all to send them to what is, in many circumstances, the antithesis of what we have so carefully taught?

Fortunately, there are enough avenues to postsecondary education that most homeschoolers can find a comfortable fit somewhere. Community college, technical school, the four-year university, an apprenticeship, an internship, or the military can offer opportunities for students' continued education beyond high school. I believe some form of postsecondary education is important for our sons and, yes, even for our daughters.

Our Sons

There is less controversy surrounding the need for our sons to continue their education beyond the high school years. Why is postsecondary training so important?

Most of our young men will someday be breadwinners. The earning power of college graduates significantly exceeds that of employees without a degree. This is not to encourage our young men to make a mad dash into whatever course of study leads to the highest paying career field. God sees our young people as individuals and has gifted them accordingly. Our sons' career goals should be prayerfully explored with a wise eye to the skills and gifts God has given them. The goal should be competence and thorough preparation for that field. In many circumstances this entails a college education.

In addition to providing adequately for their future families, our sons should pursue additional education in order to better fulfill the cultural mandate given to Adam in the garden. In Genesis 1:28 God commanded Adam to "have dominion over the fish of the sea, over the birds of the air, and over every living thing that moves on the earth." In other words, man was to rule the earth. The earth is now a complex place. To exercise leadership effectively and "take dominion" in today's world requires a level of excellence and integrity not always found in the modern workforce. Our young men need the training necessary to help them excel for Christ.

Our young men should pursue education in order to serve their fellowman more effectively. Just as Christ made Himself of no reputation and took on the form of a servant, so our sons should be willing to serve mankind. Effective service requires thoughtful preparation with goals that extend beyond the well-being of themselves and their future families.

Higher education also prepares our sons for future advancement in their occupational field. As mentioned above, my father was a competent man, yet the lack of a college education limited his ability to advance into higher managerial positions. We want our sons to be as prepared as possible for the opportunities God brings their way.

Finally, our sons should pursue higher education for the sake of offering excellence to their Creator. Ephesians 2:10 reminds us, "For we are His workmanship, created in Christ Jesus for good works, which God prepared beforehand that we should walk in them." Walking in good works is not relegated to church work only but should be evident in every area touched by our lives including the workplace. Appropriate preparation allows the good work of the hands to complement the good work of the heart.

Sometimes people question the worth of a college degree when, upon graduation, the student moves into an unrelated career field. This does not make the degree worthless. Rather, the degree sends a helpful message to employers: this man was able to set a goal and pursue it to completion. A potential employer knows that a college diploma is not earned without individual drive and the ability to be a self-starter. He also knows that the teamwork required by course projects and extracurricular activities is good preparation for the people skills necessary in the workplace. A college degree enhances employability.

OUR DAUGHTERS

On occasion I have heard homeschoolers express their family's conviction that they ought not prepare their daughters for college but should focus on homemaking skills and preparation to be a wife and mother. I have always found this comment troubling.

Like most homeschool parents, I want my girls to be wives and mothers. I do my best to train them in life skills and godly character. I want them to have sharp, biblically trained minds and a well-developed Christian worldview. I want them to be equipped to counsel their children wisely in their encounters with many different issues of life. These goals are necessary for effective motherhood and the nurturing of their own children.

In addition, however, I desire for them to have the education and skills to become breadwinners should it ever prove necessary. Life is unpredictable and, through God's sovereignty, takes twists and turns we would never expect or choose. Many girls will discover that a single life is God's will for them and will need skills to support themselves. Many wives will unexpectedly find themselves thrust into the workforce due to a husband's disability or death. Perhaps your family's history, as mine, includes stories of the hardships endured during last century's depression and world wars. Developing an educational safety net against such times is a prudent strategy.

In addition to the larger woes that can throw a family or an entire world into tumult, other troubles arise. Job security is tenuous in the modern world, with corporate loyalty to long-term employees often nonexistent. Sometimes a husband's income will need to be replaced or supplemented temporarily. Unbudgeted needs, not wants, may arise. By not preparing for life's unexpected but all too common occurrences, we potentially condemn our daughters and possibly their children to a minimum wage, poverty-level lifestyle.

Having said that, I recommend encouraging girls to enter fields that are compatible with motherhood. Education degrees prepare them for the classroom, substituting, tutoring, or capably teaching their own children. Music degrees prepare them for taking private students, holding a pianist position in the church, and enriching their family with beauty. Accounting makes way for them to keep the books for a small business or a family business of their own. Nursing can be a helpful skill for any mother and is seldom a saturated field. These career fields can either be pursued from home or offer flexible scheduling. This list is just a start; undoubtedly there are many possibilities I have missed.

Proverbs 31 contains a description of the virtuous woman. It is interesting that her enterprising activities included contributing financially to the needs of her family. She is honored for being prepared for whatever the future may hold. Consider whether college or another form of postsecondary education should be included in this preparation.

What if my student does not want to go to college?

Many students just out of high school do not want to go to college for a variety of reasons. Sometimes they have no idea what to study since their career interests are not defined. Some crave independence—the quicker, the better. Some do not seem suited for college.

A student who is unsure of a career direction can often be well served by a junior/community college situation. Tuition is usually reasonable with a wide variety of courses available. This allows some career exploration without breaking the bank. In addition, the student can often successfully juggle the flexible scheduling afforded by evening and Internet courses with work schedules. There is nothing wrong with taking a slower, scenic route through the first few years of college, especially if concurrent employment helps clarify college goals.

Instead of flipping burgers, your student should look for a job that introduces him to new career possibilities. Richard Bolles's *What Color Is Your Parachute?*, although addressed primarily to adults hunting jobs or changing careers, can also offer some practical advice to the young job seeker. My oldest son found the information on the interview process especially helpful; it helped him secure his present position. This popular book is updated regularly and should be available from your public library.

Some of our new high school graduates crave independence. They have short-term goals not extending beyond a car and freedom. Even when further training is not your student's goal, hold your student to reasonable academic standards, plan college preparatory courses, and keep adequate records. Should college become a goal at a later date, you will have helped your student make that step rather than hindering him with inadequate preparation. A few years of meeting real-life expenses with a limited income can make additional training appealing.

Some students don't seem suited for college. That may indeed be the case. However, life is far from static. People change, including students. We don't want to make a change in career or dreams impossible because we did not plan an adequate high school program.

Postsecondary Opportunities

A traditional four-year college is not the only place to prepare your student for life after high school. However, it is a path often desired. Today's colleges accommodate a wide variety of students. Some colleges require students to have the brains of a rocket scientist. Others service a student body of more moderate abilities. Still others actively accommodate bright students with learning disabilities. You can usually find a good fit for your student. If an unhealthy spiritual environment remains a concern, you can creatively reduce time spent on campus with CLEP tests, Internet courses, etc., while your student still attains the goal of a college education.

In addition to four-year college degrees, there are many one- and two-year programs. Often available at community colleges, these programs teach a variety of trades or skills. The training often culminates in a two-year associate's degree or a certification in the area of training. For our hands-on students, an education in a trade can be the right choice.

Other homeschoolers actively pursue apprenticeship opportunities. These programs can be a formal program that incorporates a mixture of classroom time and hands-on training. Look for the *Ferguson Career Resource Guide to Apprenticeship Programs* by Elizabeth Oakes in your library's reference section for help in locating apprenticeship programs.

Apprenticeships can also be a one-on-one agreement where a student moves directly into the workforce, learning a business through real-life experience. This type of apprenticeship sometimes begins as a volunteer position, that over time moves into paid employment. Apprenticeships can occur in the family's business, in that of a relative, through a community contact, or through other creative networking. The effectiveness of an apprenticeship depends on the teaching skills of the master and how well he incorporates the apprentice into daily work. When choosing an apprenticeship, take great care to be sure it will deliver all that is promised.

Another postsecondary opportunity is the military. Although not a good fit for all students, it can be the right choice for many. Uncle Sam rewards his recruits with many benefits including career training and college tuition benefits. A visit to recruiters or the Web sites of the different military branches can help you collect the information you need.

Moving On . . .

In the next section we will roll up our sleeves and look at designing an effective high school program.

SECTION FOUR

Designing the Program

Correspondence or Home-Designed Schooling?

Most homeschoolers complete their high school education in one of two ways, correspondence schools or home-designed programs. Both options have advantages and disadvantages.

CORRESPONDENCE SCHOOL BASICS

If your teen enrolls in a correspondence school, the correspondence school will provide textbooks, course requirements, and oversight of the academic work. The correspondence school generally grades and records the mailed-in tests and papers. Upon the satisfactory completion of all requirements, a diploma is issued. Some correspondence schools use videos, courses by satellite, or interaction via the Internet. Several of these schools are services of large Christian publishers.

These Christian publishers also sell their complete textbook lines, preschool to twelfth grade, without requiring enrollment in their schools. In addition to textbooks, courses on DVD (School of Tomorrow and A Beka), satellite (Bob Jones University Press), and software (Alpha Omega) are available for those homeschooling independently. If you do not choose to enroll in their correspondence schools, these publishers will be unable to issue your student a diploma. Purchasing textbooks, without the accompanying accountability of their correspondence services, does not provide the necessary verification of the student's work. In this situation the diploma will come from the parents.

Positively, correspondence schools are helpful for the parent who is overwhelmed with making curriculum decisions. They also provide an outside verification of the student's high school performance. The school will maintain the student's records and compile a transcript for college entrance. Negatively, using a correspondence school results in a loss of educational flexibility, which is one of the significant advantages to homeschooling. A correspondence school may not be able or willing to accommodate the textbooks you prefer and may not offer the classes that would most enhance your student's career goals. For this reason many homeschoolers retain some flexibility by supplementing a correspondence school program with courses of their own design.

Some parents start their high schoolers in correspondence and later move to a home-designed program. This is certainly acceptable. In this situation the student's complete transcript would be home produced, including the work done through the school and at home. The partial transcript from the correspondence school can accompany the complete transcript, providing verification for that portion of the work.

Some homeschoolers wish to move from a home-designed high school program into a correspondence school. Because of the crediting issues involved in a high school education, this transition may not be as smooth. Contact the correspondence school of interest to learn about their policies.

The following are some schools categorized under a few basic descriptions. See appendix A for address information.

CORRESPONDENCE SCHOOLS

Publishing Company Programs

A Beka* (DVD option)
Academy of Home Education* (BJU, record-keeping service)
Christian Liberty Academy*

Classical Programs

Covenant Home Curriculum*
Great Books Academy

Worktext (workbook) Programs

Alpha Omega Academy* (software option available)
Lighthouse Christian Academy* (School of Tomorrow/ACE)

Online Programs

Eagle Christian High School*
Escondido Tutorial Service* (classical emphasis)
SOLA* (Scholar's On-line Academy, classical emphasis)

Secular Accredited Programs

American School
Keystone National High School

State University Programs

Texas Tech University High School
University of Nebraska-Lincoln Independent Study High School

HOME-DESIGNED PROGRAM BASICS

The second option, a home-designed program, is what educators call an "eclectic approach." In an eclectic approach to homeschooling, an effort is made to find the best possible textbooks, living books,† and materials for

*Has a Christian worldview.
†*Living Book*. A *living* or *real* book is a homeschool description for almost any book that is not a textbook. Biographies, original sources, historical fiction, novels, etc., are examples. They are usually written by one author highly interested in the subject rather than a committee meeting mandated criteria. The premise is that living books are more interesting and, therefore, are better remembered and more meaningful. Living books can be borrowed from libraries and purchased from bookstores. Living books can either replace or enrich textbooks.

Should we use an accredited correspondence school?

Generally speaking, accreditation has minimal importance, if any, prior to the collegiate level. Accreditation is a voluntary procedure. To avoid the entanglement of unwelcome controls, many Christian correspondence schools choose not to seek accreditation from secular agencies. Some seek oversight from alternative accrediting agencies that offer accountability for Christian schools. Do not assume that a lack of secular accreditation is an indication of poor academic quality.

Accredited schools offer outside verification of the quality of their program. This reassures parents and saves them the effort of thoroughly investigating the school for themselves. However, if you insist on an accredited correspondence school, you may miss some excellent educational possibilities. If the program of a nonaccredited school appeals to your student, do your homework, learn about the school, and check its reputation with other homeschoolers. Also bear in mind that the many homeschoolers who pursue a home-designed program and receive a nonaccredited education populate colleges in growing numbers.

It is always possible that the college your child desires to attend (particularly if it is state funded) could require that your teen have a high school diploma from a secularly accredited school. However, it is not likely. A college making such a request would probably be unfriendly to the homeschooling option. Your student may want to look elsewhere for his college education.

Appearances can be deceiving, though. I know of one private college whose catalog at one time stated that the homeschooler's high school must be accredited, yet it actively recruited home-educated students who followed a home-designed program. The confusion of the earlier years of homeschooling has been largely resolved. College attitudes toward homeschooling have steadily moved from suspicion to accommodation. Although there may always be some exceptions, a nontraditional, nonaccredited high school education can find a comfortable fit at today's university.

each subject, often produced by many different publishers. While correspondence schooling usually limits curriculum flexibility, a home-designed program offers it in abundance. Why is the ability to choose school materials so important to many homeschool parents?

First, you can choose your teen's books with his strengths and weaknesses in mind. An algebra program that covers topics slowly with thorough review may be helpful to the student struggling in math while the math genius may be racing ahead into calculus. A teen interested in literature and history can read living books to his heart's content. A history textbook for this student might serve only as a framework for much broader exploration. For another student the history book may suffice. This flexibility in curriculum choice is hard to achieve in a correspondence school.

Second, you may also determine the pace of the academic work. This individualizing of pace is tremendously helpful to both the remedial student who needs more time and the accelerated student who can move ahead rapidly or desires to slow down and study something in greater depth. In our family's homeschool we spent extended time in world history, literature, and worldview studies with our third student because of his high interest level and the depth of study he desired. That love led to a college double major in English and philosophy. We would not have had the flexibility to customize his curriculum if we were using a correspondence school.

A home-designed program also provides greater flexibility in course selection. While core subjects must still be covered, electives can be effectively used to enhance the student's natural interests and abilities. Our fourth child's love of music has led to a distinct fine arts slant in the materials, courses, and activities in her school program.

Don't worry that this flexibility requires parents to develop expertise in all areas of study. No one would plan their own homeschool program if that were the case! Rather, parents of home-educated students become experts at creating a division of labor, seeking out appropriate outside instructors, courses, and materials that will enhance their student's education.

So far I have mentioned the advantages of a home-designed program. What are the drawbacks to this kind of program?

Depending on state regulations, a home-designed program offers fewer checks and balances. This means it is up to the parent and student to maintain a program that meets state standards and prepares the student for his future career goals. Failure to plan and conscientiously follow an effective high school program can have long-term consequences, significantly altering your student's ability to succeed in life. Before embarking on a home-designed plan, realistically consider your ability and drive to stay with the challenge.

In addition, although record-keeping responsibilities can be shared between parent and student, all records are produced in-house. Books such as this have been written to help you learn how to plan appropriate courses, grade and credit objectively, and compile these records into a transcript acceptable for college entrance. Although such record-keeping duties are manageable if kept current, they can assume mountainous proportions if neglected. A correspondence school will relieve you of many, but not all, of these duties.

Finally, because a self-directed program is solely under the parent's supervision, no external organization issues your student a diploma. This doesn't necessarily present a problem. A diploma, in many respects, is only a symbol of the student's achievement. The quality of your student's high school program is proved through his transcript and

When planning a home-designed program, how do you decide what materials to choose?

Many resources are available on today's homeschool market. Because of this, a homeschool parent can easily feel overwhelmed. Hopefully, earlier discussion in this book has helped you narrow your search somewhat. The course listing in section 5 can also guide you in your selections.

The course listing focuses on high quality materials. It is selective rather than exhaustive. Our family has personally used many of the products. My customers and homeschooling friends have frequently used others. Remember, these are suggestions. The best choices are those chosen with your student and situation in mind.

Most choices will represent materials from a Christian worldview. However, I will also recommend high quality secular publishers. I will leave it to the parents to sift out the occasional chaff found in these latter books.

The course listing will direct you toward some valuable resources but will not provide a thorough review of each curriculum suggested. More information and an objective review on many of the products mentioned in this book can be found in Cathy Duffy's *100 Top Picks for Homeschool Curriculum*. An Internet search for additional reviews or the opinion of a homeschool friend who has used the product you are considering can also prove helpful.

Is a home-designed program less expensive than correspondence?

Maybe. Because correspondence schools charge for both materials and the administration of your program (grading, record keeping, etc.), they can sometimes, but not always, be expensive. Planning your own program may cost less because your expense will be limited to your materials.

However, do not choose a home-designed program primarily to save money. It may not happen. Instead, see the money saved by keeping your own records as money now available to use on material to enhance your teen's education. I will gladly pay a high price for a book or program if it will light an academic fire in my teen. Don't sacrifice quality to save money. Your teen's future is too important.

college entrance scores. A parent should feel comfortable recognizing his student's accomplishments with a diploma. Attractive presentation diplomas are available through HSLDA and some state homeschool organizations.

CHOOSING BETWEEN CORRESPONDENCE SCHOOL AND A HOME-DESIGNED PROGRAM

We have looked at both correspondence and home-designed education and considered some pros and cons for each method. However, you may still be unsure which represents the best route for your family. When making a decision between the two, you may evaluate a number of factors.

Your Time. Depending on your curriculum choices, planning a home-designed program can be time-consuming. Do you have the time available?

Your Finances. Although some correspondence schools are reasonable, others offer some pretty expensive bells and whistles. Can your pocketbook handle them? Be mindful that a homeschool parent without a clear curriculum direction who makes frequent changes can also easily overspend on a home-designed program.

Your Confidence Level. If planning your own program leaves you sick in the pit of your stomach and keeps you awake at night, it is probably not the choice for you.

Your Student's Learning Style. Some students are self-directed and love to explore subjects in depth. A correspondence school might stifle this. Other students like clear directions and goals. These might welcome the structure of a correspondence school.

Your Student's Academic Ability. If your student needs his program modified to accommodate learning problems, it may be difficult with a correspondence school.

Your Student's Temperament. Some teens are anxious for independence. This can be especially true of sons ready to be men who are chafing under mom's constant oversight. A correspondence school can be the outside voice determining the direction of the program, thus removing a source of conflict between parent and student.

Camaraderie between Student and Parent. If you and your student enjoy the excitement of planning a course of study together and jointly salivate over all your book choices, follow a home-designed program. My third student and I enjoyed perusing catalogs looking for the most interesting options in historical reading.

While this book will be most helpful for those planning a home-designed program, there is plenty to help the parent choosing correspondence. Should you need to plan elective credits to supplement your student's program, you may want to consult the course listing found here. In addition, the sections on college selection, admissions, financing, and earning alternative college credit in this book will apply to all college-bound homeschoolers, regardless of their high school choice.

Working Backward to Move Forward: Planning Your Program with Future Goals in Mind

We live in a midsize city surrounded by smaller communities and open countryside. Every once in a great while, when the day is moving slowly and no obligation requires my immediate attention, I'll explore country roads. I love the leisurely pastime of turning down a road because it looks interesting, not because it brings me closer to my destination.

This nondirected cruising might be fine for a lazy afternoon but would bring disaster if applied to a high school program. Training received during the high school years will have tremendous bearing on success in both college and career. Successful preparation requires careful thought and planning. It also involves working backward to move forward.

What does "working backward to move forward" mean? It means that the most effective high school planning occurs when courses and activities are chosen with an eye toward future career goals. From this future perspective we then work backward to planning an appropriate program. A carefully customized program brought to fruition will move students forward toward a successful career and a God-honoring life.

When should high school planning begin? The best time to begin planning your high school program is during the junior high years when student strengths and interests may start coming more sharply into focus. Although the student himself may have too few or too many career ideas, mom and dad can often see the strengths of the child. Pray for wisdom and discernment and begin planning an appropriate high school program.

To help the student form career ideas, walk through daily life with your eyes open, noticing books, resource people, field trips, volunteer opportunities, and later on, work options that provide career tasting. Do not make this a tense, you-need-to-know-now situation. It's not. Encourage your teen toward a heightened awareness that God created every person with a purpose, including him. God's heart is to guide us to find and fulfill that purpose.

Our responsibility is to be diligent in developing our natural talents and strengthening our weak areas so that we can bring Him glory. Through our prayers and obedience, God will direct us in appropriate paths.

Career ideas will unfold over time. Plan to continue career investigation throughout high school. When general directions become apparent, students can seek opportunities specific to that field.

Once you have determined some areas of possible interest, begin researching to find out the educational path required to meet these potential career goals. The necessary educational path could greatly influence the design of your homeschool program. Since most paths require higher education, be sure to read the portion of this book concerning college at the beginning of your student's high-school career. The information it contains will help you plan appropriately now for the college days ahead.

My Teen Is Not College Bound

Planning the course work of a teen who is not going to college requires the same care as that of a college-bound student, perhaps even more. No school will be following after you to rub off any rough spots you have left in his education. You have to polish the gem all by yourself!

A good course of action for this student is to investigate career options, apprenticeships, and volunteer opportunities early since he will be embarking on a career sooner than college-bound students. Volunteering to help a carpenter or a plumber, do secretarial work, etc., might open the door to a future career. Be creative and thankful that homeschooling provides the flexible hours needed to pursue these opportunities.

Is a totally self-directed program wise in this situation? Perhaps not. It may be helpful if the last phase of a student's education is validated by someone other than mom and dad. For the teen who continues his education beyond high school, his certification or degree from college validates his earlier education. If the plan does not include technical school or college, correspondence school may be the best way to ensure that the quality of your teen's education is not questioned. A correspondence school can provide enough flexibility to pursue work opportunities while completing a high school education.

Be cautious in making the decision to exclude college preparation from a teen's education. Decisions made today are often reconsidered tomorrow. It would be better to be prepared should college enter the picture at a later date.

My Student Will Pursue an Apprenticeship

Although apprenticeships may not require college preparation, an employer will prefer an apprentice who is working up to his potential. Provide your student with a quality high school program. He may some day want to take technical courses or begin a college degree to enhance his skills in his chosen profession.

My Teen Will Attend Vocational/Technical School

Institutions specializing in vocational training or junior colleges with a diverse program offer vocational or technical education. Check into the schools in which your teen is interested. Find out their requirements and then design your high school program to meet them. The best way to be reassured that the high school program you are planning for your teen is sufficient is to ask questions early.

My Teen Will Attend Junior/Community College

Admission into junior/community college is less competitive than at four-year institutions. Earning modest SAT scores or passing a state-required test (should one exist) and providing a transcript of appropriate high-school courses or a GED certificate may meet requirements. Admission requirements change, so visit the office of admissions to get a college catalog and check current policies. Junior college is the first postsecondary step for many students, with enrollment in a senior university to follow.

My Teen Will Attend a Four-Year College or University

If your teen hopes to go directly to a four-year college or university, plan carefully and early. You will need to choose your homeschool direction, be it correspondence or home-designed, and all courses with both the college or university's and your state's requirements in mind.

One safe way to choose your high school program is to study the catalog and application packet from the colleges your student is considering. Catalogs will usually contain a list of preferred high school courses for applicants. Be aware of any special requirements for homeschool applicants. If the catalog lacks needed information, contact the admissions department. Plan your coursework accordingly. (Note: Due to rising costs, print copies of catalogs are rarely mailed, but are often available on a campus visit. In addition, while a bit tedious to navigate, most colleges put their entire catalog on their Web site. Applications can also often be downloaded.)

Getting college entrance information early in your high school process will allow you to strategize wisely, thus saving money and unhappy surprises. It will also reduce the anxiety that surrounds an already stressful process. Knowing what the college expects can help you plan your program in an orderly sequence, avoiding a senior-year scramble to fill academic gaps. Don't find out in your student's senior year that the college he wishes to attend requires three years of foreign language!

My Student Desires an Ivy League Education

Highly competitive Ivy League institutions have a strenuous, selective admissions process. An Ivy League student must excel in all academic areas and have stellar extracurricular activities and honors. Successful preparation includes a rigorous academic plan heavy with AP courses. Extracurricular activities for which the student has both zeal and leadership capabilities are also necessary.

With entrance into the Ivies as low as 9 percent, it is wise to have a backup plan should the dream not materialize. Such well-prepared students often receive excellent scholarships from the non-Ivies who are happy to welcome them. *Harvard Schmarvard* by Jay Mathews provides an insider's look at Ivy League admissions. It will either encourage your student to look elsewhere for his college education or teach him helpful strategies for pursuing his dream.

My Student Would Like to Attend a Conservatory or Art School

Some conservatories and art schools are independent institutions. Contact the individual school to request information and study their catalog on the Internet to develop an appropriate plan based on admission requirements. Other schools are divisions within a larger university. Admission into an art or music program at a university can require two levels of acceptance. The student may have to be accepted into the general university first, followed by an audition or portfolio review for admission into the music or art school. Sometimes the order of acceptance is reversed. Depending on the degree sought, the student may take more or fewer core classes in addition to artistic training to fulfill college graduation requirements. The best high-school preparation is a college-prep program that provides strong academics and quality art or music training.

My Teen Will Enter the Military

The opportunity to enlist in the military immediately after completing high school through homeschooling has improved significantly from the early days of homeschooling.

The most desirable candidates for the armed forces are considered Tier I applicants. In the past the military did not consider homeschooled applicants Tier I because they were not graduates of an accredited high school. It was almost impossible to enlist unless the homeschool student had completed some college work first.

In the fall of 1998, a five-year pilot program began that automatically placed homeschooled students in Tier I. During this time homeschoolers with a homeschool diploma and a transcript demonstrating completion of high school, who also successfully passed other normal eligibility requirements, could seek enlistment. The program has been a success. Homeschoolers have proved an asset to the armed forces. The military has made permanent recruitment changes for homeschoolers. Contact a recruiting office or visit the issue's area of HSLDA's Web site, www.hslda.org, for more information on homeschoolers and the military.

To prepare your student for the military, plan a high-school program that is equivalent to or better than a typical public-school program. Provide your student with a homeschool transcript and diploma (even if put together by the parent). Do not pursue a GED. A candidate whose education has been validated with a transcript and diploma receives more favor than one with a GED. However, always watch for current information as policies can change.

Students interested in applying to a military academy can find information specific to homeschoolers in the admissions area of The Naval Academy (www.usna.edu) and Air Force Academy (www.usafa.edu) Web sites. General admissions information (not homeschool-specific) can also be found for West Point (www.usma.edu) and the Coast Guard Academy (www.cga.edu).

High School Course and Credit Guidelines: What to Study When

Planning a high-school course of study would be easier if there were clear national guidelines. Thankfully, for the sake of personal freedom, this is not the case. States develop different guidelines for different goals. Private correspondence schools not regulated by the state may offer different options. A homeschool high school course of study needs to meet or exceed the standards that loosely exist to have credibility with future employees or a college admissions office.

As already mentioned, your best source for a course of study is always the college your teen is interested in attending. It will have a recommended high school course of study for general college admissions and sometimes for more specialized college majors. State requirements should also be considered. Your local or state homeschool support group can tell you any requirements peculiar to your state and their applicability to homeschoolers.

The following chart contains suggested guidelines that represent a compilation of different public, private, and correspondence school requirements. You will notice that it is divided into three career directions: noncollege bound, college bound with a liberal arts emphasis, and college bound with a science and math emphasis. Next to each subject you will find the recommended number of credits followed by courses most often taken to provide a well-rounded academic base in this subject area. When the recommended credits have a plus after them (example: English 4.00+), it means it is a good subject area in which to take additional elective credit for that career direction. Consumer math, which appears in parenthesis, is not required but is always a practical course for any career path.

Elective credits are profitable for subjects not usually included in a high-school plan. Bible, worldview studies, in-depth study in areas of special interest (especially if useful to future career plans), unusual life experiences, etc., are all excellent possibilities for elective credit.

Note: There are significant differences from state to state in high school graduation plans. You may find that your state requires fewer credits for a high school diploma. It is also possible that more credits could be recommended. My home state of Texas now recommends four years each of science and math and three years of foreign language for academically capable students, leaving little room for elective credit.

HIGH SCHOOL COURSE AND CREDIT GUIDELINES

NONCOLLEGE BOUND		COLLEGE-BOUND LIBERAL ARTS		COLLEGE-BOUND SCIENCE/ MATH	
Subject	*Credits*	*Subject*	*Credits*	*Subject*	*Credits*
English	**4.00**	**English**	**4.00+**	**English**	**4.00**
English I	1.00	English I	1.00	English I	1.00
English II	1.00	English II	1.00	English II	1.00
English III	1.00	English III	1.00	English III	1.00
English IV	1.00	English IV	1.00	English IV	1.00
Math	**3.00**	**Math**	**3.00–4.00**	**Math**	**4.00+**
Algebra I	1.00	Algebra I	1.00	Algebra I	1.00
Geometry	1.00	Geometry	1.00	Geometry	1.00
Algebra II	1.00	Algebra II	1.00	Algebra II	1.00
		(Consumer Math)	1.00	Precalculus/Other	1.00
Social Studies	**4.00**	**Social Studies**	**4.00+**	**Social Studies**	**4.00**
World Geography	1.00	World Geography	1.00	World Geography	1.00
American History	1.00	American History	1.00	American History	1.00
World History	1.00	World History	1.00	World History	1.00
Government	0.50	Government	0.50	Government	0.50
Economics	0.50	Economics	0.50	Economics	0.50
Science	**3.00**	**Science**	**3.00**	**Science**	**4.00+**
Biology	1.00	Biology	1.00	Biology	1.00
Physical Science	1.00	Physical Science	1.00	Chemistry	1.00
3rd science	1.00	Chemistry or Physics	1.00	Physics	1.00
				Advanced Lab Science	1.00
Computers	**1.00+**	**Computers**	**1.00+**	**Computers**	**1.00+**
Foreign Language	**2.00**	**Foreign Language**	**2.00–3.00**	**Foreign Language**	**2.00–3.00**
Fine Arts	**1.50**	**Fine Arts**	**1.50–3.00**	**Fine Arts**	**1.50–3.00**
Speech	0.50	Speech	0.50	Speech	0.50
Drama, Music, Art	1.00	Drama, Music, Art	1.00	Drama, Music, Art	1.00
Health	**0.50**	**Health**	**0.50**	**Health**	**0.50**
Physical Ed.	**1.50**	**Physical Ed.**	**1.50**	**Physical Ed.**	**1.50**
Career/Technology	**1.00+**				
Electives: Include as needed to meet or exceed credit minimums					
Total Credit	**24.00**		**26.00**		**26.00**

Stay Creative!

After presenting you with a structured chart of course suggestions for the high-school years, you may find the title of this section, "Stay Creative!" a bit odd. After all, that chart looked fairly rigid! Despite appearances, homeschoolers still retain the ability to be creative and flexible even at the high-school level through an enriching use of elective credit and more extensively in the methods and materials chosen to teach each course.

Homeschoolers have a great deal of freedom in book selection. However, high school level coursework usually proceeds in one of three directions: textbooks, independent reading, or hands-on projects. Sometimes a course will be a mixture of two approaches. Sometimes it will mix all three. One approach, however, will often predominate, allowing a standard to be set for crediting and grading. Let's take a look at these three approaches to coursework and discuss some of their pros and cons. In section 6 we will look at objective ways to credit and grade each.

TEXTBOOK COURSES

Textbook courses require little explanation. Most of us consider them the core of traditional schooling. We all know the routine: read the textbook for your homework, take the quiz, exchange papers to grade it, listen to the lecture, study, take the test, start all over again.

No wonder many people have an aversion to the use of textbooks! It is common in homeschooling circles to see such words as *tedious* and *boring* attached to the mention of textbooks. Broad generalizations, however, are rarely true, and both boring and interesting textbooks actually exist. Contrary to popular opinion, some students enjoy the structure of textbooks.

Advantages to This Approach

1. Textbooks are good college preparatory material. Any homeschooler entering college will have to function in a textbook world. Your student needs to be comfortable studying from a textbook and taking multiple-choice, true-and-false, and essay-based tests. If not, he may find himself overwhelmed and at a disadvantage competing with students used to this system. For at least a few courses, consider using a lecture approach

complete with reading and writing assignments, quizzes, and tests. This will give your student an accurate taste of what awaits in college. If you are hesitant to assume the role of lecturing professor, sign him up for an academic co-op or junior college class.

2. Textbooks offer the most objective crediting and grading opportunities.
3. Textbooks follow a carefully designed scope and sequence, providing reassurance that the most important skills and information are covered.
4. Planning a textbook course, particularly with the help of the teacher's manual, can be less time consuming.
5. Textbooks aren't always restricting. They can free you up to use your time and creativity in more beneficial areas.
6. Textbooks can serve as the foundation or framework for a rich, independent reading course.

Disadvantages to This Approach

1. Textbooks don't always have an appealing writing style. Their written-by-committee style often leaves much to be desired.
2. Some textbooks completely miss the human drama behind the information they present.
3. Textbooks and all the teacher helps that accompany them can be expensive.
4. Textbooks and teachers' manuals will usually provide more problems, projects, work sheets, etc., than can possibly be done in order to provide flexibility in assignments for the classroom teacher. Sometimes the homeschooler faced with such abundance has a difficult time deciding what to omit.

Can I use the same textbooks as the public schools?

Probably not. First, many textbooks used in public schools are not readily available to homeschoolers. Even when student books can be found, the accompanying teacher helps are often not available outside the public-school market. Teachers, reasonably, do not want the answers readily available to student hands.

Second, the adage "too many cooks spoil the broth" could be an appropriate caution regarding some textbooks that go through the process of state adoption. The result may not be altogether palatable with many "cooks" adding to or deleting from the textbook before it is approved. In our age of enforced political correctness and multiculturalism, you cannot be sure that the best materials for study are included in each textbook. Nor can you assume a just measure has been used to allot space to the different topics discussed.

As always, this advice is secondary to your state homeschool requirements. Presently I am not aware of any state that controls the choice of homeschool books, but homeschool laws can always change. It is your responsibility to stay informed.

Do you recommend getting all your textbooks from the same publishing company?

A number of publishing companies are homeschool friendly, making it possible to meet all your textbook needs, preschool through twelfth grade, from one company. This certainly makes homeschool shopping easy. Is it best for your situation? That depends.

On the positive side, full-line publishers work with large staffs of knowledgeable people writing and reviewing the curriculum, so material should be accurate. Carefully constructed scope and sequences mean fewer learning gaps. It is comforting to trust some decisions to someone knowledgeable and not feel you must design all your curriculum from scratch, particularly when no homeschooler can be equally adept in all subject areas on all grade levels.

In addition, textbook companies will usually follow a similar format and presentation style in all their material, making it easy for the student to move smoothly from subject to subject, avoiding what-to-use-when confusion. You may even discover some content integration between courses from time to time, which serves to highlight the interconnections that exist between subjects.

There are cautions, however. All companies will have their own educational philosophy. Their worldview will be reflected in this philosophy. Is their position compatible with your family's religious beliefs? Do the texts ever sacrifice scholarship to promote a particular viewpoint?

A publisher's educational philosophy will also determine the basic presentation of material. For example, if its pace moves faster than the norm, can your student handle it? If it moves slower, will your student get all you want him to get? Does the publisher emphasize rote recall or critical thinking?

Finally, many textbooks are published with the classroom in mind. This sometimes means there is more material and preparation time than someone teaching several grade levels can handle. Does the company you are considering have a reputation for accommodating the homeschool market and its differing needs? Do its textbooks and teacher helps reflect that commitment?

Besides the large textbook companies, many smaller companies have sprung up specifically to serve the homeschool market. Originally designed with the homeschooler in mind, they offer some curriculum gems.

Homeschooling, being a grassroots movement, often welcomes self-published material. The quality, however, can vary significantly. Always look for the author's qualifications, accuracy of information, careful work in editing, and reasonable quality in print and graphics. Try to determine the author's educational philosophy. That shouldn't be too hard; we homeschoolers tend to be openly opinionated!

When teaching high-school courses, should I stress rote memory or critical thinking?

The classical model for education offers some valuable insight. It advocates progressing from an acquisition and understanding of basic facts to the development of critical thinking skills. Without this underlying factual foundation, a student's reasoning can easily end in false conclusions. When the question, "What do you think?" is asked of a student whose head contains little more than his own thoughts, it becomes an opportunity for the student to puff up in self-importance while he spouts ignorance.

The elementary years are the best time to begin the acquisition of basic knowledge and understanding. As knowledge and understanding grow, a student's ability to accurately express, evaluate, and reshuffle information into useful combinations grows. By the junior high and high school levels the student should be encouraged and actively taught to go beyond "just the facts, ma'am."

Does this mean that the acquisition of information should take a backseat to critical thinking during the high school years? No. The best high school program prepares the student in both areas. A student's body of knowledge should continue to grow along with his ability to analyze it. College professors and courses will have differing personalities. Some will require advanced rote memory skills, An anatomy and physiology course is a grueling example! Others will require a high level of critical thinking (especially helpful in any of the social sciences where political correctness abounds). A well-rounded high-school program emphasizes both skills.

For the Christian, well-rounded knowledge and the ability to reason accurately should mark the beginnings of wisdom. Wisdom will also exhibit itself by a respect for the intellectual achievements of gifted individuals and a healthy humility when we look at ourselves in comparison. Most importantly, the student should recognize that all true wisdom in all areas of life comes from God. The Christian student should be encouraged to study the ideas, struggles, and spiritual victories of laymen and leaders who have faithfully advanced the cause of Christ through the centuries. If a student is to follow their example and actively advance the cause of Christ in today's world, he must have the ability to discern, analyze, and relate information to a Christian worldview. A student's faith needs to be both heart-and-mind engaged if he is to see his way through the ethical muddle in our world today.

INDEPENDENT READING COURSES

In independent reading courses, students pursue a topic through reading. Although the student is left largely to himself, independent reading courses may also include times of discussion. Courses of this nature often rely heavily on what homeschoolers call "living books."

A "living" book (sometimes called a "real" book) is a homeschool description for almost any book that is not a textbook. Biographies, original documents, historical fiction, novels, etc., are examples. They are generally written by one author who enjoys his subject, resulting in a well-written (and sometimes opinionated) product. The premise is that living books are more interesting and therefore better remembered and more meaningful. They can either replace or enrich textbooks. They can be borrowed from libraries and purchased from bookstores. Homeschool catalogs promoting living books offer many enticing selections.

In our homeschool this has been a favorite way to study literature and history. We take our selected historical time period and pursue it by reading biographies, historical fiction, documents and literature of the time period, and any other interesting books that cross our path.

Like any other method, an independent reading course has its pros and cons.

Advantages to This Approach

1. Independent reading courses can be a relaxing change of pace from the rigors of math and science courses.
2. They provide a wonderful flexibility that extends to the types of books read, topics studied in greater depth, and the form of evaluation used.
3. Independent reading courses stimulate intellectual growth as they provide an opportunity to begin developing expertise in areas of high interest.
4. If your reading extends to original sources and autobiographies, your student experiences the next best thing to being there.
5. The teacher's oversight can also be easier, although students reading without teacher oversight will need carefully chosen books. You may want to discuss controversial books together.
6. Independent reading courses can foster a lifelong love of reading and learning.

Disadvantages to This Approach

Although I am enthusiastic about this method, I would be remiss not to mention potential drawbacks.

1. To calculate credits and grades, course expectations are often tied to the amount of time spent reading. This may give a reluctant student an opportunity for dawdling or deception. You may find little is accomplished when you leave a reluctant reader alone to fulfill a time requirement. Don't use a method that could place undue temptation in your student's path.
2. A course based on independent reading can sometimes take a haphazard approach to a subject. You must carefully choose reading selections. To keep your focus from becoming too narrow, use at least one book or textbook that presents a broad picture of the subject you are studying. In our home we have used BJUP's *American Literature*, Clarence Carson's *The Basic History of the United States*, and Steve Wilkin's audio series *America: The First 350 Years* as we meandered our way through American history and literature.
3. A lack of checks and balances. Be sure to use some of the objective evaluations presented in section 6. Strive to set standards before the course, not after. Then your conscience will be comfortable as you prepare your student's high-school transcript.

PROJECT COURSES

Some courses are more hands-on or project oriented. Practical life-skills courses such as home economics or auto mechanics fall into this category. Courses designed to teach technical or business skills, such as learning to operate a word-processing program, are project oriented. Physical education courses based on community activities, such as participating on a swim team or in a church softball league, are also hands-on or activity based.

Some courses can be a mixture of reading, skill development, and application of these skills through community service. For example, a child care section of a home economics course could include reading assignments, CPR and basic first-aid training, and volunteering in the church nursery.

Project courses also have distinct advantages and disadvantages.

Advantages to This Approach

1. It provides a method for incorporating the teaching of practical life skills into your school program. Your student's future family will benefit!
2. It provides an opportunity to develop skills that may provide lifelong enjoyment.
3. Project courses are a welcome change to the academic side of school.
4. Students who are more hands-on have an opportunity to excel.

Disadvantages to This Approach

1. The project course is the most difficult to assess accurately. It is difficult to plan a course that is balanced (neither too easy nor too difficult for the student to achieve). Be ready to adjust your goals if necessary.
2. All high school courses do not lend themselves well to a hands-on approach.
3. Using a project approach too often or in courses where it doesn't fit naturally can significantly slow down the pace of learning.
4. Homeschoolers can be tempted to credit random life experiences by stretching them to fit into a subject's general area. All students, whether in public, private, or homeschool, have many educational experiences outside their course work. Public- and private-school students do not get academic credit for these experiences. If you give credit, be cautious in doing it. Be sure it is really worthy of crediting and not just a time filler. Time fillers replace true enrichment.

Planning a Personalized Course of Study

Now you and your teen are ready to plan his personalized high-school course of study. Strive for a careful blend of functionality and creative individualization. While basics must be covered, creative choice of materials can individualize the course for your student. Include courses and materials that enhance his talents and strengthen his areas of weakness.

The next section of this book, "A Comprehensive Homeschool Course Listing," lists possible courses with book suggestions. It will help you start making decisions on what courses your teen should take. Decisions should be made with the High School Course and Credit Guidelines in mind, which are found in the section starting on page 55.

Two forms will help you with your decision making. The Four-Year Study Plan form will help you put on paper what courses need to be taken and which year will work best to take each one. When it is completed, you will have a map directing you through all four years of high school.

Make sure the first two years of high school are full course loads setting the stage for completion of all coursework in the four years allotted. Junior and senior years often bring time pressure with such activities as apprenticeship opportunities, part-time jobs, or the beginning of a college dual-enrollment program. You will need time for visiting colleges and researching scholarship opportunities. If you lighten the junior or senior high-school load because of the pressure of nonacademic activities, make it a slight adjustment. Admissions counselors do not like a senior-year coast. Using a less intensive curriculum in a course of lower importance is a better choice than skipping the course altogether.

If your student plans to apply to a highly competitive university, all four years must be academically challenging. The competition for admission will be steep, and your student must be willing to rise to the challenge.

After the four-year plan has been decided, use the One-Year Study Plan form to list one year's courses with book or material requirements, essentially making a shopping list for the upcoming year. It can also serve as an informal record of courses and book selections.

Included on the next two pages are examples of a completed Four-Year Study Plan and One-Year Study Plan. With a total of twenty-seven credits, the sample Four-Year Study Plan may appear ambitious. However, according to the National Association of College Admission Counseling's *State of College Admissions* 2006 report, high-school graduates now earn 26 course credits on average.

Remember, these plans are only examples. You will individualize your course and material selections to meet the academic needs and career direction of your student, college requirements, and the homeschool requirements of your state. Copies of the blank One-Year Study Plan and the Four-Year Study Plan are contained on the CD-ROM in the back cover of this book.

Note: Consider obtaining a course guide (it may be called an academic planning guide or something similar) from your local high school. It can help you see what the school recommends for a four-year high-school plan because it will be in compliance with your state's requirements. It is also interesting to see the diversity in course offerings.

FOUR-YEAR STUDY PLAN for student			
9TH-GRADE COURSES	**CREDIT**	**10TH-GRADE COURSES**	**CREDIT**
English I	1.00	English II	1.00
Algebra I	1.00	Geometry	1.00
World Geography	1.00	American History	1.00
Physical Science	1.00	Biology	1.00
Word Processing	1.00	Latin II	1.00
Latin I	1.00	Private Piano	0.50
Private Piano	0.50	Church History	0.50
Bible Survey	0.50	Home Economics	1.00
P.E., ballet/tap	0.50	P.E., ballet/tap	0.50
		P.E., tennis lessons	0.50
Total	7.50	Total	8.00

11TH-GRADE COURSES	**CREDIT**	**12TH-GRADE COURSES**	**CREDIT**
English III	1.00	English 1301 & 1302 (college dual credit)	1.00
Creative Writing	0.50	Consumer Math	1.00
Algebra II	1.00	Government	0.50
World History	1.00	Economics	0.50
Latin III	1.00	Geology	0.50
Private Piano	0.50	Astronomy	0.50
Speech	0.50	Private Piano	0.50
Bible Doctrines	0.50	Worldview Studies	0.50
		Health	0.50
Total	6.00	Total	5.50

TOTAL CREDITS BY SUBJECT AREA			
Bible	2.00	Computers	1.00
English	4.50	Foreign Language	3.00
Math	4.00	Fine Arts	2.50
Science	3.00	Health and P.E.	2.00
Social Studies	4.00	Misc. Electives	1.00
FOUR-YEAR TOTAL 27.00			

ONE-YEAR STUDY PLAN

Name: __Student__   Grade: __9th__ Year: __2007–2008__

COURSE TITLE	TEXTS OR MATERIALS
English I	
Grammar and Mechanics	*Writing and Grammar 9*, BJU
Composition	*Format Writing*, paragraph styles & 5 paragraph essays
Vocabulary	*Wordly Wise 3000 6*
Literature	*The Hobbit* with Progeny Press guide
Literature	*The Yearling* with Progeny Press guide
Algebra I	*Algebra I*, Saxon
World Geography	Make geography notebook:
	Mapping the World by Heart Lite for map outlines
	Comprehensive World Reference Guide for reports
	The Internet for country reports
	The Continents, puzzles
Physical Science	School of Tomorrow *Physical Science* Paces with videos
Word Processing	project course, use resources at home
Latin I	*The Latin Road to English Grammar*
Piano	no new book
Bible Survey	read through the Bible
Physical Education	ballet/tap lessons
Notes:	

KEEPING OUR COURSE OF STUDY REALISTIC

Many wonderful homeschool books and materials seem to beg us to use them. Add to that the many things we believe our teen must know to be prepared for the future. Before long we have set such unrealistic goals that our school year cannot possibly succeed. How do we plan realistically?

Set criteria before the course begins to help keep goals realistic. Get it all on paper; then seek advice. The input of a seasoned homeschooler who has already walked the high-school path can be valuable. In addition, our spouses (who know us so well) can often discern when out-of-control idealism has created an impossible pile of challenging requirements! Our feet must be firmly planted in reality if we are going to plan a course neither too easy nor too challenging. While planning, we must remind ourselves of a few important facts.

Remind yourself that you do not have the expertise to do all subjects equally well. Know your weak areas and be especially careful when choosing materials for your teen in these subjects. Look for books or programs that require less parental involvement. In our homeschool, I have chosen to use science videos on the high school level. They may not be the most rigorous academically, but my teens definitely learn more from them than they would from me. We have also used our local junior college for both science and advanced math courses.

Remind yourself that you have limited time. This is especially true if you have more than one student. You cannot be equally involved in every subject studied. Some courses your teen will need to do with a great deal of independence while others will require more of your attention. Vary your curriculum choices so that all do not require an intense time commitment from you.

Know that some subjects will be a struggle. It is always nice when the areas you study closely together are subjects both you and your teen love. Those experiences create special moments that make homeschoolers positively glow. Unfortunately it doesn't always work that way. It is not unusual for both you and your teen to dislike or struggle with the same subject. Often you must be involved closely, or it will not get done. Choose the least painful material for both of you, hire a tutor, or join a homeschool co-op class. God will reward your faithfulness.

Plan some independent reading. High school is a wonderful time for extensive reading. The key is careful selection of reading material. Know which books to discuss to benefit from them fully and which do not require your close interaction. Vary your selections with this in mind. I have heard it said that the best way to prepare for successful college studies is to read widely and read well. That is a goal easily met through homeschooling.

A Comprehensive Homeschool Course Listing

Understanding the Course Listing

My husband and I live many miles from our extended families. Through the years this has necessitated many major treks north. Because a trip entails several weeks away from home, it must be carefully planned. For weeks the legal pad that holds my growing list is my constant companion. It becomes the brain of the operation when my own shuts down due to overload. When all is ready, the kids are in the car, the house is locked, and a prayer has been offered for a safe journey, my husband will drive slowly to the end of the street and look at me expectantly. We generally take one turnaround for something important that has been forgotten.

Planning a high-school program is similar to planning a long road trip. So many decisions! So much advance preparation! So far you have set a general direction and determined what courses are needed. It's now time to choose the books and materials, to pick up the book bag, and start packing.

The course listing that follows progresses through the following subjects: Bible and character development, English and literature, mathematics, science, social studies, unit studies, foreign language, fine arts, physical education and health, home economics and auto mechanics, computer skills, and a hodgepodge section for thinking, study skills, SAT preparation, and career exploration.

Each section begins with a short (or long!) introduction to the subject to be taught. English, which is a meshing of a number of language arts skills, is of necessity a long section. History is also long, with both nonfiction and fiction recommendations for the living book enthusiasts.

Each subject section proceeds roughly in the following order:

1. *Remedial course suggestions* are listed first. These courses represent skills that are normally mastered before high school. A parent may choose to credit and grade these courses for a student with learning disabilities who requires a significantly modified program. Under most circumstances it would not be appropriate to credit or grade remedial courses for a student planning to attend college. They will not give the student adequate preparation.

2. *Junior-high material* comes next. Some junior high materials will also be suggested for remedial high school use.

3. *Independent reading courses* follow when appropriate to the subject matter. Depending on the reading selections chosen, courses of this nature can be easy or rigorously college preparatory.

4. *Courses of average and advanced difficulty* come next. Often the same basic books will be recommended for both. Adding supplementary activity books, additional reading, projects, or writing assignments can raise the difficulty level of a course significantly, making it rigorously college preparatory. It is important to note that a book listed last in a section is not necessarily the most rigorous of the choices presented. This is true for two reasons. First, I cannot personally field test everything to make fine distinctions between solid college preparatory programs. The Johnson family, although large, is not *that* large! Second, a textbook that is difficult for one student because of content or approach may admirably suit the needs of another student. Therefore, please take my implied levels of difficulty lightly.

5. *Miscellaneous elective choices* are the last course suggestions offered.

Now that we've looked at the general progression within each subject, let's look at the information headings for each suggested course.

Course. This is a descriptive title, not necessarily the appropriate title for recording on the transcript. See the box to follow, "How Should a Course Be Titled?" for more information.

Grade(s). Suggested grade levels. When one grade level is given, this is usually a publisher's recommendation. However, the order of high-school courses is flexible provided the appropriate prerequisites have been met. This flexibility is illustrated when I suggest more than one grade level. Planning a high-school program is a customized juggle designed to meet the scheduling needs of your student and his college aspirations. Since you are your student's high-school counselor, order his courses to his best advantage. More than one grade level is also given on remedial courses because academic gaps need to be addressed regardless of the grade of the student.

Prerequisite. Course(s) that must be completed before beginning this course (e.g., algebra I must precede algebra II).

Main Text or Materials. Suggested textbook(s), living books, videos, etc. Sometimes there will be several. The author and/or publisher of the recommended book usually follows the title. Living books commonly available at large bookstores or via Internet sales do not always give publisher information.

Additional Materials. Sometimes these are necessary to the course. Sometimes they are nice extras.

Teacher Helps. What support materials (teacher's manual, tests, work sheets, etc.) are available to help teach the course.

Description. A general description of the course or book.

Credit Recommendations. Actually, you will not find any! Your requirements and design of any particular course will determine the number of credits to award. The grading and crediting suggestions offered in section 6 will help you set objective standards. Please note that independent reading courses are not necessarily complete courses but may be effectively combined to create one larger course. For example, the Study of God and Studies in Theology courses may together represent one-half credit based on time spent and books read. These two courses could be combined and recorded on the transcript as Bible Doctrines.

After a look at four major homeschool publishers, the course listing begins. There is nothing inspired about this course listing. Many core course suggestions are based on personal or customer observations of different textbooks and their level of difficulty. Independent reading courses often use favorite living books worthy of a teen's time. Other elective courses may be based on skills that are important for everyone to master. As you browse through the course ideas, you will hopefully be motivated to create your own courses using favorite study-worthy books.

It is not my intention to give you thorough descriptions of all the different materials available. Rather, I will point to a few tried-and-true, readily available resources. On a few occasions I may include an excellent resource that may take some work to get but is worth the effort. When a product is reviewed in Cathy Duffy's *100 Top Picks for Homeschool Curriculum*, I will precede that book with an asterisk. Her reviews should help you determine if a particular recommendation is suitable for your student. Plan to use the Internet and the homeschool grapevine for information on programs not covered in Cathy Duffy's book or for the most current information.

I would like to encourage you once again to match the difficulty of a course to the needs of the student. Courses of average difficulty would be appropriate for the student who is not college bound or for areas outside your college-bound student's choice of study. An example is the liberal arts student who struggles in math. A sequence of math courses preparing him for college algebra will probably be all that is required. Calculus studies in high school will not be necessary. Such advanced-level courses are best for the student planning to apply to a competitive college, capable of rigorous study in all academic areas, or planning a college major that will require high level studies in this academic area.

The course listing includes asterisks in front of some book titles. What does that mean?

As mentioned above, the asterisk before a book title indicates the book is reviewed in Cathy Duffy's *100 Top Picks for Homeschool Curriculum*. Products not reviewed in *100 Top Picks* are sometimes included on her Web site, www.cathyduffyreviews.com. An Internet search will often turn up reviews available on other sites.

How should a course be titled?

As you read this course listing, you will probably come across courses with titles different from any you took in high school. These titles are descriptive to help you see the direction of a course. *They are not necessarily meant to be the course title on your teen's transcript.*

When colleges look at your teen's transcript, they want reassurance that your teen has been well-prepared for the academic rigors of college. Both grades and course titles should provide that reassurance. The titles on core courses, such as algebra I, geometry, algebra II, biology, chemistry, etc., should signify that the basics have been taught. Creative titles here may raise doubts as to the content of your course.

In other areas more descriptive titles might be helpful. For example, titles such as Grammar and Composition, American Literature, etc. may help define the content of those nebulously titled English I through English IV courses.

Creative titles may be most helpful with elective courses. Here a creative title may indicate dedicated pursuits that go well beyond the normal high-school course of study. For example, a course titled Constitutional Law in addition to the required government credit indicates that your teen is a serious political science student. As a general rule, use course titles to reassure admissions counselors that basic course work has been successfully completed and that noteworthy elective credit was also earned.

Perhaps creativity is used to its best purpose in your curriculum selection. An English course might include participation in a summer Shakespearean festival. An American history course might include a creative and enriching choice of living books and a visit to a historical reenactment. Although mundanely called "American History" to show that the basics have been covered, your course contract and reading list will reveal the course in all its glory should a college admissions officer be interested. Exceptional activities in which your student has extensive participation or a leadership role can also be included in the extracurricular activities listed on his college application form or page 2 of his transcript. In course titles or materials selection, as in all of your curriculum planning, use your homeschool flexibility to your student's advantage.

Full-Service Publishers

Several Christian publishers—A Beka Books, Bob Jones University Press, Alpha Omega, and School of Tomorrow (ACE)—offer their kindergarten through twelfth-grade programs for use in the homeschool market. While the programs have similarities, they also have distinct differences. An examination of their style of material, educational philosophy, support materials, and availability of material will point out some of those differences.

A BEKA BOOKS

A Beka Books publishes textbooks from a Christian perspective with a strong patriotic flavor. Their very conservative viewpoints in both religion and politics include use of the King James Bible and an emphasis on personal responsibility, initiative, and love of God and country.

Academically rigorous textbooks emphasize the presentation of fact and detail. This emphasis works well with detail-oriented students having excellent memorization skills but may be less successful with students who think more globally or conceptually. Students with learning difficulties may also struggle with retaining the many details.

A Beka's emphasis on detail can be most appropriately applied to subjects that rely heavily on fact accumulation. For the development of critical thinking, it may be helpful to branch out beyond A Beka.

A Beka textbooks are full-color, quality paperback editions. (Their life can be extended with the addition of rigid plastic covers, such as those put out by the Kapco Company.)

A full complement of teacher's manuals, tests, and quizzes is available. Because A Beka materials are designed primarily for the classroom, you will often find more material than you can use in the homeschool setting. Rely on the advice of other homeschool A Beka users as to which materials are necessary and what can be eliminated. A Beka materials are available directly from A Beka Books.

In addition to textbooks, A Beka Books also offers a DVD-rental program. If enrolling in the DVD program, your high schooler will follow a traditional school program of standard-length classes and follow-up homework assignments. These courses are taught by teachers from the Pensacola Christian Academy. Both the academy and the publishing house are affiliated with Pensacola Christian College and Pensacola Theological Seminary.

A Beka Books offers correspondence options for homeschoolers wanting to use just their textbooks or both textbooks and DVDs. See www.abekaacademy.org for details.

You will notice that A Beka Books are absent from the course listing in this book. This does not mean that they cannot be a good choice for your homeschool. I am simply limited in my own exposure to them. A Beka Books are not available in the homeschool retail market, so I have not developed the same day-to-day working knowledge of A Beka materials that I have developed for other homeschool publishers.

BOB JONES UNIVERSITY PRESS

Bob Jones University Press is another full-line, conservative Christian textbook publisher. BJUP believes that understanding is vital to the learning of skills and concepts. Practically, this means a child's readiness precedes the presentation of a skill. It also means that understanding precedes memorization. BJUP believes the teacher is the key to high quality education. Therefore, this is not a wind-them-up-and-let-them-go curriculum.

BJU's high-school texts are high quality, full-color books. The hardbacks that had been the rule are, regrettably for the homeschooler, being replaced by softback editions. I used the American and British literature books with my older three students, enjoying both books immensely. One of my high schoolers actually read through the American literature book twice. (A feat never accomplished by any other textbook in the history of our homeschool!) BJU texts present information in a scholarly, evenhanded presentation unlikely to offend anyone in the evangelical market. Our decision to use BJU's HomeSat program for selected courses with our younger two children has increased our use of Bob Jones materials. The HomeSat program is discussed below.

Support materials include teacher's guides, activity books, teacher's guides to the activity books, tests, and keys. The teacher's guides I used were helpful in presenting the type of college preparatory courses we were pursuing. For parents desiring to customize their student's tests, *Testbuilder 2* software is available. Although a bit pricey, the software includes test questions for a large number of courses. If you plan to use BJU materials for several courses and like to personalize your tests, it would be a worthwhile expenditure.

Through the years BJUP has shown itself sensitive to the homeschool market. Its academic testing service and its satellite program, HomeSat, are two noteworthy examples. BJUP books are widely available through homeschool catalogs and the newer homeschool retail market. You may also purchase them directly from the company. A number of BJUP books are included in the course listing.

Bob Jones also serves homeschoolers through its Academy of Home Education. In addition to record-keeping services, they offer opportunities for academy students to interact during annual Open House Days, summer camp opportunities, and a yearly multiday graduation event.

Bob Jones HomeSat Program

If you prefer the ultimate in teaching help, BJUP's HomeSat now provides courses through satellite. Through the purchase of a satellite from BJUP and a monthly subscription fee, a homeschool family can view and record any of the broadcasting available. Courses are offered for four-year-old kindergarten through the twelfth grade. All the core high-school subjects are covered: English, math, social sciences, natural sciences, and foreign language. Bible electives are also offered. All programming uses Bob Jones textbooks and materials.

High-school programming comes in two formats. Some courses are prerecorded in a studio and are shorter in length. These include English, social science, and Bible classes. Other courses are part of the BJ Linc program. Linc courses are live and interactive traditional classrooms offered to Christian schools. Homeschoolers who take Linc classes can listen in but do not have the equipment to participate actively. Linc courses, available in the high-school maths, sciences, and two foreign languages, (Spanish and French) can be watched daily at a set time or recorded once weekly via a block field.

While employing lecture-style instruction with screen shots of key facts, HomeSat courses add interest with additional presentations. For example, American history includes monologues by historical characters, fun facts and slide shows of different areas of the United States, and music of the time period.

Special programs for parents and students are also available. Panel discussions, a cooking program, films for family viewing, and inspirational programming are just some of the options.

I considered using HomeSat for several years before we actually took the plunge. When my fourth child hit high school and her voice teacher suggested she study French, I knew we needed help. I had several reservations about using the HomeSat program. First, I perceived an inefficiency and time waste in the Linc classes. Second, I was unwilling, in a storage-challenged home, to accumulate a closetful of videotapes.

To date, French has been our only use of Linc programming. Most of our HomeSat use has been the shorter studio courses. Rather than causing restlessness, we have found the live course teacher-student exchanges reassuring. Since my daughter had only taken a few high school co-op courses, I had limited reliable information on how she would measure up to her peers in a college-prep class. Using Linc has helped reassure me that she is capable of holding her own. (And should she ever see this, we have enjoyed Mrs. Anderson, the French teacher, tremendously!)

My second concern was storage. To solve the problem, we purchased a DVD burner with hard drive. Although requiring more technological savvy than I possess, such machines are within my husband's capabilities. Each week he records our chosen courses via block feed onto the hard drive. He later fast-forwards through the block feeds, breaking each course into chapters representing a daily lesson. They are then ready to burn to a weekly course disk. In three years of taping for two students, we have only accumulated a few neatly organized binders of DVDs. The whole process has been preferable to that of a mom I know who was taping so many classes she had to get up at night to change videotapes. It was much like having a newborn in the home!

As with any program dependent on technology, there will be some glitches. Installation of the satellite went pretty smoothly, but we had a few problems with loss of signal after storms before we anchored the satellite more tightly. We also experienced some early problems with the receiver. These were corrected with an upgrade in HomeSat software and have not recurred.

We have found technical support helpful when needed. If you have a recurrent problem, be sure to get the name of the person assisting you. Follow-up contact will be more efficient if the problem does not need to be reexplained each time and unsuccessful corrections don't have to be repeated.

Finally, if the challenge of mastering the technology seems overwhelming, it's also possible to lease prerecorded DVDs of the junior-high and high-school level courses. While not as economical as the satellite program, the ease-of-use factor jumps considerably making it appealing for many homeschoolers.

That's our HomeSat adventure to this point. I have a little more parting advice should you decide to give it a try. First, I recommend registering for the classes. On the high-school level we have actively used the tests, quizzes, study guides, etc., included in the HomeSat teaching material. Second, unless your student revels in academics, do not try to use HomeSat for every course. A BJU course without HomeSat requires reading the text, answering questions, and taking tests. Activity sheets and various projects may also be recommended. A HomeSat course requires all of that *plus* the time spent watching the class. If your student has many outside co-op classes, extracurricular activities, or a part-time job, you will soon be sinking under the load. Use HomeSat where it will be most helpful to your student and modify the course recommendations if necessary. Take a less intense approach to a course of lower future career significance.

ALPHA OMEGA

Alpha Omega Lifepacs offer a consumable workbook approach to Christian education. Each set of ten Lifepacs contains a full year's work in one subject. They are available in five core subjects: Bible, language arts, math, history and geography, and science. In addition, elective courses such as accounting, art, American literature, British literature, civics, consumer math, essentials of communication, foundations for living, home economics, and Spanish are also available.

Alpha Omega's educational philosophy stresses both understanding and memorization. This is evidenced by solid study strategies that are an integral part of each Lifepac's organization. Main objectives and vocabulary introduce each booklet and section; this provides immediate memory hooks on which to place the forthcoming information. Constant review of main objectives, presented in various questioning formats, aids mastery of the material and extends the learning beyond simple recall. Periodic self-tests and a final pull-out test are included in each Lifepac. Students who underperform can retest on an alternate test provided in the teacher's manual.

Alpha Omega Lifepacs allow the student a great deal of academic independence. Parental involvement is still needed but not as intensively as with some other materials. If the student reads well, likes well-defined goals and a consistent approach, and desires a high measure of independence, this type of study may prove enjoyable for him. In addition to the Lifepacs, a helpful supplemental experiment video or DVD is available for the science program. When time or scientific equipment are not available, viewing the video can provide the necessary continuity.

Students who prefer a high level of independence in their studies and also enjoy computers may do well with Switched on Schoolhouse. SOS is a computerized version of the Lifepac. Since Switched on Schoolhouse was first introduced, Alpha Omega has worked continually to enhance the learning experience by making it more student interactive, visually appealing, and user-friendly for both parent and student. Enhancements have included adding varied graphics to personalize the student's computer screen, games, video clips, links to Web sites, and careful step-by-step instructions for personalizing your record keeping.

If your homeschool has become an impossible juggle of subjects and children, you may find yourself glancing wistfully at a workbook approach. A teacher's manual includes all the parental help needed. Parents will also appreciate the ease in grading the pull-out tests. If Switched on Schoolhouse sounds appealing, you may be even more attracted by the considerable amount of grading this program does for you. (Short answer and essay questions will still need teacher grading.) Alpha Omega products are widely available through homeschool catalogs and the newer homeschool retail market. They can also be ordered directly from the company.

Alpha Omega Academy, www.aop.com, offers both a traditional program using the Lifepacs or a software option that uses Switched on Schoolhouse.

Titling Alpha Omega Courses on a Transcript

If you are interested in using the Alpha Omega Lifepacs, you will soon notice the generic titles for the courses. How do you record History and Geography 10 or Math 9 on a transcript? Fortunately, Alpha Omega's scope and sequence provides the information needed to title most classes with traditional high-school names. These titles will work with either the Lifepacs or the Switched on Schoolhouse computerized version.

The following titles reflect the content of the various Lifepacs.

BIBLE

9th: New Testament Survey*
10th: Old Testament Survey*
11th: Major Biblical Themes I*
12th: Major Biblical Themes II*

LANGUAGE ARTS

9th: English I
10th: English II
11th: English III
12th: English IV

*Bible courses will most likely be viewed as electives and not academic core courses. Therefore, their transcript titles are not of great concern.

MATH

9th: Algebra I
10th: Geometry
11th: Algebra II
12th: Precalculus

HISTORY

9th: Social Studies**
10th: World History
11th: U.S. History
12th: Government/Economics

SCIENCE

9th: Physical Science***
10th: Biology
11th: Chemistry
12th: Physics

SCHOOL OF TOMORROW/ACCELERATED CHRISTIAN EDUCATION (ACE)

School of Tomorrow also offers a workbook approach to learning. Twelve workbooks, or Paces, are required to finish each full-year course. School of Tomorrow's Christian emphasis includes a conscientious effort to weave character building into each of its courses.

The program is self-instructional and does not rely heavily on the teacher. The Paces themselves are colorful and attractive. Excellent videos, which greatly enhance the Paces, are available for purchase in the high-school sciences, maths, and Spanish.

Our experience has been limited to the biology, physical science, and geometry courses, where we used both the worktexts and videos. The biology videos drew the attention of the whole family; other work often stopped while we all enjoyed them together. In the physical science course, we found the easy-to-follow, step-by-step presentation of the math concepts helpful. The videos made a difficult subject accessible and interesting. The geometry was thorough, with significant time spent on proofs.

The biology material seemed less in-depth than some other choices, but perhaps the enjoyable format made it seem easier. Students who plan a career in the sciences will need to add hands-on lab work of their own in addition to watching the video demonstrations. Serious science students may also find the biology course more appropriate for junior high work. School of Tomorrow materials are available directly from the company. See appendix A for ordering information.

**Ninth-grade history and geography is a general study of civics, careers, and world geography. This is the hardest course to title. While Social Studies would be an appropriate title, it is not typical for a high school course. Consider supplementing with additional geography reading and activities and call it World Geography. If you want a workbook course that is only geography, use their half-year *Geography* Lifepac Select and supplement with map making, report writing, etc., to make a full-year course.
***If you prefer an integrated physics and chemistry course (IPC) to a more general physical science, you may want to pick and choose Lifepacs from grades eight and nine to focus on those two areas. IPC courses are often taken by students who are not planning to take a full year of either chemistry or physics.

Bible and Character Development Courses

Although biblical studies are not usually offered in a secular high school, they should be foundational for the Christian homeschooler. The greatest contribution we can make toward our teen's future is a vibrant Christian faith. Nothing else is eternal.

Any biblical studies plan should contain systematic Bible reading. I strongly encourage you to implement a plan for reading through the Scriptures at least once during the high-school years. Many plans do this. Some are just a schedule sheet where the daily reading is checked off when completed. Another possibility is a one-year Bible, which divides the Bible into daily readings.

In addition to ongoing Bible reading, I recommend other areas of biblical studies. The character of God, apologetics, theology, and Christian growth are some of the areas included. Church history also deserves our attention. It teaches students that Christianity is much bigger than themselves, their parents, and the churches they attend. In both our American and homeschool individualism, we have too often neglected our connection to the corporate body of Christ, both in the world today and in previous centuries. Salvation is not just a private matter; it places each of us into a family that transcends time and place. Today we stand on the shoulders of God's faithful servants who have preceded us into eternity. Introduce your teen and yourself, perhaps for the first time, to these heroes. Church history suggestions are located in the social studies section of the course listing immediately following world history.

Another important area is worldview studies. Worldview studies will help your teen understand both his Christian faith and the underlying premises of philosophies opposed to Christianity. Worldview courses, because of their emphasis on history, are listed in the social studies course listing but could be considered Bible, philosophy, or social studies electives.

Browse through the course suggestions and consider adding a few as electives to your teen's course of study. All books recommended for Bible courses adhere to the basic tenets of the historic Christian faith.

BIBLE

Course: Bible reading	*Grades:* 9–12	*Prerequisite:* None

MAIN TEXT OR MATERIAL: Daily Bible reading plan or the one-year Bible, publishers vary according to translation

ADDITIONAL MATERIALS: *The Victor Journey through the Bible*, V. Gilbert Beers, *Then and Now Bible Map Book*, Rose Publishing

TEACHER HELPS: Independent reading course, no teacher helps needed

DESCRIPTION: A systematic reading through the entire Bible. Arranged chronologically, *The Victor Journey through the Bible* includes interesting cultural information to enrich the study. In full color, the *Then and Now Bible Map Book's* transparent overlays compare biblical locations to modern-day maps.

Course: Bible study (for the serious Bible student)	*Grades:* 9–12	*Prerequisite:* None

MAIN TEXTS OR MATERIAL: *Knowing Scripture*, R. C. Sproul, *The Reformation Study Bible*, Ligonier Ministries

ADDITIONAL MATERIALS: *The Victor Journey through the Bible*, V. Gilbert Beers, *Then and Now Bible Map Book*, Rose Publishing

TEACHER HELPS: Independent reading course, no teacher helps needed

DESCRIPTION: R. C. Sproul's book gives a good overview on how to study the Bible effectively. The notes in *The Reformation Study Bible* (English Standard version) are written by dependable Bible scholars; R. C. Sproul was the general editor. Arranged chronologically, *The Victor Journey through the Bible* includes interesting cultural information to enrich the study. In full color, the *Then and Now Bible Map Book's* transparent overlays compare biblical locations to modern-day maps.

Course: Old Testament Bible study	*Grades:* 9–12	*Prerequisite:* None

MAIN TEXT OR MATERIAL: *A House for My Name*, Peter Leithart, the Bible

ADDITIONAL MATERIALS: *The Victor Journey through the Bible*, V. Gilbert Beers, *Then and Now Bible Map Book*, Rose Publishing

TEACHER HELPS: Independent reading course, no teacher helps needed

DESCRIPTION: Leithart's Old Testament survey presents Scripture in historical context and shows how all of Scripture points to Christ. *The Victor Journey through the Bible* and *Then and Now Bible Map Book* are helpful supplements.

Course: Study of God	*Grades:* 9–12	*Prerequisite:* None

MAIN TEXTS OR MATERIAL (CHOOSE FROM): *Knowing God*, J. I. Packer, *A Heart for God*, Sinclair Ferguson, *The Attributes of God*, A. W. Pink, *The Holiness of God*, R. C. Sproul

TEACHER HELPS: Independent reading course, no teacher helps needed

DESCRIPTION: A study on the character of God. Understanding His character is foundational to every Christian's faith. All of these books make excellent choices.

Course: Christian apologetics	*Grades:* 11–12	*Prerequisite:* None

MAIN TEXTS OR MATERIAL (CHOOSE FROM): *Can Man Live without God*, Ravi Zacharias, *Jesus among Other Gods*, Ravi Zacharias, *Deliver Us from Evil*, Ravi Zacharias

TEACHER HELPS: Independent reading course, no teacher helps needed

DESCRIPTION: Ravi Zacharias is an articulate, thought-provoking defender of the Christian faith. Many of his messages and seminars can be purchased in video or audio formats.

Course: God's sovereignty in suffering	*Grades:* 9–12	*Prerequisite:* None

MAIN TEXT OR MATERIAL: *When God Weeps*, Joni Erickson Tada and Steven Estes

TEACHER HELPS: Independent reading course, no teacher helps needed

DESCRIPTION: It is difficult to see God's children suffer. It is especially difficult when it is a family member, a close friend, or ourselves. This well-written, deeply meaningful book explains God's purposes in man's suffering. Joni Erickson Tada and Steven Estes are well qualified to speak on the subject.

Course: Studies in theology	Grades: 9–12	Prerequisite: None

MAIN TEXT OR MATERIAL (CHOOSE ONE): *Essential Truths of the Christian Faith*, R. C. Sproul, *Concise Theology: A Guide to Historic Christian Beliefs*, J. I. Packer
TEACHER HELPS: Independent reading course, no teacher helps needed
DESCRIPTION: Both of these readable books will provide the student with a strong foundation in the major tenets of the Christian faith.

Course: Christian growth	Grades: 9–12	Prerequisite: None

MAIN TEXTS OR MATERIAL: *Basic Christianity*, John R. Stott, *Profiting from the Word*, A. W. Pink, *The Cost of Discipleship*, Dietrich Bonhoeffer
TEACHER HELPS: Independent reading course, no teacher helps needed
DESCRIPTION: A study designed to aid in personal growth through an understanding of the work of Christ, the value of the Word of God, and discipleship.

Course: The history of Christianity	Grades: 9–12	Prerequisite: None

MAIN TEXT OR MATERIAL: *Sketches from Church History*, S. M. Houghton, Banner of Truth
TEACHER HELPS: Independent reading course, no teacher helps needed
DESCRIPTION: An excellent study of the Christian church through the ages, providing the student information on the richness of his spiritual heritage.

Course: Classic Christian reading	Grades: 11–12	Prerequisite: None

MAIN TEXT OR MATERIAL: *The City of God* or *Confessions of St. Augustine*, Augustine, *Imitation of Christ*, Thomas á Kempis, *Bondage of the Will*, Martin Luther, *Institutes of the Christian Religion*, John Calvin, (in one volume, Tony Lane, editor, Baker Books), *Pilgrim's Progress*, John Bunyan
TEACHER HELPS: Independent reading course, no teacher helps needed
DESCRIPTION: This is a challenging independent study for the serious Bible and church history student. All of the selections represent books that have had a far-reaching effect on the history of the Christian church. *The City of God* profoundly affected the reformers hundreds of years after its publication. *Confessions* is the testimony of Augustine's conversion. The *Imitation of Christ*, perhaps the most widely read Christian devotional book in the world for the past five hundred years, is both simple and moving. Luther's *The Bondage of the Will* and Calvin's *Institutes* were the great reformers' most influential works. *Pilgrim's Progress* remains a widely read Christian classic.

Course: Readings in C. S. Lewis (or . . .)	Grades: 9–12	Prerequisite: None

TEACHER HELPS: Independent reading course, no teacher helps needed
DESCRIPTION: An independent study concentrating on an individual author's work. Although I highly recommend C. S. Lewis, you may want to consider Martyn Lloyd-Jones, A. W. Pink, Francis Schaeffer, Charles Spurgeon, and A. W. Tozier. In addition, there are many popular modern choices, such as Charles Colson, Sinclair Ferguson, John MacArthur, J. I. Packer, John Piper, R. C. Sproul, Chuck Swindoll, and Ravi Zacharias.

CHARACTER DEVELOPMENT

Course: Godly character for young men	Grades: 9–12	Prerequisite: None

MAIN TEXTS OR MATERIAL, (CHOOSE FROM): *Thoughts for Young Men*, J. C. Ryle, *The Mark of a Man*, Elisabeth Elliot, *Passion and Purity*, Elisabeth Elliot, *God's Gift to Women*, Eric Ludy
ADDITIONAL MATERIALS: Choose a dating/courtship book. (See Dating/Courtship below.)
TEACHER HELPS: Independent reading course, no teacher helps needed
DESCRIPTION: A study designed to help young men develop character that is pleasing in the sight of God.

Course: Godly character for young women	Grades: 9–12	Prerequisite: None

MAIN TEXTS OR MATERIAL, (CHOOSE FROM): *Let Me Be a Woman*, Elisabeth Elliot, *Passion and Purity*, Elisabeth Elliot, *Lady in Waiting*, Jackie Kendall and Debby Jones, *Authentic Beauty*, Leslie Ludy
ADDITIONAL MATERIALS: Choose a dating/courtship book. (See Dating/Courtship below.)
TEACHER HELPS: Independent reading course, no teacher helps needed
DESCRIPTION: A study designed to help young women develop character that is pleasing in the sight of God.

Course: Dating/courtship	Grades: 9–12	Prerequisite: None

MAIN TEXTS OR MATERIAL (CHOOSE FROM): *Dating with Integrity*, John Holzmann, *I Kissed Dating Good-bye*, Josh Harris, *Boy Meets Girl*, Josh Harris, *Passion and Purity*, Elisabeth Elliot, *When Dreams Come True*, Eric Ludy, *When God Writes Your Love Story*, Eric Ludy, *Sex Is Not the Problem, Lust Is*, Josh Harris, *Not Even a Hint: Guarding Your Heart against Lust*, Josh Harris
TEACHER HELPS: Independent reading course, no teacher helps needed
DESCRIPTION: Some excellent books are available on this topic now. They may have different views on dating and courtship, but all have the common goal of promoting purity before marriage. You may want to preread these titles. The stories aren't only about remaining pure before marriage; sometimes they are also about God's reclamation after a fall into sin.

Should My Student Date or Court?

Now that's a topic for a lively debate! While individuals may have varying views on what courtship entails and the wisdom of dating, there is at least one point on which everyone agrees. Of deep concern is promoting personal purity, a saving of yourself both emotionally and physically for the spouse of God's choosing. With that in mind, search out God's direction for your family.

English and Literature Courses

Although mentioned earlier, it is worth repeating: God holds language in high esteem. With the entire universe at His disposal, He chose the printed word as a primary means of communicating His loving plan of redemption to man. As His image bearers (marred though the image is), we should follow God's example. A thoughtful and careful honing of communication skills shows that we also hold language in an elevated position. Let's examine these skills one by one.

ELEMENTS OF AN ENGLISH PROGRAM

Grammar is the study of word usage. Our earliest grammar study begins as infants and toddlers learning to speak. Parents who model correct speech in their everyday conversation have given their children a decided advantage in learning grammar skills. It is always easier to learn something correctly from the beginning than to try to correct wrong usage once it's imbedded in the memory. During elementary school, students begin learning the different parts of speech: nouns, pronouns, verbs, adjectives, adverbs, prepositions, conjunctions, and interjections. As the student progresses through his school years, he will learn increasingly complex rules that govern their proper use.

Mechanics includes the study of other details necessary for successful writing, primarily capitalization and punctuation. Most grammar books also cover mechanics. Like grammar, this study begins in the elementary grades and continues until mastered.

Some homeschoolers finish formal grammar and mechanics studies in the ninth grade. A writing handbook would then become a constant reference when grammatical or mechanical problems arise. However, if desired, it is also possible to use grammar workbooks, such as those from A Beka or Bob Jones University Press, through all four high school grades.

The end result of all this study is (hopefully!) students who can use language with great skill in both speaking and writing. This is best achieved by practically applying these skills to the regular writing of compositions along with some opportunity for public speaking.

Composition is the art of expressing oneself in writing. It includes learning the various standard formats for constructing sentences, paragraphs, and larger works. It also involves developing a personal style of writing. High school level composition will show the most progress if grammatical and mechanical skills are already well developed.

While overlap exists, two basic directions are included in the study of composition: creative and informational writing. At their best both types of writing bring glory to God.

Creative writing offers the greatest freedom for personal expression through the writing of poetry, short stories, novels, plays, etc. At its best it makes us laugh, cry, or wonder at its beauty. Creative writing is not only creative expression. It also includes learning effective formats for each of the different writing genres.

Informational or expository writing organizes ideas, information, or processes. This promotion of order helps daily life flow more smoothly. It includes countless day-to-day writing tasks. In the home it means writing grocery lists, recipes, letters to friends, and a letter to the editor. In the business world it includes writing business letters, resumes, e-mail correspondence, employee directives, and speeches. In school it includes learning the formats for proper paragraphing (vital for essay questions on tests), summarization skills, research papers, book reports, and speech writing.

Not all students will choose to write creatively. However, everyone is required in life to write informationally. How do these thoughts direct us in making academic choices for our students? Consider putting the greatest composition efforts into learning the writing formats necessary for success in the academic and business world. For those students who are more creatively gifted, an elective course in creative writing could be offered. Check the course listing for some excellent resources.

Dictionary and research skills include learning the proper use of the tools needed for study. These tools include the dictionary, encyclopedia, the library classification systems (Dewey Decimal and Library of Congress), and various common reference works found in libraries. Using these library tools, the student should learn how to search for appropriate books and magazines on the topic he is pursuing. Of great importance in the world today is knowing how to navigate the Internet and its vast resources with ease. Dictionary and research skills are not always a separate area of study. The completion of several research projects and instruction from a helpful librarian can often teach these skills adequately.

Vocabulary is the study of word meanings. This study is preceded by a focus on spelling during the elementary grades. After the sixth grade it is not unusual for the emphasis to switch to vocabulary development. Some students are not ready for this switch. If your older student has not mastered spelling, it is important to revisit this skill while continuing ahead with vocabulary. Keep the future in mind. In the workforce poor spelling can make someone appear illiterate, regardless of how well he reads and how hard he works. Although spell-checkers are great, they will not be available for every writing situation on the job. And they are not always accurate!

There are different ways to approach the study of vocabulary. Vocabulary words can be drawn from the literature, history, and science being studied. They can also be studied through separate vocabulary workbooks. A thorough program may include both. For the college-bound student, a study of Latin or Greek roots is an appropriate addition to vocabulary studies. Studying Latin roots in particular, or the language itself, can enhance scores on college entrance exams.

Literature involves reading and analyzing written works that have shown themselves of lasting value through the test of time. It includes studying the elements contained in the different literary genres. For example, studying short stories or novels includes an examination of setting, characterizations, types of conflict, etc. Essays might be examined for persuasive devices used and the possible presence of propaganda techniques.

With so much available to read, how do you choose where to concentrate your efforts? Actually, it is amazing how much agreement there is on what literature is truly great. Many lists and reading plans are available. This book includes lists of American, English, and world literature known for its lasting value. There is, however, a limit to how many whole books can be read in four years. Should you prefer a wider exposure to more literary choices, A Beka and Bob Jones University Press publish high-school literature books. These books concentrate on poems, short stories, and excerpts from longer works. An anthology of this nature is especially helpful in providing a historical overview of a literary time period.

A prerequisite to literature studies is well-developed reading skills. In fact, strong reading skills are necessary for success in every academic subject and almost any future career. If your student struggles in reading, I strongly encourage you to continue working on reading skills. The literature course listing includes some suggestions for remedial reading.

ORGANIZING YOUR ENGLISH PROGRAM

Now that we've looked at the pieces of an English course, let's look at different ways to put it together. This is where you and your student consider your personalities, future goals, and your present situation when making a decision. There are three basic approaches, all academically sound:

1. *Use a workbook approach*, such as Alpha Omega, where all the skills are integrated. This is the easiest approach for the parent. No juggling required! However, if you find that your student needs additional work in a specific skill, supplement in that area.

2. *Choose materials from one publisher* such as Bob Jones University Press or A Beka Books. They may have separate grammar, literature, and vocabulary books to juggle, but the different components of their program will share the same educational philosophy and work well with one another.

3. *Choose different materials to teach each skill separately.* This is undoubtedly the most difficult but also the most flexible way to proceed. Possible reasons for integrating your English program yourself include the desire:

- To use a favorite program that covers only one particular skill.
- To work at different levels in different skills.
- To choose composition topics that integrate with other subjects.
- To teach dictionary and research skills through practical use.
- To study Latin as a foreign language rather than using a vocabulary text.
- To choose literature that integrates with your history studies.
- To study literature through the use of whole books instead of excerpts.

If you choose to integrate your English program yourself, you will need to decide how to order the teaching of skills. The following is a possible timetable for teaching the various English skills.

9th grade	emphasize grammar, mechanics, include short compositions, some vocabulary, read a few novels, begin studying the elements of literature
10th grade	if grammar skills are strong, discontinue use of grammar workbooks and use an English handbook when grammar or mechanical problems arise, increase length and variety of compositions, for the college-bound study Greek and Latin roots for vocabulary, increase the amount of literature studied, continue studying the elements of literature
11th grade	continue to refer to English handbook as needed, increase length and variety of compositions with an emphasis on SAT essay preparation, continue with vocabulary work using an SAT or ACT preparation guide in addition to studying Greek and Latin roots, include a historical anthology of literature (American) and study several novels
12th grade	continue to refer to English handbook as needed, increase length and variety of compositions—including fall work on college essays, continue vocabulary work (can use words in literature), include a historical anthology of literature (British or world) and study several novels

If including all these elements in your English program is overwhelming, don't panic. Instead, make some adaptations. Consider the following ideas:

1. Divide your areas of English study into semesters. Example: first semester study grammar, mechanics, and composition. Second semester study vocabulary, literature, and write book reports. This timetable could be further divided into quarters, emphasizing different skills at different times.
2. Study different skills on different days of the week.
3. If your teen has already mastered an area (like grammar or mechanics), don't restudy. Instead use an English handbook as a reference when problems arise.
4. Reduce the size of workbook assignments when it can be done without hampering learning. Do only odd or even questions. Do the first half. Often there is more work than the student needs for concept mastery.
5. Carry some work into the next school year if necessary.
6. Adapt the amount of work required according to the abilities and future ambitions of each student.

Even in adapting the amount of work, bear in mind that communication skills are important in most career fields. Therefore, the mastery of English should be emphasized for all students. For that reason you may want to keep your English courses fairly ambitious.

Possible resources for most of the English skills we have discussed are included. However, no separate dictionary and research suggestions are offered. Remedial suggestions are included under the appropriate headings (examples: spelling with vocabulary, reading with literature). A book report form, a list of self-editing questions, and a checklist for a research paper are included after the composition resources. American, British, and world literature novel choices follow the literature section. When Christian study guides are available, that is also noted.

To illustrate subject integration in an English course, the final entry contains sample standard and advanced classes for all four years. Please do not burden yourself by trying to follow these suggestions exactly. Instead, interact with them as you set your own expectations. I have not included sample remedial classes. The format of remedial

Which English reference books are most helpful?

First, every student needs a good dictionary. Both the *Merriam-Webster's Collegiate Dictionary* and *Webster's Third Edition New International Dictionary* are considered authoritative by the *Chicago Manual of Style*. In addition, many homeschoolers appreciate the *Webster's 1828 Dictionary*. Its use can be an interesting lesson in the fluidity (not always for the better) of the English language, but it will not be helpful with modern English standards. In fact, English can change so rapidly that the dictionary you used as a child may not give accurate help.

A thesaurus is another valuable tool for any writer. A thesaurus provides synonym and antonym help. For students it is a helpful means of increasing their vocabulary and improving the variety of word choice in their writing. (We older folk find it helpful when the right word can't quite escape our brain!) If you don't have a thesaurus, both *Roget's International Thesaurus* and *Rodale's Synonym Finder* are good choices.

An English handbook is the next important item. The answers to questions concerning grammar, punctuation, capitalization, and other language mechanics can be found quickly. Bob Jones University Press's *The Writer's Toolbox* is one good choice. A trip to a college bookstore may offer choices that can be used in high school and college. Finally, no writer's bag of tricks would be complete without Strunk and White's *The Elements of Style*. This small book contains succinct help for improving writing.

courses should be based on the immediate needs of the student. Remember that remedial materials are generally not considered high school level; use your own discretion about how best to incorporate them into your program.

Encourage summer reading to supplement school year assignments. The more your teen reads, the greater will be his academic success. Both reading and writing skills improve with exposure to good literature. If you would like additional reading suggestions, a book worth consulting is *Invitation to the Classics* by Louise Cowan and Os Guinness.

GRAMMAR AND MECHANICS

English skill: Grammar	*Grades:* Elementary and up, remedial 9–12	*Prerequisite:* None

MAIN TEXT OR MATERIAL: **Winston Grammar* student book, cue cards, Precious Memories

TEACHER HELPS: Teacher's manual

DESCRIPTION: *Winston Grammar* is appropriate for the student with little or no grammar background. Cue cards are used, which offer picture clues and short phrases to describe parts of speech and noun functions. Each lesson begins with the teacher writing out sample sentences which the student analyzes using the cue cards learned thus far. A student workbook follows up the lesson with sentences that the student marks using a simple system as an alternative to diagramming. If this approach works well for you, *Advanced Winston Grammar,* which includes types of pronouns, present and past participles, gerunds, infinitives, and other topics, is also available.

English skill: Grammar	*Grades:* 5+up, remedial 9–12	*Prerequisite:* None

MAIN TEXT OR MATERIAL: *Rules of the Game* Books 1–3, EPS

TEACHER HELPS: Three answer keys

DESCRIPTION: A set of three workbooks that help students discover grammar rules through a series of questions and examples. All three workbooks are needed to supply basic grammatical instruction. Written for junior high, it may also be appropriate for the high school student needing a fresh start in grammar.

English skill: Remedial grammar and mechanics	*Grades:* Remedial 9–12	*Prerequisite:* None

MAIN TEXT OR MATERIAL: *English Worksheets,* Rod and Staff

TEACHER HELPS: Teacher's edition

DESCRIPTION: This series of three workbooks covers parts of speech, the sentence, and punctuation and capitalization. They are inexpensive and uncomplicated.

English skill: Grammar and mechanics	*Grades:* 5–8, remedial 9–12	*Prerequisite:* None

MAIN TEXT OR MATERIAL: **Easy Grammar 5 & 6,* Isha

ADDITIONAL TEXT: **Easy Grammar Plus,* Isha, can be used as a standard high-school text

TEACHER HELPS: Teacher's manual

DESCRIPTION: *Easy Grammar* is a large fill-in-the-blank workbook teaching parts of speech, punctuation, and capitalization. Prepositions are taught first. The student memorizes them so he can successfully eliminate prepositional phrases from sentences, making it easier to find the simple sentence and its parts. *Easy Grammar's* various books begin with *Easy Grammar 3 & 4* (third and fourth grade) and progress to *Easy Grammar Plus* for high school. All build on one another. *Easy Grammar 5 & 6* is an upper elementary/early junior-high book, making it appropriate for remedial work. *Easy Grammar Plus* is designed for junior high through adult. Remedial high school students may also find it works fine since it is easier than many grammars. The teacher's manual contains the answers and blank student pages that may be photocopied, although purchasing the separate student workbook is usually more cost effective than photocopying. I hope someday they will put out a teacher's manual with only answers; it would be more cost effective for the homeschooler.

| *English skill:* Grammar and mechanics | *Grades:* 6–8, 9–12 | *Prerequisite:* None |

MAIN TEXT OR MATERIAL: *Editor in Chief B1, B2, C1, C2*, Bright Minds (part of Critical Thinking Press)

TEACHER HELPS: Answers in back of student workbook

DESCRIPTION: *Editor in Chief* teaches the student to sharpen his editing skills by finding the errors contained in the reading selection for each lesson. With mixed errors on each page, the practice resembles a real-life editing task. An editing checklist, grammar guide, and thoroughly explained answers makes this approximately 130-page book a good supplemental resource. *B1* and *B2* are for grades 6–8, *C1* and *C2* for grades 9–12. (If working below level, books *A1* and *A2* for grades 4–5 could be used.)

| *English skill:* Grammar and mechanics | *Grades:* 7–12 | *Prerequisite:* None |

MAIN TEXT OR MATERIAL: *Jensen's Grammar, Jensen's Punctuation*, Wordsmith

TEACHER HELPS: Key in back of student workbooks

DESCRIPTION: *Jensen's Grammar* is a thorough one-year program that should effectively polish off your high school grammar program. It may also be used with an academically strong junior high student. Exercises that require writing a sentence based on a given grammar formula make this a challenging book. *Jensen's Punctuation* is also thorough in its coverage of punctuation. There are no bells and whistles here but plenty of opportunity for practice in these consumable workbooks.

| *English skill:* Grammar and mechanics | *Grades:* 7–12 | *Prerequisite:* None |

MAIN TEXT OR MATERIAL: *Writing and Grammar*, Bob Jones University Press

TEACHER HELPS: Teacher's manual, tests, and test key

DESCRIPTION: Content from book to book includes the same basic topics with a steady growth in the concepts taught. Junior-high grades emphasize grammar while still providing composition opportunities. By the tenth grade the emphasis begins to move toward more advanced composition and shorter but more intense grammar lessons. Eleventh and twelfth grades continue the move into more advanced composition. Because grades eight and nine both provide a thorough presentation of grammar, some homeschoolers may feel that successful completion of these books provides sufficient formal grammar instruction, freeing more time for composition, literature, and vocabulary studies. Students planning a college major in English will find all the challenge they need in the upper-level books. The best preparation for these eleventh- and twelfth-grade books is the use of the series in previous grades. Coming into an upper-level book without prior instruction might be too great of a challenge. Other skills addressed include mechanics, tricky spelling, and library and study skills. Teacher's guides contain teaching and scheduling helps, workbook answers, reproducible work sheets, and helps for objectively grading compositions.

COMPOSITION

| *English skill:* Composition | *Grades:* 7–12 | *Prerequisite:* None |

MAIN TEXT OR MATERIAL: *Composition* Lifepac Select, Alpha Omega

TEACHER HELPS: Teacher's guide

DESCRIPTION: Alpha Omega Select electives consist of five workbooks topically chosen to create a one-semester course. Since the course includes both junior high and high school level workbooks, it will be less challenging than some other choices.

| *English skill:* Composition | *Grades:* All grades | *Prerequisite:* None |

MAIN TEXT OR MATERIAL: **Teaching Writing: Structure and Style*, The Institute for Excellence in Writing

TEACHER HELPS: DVDs, syllabus, no student text or workbook, teacher directed

DESCRIPTION: Andrew Pudewa has a unique methodology for teaching both expository and creative writing to all age levels. The videos record Mr. Pudewa teaching adults to use his methods. Additional videos show him working with children in various age groups. His note-taking techniques are valuable for learning summarization skills, organizing writing, and avoiding plagiarism. They can be used for both oral and written presentations. His stylistic techniques teach objective methods for improving the creativity of sentence structure and language. These techniques are sometimes criticized as encouraging students to write in a stilted, less natural fashion. Use of the techniques does not have to result in formula writing but can appropriately broaden a student's knowledge of the writing tools available for his use. The information presented in the videos is also in the accompanying syllabus. Although pricey, this program sets a good foundation for any type of writing. Check www.writing-edu.com for other teaching video combinations.

English skill: Composition	*Grades:* 10–12	*Prerequisite:* None

MAIN TEXT OR MATERIAL: **Wordsmith Craftsman*, Janie Cheaney, Common Sense Press
TEACHER HELPS: None needed, student directed
DESCRIPTION: *Wordsmith Craftsman* polishes practical writing skills. These skills include taking notes, outlining, letters, summaries, reports, paragraphing, writing techniques, and various forms of essays. Janie Cheaney directly addresses the student using her delightful writing style.

English skill: Composition	*Grades:* 7–12	*Prerequisite:* None

MAIN TEXT OR MATERIAL: **Format Writing*, Frode Jensen, Wordsmith
TEACHER HELPS: Grading rubrics in back of book
DESCRIPTION: *Format Writing*, while not flashy, offers effective instruction in the art of composition. The book progresses from various forms of paragraphs to five paragraph essays. The strong emphasis on these early skills will provide an excellent foundation for the writing portions of the SAT and ACT. After thoroughly addressing paragraphing, the book then moves to the precis (summarizations) and research papers. The book could be effectively used as a teacher reference or student guidebook as the student builds his skills through junior high and high school.

English skill: Composition	*Grades:* 9–12	*Prerequisite:* None

MAIN TEXT OR MATERIAL: *Writing Strands*, David Marks, National Writing Institute
TEACHER HELPS: None needed, student directed
DESCRIPTION: Writing Strands is a series of thin, spiral-bound books, which gradually move the student through all the necessary writing skills. High schoolers will begin anywhere from Level 4 on up, depending on their previous composition experience. Both creative and expository writing are taught. The books directly address the student. Teacher involvement will be correcting and discussing compositions.

English skill: Composition	*Grade:* 9	*Prerequisite:* None

MAIN TEXT OR MATERIAL: **Skills for Rhetoric*, James Stobaugh, Broadman & Holman
TEACHER HELPS: Teacher's edition
DESCRIPTION: *Skills for Rhetoric* is a challenging course that focuses on the effective use of words, both written and spoken. Assignments emphasize public speaking and various forms of expository writing, culminating with a research paper. Daily reading is recommended and a suggested reading list is provided. A suggested weekly schedule is also provided. Although a challenging course, parents are encouraged to customize the program to fit their need. Always presenting a conscientiously Christian worldview, this is the second book in the Encouraging Thoughtful Christians to Be World Changers series.

English skill: Research paper writing	*Grades:* 9–12	*Prerequisite:* None

MAIN TEXT OR MATERIAL: *Writing a Research Paper*, Edward J. Shewan, Christian Liberty Press
TEACHER HELPS: None needed, student directed

DESCRIPTION: This little inexpensive booklet provides an excellent nutshell presentation of writing a research paper.

English skill: Research paper writing	*Grades:* 9–12	*Prerequisite:* None

MAIN TEXT OR MATERIAL: *Writing Research Papers with Confidence*, Sheila Moss, Broadman & Holman

TEACHER HELPS: Teacher edition

DESCRIPTION: *Writing Research Papers with Confidence* is a thorough presentation of the process a student undergoes when writing a research paper. Early assignments include scheduling a tour of the library to learn how to access information, interviewing others on their researching experiences, and learning the language of research. The student is then taken step-by-step through the research process. In addition, each chapter provides practice with the SAT's writing test. Exercises are modeled on SAT usage questions and essay prompts. The prompts presented are largely related to the course material, and some students may find it difficult to take a position and write persuasively on the suggested topic. Modify the prompt if necessary rather than discard this important activity. A student who learns researching through this book should be well prepared for college-level work.

English skill: Creative writing	*Grades:* 7–12	*Prerequisite:* None

MAIN TEXT OR MATERIAL: **Wordsmith*, Janie Cheaney, Common Sense Press

TEACHER HELPS: Teacher's guide

DESCRIPTION: This excellent guide for creative writing is geared to students in junior high and up. Written directly to the student, the writing is both concise and entertaining. It makes an excellent elective course. The teacher's guide includes teaching and scheduling helps.

English skill: Short story writing	*Grades:* 10–12	*Prerequisite:* None

MAIN TEXT OR MATERIAL: *The Exciting World of Creative Writing*, Ruth McDaniels, Christian Liberty Press

TEACHER HELPS: None required, student directed

DESCRIPTION: An excellent guide that carefully walks the student through the process of writing a short story, this friendly and encouraging book contains a wealth of information for the budding writer. Consider using it for an elective course in creative writing.

BOOK REPORT FORMAT

NAME _____ DATE _____

TITLE: (underlined or in italics)

AUTHOR:

PUBLISHER:

COPYRIGHT YEAR:

BOOK TYPE: (biography, fiction, historical fiction, short story, nonfiction, Christian fiction, etc.)

SETTING: Tell where and when the story takes place.

SUMMARY: Write at least one paragraph of five or six sentences summarizing the plot.

CHARACTER SKETCH: Choose one character to describe. Look for both positive and negative characteristics. How did these characteristics affect the action of the book?

THEME: What do you believe is the overall theme or moral of this book? What do you think the author was trying to say or teach?

RECOMMENDATION: Would you recommend this book? Tell why or why not.

		Editing Checklist
YES	**NO**	
		Did I write with my reader in mind?
		Did I follow my outline or organizational plan?
		Can the reader follow my thought progression easily?
		Have I used strong nouns and verbs?
		Have I used adjectives and adverbs lightly?
		Have I selected the best words for my purposes rather than the most impressive?
		Are there any unnecessary words I can leave out? Check sentence by sentence.
		Did I show, not tell? (Ex.: "Her lip quivered," not "she began to cry.")
		Have I varied my sentence styles?
		Is the writing style I'm using natural for me?
		Is my final draft free of spelling, punctuation, and grammar mistakes?
		Self-editing has its limitations. Am I brave enough to give my paper to someone else to critique?
		Does my final polished copy glorify God both in content and presentation?
	Additional editing hints for an excellent paper. Have you:	
		Read it slowly out loud, word by word? You'll catch more errors.
		Used a different color ink to mark the errors you find? Red shows best.
		Read it through several times looking for different problems? (Ex.: Read it once for spelling, once for punctuation, once for word clarity, etc.)
		Learned how to use a word-processing program on your computer? It makes editing much easier.
		Started fresh with a clean copy after making your initial corrections in order to catch more mistakes? If the paper gets too messy with corrections, you can no longer see additional errors. On a clean copy, errors you missed may jump out at you!
		Be on the look out for repetitive errors.
"Whatever things are true, whatever things are noble, whatever things are just, whatever things are pure, whatever things are lovely, whatever things are of good report, if there is any virtue and if there is anything praiseworthy—meditate [editor's note: and write!] on these things" (Phil. 4:8).		

Research Paper Checklist

Check off and date when each assignment is completed.   Paper due on:

☒	Date	Assignment
		Week One
		I. Preliminary reading on research papers. (Consider *Format Writing*, the section on major papers or *Writing a Research Paper* by CLP.)
		II. Gather information. Use guidelines in above publications for cards.
		A. Keep a bibliography card for each source.
		B. Read and collect information on note cards about your topic.
		C. Turn in for evaluation.
		III. Organize information.
		A. Separate note cards into topical piles.
		B. Write your outline using your note card piles as your guide.
		C. Turn in for evaluation.
		Week Two
		IV. Write your rough draft. Follow your outline, refer to note cards, and be sure to include in-text citations as you go. Include:
		A. An introductory paragraph with a thesis sentence.
		B. Body paragraphs.
		C. A conclusion paragraph that directs the reader back to the thesis sentence or recaps main points.
		D. Organize "works cited" page.
		E. Use a bibliography page for additional reading not cited in the paper.
		V. Put the paper up for several days and forget about it.
		Week Three
		VI. With a fresh mind polish your rough draft looking for the following errors:
		A. Errors in structure.
		1. Not following your outline.
		2. Disorderly sequence of thoughts within a paragraph.

☒	Date	*Check off and date when each assignment is completed. Paper due on:*
		Assignment
		Week Three continued
		B. Errors in style:
		1. Wordiness—Ask yourself:
		a. What sentences or phrases can I take out and not miss?
		b. What words are unnecessarily difficult when a simpler word will do?
		2. Ambiguity—Ask yourself:
		a. Is this the clearest way to say this?
		b. Will my audience understand this?
		C. Errors in mechanics—Check for errors in:
		1. Spelling
		2. Punctuation
		3. Sentence fragments
		4. Run-on sentences
		5. Grammar
		D. Errors in form—Follow the format rules taught in your preliminary reading for the following items:
		1. Title page
		2. Body of paper
		a. Double space
		b. Include in-text citations
		3. "Works Cited" page
		4. "Bibliography" page, if included
		VI. Complete second draft and turn in for evaluation.
		Week Four
		VII. Make corrections and submit in final form for grading.

Additional Notes:

VOCABULARY

English skill: Remedial spelling	*Grades:* all grades	*Prerequisite:* None

MAIN TEXT OR MATERIAL: *Spelling Power, 4th ed.*, Castlemoyle Books

TEACHER HELPS: Everything needed is in the teacher's book, CD-ROM and DVD included in price of book; student record books available separately.

DESCRIPTION: *Spelling Power* begins with diagnostic tests that help you place your student at the appropriate level in the extensive spelling lists. Each day, for 15 minutes, words are dictated, written, spelled aloud, and immediately corrected. A check sheet presents a systematic, multisensory routine for learning the misspelled words. Activities are recommended to reinforce the spelling words. The fourth edition includes all the printable forms on a *Teacher's Resource CD-ROM*. The *Quick Start DVD* walks you through the steps needed to use the program effectively.

English skill: Vocabulary	*Grades:* 6–12 (elementary grades also available)	*Prerequisite:* None

MAIN TEXT OR MATERIAL: *Vocabu-Lit, Books F–L*, Perfection Learning Company

TEACHER HELPS: Teacher's editions

DESCRIPTION: *Vocabu-Lit* is a literature-based vocabulary series for grades six through twelve. Excerpts from a wide range of classic stories, novels, poems, essays, and speeches provide the words to study.

English skill: Vocabulary	*Grades:* 7–12	*Prerequisite:* None

MAIN TEXT OR MATERIAL: *Vocabulary: Level A–F*, Bob Jones University Press

TEACHER HELPS: Teacher's edition

DESCRIPTION: Areas studied over the course of the series include Latin and Greek prefixes and roots, words borrowed from other languages, using context to discover word meaning, proper word selection to enhance writing, and terminology pertinent to vocabulary studies.

English skill: Vocabulary	*Grades:* 4–12	*Prerequisite:* None

MAIN TEXT OR MATERIAL: *Wordly Wise 3000 Books 1–9*, Educator's Publishing Service

TEACHER HELPS: Answer key

DESCRIPTION: Wordly Wise is a vocabulary series that has long been popular with homeschoolers. *Wordly Wise 3000* contains the same helpful variety of activities as the original series with the added feature of using a short narrative to study the vocabulary words in context. Some words are included that frequently appear on SAT tests. An inexpensive answer key is also available. The series starts at the fourth-grade level with book 1. Counting upward, this places book 9 at the twelfth grade level. A bit confusing but a good vocabulary series nonetheless.

English skill: Vocabulary	*Grades:* 5–11	*Prerequisite:* None

MAIN TEXT OR MATERIAL: *Vocabulary from Classical Roots, Books A–E*, Educator's Publishing Service

TEACHER HELPS: Answer key

DESCRIPTION: Latin and Greek roots are studied through a variety of exercises. This series is valuable for enriching vocabulary and for SAT preparation. Book A is the seventh grade book. Book E brings the series through the eleventh grade. The newer books for grades five and six are called *Vocabulary from Classical Roots 5* and *6* respectively.

English skill: Vocabulary	*Grades:* 9–12	*Prerequisite:* None

MAIN TEXT OR MATERIAL: *Jensen's Vocabulary*, Frode Jensen, Wordsmith

TEACHER HELPS: Answers in back of book

DESCRIPTION: This challenging book contains master lists of Latin or Greek prefixes, roots, and suffixes. Using these lists, students dissect an English word into parts, searching for its meaning in the original language. They then apply this knowledge to choosing a current definition from the list provided. The approach is challenging, requiring careful thought and analysis. It should make excellent SAT/ACT preparation.

READING AND LITERATURE

English skill: Remedial phonics reading   **Grades:** Any age needing remedial phonics   **Prerequisite:** None

MAIN TEXT OR MATERIAL: *Alpha Phonics*, Samuel Blumenfeld, Paradigm Company
TEACHER HELPS: Suggested lessons in back of book
DESCRIPTION: Samuel Blumenfeld was an early activist in promoting a return to phonics. His *Alpha Phonics* provides a simple no-nonsense drill for practicing phonics skills. Because the program returns to the earliest phonics skills, it is most appropriate for new readers, students with severe reading problems, or students who were taught to read by a method that did not teach letter sounds systematically or thoroughly. The lack of childish graphics makes it inoffensive to the adult learner. Teacher preparation is located in the back of the book and is simple and straightforward.

English skill: Remedial reading   **Grades:** Any age needing remedial phonics   **Prerequisite:** None

MAIN TEXT OR MATERIAL: *Phonics Tutor*, software, reader, and workbook, 4:20 Communications
TEACHER HELPS: Teacher's manual available separately
DESCRIPTION: *Phonics Tutor* is a self-instructional computer program with a thorough and systematic presentation of phonics, as presented in *Alpha Phonics*. Like *Alpha Phonics*, it begins at the beginning of phonics instruction and moves forward. This makes it most appropriate for new readers, students with severe reading problems, or students who were taught to read by a method that did not teach letter sounds systematically or thoroughly. The lack of childish graphics makes it inoffensive to the adult learner. A companion program, *Frequent Words*, expands the number of words taught.

English skill: Remedial reading   **Grades:** 4–adult   **Prerequisite:** None

MAIN TEXT OR MATERIAL: *Phonics Intervention*, Saxon
TEACHER HELPS: Teacher's manual, classroom materials kit
DESCRIPTION: *Phonics Intervention* is designed for the older student who has reading and spelling difficulty. The student workbook serves as both a reference and practice book. The teacher's manual provides a scripted dialogue for teaching the material, lesson plans, and supplementary materials. A material kit contains card decks and an audiotape for reviewing learned skills. Saxon is now owned by Harcourt Achieve. Go to www.harcourtachieve.com for more information.

English skill: Remedial reading   **Grades:** Any age needing remedial phonics   **Prerequisite:** None

MAIN TEXT OR MATERIAL: *Developing Better Reading*, Rod and Staff
TEACHER HELPS: Teacher's manual
DESCRIPTION: *Developing Better Reading* is an inexpensive workbook presenting a review of basic phonics, spelling, and syllabication rules for the remedial reading student.

English skill: Remedial reading   **Grade:** Any age needing remedial reading   **Prerequisite:** None

MAIN TEXT OR MATERIAL: *Classics*, *Easy Shakespeare* workbooks, Edcon
TEACHER HELPS: Answer key included in student workbook
DESCRIPTION: Edcon's reading workbooks adapt children's classics and Shakespeare's plays to first- through fifth-grade reading levels. Condensed, simplified, and presented in a ten-chapter format with comprehension questions. There are many titles from which to choose.

English skill: Literary interpretation   **Grades:** 5–12   **Prerequisite:** None

MAIN TEXT OR MATERIAL: *Progeny Press*, work sheets, novel purchased separately

TEACHER HELPS: Answers included with work sheets

DESCRIPTION: Those who enjoy a living-book approach will appreciate the Progeny Press study guides for literature. The study guides are loose-leaf, ready for insertion into a three-ring binder. Approximately thirty guides are available for the middle school grades (5–8) and another thirty are available for high school, but the list is always growing. Questions reflect a Christian worldview so that even controversial novels can be discussed profitably. A synopsis of the novel, vocabulary activities, composition suggestions, basic reading comprehension, and more advanced critical thinking questions are all included. Guides are also available for earlier grades.

English skill: Literary interpretation	*Grades:* 5–12	*Prerequisite:* None

MAIN TEXT OR MATERIAL: *Total Language Plus*, workbook, novel purchased separately

Teacher helps: Answers included with workbook

DESCRIPTION: Like Progeny Press above, Total Language Plus guides students through studying a novel. Skills include spelling, vocabulary, comprehension, grammar and mechanics, critical thinking, and composition. More than thirty guides are available for junior high and high school use. Guides are also available for younger children.

English skill: Literature approach to language skills	*Grade:* 7	*Prerequisite:* None

MAIN TEXT OR MATERIAL: *Learning Language Arts through Literature, Green Book*, Common Sense Press

TEACHER HELPS: Teacher's guide

DESCRIPTION: Students study *Star of Light, Adam and His Kin, Much Ado about Nothing*, and numerous book quotations to learn about comprehension, literary terms, spelling, grammar, composition, research skills, and critical thinking.

English skill: Literature approach to language skills	*Grade:* 8	*Prerequisite:* None

MAIN TEXT OR MATERIAL: *Learning Language Arts through Literature, Gray Book*, Common Sense Press

TEACHER HELPS: Teacher's guide

DESCRIPTION: Students study *Across Five Aprils, A Lantern in Her Hand, Eric Liddell, God's Smuggler*, and numerous book quotations to learn about comprehension, literary terms, spelling, grammar, composition, research skills, and critical thinking.

English skill: Literary interpretation	*Grades:* 6–8, early high school	*Prerequisite:* None

MAIN TEXT OR MATERIAL: *Drawn into the Heart of Reading*, Heart of Dakota, student book, student or parent-selected novels

TEACHER HELPS: Teacher's guide

DESCRIPTION: *Drawn into the Heart of Reading* provides both the guidance and the flexibility to use living books effectively in your homeschool program. The student book provides activities for books in nine different genres: biography, adventure, historical fiction, fantasy, mystery, folk tales, nonfiction, humor, and realistic fiction. Story elements, vocabulary, discussion, godly character traits, and project ideas are interwoven into the program. The teacher's guide covers the entire program, including the two books for younger grades, 2/3 and 4/5. The student workbook for 6/7/8 can also be used with high school students as an introduction to literature course. I wish this program had been around when my older students were young! For additional information see the listing for Heart of Dakota in appendix A.

English skill: Literary interpretation	*Grades:* 9–12	*Prerequisite:* None

MAIN TEXT OR MATERIAL: *Movies as Literature*, Design a Study

TEACHER HELPS: Student pages and teacher's guide in one combined volume

DESCRIPTION: This one-year high school study uses seventeen classic movies to teach the elements of literary analysis. In addition to English skills learned, students will learn to watch movies actively rather than passively absorbing the movie's content. Some of the movies studied are suitable for junior high.

| *English skill:* Literary interpretation | *Grades:* 7–12 | *Prerequisite:* None |

MAIN TEXT OR MATERIAL: *Literary Lessons from The Lord of the Rings*, HomeScholar Books
TEACHER HELPS: Teacher's guide
DESCRIPTION: For Tolkien lovers this program is a real gem. Amelia Harper has written an easy-to-use guide to both the Lord of the Rings series and the ancient literature that inspired it. Student books include fill-in-the-blank chapter reviews, while chapter notes provide background information and a study of literary terms. Smaller unit studies within the larger study cover literary concepts and the ancient and Arthurian literature that hold a creative link to Middle Earth. Quizzes, tests, and all answers are provided. This self-directed study couldn't be easier to use. For high-school transcript purposes, Ms. Harper suggests entitling the course, An Introduction to Literary Analysis. This one-year course could appropriately replace one general literature course, such as those offered in seventh through tenth grade. She does not recommend using it as a replacement for American or British literature. Information for contacting HomeScholar Books, publisher of this guide, is available in appendix A.

| *English skill:* Literary analysis | *Grades:* 8–early high school | *Prerequisite:* None |

MAIN TEXT OR MATERIAL: *Skills for Literary Analysis*, James Stobaugh, Broadman & Holman
TEACHER HELPS: Teacher's edition
DESCRIPTION: *Skills for Literary Analysis* is a challenging course which, when successfully completed, will give students a thorough understanding of literary terms and the ability to discuss their use intelligently. Terms are amply illustrated through literary examples. An aggressive reading schedule requires careful planning and advance reading to stay current with lessons. Writing projects include a daily prayer journal, several weekly essays, and literary reviews. Although this is a challenging course, parents are encouraged to customize the program to fit their needs. Always presenting a conscientiously Christian worldview, this is the first book in the Encouraging Thoughtful Christians to Be World Changers series.

| *English skill:* Literary interpretation | *Grade:* 9 | *Prerequisite:* None |

MAIN TEXT OR MATERIAL: *Fundamentals of Literature*, Bob Jones University Press
TEACHER HELPS: Teacher's edition, tests and test key, or *Testbuilder 2* software
DESCRIPTION: Analyzes various reading selections for the following elements: conflict, character, theme, structure, point of view, and moral tone. The student text includes introductory text for each selection, author biographies, and thought and discussion questions. *Cyrano de Bergerac* is studied in full. The teacher's edition contains the student pages with additional helpful information for guiding discussion. Answers to the questions in the student text are also included. Questions for producing customized tests are available on the *Testbuilder 2* software.

| *English skill:* Literary interpretation | *Grade:* 10 | *Prerequisite:* None |

MAIN TEXT OR MATERIAL: *Elements of Literature*, Bob Jones University Press
TEACHER HELPS: Teacher's edition, tests and test key, or *Testbuilder 2* software
DESCRIPTION: This text moves into advanced literary concepts with a study of different genres. The Shakespearian play *Romeo and Juliet* is studied in full. The teacher's edition has the same helpful features as other BJUP literature books. See ninth-grade book *Fundamentals of Literature* for more information. Questions for producing customized tests are available on *Testbuilder 2* software.

| *English skill:* American literature | *Grades:* 7–12 | *Prerequisite:* None |

MAIN TEXT OR MATERIAL: *American Literature*, Alpha Omega, also available in Switched on Schoolhouse format
TEACHER HELPS: Teacher's manual for Lifepacs
DESCRIPTION: This one-semester course progresses chronologically, dividing the examination of American literature into five time periods. It can be used as a supplement to Alpha Omega's *Language Arts* Lifepacs or any other

English program you are using. A workbook approach to learning is used in this course. Its adaptability to grades seven to twelve means it will be less rigorous than some choices.

English skill: American literature	*Grades:* 9–12	*Prerequisite:* None

MAIN TEXT OR MATERIAL: *The Gold Book: American Literature*, Common Sense Press novels, two anthologies

TEACHER HELPS: One book for teacher or self-directed student use

DESCRIPTION: *The Gold Book: American Literature* is part of the Learning Language Arts through Literature series. It is organized by genre rather than chronology. Genres studied include the short story, the novel, and poetry. Three essay assignments—expository, descriptive, and narrative—are also included. Students will need to purchase the recommended novels and anthologies which include *Great American Short Stories, the Mentor Book of Major American Poets, The Old Man and the Sea, The Red Badge of Courage,* and *The Pearl.* Unlike other LLATL titles, this level has only one text for either teacher or self-directed student use.

English skill: American literature	*Grade:* 11	*Prerequisite:* None

MAIN TEXT OR MATERIAL: *American Literature*, Bob Jones University Press

TEACHER HELPS: Teacher's edition, tests and test key, or *Testbuilder 2* software

DESCRIPTION: This text takes a chronological walk through American literature. Introductions explaining each major time period are accompanied by a time line. Biographical information on the various authors precedes the selections. Using this book in conjunction with American history makes it doubly effective. The teacher edition contains student pages and plenty of help for preparing an excellent college-preparatory course. Questions for producing customized tests are available on the *Testbuilder 2* software.

English skill: American literature	*Grade:* 10	*Prerequisite:* None

MAIN TEXT OR MATERIAL: *American Literature*, James Stobaugh, Broadman & Holman

TEACHER HELPS: Teacher's edition

DESCRIPTION: *American Literature* is a chronological study of the literature of our nation. Stobaugh's program, while including poetry and other short works, also requires a large number of full-length novels. With recommended reading requiring thirty-five to fifty pages nightly, even voracious readers will be significantly challenged. Advance summertime reading will help your student meet the challenge. Vocabulary building and essay writing are emphasized as they are in all books in this series. The student textbook is well written and interesting. Critical thinking questions require significant thought and should spark interesting discussion. The exceptional English student will find all the intellectual stimulation he needs in this challenging course. For those who find the lesson plans too daunting, Stobaugh encourages adapting the program as needed. Always presenting a conscientiously Christian worldview, this book is part of the Encouraging Thoughtful Christians to Be World Changers series.

English skill: British literature	*Grades:* 7–12	*Prerequisite:* None

MAIN TEXT OR MATERIAL: *British Literature*, Alpha Omega, also available in Switched on Schoolhouse format

TEACHER HELPS: Teacher's manual for Lifepacs

DESCRIPTION: This one-semester chronological British literature course can be used as a supplement to Alpha Omega's Language Arts Lifepacs or any other English program you are using. The workbook approach to learning is used in this course. Its adaptability to grades seven to twelve means it will be less rigorous than some choices.

English skill: British literature	*Grades:* 9–12	*Prerequisite:* None

MAIN TEXT OR MATERIAL: *The Gold Book: British Literature*, Common Sense Press, five novels, one anthology

TEACHER HELPS: One book for teacher or self-directed student use

DESCRIPTION: *The Gold Book: British Literature* is the final book in the Learning Language Arts through Literature series. Books studied include: *Frankenstein, Emma, A Tale of Two Cities, The Time Machine, Animal Farm*, and *The Mentor Book of Major British Poets*. Composition requirements are included. Unlike other LLATL titles, this level has only one text for either teacher or self-directed student use.

English skill: British literature	*Grade:* 12	*Prerequisite:* None

MAIN TEXT OR MATERIAL: **British Literature*, Bob Jones University Press
TEACHER HELPS: Teacher's edition, tests and test key, or *Testbuilder 2* software
DESCRIPTION: This text takes a chronological walk through British literature. Introductions explaining each major time period are accompanied by a time line. Biographical information on the various authors precedes the selections. The teacher edition contains student pages and plenty of help for preparing an excellent college preparatory course. Questions for producing customized tests are available on the *Testbuilder 2* software. This text is a favorite of mine.

English skill: British literature	*Grade:* 11	*Prerequisite:* None

MAIN TEXT OR MATERIAL: **British Literature*, James Stobaugh, Broadman & Holman
TEACHER HELPS: Teacher's edition
DESCRIPTION: Arranged chronologically, *British Literature* is a challenging course for the serious literature student. *British Literature* requires reading both literary excerpts and complete novels. Authors range from Venerable Bede and Chaucer, representing England's earliest literary history, to C. S. Lewis and Tolkien, whose writings are well-known to many students. A smart student will use summer to get a jump on reading assignments. In addition to stimulating but daunting reading requirements, students will also make vocabulary cards and write several essays weekly. Parents are encouraged to customize the program to fit their needs. Always presenting a conscientiously Christian worldview, this book is part of the Encouraging Thoughtful Christians to Be World Changers series.

English skill: World literature	*Grade:* 12	*Prerequisite:* None

MAIN TEXT OR MATERIAL: **World Literature*, James Stobaugh, Broadman & Holman
TEACHER HELPS: Teacher's edition
DESCRIPTION: *World Literature* is a challenging course in the Encouraging Thoughtful Christians to Be World Changers series. All of Stobaugh's literature books stress the same elements: extensive reading, vocabulary accumulation, thought-provoking questions, a significant volume of essay writing, and a conscientiously Christian worldview. *World Literature* spends ample time with early Greek and Roman writers before moving to early church fathers and Eastern writings. Dante's *Divine Comedy*, Goethe's *Faust*, Tolstoy's *War and Peace*, Dostoevsky's *Crime and Punishment*, and Paton's *Cry, the Beloved Country* are some of the literature selections that bring us from the Middle Ages to modern times. Summer reading is encouraged for some of the weightier tomes. As with all Stobaugh's books, expect a stimulating challenge and adapt for time constraints if necessary.

English skill: Ancient literature	*Grade:* 12	*Prerequisite:* Most effective if taught concurrently with ancient world history

MAIN TEXT OR MATERIAL: *Heroes of the City of Man*, Peter Leithart, Canon Press
TEACHER HELPS: None
DESCRIPTION: Peter Leithart analyzes the ancient Greek and Roman classics—*The Iliad, The Odyssey*, and *The Aeneid*—from a Christian worldview. Thought-provoking questions conclude each section. *Heroes* is a valuable introduction for the Christian student who may cover this material again (from a vastly different viewpoint) in a secular college course.

English skill: Writings of Jane Austen	*Grades:* 11–12	*Prerequisite:* After or concurrent with British literature

MAIN TEXT OR MATERIAL: *Miniatures and Morals*, Peter Leithart, Canon Press
TEACHER HELPS: None
DESCRIPTION: For all the Jane Austen lovers, Peter Leithart summarizes each of Austen's books. Character and theme are analyzed, and helpful thought and review questions conclude each section. The title, *Miniatures and Morals*, refers to Austen's careful, detailed writing style and her concern that Christian virtues be part of the fabric of life.

English skill: Shakespeare	*Grades:* 11–12	*Prerequisite:* After or concurrent with British literature

MAIN TEXT OR MATERIAL: *Brightest Heaven of Invention*, Peter Leithart, Canon Press
TEACHER HELPS: None
DESCRIPTION: Another Peter Leithart book, which this time walks the student through six of Shakespeare's plays. Two historical plays, two tragedies, and two comedies are included. *Brightest Heaven of Invention* is an in-depth study from a Christian worldview.

English skill: Shakespeare	*Grades:* 11–12	*Prerequisite:* After or concurrent with British literature

MAIN TEXT OR MATERIAL: *William Shakespeare: Comedies, Histories, and Tragedies*, The Teaching Company
TEACHER HELPS: None
DESCRIPTION: The Teaching Company offers DVD or audio instruction from well-respected, excellent instructors from across the United States. Course outlines are included with each DVD or CD set. If desired, a complete course transcript can be purchased for an additional fee. Offering more than two hundred college-level courses, their catalog is a feast for learning-addicted homeschoolers. Undoubtedly there are some courses to avoid, but the generous course descriptions make appropriate selections easy. For more information visit www.teach12.com or call the company for a catalog. Sales run regularly, rotating through the different courses. The catalog will alert you to current offers.

English skill: Spenser	*Grades:* 11–12	*Prerequisite:* After or concurrent with British literature

MAIN TEXT OR MATERIAL: *Fierce Wars and Faithful Loves*, Roy Maynard, Canon Press
TEACHER HELPS: None
DESCRIPTION: For the motivated student of English literature, Roy Maynard has updated and annotated book one of *The Faerie Queene* by Edmund Spenser. Maynard's Christian worldview is evident in his commentary. "Sword Talk" at the end of each chapter provides a vocabulary list and questions.

English skill: Literary genres/history of literature	*Grades:* 9–12	*Prerequisite:* None

MAIN TEXT OR MATERIAL: *Reading Between the Lines*, Gene Edward Veith, Crossway
TEACHER HELPS: None
DESCRIPTION: *Reading Between the Lines* is an excellent introduction to the forms and history of literature. A literary history course could be designed using *Reading Between the Lines* as a guide to choosing selections from different literary genres or time periods. While we used it as a high school text, my son studied it again at the Christian college he attended. This is one of my favorite books.

English skill: Critical reading	*Grades:* 9–12	*Prerequisite:* None

MAIN TEXT OR MATERIAL: *How to Read a Book*, Mortimer Adler, Simon & Schuster

TEACHER HELPS: None

DESCRIPTION: *How to Read a Book* is subtitled *The Classic Guide to Intelligent Reading.* A well-respected guide for over sixty years, it teaches the reader to interact actively and intelligently with his reading material. Different levels and techniques of reading are taught, which can be employed when reading various types of books. This book would be especially helpful for any college-bound student.

A NOTE ON POETRY

No study of literature would be complete without attention to the beauty of poetry. Many sources are available. Student literature textbooks will usually contain a liberal sprinkling of poetry. This is especially helpful when the poetry is placed in historical context, as in American, British, and world literature texts. *The Top 500 Poems*, edited by William Harmon, chooses the works that most often appear in English poetry anthologies. Arranged chronologically, each entry includes information on the work and the poet. "The Poems in Order of Popularity" listing concludes the book. This quality hardcover is a fine beginning to a student's poetry library.

Paperback poetry collections are also available. *The Harp and Laurel Wreath: Poetry and Dictation for the Classical Curriculum* by Laura Berquist contains both poetry and prose dictation or recitation selections for all ages, arranged by grade level. Study questions follow selections for older students, with answers in the back of the book. Poetry collections such as *The Mentor Book of American Poetry* (also *Major British Poets*) or Dover Publications thrift editions, available through many bookstores, provide inexpensive means for providing poetry studies for your homeschool. Two lists follow of well-recognized American and British poets. Although certainly not exhaustive, it gives you a place to start.

American poets: Anne Bradstreet, William Cullen Bryant, Henry Wadsworth Longfellow, John Greenleaf Whittier, James Russell Lowell, Oliver Wendall Holmes, Walt Whitman, Sidney Lanier, Emily Dickinson, Robert Frost, Edna St. Vincent Millay, Carl Sandburg, E. E. Cummings, and T. S. Eliot.

British poets: Edmund Spenser, William Shakespeare, John Donne, George Herbert, John Milton, Isaac Watts, Robert Burns, William Blake, William Wordsworth, Samuel Coleridge, Percy Bysshe Shelley, John Keats, Lord Tennyson, Robert Browning, and Christina Rossetti.

For help in reading poetry, consider *How to Read a Poem* by Burton Raffel. *The Roar on the Other Side: A Guide for Student Poets* by Suzanne Clark instructs our creative students in the basics of writing poetry.

KEY TO LITERATURE GUIDES

Progeny Press: PP
Total Language Plus: TLP
Alpha Omega: AO with the Lifepac number
Learning Language Art through Literature Gold Books: LLATL AM (American) or LLATL BR (British)
Fierce Wars and Faithful Loves: FWFL
Brightest Heaven of Invention: BHI
Heroes of the City of Man: HCM
HomeScholar Books: HSB
Miniatures and Morals: MM

American Literature Reading List		
This list of suggested high-school American literature is by no means a complete list. Many other excellent books are worth reading that are not listed here. When a study guide is available for a book, this is listed after the author.		
Title	**Author**	**Guides**
The Adventures of Huckleberry Finn	Mark Twain	PP
The Adventures of Tom Sawyer	Mark Twain	PP
Billy Budd, Moby Dick	Herman Melville	
The Call of the Wild	Jack London	TLP
The Chosen	Chaim Potok	
The Day No Pigs Would Die	Robert Newton Peck	PP
The Deerslayer, The Last of the Mohicans	James Fenimore Cooper	
Fahrenheit 451	Ray Bradbury	PP
The Great Gatsby	F. Scott Fitzgerald	PP
The Good Earth	Pearl Buck	
Great American Short Stories	Dell Publishing	LLATL AM
The Song of Hiawatha, Evangeline	Henry Wadsworth Longfellow	
The House of Seven Gables	Nathaniel Hawthorne	
In His Steps	Charles Sheldon	AO 1009
The Incredible Journey	S. Burnford	
The Island of the Blue Dolphin	Scott O'Dell	PP
Little Women	Louisa May Alcott	
The Mentor Book of American Poetry	Oscar Williams	LLATL AM
The Merry Adventures of Robin Hood	Howard Pyle	
The Miracle Worker	William Gibson	AO 908
My Antonia	Willa Cather	
The Old Man and the Sea	Ernest Hemingway	AO 1108, LLATL AM, PP
Our Town	Thornton Wilder	AO 1107
The Pearl	John Steinbeck	LLATL AM
The Red Badge of Courage	Stephen Crane	PP
The Scarlet Letter	Nathaniel Hawthorne	PP, TLP
To Kill a Mockingbird	Harper Lee	PP, TLP
The Yearling	Majorie Rawlings	PP, TLP

British Literature Reading List

This list of suggested high-school literature is by no means a complete list. Many other excellent books are worth reading that are not listed here. When a Christian study help is available for a book, this is listed after the author. See the key provided on page 100 for a description of the guide abbreviations.

Title	Author	Guides
Adventures of Sherlock Holmes	Sir Conan Doyle	
Alice's Adventures in Wonderland	Lewis Carroll	
Through the Looking Glass	Lewis Carroll	
Animal Farm	George Orwell	LLATL BR
1984	George Orwell	
Anne of Green Gables	Lucy Maude Montgomery	TLP
As You Like It	William Shakespeare	
A Tale of Two Cities	Charles Dickens	LLATL BR
Best of Father Brown	G. K. Chesterton	
Best of James Herriot	James Herriot	
The Black Arrow	Robert Louis Stevenson	
Captains Courageous	Rudyard Kipling	
A Christmas Carol	Charles Dickens	PP
The Canterbury Tales	Geoffrey Chaucer	
David Copperfield	Charles Dickens	
Emma	Jane Austen	LLATL BR, MM
The Faerie Queene	Edmund Spenser	FWFL
Frankenstein	Mary Shelley	LLATL BR, PP
Gray Wolf	George MacDonald	
Great Expectations	Charles Dickens	
Gulliver's Travels	Jonathan Swift	
Hamlet	William Shakespeare	AO 1206, PP, BHI
Heart of Darkness	Joseph Conrad	PP
Henry V	William Shakespeare	BHI
The High King	Lloyd Alexander	TLP
The Hobbit	J. R. R. Tolkein	PP TLP
The Hound of the Baskervilles	Sir Conan Doyle	
Ivanhoe, The Talisman, and/or other titles	Sir Walter Scott	
Jane Eyre	Charlotte Bronte	PP TLP
Julius Caesar	William Shakespeare	BHI
Kidnapped	Robert Louis Stevenson	
Kim	Rudyard Kipling	
Lord of the Flies	William Golding	PP
The Lord of the Rings Trilogy	J. R. R. Tolkien	HSB
Macbeth	William Shakespeare	BHI
Merchant of Venice	William Shakespeare	PP

Much Ado about Nothing	William Shakespeare	BHI
Oliver Twist	Charles Dickens	TLP
Out of the Silent Planet	C. S. Lewis	PP
Paradise Lost	John Milton	
Perelandra	C. S. Lewis	PP
Pilgrim's Progress	John Bunyan	
Pride and Prejudice	Jane Austen	TLP, MM
Pygmalion	George Bernard Shaw	
Robinson Crusoe	Daniel DeFoe	
Romeo and Juliet	William Shakespeare	PP
The Screwtape Letters	C. S. Lewis	PP
Sir Gawain and the Green Knight	J. R. R. Tolkien version	
The Strange Case of Dr. Jekyll and Mr. Hyde	Robert Louis Stevenson	PP
A Tale of Two Cities	Charles Dickens	PP
Tales from Shakespeare	Charles and Mary Lamb	
Taming of the Shrew	William Shakespeare	BHI
That Hideous Strength	C. S. Lewis	
The Time Machine	H. G. Wells	LLATL BR
Treasure Island	Robert Louis Stevenson	TLP
Wuthering Heights	Emily Bronte	

World Literature Reading List		
This list of suggested high-school literature is by no means complete. Many other excellent books are worth reading that are not listed here. When a Christian study guide is available for a book, this is listed after the author. See the key provided on page 100 for a description of the guide abbreviations.		
Title	**Author**	**Guides**
The Aeneid	Virgil	HCM
Anna Karenina	Leo Tolstoy	
Arabian Nights	Andrew Lang	
Around the World in Eighty Days	Jules Verne	TLP
The Brothers Karamazov	Fyodor Dostoevsky	
Crime and Punishment	Fyodor Dostoevsky	
Cry, the Beloved Country	Alan Paton	
Cyrano de Bergerac	Edmond Rostand	
Don Quixote	Miguel de Cervantes	
The Iliad	Homer	HCM
The Odyssey	Homer	HCM
Hunchback of Notre Dame	Victor Hugo	
Kon Tiki	Thor Heyerdahl	
Les Miserables	Victor Hugo	
Quo Vadis	Henry Sienkiewicz	
Swiss Family Robinson	Johann Wyss	TLP
Twenty Thousand Leagues under the Sea	Jules Verne	AO 909
War and Peace	Leo Tolstoy	

Following are examples of standard and advanced English courses for grades 9–12. They illustrate various ways textbooks can be combined in a course and English topics integrated. They may or may not be appropriate for your student.

STANDARD ENGLISH COURSE EXAMPLES

Course: English I   **Grade: 9**   **Prerequisite: None**

TEXT: *Writing and Grammar 9*, Bob Jones University Press or *Jensen's Grammar* and *Jensen's Punctuation*, Wordsmith

Format Writing, Wordsmith

Wordly Wise 3000 #6, Educator's Publishing Service

Selected novels

DESCRIPTION: This is a standard English I course. A combination of grammar, mechanics, composition, vocabulary, and literature will be studied at this level. BJUP's *Writing and Grammar* worktext covers writing and grammar. If you like the format and price of *Jensen's* grammar and punctuation books, these can be used instead. Regardless of your grammar choice, all students use *Format Writing's* first section, "Single Paragraph Formats." Since only this section will be done, it would be appropriate to assign more than one of each paragraph type. (BJUP's *Writing and Grammar* users may need to be selective in the composition exercises used from the BJU book. However, I'd still recommend completing all the paragraph forms in section 1 of *Format Writing*.) For *Jensen's* users, consider doing half of each exercise in *Jensen's Punctuation* so skills can be reviewed again next year. Vocabulary can be studied using *Wordly Wise 3000, Book Six*. Read one novel a semester, writing a book report on each. Choose to coincide with the topic being studied in history if desired. See the various literature lists for guide availability. Encourage summer reading.

Course: English II   **Grade:** 10   **Prerequisite:** English I

TEXT: *Format Writing*, Wordsmith
Jensen's Punctuation, Wordsmith
Wordly Wise 3000 #7, Educator's Publishing Service
Reading between the Lines, Gene Veith/Crossway Books or selected novels
DESCRIPTION: This is a standard English II course. Composition, vocabulary, and literature are studied. For composition work, continue with *Format Writing* "Section Two, Five Paragraph Essays: Elements and Formats." Complete *Jensen's Punctuation* if you reserved "half exercises" for use this year. Vocabulary work continues with *Wordly Wise 3000, Book Seven*. For literature, use *Reading between the Lines*. This is a challenging but readable book on how Christians should respond to literature. I highly recommend it. Grading can include discussion along with chapter and book summaries. If you feel this book is too challenging for your teen, consider having him read several novels using literature guides. This course could easily be divided into semesters, concentrating on composition and punctuation the first semester and vocabulary and literature the second. (If grammar work is desired, the student can stay fresh with *Easy Grammar Plus*.)

Course: English III   **Grade:** 11   **Prerequisite:** English II

TEXT: *Format Writing*, Wordsmith
The SAT Writing Workbook, Kaplan
Wordly Wise 3000 #8, Educator's Publishing Service
Learning Language Arts through Literature Gold Book: American Literature, Common Sense Press
DESCRIPTION: This is a standard English III course. A combination of composition, vocabulary, and American literature will be studied. For composition, continue with *Format Writing*. With SAT and ACT testing around the corner, the student might benefit most by continuing with "Section Two, Five Paragraph Essays: Elements and Formats" adding SAT prompts, or moving to an SAT writing prep book such as Kaplan's *The SAT Writing Workbook*. (Note: The Kaplan book, while excellent, does not stress the use of literary or historic examples in the body paragraphs of the essay. *Princeton Review*'s *Cracking the SAT* places a stronger emphasis on this type of support.) Vocabulary continues with *Wordly Wise 3000, Book Eight*. For literature use *Learning Language Arts through Literature Gold Book: American Literature*.

Course: English IV   **Grade:** 12   **Prerequisite:** English III

TEXT: *Format Writing*, Wordsmith
Wordly Wise 3000 #9, Educator's Publishing Service
Learning Language Arts through Literature Gold Book: British Literature, Common Sense Press
DESCRIPTION: This is a standard English IV course. A combination of composition, vocabulary, and literature will be studied. For composition continue in *Format Writing* "Sections Three and Four: The Principle of Condensation and Major Papers." If college applications require essays, concentrate on these essays first semester and save *Format Writing*'s major papers until second semester. Vocabulary continues with *Wordly Wise 3000, Book Nine*. For literature use *Learning Language Arts through Literature Gold Book: British Literature*.

ADVANCED ENGLISH COURSE EXAMPLES

Course: English I Advanced	*Grade:* 9	*Prerequisite:* None

TEXT: *Writing and Grammar 9*, Bob Jones University Press or use *Jensen's Grammar* and *Jensen's Punctuation*, Wordsmith

Format Writing, Wordsmith

Jensen's Vocabulary, Wordsmith, or *Vocabulary from Classical Roots C*, Educators Publishing Service

Fundamentals of Literature, Bob Jones University Press

Selected novels

DESCRIPTION: This course is similar to Standard English 9 but has the addition of a literature book, which greatly accelerates the pace of the work to be accomplished. If you like the format and price of *Jensen's* grammar and punctuation books, these can be used instead of BJU's *Writing and Grammar 9*. Regardless of your grammar choice, all students use *Format Writing's* first section, "Single Paragraph Formats." Continue into "Section Two" on five paragraph essays if time permits. (BJUP's *Writing and Grammar* users may need to be selective in the composition exercises used from the BJU book in order to complete the paragraph exercises in *Format Writing*.) For vocabulary, use *Jensen's Vocabulary* or *Vocabulary from Classical Roots C*. BJUP's *Fundamentals of Literature* is used for literature. A novel or two can be read during the school year or during the summer if necessary. Book reports can be assigned or a literature guide used. See the various literature lists for guide availability. Novels can be chosen to coincide with the topic studied in history if desired.

Course: English II Advanced	*Grade:* 10	*Prerequisite:* English I Advanced

TEXT: *Writing and Grammar 10*, Bob Jones University Press

Format Writing, Wordsmith

Jensen's Vocabulary, Wordsmith, or *Vocabulary from Classical Roots D*, Educators Publishing Service

Reading Between the Lines, Gene Veith/Crossway Books or *Elements of Literature*, Bob Jones University Press

Selected novels

DESCRIPTION: In advanced English II the pace is accelerated, requiring more of the student. BJUP's *Writing and Grammar 10* provides a thorough college-prep presentation but will be difficult if the student is not already well-grounded in grammar. To stay up with the volume of work, review the material and don't assign a lot of repetition if the student has mastery of the skill. For example, the student can do odd or even problems, first five, etc. For composition choose from the activities in the BJU book but concentrate on *Format Writing*, section 2, continuing into sections 3 and 4: "The Principle of Condensation and Major Papers," only after the student has thoroughly mastered five-paragraph essays. Mastery of the five-paragraph essay is very important for college entrance tests. For vocabulary, use *Jensen's Vocabulary* or *Vocabulary from Classical Roots D*. For literature use *Reading between the Lines*. This is a challenging but readable book on how Christians should respond to literature. I highly recommend it. Grading can include discussion along with chapter and book summaries. If you prefer a textbook, use BJU's *Elements of Literature*. Study a novel if time permits or add a few for summer reading. See the various literature lists for guide availability.

Course: English III Advanced	*Grade:* 11	*Prerequisite:* English II Advanced

TEXT: *The SAT Writing Workbook*, Kaplan

Format Writing, Wordsmith

Jensen's Vocabulary, Wordsmith, or *Vocabulary from Classical Roots E*, Educators Publishing Service

American Literature, Bob Jones University Press

Selected novels

For extra eager beavers: *Writing and Grammar 11*, Bob Jones University Press

DESCRIPTION: In advanced English III the pace is accelerated, requiring more of the student. With the SAT now requiring an essay, skill with the essay is important. Therefore, you may want to begin the year studying *The SAT*

Writing Workbook by Kaplan. (Note: The Kaplan book, while excellent, does not stress the use of literary or historic examples in the body paragraphs of the essay. *Princeton Review*'s *Cracking the SAT* places a stronger emphasis on this type of support.) Upon completion, continue in *Format Writing* with mastery of sections 3 and 4: "The Principle of Condensation and Major Papers." Require a major paper second semester. Vocabulary can continue with *Jensen's* if not already used, or *Vocabulary from Classical Roots E*. For literature, use the excellent *American Literature* anthology from Bob Jones University Press. The teacher's guide has a one-semester scheduling option. Reading a full-length novel each semester or saving it for summer reading, if necessary, would be appropriate. See the various literature lists for guide availability. (A student who has done well in Bob Jones' *Writing and Grammar* may wish to continue this series. If he does the large number of writing activities, he will need to discontinue *Format Writing*. However, I would still include some of the SAT-directed essay preparation. Plan on streamlining grammar exercises and omitting some writing assignments in the BJU book.)

Course: English IV Advanced	*Grade:* 12	*Prerequisite:* English III Advanced

TEXT: *Format Writing*, Wordsmith
British Literature, Bob Jones University Press
Selected novels
For extra eager beavers: *Writing and Grammar 12*, Bob Jones University Press
DESCRIPTION: In advanced English IV the pace is accelerated, requiring more of the student. For composition continue practicing the skills learned in *Format Writing*. If college applications require essays, concentrate on these essays first semester and save *Format Writing's* major papers until second semester. *Vocabulary from Classical Roots* ends at the eleventh grade so there is no recommended vocabulary book. *Vocabu-Lit* or *Wordly Wise 3000* could be used if more vocabulary work is desired. For literature use the excellent anthology from Bob Jones University Press. Add two to four full-length novels with accompanying book reports or longer opinion papers. (A student who has done well in Bob Jones' *Writing and Grammar* may wish to continue this series. If he does the large number of writing activities, he will need to discontinue *Format Writing* and concentrate on the exercises in this book. Plan on streamlining grammar exercises.)

Mathematics Courses

Many of us feel inadequate when it comes to higher level math. If struggles arise, you might:

1. Learn along with your student.
2. Hire a tutor for your teen (maybe an older homeschooled student).
3. Stretch an advanced math text over an extra semester or year.
4. Look for or start a cooperative class for homeschooled students.
5. Use a program designed for independent student use.
6. Look into the availability of junior or community college math courses.

Suggestions for mathematics courses represent publishers widely available through homeschool retail departments, catalogs, or the Internet. For a wider look at mathematics products and a more complete look at some of the products mentioned here, I once again point you to Cathy Duffy's *100 Top Picks for Homeschool Curriculum*. Programs reviewed in her book have been marked with an asterisk.

The normal progression for high-school math is algebra I, geometry, algebra II, and precalculus. Students who begin algebra in eighth grade may begin college math courses, such as calculus, their senior year.

Time your math courses carefully in relation to college entrance tests. Students will perform better on the PSAT if they have studied geometry prior to taking the test. This has proved a dilemma with Saxon that incorporates geometry into *Algebra I*, *Algebra II*, and *Advanced Math*. The dilemma can be solved with an eighth-grade start to algebra I if the student is ready. The SAT and ACT are generally taken in the spring of the eleventh grade, the following summer, and possibly again in the fall of twelfth grade. These tests demand knowledge of algebra I, algebra II, and geometry. Taking algebra II in eleventh grade ensures that the information is fresh in the student's mind. Students who complete their math in tenth grade and do not take math in eleventh grade create a year time lag between their last math course and college entrance tests. In all probability, without an SAT review course, it will affect test scores negatively.

Homeschoolers tend to have strong opinions on math programs and for good reason. We are all individuals, assimilating information in different ways. Some people think mathematically; others do not. It is no wonder a program that works well with one student may not work well with another. Before choosing a math program, use the Internet to good advantage, looking for pros and cons. Look for background information about the reviewer. My family may not do well in a math program that an electrical engineer parent loves. Our brains work differently. Note how long the reviewer has used the program. It's easy to give high marks in the first month of use. Reviews from longtime users carry more weight. Make math purchases with your eyes wide open.

In choosing a math program, there are a number of important considerations.

Do you prefer an emphasis on mathematical processes or conceptual understanding? Different books take different approaches. A Beka Books and Saxon tend to emphasize processes, while Bob Jones, Jacobs, and Math U See emphasize conceptual understanding. Mathematically strong students who intuitively understand the concept behind the process may do well with either approach. Other students, whose strengths lie in areas other than math, may find greater understanding when the underlying concepts are also emphasized. It is not surprising that many of my mathematically strong friends enjoy Saxon while my own preference leans toward more conceptual presentations.

What is the overall difficulty of the book? Some students will not go beyond college algebra and do not need as rigorous a book as the student bound for the maths and sciences. Since many students will need parental help, the amount of aid given through teacher's guides and solutions manuals should also be considered.

Is the material suitable for independent work? Several programs facilitate the ability of the student to work without parental aid. Examples include Chalk Dust and Teaching Textbooks. Saxon, already designed for independent student use, can be enhanced with supplementary software or videos, such as those from D.I.V.E. into Math (www.diveintomath.com) and Teaching Tapes (www.teachingtapes.com). Bob Jones HomeSat and A Beka's DVD programs also significantly reduce parental involvement.

What added features would be helpful? Math manipulatives, DVDs, and videos are an integral part of many math programs. Other programs offer a traditional student textbook and teacher's guide.

The chart below lists popular homeschool math publishers and special features that add to their appeal. Following the chart is additional information on some of the programs. Courses are arranged in the order they are normally taken, and then roughly by difficulty. Since difficulty of use can relate to both the usability of the materials and the content contained and because I have not had personal experience with each program, this ordering is highly subjective. Most of the programs, successfully completed, will do an admirable job of preparing your student for postsecondary education.

High School Math Publishers

	Textbook	Workbook	DVDs	Manipulatives	Satellite	Software
A Beka Books	X		X			
Alpha Omega		X				X
Bob Jones University Press	X	X*	X		X	
Chalk Dust Company	X		X			
Harold Jacobs (W. H. Freeman)	X					
Key Curriculum Press		X				
Math U See		X	X	X		
Saxon	X		X**			
School of Tomorrow (ACE)		X	X			
Teaching Textbooks		X				X
Videotext		X	X			

*Activity books available for some levels.
**Videos for use with Saxon are available from D.I.V.E. into Math and Teaching Tape Technology

Course: Remedial math: drill   **Grade:** Anyone who needs to build math speed   **Prerequisite:** None

MAIN TEXT OR MATERIAL: *Calculadder 1-6*, Providence Project

TEACHER HELPS: Keys included with workbook

DESCRIPTION: *Calculadder* is a series of drill workbooks with the goal of building speed in all math processes. The program has six levels that progress from basic addition and subtraction through multiplication, division, estimation, fractions, decimals, common denominators, improper fractions, percents, units of measure, unit conversions, geometry definitions, Roman numerals, and more. Each level is made up of sixteen different work sheets with twelve copies of each. This provides plenty of practice, if needed, before moving on to the next work sheet. *Calculadder* is not a stand-alone program but supplements your main math program. In my own use of the program, I found it helpful to do more than one page a day. Generally my students were just getting warmed up on the first work sheet and performed better on the second. When the timer buzzed, they would circle the problem they were on, then complete the work sheet. From day to day they could check their circled problems to see if they were making progress.

Course: Remedial math   **Grades:** 6–12, students needing skill mastery   **Prerequisite:** None

MAIN TEXT OR MATERIAL: *Keys to Fractions, Keys to Decimals, Keys to Percents, Keys to Measurement, Keys to Metric Measurement*, Key Curriculum Press

TEACHER HELPS: Separate answer keys and tests

DESCRIPTION: Each set consists of four workbooks and one answer key that shows solutions on reduced copies of student workbook pages. Each set starts at the beginning of the targeted concept and increases slowly in difficulty. Plenty of white space on each page keeps the appearance nonthreatening. The *Keys to* program is a good choice for summer review before beginning prealgebra or algebra.

Course: Basic math   **Grades:** 6–7   **Prerequisite:** Fifth- or sixth-grade math

MAIN TEXT OR MATERIAL: **Basic Math* Videos or DVDs, Chalk Dust
Basic Math, 2nd ed., Aufmann, Barker, and Lockwood, Houghton Mifflin

ADDITIONAL MATERIALS: Solutions guide

TEACHER HELPS: Program is self-directed

DESCRIPTION: *Basic Math* is a video presentation that offers thorough instruction for the accompanying textbook. Video instructor Dana Mosely brings many years of experience and a relaxed, easy-to-understand teaching style to his presentations. The solutions guide offers complete solutions to textbook problems. Many students are able to work without parental help. Tests are included in the textbook. Sixth-grade use prepares the student for algebra in eighth grade. Using this book in seventh grade would be appropriate for a weaker math student or one choosing to start algebra in ninth grade.

Course: Math 7   **Grade:** 7   **Prerequisite:** Sixth-grade math

MAIN TEXT OR MATERIAL: *Math 7* student text, Teaching Textbooks

ADDITIONAL MATERIALS: *Lecture and Practice CDs, Solutions CDs, Test Solutions CDs*

TEACHER HELPS: Tests and answer keys, course is student directed

DESCRIPTION: Teaching Textbooks offers thorough instruction and support for the self-directed math student. Textbooks are written directly to the student and have an easy conversational style. Throughout the student text, key concepts are highlighted. (While helpful for some students, it may be visually busy for others.) Three sets of CDs offer support for the student textbook. The *Lecture and Practice CDs* teach the lesson and provide step-by-step solutions to the practice problems for the new skill. After completing the practice problems, the student then completes the homework assignment. If these problems present any difficulty, the *Solutions CDs* offer complete solutions to every problem. Finally, the *Test Solutions CDs* walk the student through any problems missed on the test. For more information on the program see www.teachingtextbooks.com.

Course: Math 7   **Grade:** 7   **Prerequisite:** Sixth-grade math

MAIN TEXT OR MATERIAL: *Fundamentals of Math*, Bob Jones University Press

ADDITIONAL MATERIALS: *Student Activities Book*

TEACHER HELPS: teacher's edition, tests and key, teacher's edition for student activity book

DESCRIPTION: This book offers a thorough review of all math skills, making next year's transition to prealgebra easier. I moved one student from another program into this book when math scores were not what we wanted. It was a good decision for both student and teacher. The student activity book is supplementary. Bob Jones courses are designed for teacher interaction. If parents feel inadequate or have limited time, instruction is also available on BJU's HomeSat or by DVD rental.

Course: Math 7   **Grade:** 7   **Prerequisite:** Sixth-grade math

MAIN TEXT OR MATERIAL: **Math 87, 3rd ed., Tests and Worksheets Booklet*, Saxon

TEACHER HELPS: Solutions manual

DESCRIPTION: *Math 87* reviews math skills then moves into prealgebra instruction. Saxon is known for its incremental skill-building approach and thorough review. Each lesson is directed to the student and begins with warm-up exercises and a presentation of that day's new material. A practice set follows, with problems focusing on the new skill. A problem set then provides review on previously taught skills. With *Math 87*'s new focus on prealgebra, Saxon no longer advises excellent math students to skip this text. Supplementary CDs and video instruction are available from www.diveintomath.com and www.teachingtape.com.

Course: Prealgebra   **Grades:** 7–8   **Prerequisite:** Seventh-grade math

MAIN TEXT OR MATERIAL: **Prealgebra* Videos or DVDs, Chalk Dust
Prealgebra, a Worktext, 2nd ed., Aufmann, Barker, and Lockwood, Houghton Mifflin

ADDITIONAL MATERIALS: Solutions guide

TEACHER HELPS: Program is self-directed.

DESCRIPTION: *Prealgebra* is a video presentation that offers thorough instruction in the accompanying textbook. Video instructor Dana Mosely brings many years of experience and a relaxed, easy-to-understand teaching style to his presentations. The solutions guide offers complete solutions to textbook problems. Tests are included in the textbook. Many students are able to work without parental help. Use in seventh grade prepares the student for first-year algebra in eighth. Eighth-grade use offers a slower pace for students who find math challenging.

Course: Prealgebra   **Grade:** 8   **Prerequisite:** Seventh-grade math

MAIN TEXT OR MATERIAL: *Pre-Algebra* student text, Teaching Textbooks

ADDITIONAL MATERIALS: *Lecture and Practice CDs, Solutions CDs, Test Solutions CDs*

TEACHER HELPS: Tests and key, program is self-directed.

DESCRIPTION: Teaching Textbooks offers thorough instruction and support for the self-directed math student. Textbooks are written directly to the student and have an easy conversational style. Throughout the student text, key concepts are highlighted. (While helpful for some students, it may be visually busy for others.) Three sets of CDs offer support for the student textbook. The *Lecture and Practice CDs* teach the lesson and provide step-by-step solutions to the practice problems for the new skill. After completing the practice problems, the student then completes the homework assignment. If these problems present any difficulty, the *Solutions CDs* offer complete solutions to every problem. Finally, the *Test Solutions CDs* walk the student through any problems missed on the test. For more information on the program see www.teachingtextbooks.com.

Course: Prealgebra   **Grade:** 8   **Prerequisite:** Seventh-grade math

MAIN TEXT OR MATERIAL: **Algebra ½*, Saxon

ADDITIONAL MATERIALS: *Algebra ½ Solutions Manual*

TEACHER HELPS: Answers and tests included in homeschool kit

DESCRIPTION: Saxon is known for its incremental skill-building approach and thorough review. Each lesson is directed to the student and begins with a presentation of that day's new material. A practice set follows with problems focusing on the new skill. A problem set then provides review on previously taught skills. For excellent math students desiring to skip a Saxon text, Saxon now advises students to skip *Algebra ½*, moving from *Math 87, 3rd ed.* directly into *Algebra 1*.

Course: Prealgebra	*Grade:* 8	*Prerequisite:* Seventh-grade math

MAIN TEXT OR MATERIAL: *Pre-Algebra*, Bob Jones University Press

ADDITIONAL MATERIALS: *Student Activities Book*

TEACHER HELPS: Teacher's edition, tests and key, teacher's edition for student activity book

DESCRIPTION: This book offers a thorough review of all math skills before introducing negative numbers and the use of variables in algebraic expressions. Practical math lessons include consumer-related applications to daily life. A supplementary activity book is available. Bob Jones courses are designed for teacher interaction. If parents feel inadequate or have limited time, instruction is also available on BJU's HomeSat or by DVD rental.

Course: Prealgebra, Algebra I, Algebra II	*Grade:* 8	*Prerequisite:* Seventh-grade math

MAIN TEXT OR MATERIAL: **Videotext, Modules A-F* DVDs or videos, Videotext

ADDITIONAL MATERIALS: *Course Notes, Worktext, Solutions Manual*

TEACHER HELPS: *Progress Tests and Quizzes, Instructors Guide* (with solutions)

DESCRIPTION: *Videotext* is a set of six modules that take you from prealgebra through algebra II. Other topics commonly included in prealgebra are not covered. Videos are high quality, presenting math concepts with clear sequential graphics. After watching the short video lesson, students complete the nonconsumable worktext page. Quizzes and tests provide an easy grading method. This program should work well with strong math students. Weaker math students may need help applying the skills taught on the DVD to the problems in the worktext.

Course: Algebra I	*Grade:* 8-9	*Prerequisite:* Prealgebra

MAIN TEXT OR MATERIAL: *Keys to Algebra*, Key Curriculum Press

TEACHER HELPS: Separate answer keys and tests

DESCRIPTION: A slower workbook approach that introduces one concept at a time. This program is a good precursor to a more in-depth algebra course. It may be sufficient for junior-college entrance for the student who struggles with math, but the course will probably not contain enough content for the student planning a rigorous math program.

Course: Algebra I	*Grade:* 9	*Prerequisite:* Prealgebra

MAIN TEXT OR MATERIAL: **Algebra I*, Math U See

ADDITIONAL MATERIALS: Math manipulatives, test booklet

TEACHER HELPS: Teacher's manual, DVDs or videos

DESCRIPTION: Math U See is a full-line math curriculum available for all grade levels. DVDs explain the new concept using manipulative blocks and algebra/decimal inserts whenever possible. Although originally designed for instructing the teacher, students often enjoy watching the DVDs with the parent. The home teacher then presents the lesson to the student, working with him as needed for skill mastery. Workbook pages include practice in the new skill and review of previously taught concepts. A test booklet is included in the student kit. Students who struggle with math will find Math U See's approach friendlier and less intense than other programs. For students wanting additional challenge, a supplement of honor problems is also available. For junior high students, the seventh-grade book, *Zeta*, and the eighth-grade book, *Pre-Algebra*, are also available. To purchase, go to www.mathusee.com to find a distributor in your area.

Course: Algebra I	*Grade:* 9	*Prerequisite:* Prealgebra

MAIN TEXT OR MATERIAL: *Algebra I* Paces, School of Tomorrow

ADDITIONAL MATERIALS: Videos (optional)

TEACHER HELPS: Answer keys

DESCRIPTION: This program offers a self-paced approach to algebra. Twelve workbooks guide the student through a year's algebra instruction. Videos, which may be purchased separately, provide daily instruction and are a helpful enhancement to this workbook approach.

Course: Algebra I	*Grade:* 9	*Prerequisite:* Prealgebra

MAIN TEXT OR MATERIAL: Lifepac *Math 9* or Switched on Schoolhouse *Math 9*, Alpha Omega

TEACHER HELPS: Teacher's edition for Lifepacs

DESCRIPTION: Ten workbooks walk your student through a standard-paced algebra course. Each workbook has several self-tests and a middle pullout test that make determining a grade easy. The teacher guide provides step-by-step solutions. Some students find the smaller individual workbooks less intimidating than a large textbook. For students who enjoy working on the computer, algebra is also available in the computerized Switched on Schoolhouse format. SOS offers colorful graphics for the student and significantly streamlines grading and record keeping for the teacher.

Course: Algebra I	*Grade:* 9	*Prerequisite:* Prealgebra

MAIN TEXT OR MATERIAL: *Algebra I* student text, Teaching Textbooks

ADDITIONAL MATERIALS: *Lecture and Practice CDs, Solutions CDs, Test Solutions CDs*

TEACHER HELPS: Tests and key, program is self-directed.

DESCRIPTION: Teaching Textbooks offers thorough instruction and support for the self-directed math student. Textbooks are written directly to the student and have an easy conversational style. Throughout the student text, key concepts are highlighted. (While helpful for some students, it may be visually busy for others.) Three sets of CDs offer support for the student textbook. The *Lecture and Practice CDs* teach the lesson and provide step-by-step solutions to the practice problems for the new skill. After completing the practice problems, the student then completes the homework assignment. If these problems present any difficulty, the *Solutions CDs* offer complete solutions to every problem. Finally, the *Test Solutions CDs* walk the student through any problems missed on the test. For more information on the program see www.teachingtextbooks.com.

Course: Algebra I	*Grades:* 8–9	*Prerequisite:* Seventh-grade math

MAIN TEXT OR MATERIAL: **Algebra I* Videos or DVDs, Chalk Dust
Algebra 1, 2nd ed., Larson, Roland, and Hostetler, Houghton Mifflin

ADDITIONAL MATERIALS: *Solutions Guide*

TEACHER HELPS: Program is self-directed.

DESCRIPTION: *Algebra I* is a video presentation that offers thorough instruction in the accompanying textbook. Video instructor Dana Mosely brings many years of experience and a relaxed, easy-to-understand teaching style to his presentations. The solutions guide offers complete solutions to textbook problems. Tests are included in the textbook. Many students are able to work without parental help. For more information visit www.chalkdust.com.

Course: Algebra I	*Grade:* 9	*Prerequisite:* Prealgebra (Saxon *Math 87* or *Algebra ½*)

MAIN TEXT OR MATERIAL: **Algebra I*, Saxon

ADDITIONAL MATERIALS: *Algebra I Solutions Manual*

TEACHER HELPS: Answers and tests included in homeschool kit

DESCRIPTION: A thorough algebra I course that also incorporates beginning geometry. Saxon follows an incremental approach, teaching little piece by little piece. Practice sets provide daily practice on new instruction. The longer problem set provides comprehensive practice on skills from previous lessons. If the student has mastered all basic mathematical operations, a calculator can be introduced when using this text. It is important to note that this book is only an introduction to geometry. For SAT preparation it is important to continue this program through *Advanced Math* to get a full year of geometry instruction.

| *Course:* Algebra I | *Grade:* 9 | *Prerequisite:* Prealgebra |

MAIN TEXT OR MATERIAL: *Elementary Algebra*, Harold Jacobs, W. H. Freeman

TEACHER HELPS: Teacher's guide, testbank

DESCRIPTION: In my work at the bookstore, I get a lot of calls for this book. Its strong emphasis on conceptual understanding makes it popular among classical homeschoolers. Jacobs gains the attention of reluctant students unconventionally, through anecdotes, cartoons, and puzzles. Some answers are found in the back of the student text. The rest are found in the teacher's guide. No solutions are available.

| *Course:* Algebra I | *Grade:* 9 | *Prerequisite:* Prealgebra |

MAIN TEXT OR MATERIAL: *Algebra I*, Bob Jones University Press

ADDITIONAL MATERIALS: *Student Activities Book*

TEACHER HELPS: Teacher's edition, tests and key, teacher's edition for student activity book

DESCRIPTION: A strength of BJUP materials lies in its emphasis on building conceptual understanding. Word problems, real-life applications, and biographical sketches on mathematicians are included in addition to standard algebra I concepts. Solutions are contained in the teacher's edition. The supplementary activity book is a mixture of enrichment, drill, and review from which the parent chooses. Use of the graphing calculator is included. In my work at the bookstore, I have often found this book to be helpful for the student who has struggled with other algebra programs. Bob Jones courses are designed for teacher interaction. If parents feel inadequate or have limited time, instruction is also available on BJU's HomeSat or by DVD rental.

| *Course:* Remedial Geometry | *Grades:* 7–12 | *Prerequisite:* None |

MAIN TEXT OR MATERIAL: *Keys to Geometry*, Key Curriculum Press

TEACHER HELPS: Separate keys

DESCRIPTION: A slower paced, workbook approach to geometry that provides a simple introduction to geometric constructions and terminology. You will need to supplement for college preparation, or use it as a junior high introduction to a more thorough geometry program.

| *Course:* Geometry | *Grade:* 10 | *Prerequisite:* Algebra I |

MAIN TEXT OR MATERIAL: *Geometry*, Math U See

ADDITIONAL MATERIALS: Test booklet

TEACHER HELPS: Teacher's manual, DVDs or videos

DESCRIPTION: *Geometry* continues to use DVDs to introduce teachers to mathematical concepts. The manipulatives are shown on the DVD (more frequently at the beginning of the course) but do not need to be purchased for student use. The home teacher then presents the lesson to the student, working with him as needed for skill mastery. Workbook pages include practice in the new skill and review of previously taught concepts. Geometric proofs are used but not to the extent of some other courses. A test booklet is included in the student kit. Students who struggle with math will find Math U See's approach friendlier and less intense than other programs. A booklet of honors problems is also available. To purchase, go to www.mathusee.com, to find a distributor in your area.

| *Course:* Geometry | *Grade:* 10 | *Prerequisite:* Algebra I |

MAIN TEXT OR MATERIAL: *Geometry Paces*, School of Tomorrow

ADDITIONAL MATERIALS: Videos (optional)

TEACHER HELPS: Answer keys

DESCRIPTION: This is a complete geometry course. Its logical sequence teaches properties and theorems with plenty of application to geometric proofs. Twelve workbooks or Paces, guide the student through a year's geometry instruction. The videos provide a helpful enhancement to this workbook approach.

Course: Geometry	*Grade:* 10	*Prerequisite:* Algebra I

MAIN TEXT OR MATERIAL: Lifepac *Math 10* or Switched on Schoolhouse *Math 10*, Alpha Omega
TEACHER HELPS: Teacher's edition for Lifepacs
DESCRIPTION: Ten workbooks walk your student through a standard-paced geometry course. Each workbook has several self-tests and a middle pullout test that make determining a grade easy. The teacher guide provides step-by-step solutions. Some students find the smaller individual workbooks less intimidating than a large textbook. For students who enjoy working on the computer, geometry is also available in the computerized Switched on Schoolhouse format. SOS offers colorful graphics for the student and significantly streamlines grading and record keeping for the teacher.

Course: Geometry	*Grade:* 10	*Prerequisite:* Algebra I

MAIN TEXT OR MATERIAL: *Geometry*, student text, Teaching Textbooks
ADDITIONAL MATERIALS: *Lecture and Practice CDs, Solutions CDs, Test Solutions CDs*
TEACHER HELPS: Tests and key, program is self-directed.
DESCRIPTION: Teaching Textbooks offers thorough instruction and support for the self-directed math student. Textbooks are written directly to the student and have an easy conversational style. Throughout the student text, key concepts are highlighted. (While helpful for some students, it may be visually busy for others.) Three sets of CDs offer support for the student textbook. The *Lecture and Practice CDs* teach the lesson and provide step-by-step solutions to the practice problems for the new skill. After completing the practice problems, the student then completes the homework assignment. If these problems present any difficulty, the *Solutions CDs* offer complete solutions to every problem. Finally, the *Test Solutions CDs* walk the student through any problems missed on the test. For more information on the program see www.teachingtextbooks.com.

Course: Geometry	*Grades:* 9–10	*Prerequisite:* Algebra I

MAIN TEXT OR MATERIAL: **Geometry* Videos or DVDs, Chalk Dust
Geometry: An Integrated Approach, Larson, Boswell, and Stiff, D. C. Heath & Company
ADDITIONAL MATERIAL: *Solutions Guide*
TEACHER HELPS: Program is self-directed.
DESCRIPTION: *Geometry* is a video presentation that offers thorough instruction in the accompanying textbook. Video instructor Dana Mosely brings many years of experience and a relaxed, easy-to-understand teaching style to his presentations. The solutions guide offers complete solutions to textbook problems. Tests are included in the textbook. Many students are able to work without parental help. For more information visit www.chalkdust.com.

Course: Geometry	*Grade:* 10	*Prerequisite:* Algebra I

MAIN TEXT OR MATERIAL: *Geometry*, Bob Jones University Press
ADDITIONAL MATERIALS: *Student Activities Book*
TEACHER HELPS: Teacher's manual, tests and key, teacher's edition to student activities book
DESCRIPTION: Unlike Saxon, Bob Jones geometry is offered in a separate textbook. This is especially helpful for the student whose high school plan does not include four years of mathematics. The groundwork is laid for a thorough presentation of geometric proofs. Biographical sketches of mathematicians and features on "Geometry Around Us" appear periodically. Trigonometry is introduced at the end of the book. The supplementary activity book contains additional practice, cumulative reviews, and enrichment activities. A graphing calculator is needed. Bob Jones courses are designed for teacher interaction. If parents feel inadequate or have limited time, instruction is also available on BJU's HomeSat or by DVD rental.

Course: Geometry **Grade:** 10 **Prerequisite:** Algebra I

MAIN TEXT OR MATERIAL: *Geometry: Seeing, Doing, Understanding, 3rd ed.*, Harold R. Jacobs, W. H. Freeman

TEACHER HELPS: Teacher's guide, testbank

DESCRIPTION: *Geometry: Seeing, Doing, Understanding* shares the popularity of Jacob's algebra book. His engaging introductions to math concepts catch the interest of most students. There is a strong emphasis on understanding rather than on following rote processes. Proofs are informal, following current NCTM (National Council of Teachers of Math) standards. SAT topics are addressed. Some answers are found in the back of the student text. All are found in the teacher's guide. A testbank is also available.

Course: Algebra II **Grades:** 11 **Prerequisite:** Algebra I

MAIN TEXT OR MATERIAL: *Algebra II*, Math U See

ADDITIONAL MATERIALS: Test booklet

TEACHER HELPS: Teacher's manual, DVDs or videos

DESCRIPTION: *Algebra II* continues to use DVDs to introduce teachers to mathematical concepts although the use of manipulatives is discontinued at this level. The home teacher then presents the lesson to the student, working with him as needed for skill mastery. Workbook pages include practice in the new skill and review of previously taught concepts. A test booklet is included in the student kit. Many students will find Math U See's approach friendlier and less intense than other programs. They often enjoy watching the instructional video, too. A booklet of honors problems is also available. To purchase, go to www.mathusee.com, to find a distributor in your area.

Course: Algebra II **Grade:** 11 **Prerequisite:** Algebra I

MAIN TEXT OR MATERIAL: *Algebra II* Paces, School of Tomorrow

ADDITIONAL MATERIALS: Videos (optional)

TEACHER HELPS: Answer keys

DESCRIPTION: Twelve workbooks guide the student through a year's Algebra II instruction. Pullout tests make determining a grade easy. The videos provide a helpful enhancement to this workbook approach.

Course: Algebra II **Grade:** 11 **Prerequisite:** Algebra I

MAIN TEXT OR MATERIAL: Lifepac *Math 11* or Switched on Schoolhouse *Math 11*, Alpha Omega

TEACHER HELPS: Teacher's edition for Lifepacs

DESCRIPTION: Ten workbooks walk your student through a standard-paced algebra II course. Each workbook has several self-tests and a middle pullout test that make determining a grade easy. The teacher guide provides step-by-step solutions. Some students find the smaller individual workbooks less intimidating than a large textbook. For students who enjoy working on the computer, this course is also available in the computerized Switched on Schoolhouse format. SOS offers colorful graphics for the student and significantly streamlines grading and record keeping for the teacher.

Course: Algebra II **Grade:** 11 **Prerequisite:** Algebra I

MAIN TEXT OR MATERIAL: *Algebra II*, student text, Teaching Textbooks

ADDITIONAL MATERIALS: *Lecture and Practice CDs, Solutions CDs, Test Solutions CDs*

TEACHER HELPS: Tests and key, program is self-directed.

DESCRIPTION: Teaching Textbooks offer thorough instruction and support for the self-directed math student. Textbooks are written directly to the student and have an easy conversational style. Throughout the student text, key concepts are highlighted. (While helpful for some students, it may be visually busy for others.) Three sets of CDs offer support for the student textbook. The *Lecture and Practice CDs* teach the lesson and provide step-by-step solutions to the practice problems for the new skill. After completing the practice problems, the student then completes the homework assignment. If these problems present any difficulty, the *Solutions CDs* offer complete solutions to every problem. Finally, the *Test Solutions CDs* walk the student through any problems missed on the test. For more information on the program see www.teachingtextbooks.com.

Course: Algebra II   *Grades:* 10–11   *Prerequisite:* Algebra I

MAIN TEXT OR MATERIAL: *Algebra II* Videos or DVDs, Chalk Dust
Algebra II, 2nd ed., Larson and Hostetler, Houghton Mifflin
ADDITIONAL MATERIALS: *Solutions Guide*
TEACHER HELPS: Program is self-directed.
DESCRIPTION: *Algebra II* is a video presentation that offers thorough instruction in the accompanying textbook. Video instructor Dana Mosely brings many years of experience and a relaxed, easy-to-understand teaching style to his presentations. The solutions guide offers complete solutions to textbook problems. Tests are included in the textbook. Many students are able to work without parental help. Students planning future studies in the humanities may end their high school math at this level. Following this course with Chalk Dust's *College Algebra* will prepare students for the CLEP, if desired. For information on college algebra visit www.chalkdust.com. (For information on CLEP testing, see section 11.)

Course: Algebra II   *Grade:* 11   *Prerequisite:* Algebra I

MAIN TEXT OR MATERIAL: *Algebra II*, Bob Jones University Press
ADDITIONAL MATERIALS: *Student Activities Book*
TEACHER HELPS: Teacher's manual, tests and key, teacher's edition for student activities book
DESCRIPTION: *Algebra II* reviews and extends the learning presented in *Algebra I*. The graphing calculator is used throughout the year. Solutions are contained in the teacher's edition. The supplementary activity book contains remediation and enrichment activities. As with all Bob Jones textbooks, the teacher is viewed as an integral part of the course. For the mathematically challenged parent, this course can be studied on BJU's HomeSat or by DVD rental.

Course: Algebra II   *Grade:* 10   *Prerequisite:* Algebra I

MAIN TEXT OR MATERIAL: *Algebra II*, Saxon
ADDITIONAL MATERIALS: *Algebra II Solutions Manual*
TEACHER HELPS: Answers and tests included in homeschool kit
DESCRIPTION: A thorough algebra II course that continues incorporating geometry. Math problems at this level often have multiple steps requiring extensive computation. If answers are rounded before the final step, they will not match the answer key. For this reason consider using a calculator with this text.

Course: Precalculus   *Grades:* 12   *Prerequisite:* Algebra I and II, Geometry

MAIN TEXT OR MATERIAL: *PreCalculus*, Math U See
ADDITIONAL MATERIALS: Test booklet
TEACHER HELPS: Teacher's manual, solutions, DVDs or videos
DESCRIPTION: Originally a trigonometry course, additional lessons have earned this book a new title. Teacher instruction via video or DVD continues. New material and old skills are reinforced in each lesson. Solutions are contained in a separate book. Honors problems are now available for this level. To purchase, go to www.mathusee.com to find a distributor in your area.

Course: Trigonometry   *Grades:* 11–12   *Prerequisite:* Algebra II

MAIN TEXT OR MATERIAL: *Trigonometry* Videos or DVDs, Chalk Dust
Trigonometry, 6th ed., Larson and Hostetler, Houghton Mifflin
ADDITIONAL MATERIALS: *Solutions Guide*

TEACHER HELPS: Program is self-directed.

DESCRIPTION: *Trigonometry* is a video presentation that offers thorough instruction in the accompanying textbook. Video instructor Dana Mosely brings many years of experience and a relaxed, easy-to-understand teaching style to his presentations. The solutions guide offers complete solutions to textbook problems. Tests are included in the textbook. Many students are able to work without parental help. Students planning to take precalculus should skip this course to avoid redundancy. Additional higher level courses are available. For more information visit www.chalkdust.com.

Course: Precalculus   **Grade:** 12   **Prerequisite:** Algebra II

MAIN TEXT OR MATERIAL: *Precalculus*, Bob Jones University Press

TEACHER HELPS: Teacher's manual, tests and key

DESCRIPTION: Course includes a continuation of algebraic principles, graphing, trigonometry, and an introduction to differential calculus. The graphing calculator is used all year. There is no student activity book for this text. Unless math is your strength, consider using BJU's HomeSat or DVD rental. (We left it to the junior college!)

Course: Precalculus   **Grades:** 11–12   **Prerequisite:** Algebra II

MAIN TEXT OR MATERIAL: **Precalculus* Videos or DVDs, Chalk Dust
Precalculus with Limits, 3rd ed., Larson, Hostetler, Edwards, Houghton Mifflin

ADDITIONAL MATERIALS: *Solutions Guide*

TEACHER HELPS: Program is self-directed.

DESCRIPTION: *Precalculus* is a video presentation that offers thorough instruction in the accompanying textbook. Video instructor Dana Mosely brings many years of experience and a relaxed, easy-to-understand teaching style to his presentations. The solutions guide offers complete solutions to textbook problems. Tests are included in the textbook. Many students are able to work without parental help. This course combines college algebra and trigonometry. Upon completion, students will be ready to proceed into college-level calculus. For information on college-level courses offered, see www.chalkdust.com.

Course: Precalculus   **Grades:** 11–12   **Prerequisite:** Algebra II

MAIN TEXT OR MATERIAL: **Advanced Mathematics*, Saxon

ADDITIONAL MATERIALS: *Advanced Mathematics Solutions Manual*

TEACHER HELPS: Answers and tests included in homeschool kit

DESCRIPTION: A challenging precalculus course that includes one half year of plane geometry. This book can be taken over the course of two to four semesters. Calculator use is recommended. The graphing calculator is introduced.

Course: Calculus   **Grade:** 12   **Prerequisite:** Advanced math

MAIN TEXT OR MATERIAL: *Calculus*, Saxon

ADDITIONAL MATERIALS: *Calculus Solutions Manual*

TEACHER HELPS: Answers and tests included in homeschool kit

DESCRIPTION: This course is equivalent to two semesters of college calculus. If successfully completed, the student is ready to take the College Board's Advanced Placement exam in Calculus. (See section 11 concerning AP exams.)

Course: Consumer math elective   **Grades:** 9–12   **Prerequisite:** None

MAIN TEXT OR MATERIAL: *Consumer Math*, Alpha Omega, also available in Switched on Schoolhouse format

TEACHER HELPS: Teacher's guide for Lifepacs

DESCRIPTION: Consumer math teaches careful stewardship of our personal resources. Topics covered include basic math, family finances, occupations, business, and transportation. This course is available in ten Lifepacs or in the computerized Switched on Schoolhouse format. Consumer math is always a wise elective course.

Course: Consumer math elective   **Grades:** 9–12   **Prerequisite:** Algebra I

MAIN TEXT OR MATERIAL: *Stewardship* student text

TEACHER HELPS: Teacher manual, devotional, DVDs or videos

DESCRIPTION: This new offering from Math U See covers practical consumer math topics: taxes, banking, checking, interest, credit cards, comparison shopping, and more. A separate devotional offers thirty-eight biblically-based financial lessons. For more information go to www.mathusee.com.

Course: Consumer math elective   **Grades:** 9–12   **Prerequisite:** None

MAIN TEXT OR MATERIAL: *Consumer Math*, Bob Jones University Press

TEACHER HELPS: Teacher's guide, tests and key

DESCRIPTION: *Consumer Math* teaches careful stewardship of our personal resources. Topics covered include budgeting, banking, interest, savings accounts, loans, and credit cards. Lessons on the cost of goods and services such as transportation, food, clothing, housing, utilities, insurance, and vacations are also included. Although not required for college, it is certainly a wise elective course.

Course: Accounting   **Grades:** 7–12   **Prerequisite:** None

MAIN TEXT OR MATERIAL: *Accounting*, Alpha Omega

TEACHER HELPS: Teacher's guide

DESCRIPTION: This Lifepac program includes an overview of accounting, debits and credits, posting transactions, statements, payroll, and taxes. A business simulations activity is also included. This course could be considered a math or business elective.

Science Courses

My high-school memories of biology are positive. My memories of chemistry are entirely different. My chief recollection is of two girlfriends and myself holding back tears and sniffing our way through yet another test we did not understand. I passed chemistry, not on merit but on the kindness of a merciful teacher. The grief of chemistry motivated me to persuade my counselor not to include physics in my next year's studies. If your memories are similar, take courage. There is hope! Thanks to homeschool-friendly textbooks, satellite technology, and DVDs, options for teaching these difficult courses at home are increasing.

Apologia science heads the list of homeschool-friendly science textbooks. Dr. Jay Wile's seventh through college-level texts enjoy a growing popularity among homeschool parents and students. Rather than containing material-dense sentences that take multiple readings to decipher, Dr. Wile's books employ a conversational style that makes the material more accessible. Experiments also take into account the needs of homeschoolers, using common household items whenever possible. Most remarkable of all, the experiments usually work! The author's classroom experience shows itself through carefully written experiments that leave less to go wrong. On Your Own Questions scattered throughout each chapter encourage the student to think critically about science. Students who thoughtfully complete the end-of-chapter study guide should do well on the test. In addition, the author's Christian worldview is clearly expressed throughout the series. Apologia texts are available in traditional textbook form or in a CD-ROM version. An MP3 Audio CD is available for students who learn better by hearing the text read while they follow along in the book. Students choosing the textbook format can purchase a companion CD-ROM that contains the video clips, animations, and other helps contained on the computerized book. Second edition books contain icons in the page margins that alert the student that a corresponding clip is available on the companion CD-ROM. Students can also take a number of Apologia science courses online through The Potter's School. See appendix A for address information.

A second option for science at home can be found in the Bob Jones University Press texts. Used in conjunction with their HomeSat program, the college prep sciences become much more doable. Families can either subscribe to the HomeSat program or rent DVDs. Students view daily lessons, listen to interaction between teacher and students from Christian schools across the nation, and complete the same requirements as their video classmates. Lab work can be observed on the video and/or completed hands-on at home. When possible, experiments use locally available materials. Other supplies will need to be ordered. For additional information on the HomeSat program, see the introduction to the course listings in this book or get the full story at www.bjup.com.

The School of Tomorrow video courses, which include the high school sciences, are another possible choice. Students watch each day's video lesson and then complete the accompanying workbook (Paces). Videos are of a high quality and offer an interesting presentation. Instead of doing experiments, students watch them on video, recording the results on lab work sheets. Since a lab science normally includes approximately 20 percent lab work, it would be best to include some hands-on lab. However, for the student not headed into the maths and sciences, this program may get a difficult course completed adequately. It is possible to do the School of Tomorrow courses without the videos, but much of the course's student appeal will be lost.

Another strategy for fulfilling lab science requirements is to take them through early admissions at your local junior college. College courses will include work with higher quality lab equipment than can usually be afforded for home use. In addition, successful course completion usually earns the student both high school and college credit. Check with your local junior or community college for requirements and information.

My goal is not to make an exhaustive list but to include some of the easiest to use or most widely available science materials on the homeschool market. There are other academically sound products available.

| *Course:* General science | *Grade:* 7 | *Prerequisite:* None |

MAIN TEXT OR MATERIAL: *Exploring Creation with General Science*, Dr. Jay Wile, Apologia

ADDITIONAL MATERIALS: Companion CD, MP3 audio CD, full course CD-ROM

TEACHER HELPS: Solutions and test book

DESCRIPTIONS: *Exploring Creation with General Science* provides a solid general introduction to science. The sixteen modules include topics on scientific method, designing experiments, simple machines, archaeology, geology, paleontology, biology, and the human body. It is available in textbook or CD-ROM format. Although the author's primary recommendation is to use this in seventh grade, it can also be used on the eighth-grade level for those needing an easier text. See general information on Apologia science at the beginning of this chapter.

| *Course:* General science | *Grades:* 7–8 | *Prerequisite:* None |

MAIN TEXT OR MATERIAL: *The Rainbow*, Beginnings Publishing House, Inc.

ADDITIONAL MATERIALS: *The Rainbow Home Laboratory* with student workbook

TEACHER HELPS: *Teacher's Helper*

DESCRIPTION: This colorful two-year lab course introduces students to physics, chemistry, and biology. The final quarter applies what has been learned through lessons on geology, weather, and astronomy. *The Rainbow Home Laboratory* contains all the materials needed to complete all experiments. Even chemicals are premeasured. Any student who has seen this kit at a homeschool book convention may decide this program is the one for him! For more information visit www.beginningspublishing.com.

| *Course:* Earth science | *Grade:* 8 | *Prerequisite:* None |

MAIN TEXT OR MATERIAL: *Space and Earth Science*, 3rd ed., Bob Jones University Press

TEACHER HELPS: Teacher's edition, tests and answer key

DESCRIPTION: This attractive, colorful volume begins with a discussion of the origins of the earth, affirming a young-earth, creationist perspective, and then turns to a study of space (sun, stars, planets, moon, etc.) and our Earth (meteorology, geology, oceanography). *Space and Earth Science, 3rd ed.*, utilizes the P.I.L.R. (Personal Interactive Learning Resource) concept. This concept results in a friendly book with plenty of white space, facilitating the student's ability to take notes, highlight key information, and answer questions within the book. Activity sheets are now contained within the student text. Replacement sheets are available, making the text reusable for a second student. This course is available on HomeSat.

Course: Physical science   **Grade:** 10, or after completion of Algebra I   **Prerequisite:** Algebra I

MAIN TEXT OR MATERIAL: *Physical Science* Paces, School of Tomorrow

ADDITIONAL MATERIALS: Videos

TEACHER HELPS: Answer keys

DESCRIPTION: *Physical Science* is an introduction to both chemistry and physics, sometimes called an IPC (integrated physics and chemistry) course. It can serve as one of the lab sciences for the nonscience-bound student. It can also provide an introduction for the student who plans to include both chemistry and physics in his high school program. An interesting and professional video presentation makes these workbooks a good choice. Although the course can be done with workbook only, the videos greatly enhance the course. The course teaches itself and is easy to grade. For those preferring to purchase the Paces only, a separate DVD that contains lab work only is also available.

Course: Physical science   **Grade:** 9   **Prerequisite:** None

MAIN TEXT OR MATERIAL: *The Physical World*, Bob Jones University Press

ADDITIONAL MATERIALS: Student Lab Manual

TEACHER HELPS: Teacher's edition, tests and answer key, teacher's edition for student lab manual

DESCRIPTION: *The Physical World* is an introduction to chemistry and physics. Some parents teach this course using the textbook, answering textbook questions (answers in the teacher's manual), and taking tests. Using the student laboratory manual adds to the thoroughness of the course and provides the lab content that a college-prep lab science should include. This course is available on BJU's HomeSat or through their DVD rental program.

Course: Physical science   **Grade:** 8   **Prerequisite:** Seventh-grade math

MAIN TEXT OR MATERIAL: **Exploring Creation with Physical Science*, 2nd ed.*, Dr. Jay Wile, Apologia

TEACHER HELPS: Solutions and test book

ADDITIONAL MATERIALS: Companion CD-ROM, full course CD-ROM

DESCRIPTIONS: *Exploring Creation with Physical Science* was recently released in a 2nd edition. The book provides a solid introduction in the physical sciences. The sixteen modules include topics on the atmosphere, hydrosphere, weather, structure of the Earth, environmentalism, and various physics topics. Special attention is given to the myths propagated by extreme environmentalists. This book is intended for eighth graders. However for students who are not science oriented, it may also be appropriate to use this course with a ninth grader. See general information on Apologia science at the beginning of this chapter. Visit www.apologia.com for more information.

Course: Life science   **Grades:** 7–12   **Prerequisite:** None

MAIN TEXT OR MATERIAL: *Life Science* Lifepac Select, Alpha Omega

TEACHER HELPS: Teacher's guide

DESCRIPTION: Alpha Omega Select electives are Lifepacs topically chosen to create a one-semester course. Since Lifepac Select courses include both junior high and high school level Lifepacs, this course will be less challenging than some other choices.

Course: Life science or biology   **Grades:** 7–10   **Prerequisite:** None

MAIN TEXT OR MATERIAL: *Life Science*, 3rd ed.*, Bob Jones University Press

TEACHER HELPS: Teacher's edition, tests and answer key, *Testbuilder 2* software

DESCRIPTION: This seventh-grade text provides a good survey course in preparation for high school biology. It could also be used by the high school student needing a less challenging biology text. If used on the high school level, title the course "biology" on the transcript. This recently revised text has the same friendly appearance as

BJ's *Space and Earth Science*. Activity sheets are now contained in the student text. Replacement sheets are available, making the text reusable. The biology dissection kit and video, also available from BJUP, can be successfully used with the text.

Course: Biology	*Grades:* 7–9	*Prerequisite:* None

MAIN TEXT OR MATERIAL: *Biology* Paces, School of Tomorrow

ADDITIONAL MATERIALS: Videos

TEACHER HELPS: Answer keys

DESCRIPTION: An interesting and professional video presentation makes these workbooks a good choice for some students. Although the course can be done with workbook only, the videos greatly enhance the course. Less difficult than most biology courses, a junior high student might tackle it as a life science, using a more difficult program for the high school years. High school students that are not science bound may find it a sufficient high school credit. The course teaches itself and is easy to grade. For those preferring to purchase the Paces only, a separate DVD that contains lab work only is also available.

Course: Biology	*Grade:* 10	*Prerequisite:* None

MAIN TEXT OR MATERIAL: *Biology, 3rd ed.*, Bob Jones University Press

ADDITIONAL MATERIALS: Dissection kit and video

TEACHER HELPS: Teacher's edition, tests and answer key, teacher's edition of lab manual, *Testbuilder 2* software

DESCRIPTION: *Biology, 3rd ed.* will give any student headed into the sciences an excellent background. In addition to standard biology topics, Christian positions on a number of issues are presented: biotechnology, abortion, evolution, homosexuality, ecology, disease, and drugs. This text uses the P.I.L.R. (personal interactive learning resource) concept. This concept results in a friendly book with plenty of white space, facilitating the student's ability to take notes, highlight key information, and answer questions within the book. Lab sheets are now contained within the student text with replacement sheets available. A dissection kit (complete with specimens) provides all you need to do dissection at home. A dissection video is also available. This course is available through BJU's HomeSat program. Questions for this course are included on the *Testbuilder 2* software.

Course: Biology	*Grades:* 9–10	*Prerequisite:* Take concurrently with Algebra I

MAIN TEXT OR MATERIAL: **Exploring Creation with Biology, 2nd ed.*, Dr. Jay Wile, Apologia

ADDITIONAL MATERIALS: Companion CD, MP3 audio CD, full course CD-ROM

TEACHER HELPS: Solutions and test book

DESCRIPTION: A solid college prep choice, *Exploring Creation with Biology* includes scientific methods, the five-kingdom classification system, microscopy, biochemistry, cellular biology, genetics, evolution, dissection, and ecosystems. Anatomy and physiology are covered in Apologia's advanced biology course, *The Human Body*. Instructions for lab work are contained in the student text. Helpful features added to the second edition include an appendix with questions that cover the whole course and a separate test booklet with perforated, pullout tests. See general information on Apologia science at the beginning of this chapter or go to www.apologia.com.

Course: Advanced biology	*Grade:* 12	*Prerequisite:* Biology I and chemistry I

MAIN TEXT OR MATERIAL: **The Human Body: Fearfully and Wonderfully Made*, Dr. Jay Wile, Apologia

ADDITIONAL MATERIALS: Companion CD, full course CD-ROM

TEACHER HELPS: Solutions and test book

DESCRIPTION: For those students desiring an advanced biology course, Apologia offers *The Human Body: Fearfully and Wonderfully Made*. This anatomy and physiology course covers all eleven of the body's systems. Students who have already taken *Exploring Creation with Biology* will have the equivalent of a college-level biology course when

The Human Body is successfully completed. Interested students will be well prepared for either an AP or CLEP exam. General information on Apologia science can be found at the beginning of this chapter.

Course: Chemistry   **Grade:** 11 **Prerequisite:** Algebra I, biology, physical science
MAIN TEXT OR MATERIAL: *Chemistry* Paces, School of Tomorrow
ADDITIONAL MATERIALS: Videos
TEACHER HELPS: Answer keys
DESCRIPTION: It is my tendency to view every chemistry course as advanced. I have no personal experience with this course, but judging from our experience with other School of Tomorrow sciences, I assume its video presentation makes it more accessible than other chemistry courses. Although the course can be done with workbook only, if the video quality is as good as the other science courses we have used, it should greatly enhance the course. For those preferring to purchase the Paces only, a separate DVD that contains lab work only is also available.

Course: Chemistry   **Grade:** 11   **Prerequisite:** Algebra I (although more math is better)
MAIN TEXT OR MATERIAL: *Chemistry*, Bob Jones University Press
ADDITIONAL MATERIALS: *Lab Manual*
TEACHER HELPS: Teacher's edition, tests and keys, teacher's edition for lab manual
DESCRIPTION: This challenging course will give any student headed into the sciences an excellent background. This course is also available through BJU's HomeSat program.

Course: Chemistry   **Grades:** 10–11 (11–12 if nonscience oriented)   **Prerequisite:** Algebra I
MAIN TEXT OR MATERIAL: *Exploring Creation with Chemistry, 2nd ed.*, Dr. Jay Wile, Apologia
ADDITIONAL MATERIALS: Companion CD, MP3 audio CD, full course CD-ROM
TEACHER HELPS: Solutions and test book, separate test booklet also available
DESCRIPTION: *Exploring Creation with Chemistry* is designed to be a rigorous college prep chemistry course. The updated second edition includes additional optional lab experiments and a Web site with links for additional information. Testing now includes a point system to help with grading quarterly, semester, and final exams, and a perforated test booklet. For general information on Apologia science, go to the beginning of this chapter or visit www.apologia.com.

Course: Advanced chemistry   **Grade:** 12   **Prerequisite:** Algebra II and chemistry I
MAIN TEXT OR MATERIAL: *Advanced Chemistry in Creation*, Dr. Jay Wile, Apologia
TEACHER HELPS: Solutions and test book
DESCRIPTION: Not for just any high school student, *Advanced Chemistry in Creation* is the equivalent of a college-level course. Students taking the course successfully will be prepared for the AP exam. Prerequisites include successful completion of one year of high-school chemistry and algebra II.

Course: Physics   **Grade:** 12   **Prerequisite:** Algebra I, physical science
MAIN TEXT OR MATERIAL: *Physics* Paces, School of Tomorrow
ADDITIONAL MATERIALS: Videos
TEACHER HELPS: Answer keys
DESCRIPTION: Although the course can be done with workbook only, if the video quality is as good as the other science courses we have used, it should greatly enhance the course. For those preferring to purchase the Paces only, a separate DVD that contains lab work only is also available.

Course: Physics   **Grade:** 12   **Prerequisite:** Algebra II

MAIN TEXT OR MATERIAL: *Physics*, Bob Jones University Press

ADDITIONAL MATERIALS: *Lab Manual*

TEACHER HELPS: Teacher's edition, teacher's edition for student lab manual, lab manual supplement for home educators, testbank

DESCRIPTION: This challenging course will provide the background needed for the young math and science scholar. If this one is way over your head, consider the BJU HomeSat program.

Course: Physics   **Grade:** 12   **Prerequisite:** Algebra II

MAIN TEXT OR MATERIAL: *Physics*, Saxon

ADDITIONAL MATERIALS: *Solution Manual*

TEACHER HELPS: Answer key and tests available in homeschool kit

DESCRIPTION: This is the last textbook in the Saxon series. Students completing this course successfully will be ready for the advanced-placement physics exam and for majoring in college math and sciences.

Course: Physics   **Grades:** 11–12   **Prerequisite:** Algebra II, one semester of trigonometry

MAIN TEXT OR MATERIAL: **Exploring Creation with Physics, 2nd ed.*, Dr. Jay Wile, Apologia

ADDITIONAL MATERIALS: Companion CD, MP3 audio CD, full course CD-ROM

TEACHER HELPS: Solutions and test book, separate test booklet available

DESCRIPTION: This college-prep course requires a complete understanding of Algebra II and a beginning understanding of trigonometry. The updated second edition has increased the number of lab experiments 50 percent. Testing now includes a point system to help with grading quarterly, semester, and final exams, and a perforated test booklet. For specific course content see www.apologia.com. General information on Apologia science is found at the beginning of this chapter.

Course: Advanced physics   **Grade:** 12   **Prerequisite:** Precalculus

MAIN TEXT OR MATERIAL: *Advanced Physics in Creation*, Dr. Jay Wile, Apologia

TEACHER HELPS: Solutions and test book

DESCRIPTION: Not for just any high school student, *Advanced Physics in Creation* is the equivalent of a college-level course. Students taking the course successfully will be prepared for the AP exam. Prerequisites include successful completion of precalculus.

Course: Marine biology elective   **Grades:** 11–12   **Prerequisite:** One year of high school biology

MAIN TEXT OR MATERIAL: *Exploring Creation with Marine Biology*, Sherri Seligson, Apologia

ADDITIONAL MATERIALS: Companion CD, full course CD-ROM

TEACHER HELPS: Solutions and test book

DESCRIPTION: *Exploring Creation with Marine Biology*, while not written by Dr. Wile, retains the writing flavor of the Apologia series. Students desiring to take marine biology should have completed one year of high school biology. The course surveys marine animals from every animal kingdom. Labs include household, microscope, and dissection activities. Only the household labs are required. Completing the other labs depends on the desire of the student and resources of the family.

Course: Astronomy/geology high school elective credit   **Grades:** 9–12   **Prerequisite:** None

MAIN TEXT OR MATERIAL: *Space and Earth Science, 3rd ed.*, Bob Jones University Press

TEACHER HELPS: Teacher's edition, tests and answer key

DESCRIPTION: This junior high book can provide a third science credit for the high-school student not headed into the sciences. This course could serve as two one-semester courses: astronomy and geology. See full description under Earth Science in the junior high section. This course is available on HomeSat.

Course: Geology elective	*Grades:* 7–12	*Prerequisite:* None

MAIN TEXT OR MATERIAL: *Geology* Lifepac Select, Alpha Omega
TEACHER HELPS: Teacher's manual
DESCRIPTION: *Geology* Lifepac Select uses Lifepacs chosen from Alpha Omega's junior-high and high-school level science courses. This makes the study less challenging and appropriate for the noncollege-bound or nonscience-bound student. This is a half year course and would earn one-half credit. You could pair it with the half credit *Astronomy* Lifepac Select for a full third year of science.

Course: Astronomy elective	*Grades:* 7–12	*Prerequisite:* None

MAIN TEXT OR MATERIAL: *Astronomy* Lifepac Select, Alpha Omega
TEACHER HELPS: Teacher's manual
DESCRIPTION: *Astronomy* Lifepac Select uses Lifepacs chosen from Alpha Omega's junior-high and high-school level science courses. This makes the study less challenging and appropriate for the noncollege-bound or nonscience-bound student. This is a half year course and would earn one half credit. You could pair it with the half credit *Geology* Lifepac Select for a full third year of science.

Course: Creation science elective	*Grades:* 9–12	*Prerequisite:* None

MAIN TEXT OR MATERIAL: *Darwin's Black Box*, Michael Behe, *Unlocking the Mysteries of Creation*, Dennis Peterson
TEACHER HELPS: None available
DESCRIPTION: *Darwin's Black Box* is a book supporting intelligent design of the universe. It is written from a Christian perspective and is very readable. (One of my students read this book after reading Darwin's *Origin of the Species*. He then wrote a paper to compare the two.) *Unlocking the Mysteries of Creation* is a large format, heavily illustrated book with a question-and-answer format that explores many interesting facts. Many other living books on creation science can be found at Christian bookstores.

Social Studies Courses

Social studies refers to a wide variety of courses. History, geography, government, economics, and worldview studies fall within this broad category. We will look at course options for all of these areas.

Geography is the first area considered. Recommendations include project and textbook suggestions. Project courses will challenge your student's abilities in map drawing, researching, and report writing. Textbook courses are offered for those wanting a more traditional approach.

World, church, and American history are next. For most of our world's history, church and state have been closely intertwined. Only in recent centuries has there been a marked division between the two. This makes a church history book an appropriate choice for a world history survey. Therefore, you will find church history resources after the world history recommendations. American history follows, as the newest kid on the historical block.

History course recommendations offer a mixture of independent reading and textbooks. Living books (high-interest nonfiction, biographies, and historical fiction books) add spark to a textbook course. If using living books exclusively, consider using a time line or textbook to provide a framework for your course. This can be read by the student or used as a reference.

At the end of the world/church and American history sections are lists of nonfiction and historical fiction books worthy of your consideration. Not every book recommended is challenging. You will find some junior-high level books included. While it may be important to challenge the reader in a literature course, history reading should bring emotion and life to people and events of the past. Reading level becomes secondary to the power of the story. I have also found that some easily read books have content more appropriate for a high school student. For example, *The Bronze Bow*, a Newbery award book, is easily read by an upper elementary student. However, Daniel's struggle whether to follow the zealots and avenge his family's suffering or follow Christ is more fully appreciated by an older reader. When a book tells an appealing, thought-provoking story, it may make it to my list regardless of the difficulty.

American nonfiction and fiction choices are fairly eclectic. I grew up in Illinois, the "land of Lincoln," and gradually migrated through a number of Southern states before settling in Texas. Therefore, you will find both northern and southern Civil War viewpoints in my book selections. If you are Yankee raised like me, you may find a biography on Stonewall Jackson or Robert E. Lee an interesting change in perspective.

History is followed by government and economics courses. All suggestions are conservative, promoting self-responsibility, limited government, and free-market economics. Use these courses to help build your teen into a thoughtful, responsible American citizen.

Worldview studies will help your teen understand both his Christian faith and the underlying premises of philosophies opposed to Christianity. This serves a twofold purpose. First, it will ground your student in his faith in preparation for those who might seek to destroy it. Second, it will equip him to defend and share his faith in the world's vast arena of ideas. This equipping is important even if your teen will be attending a Christian college. Many schools retain the name *Christian* but have left orthodox Christian belief behind. While worldview courses are listed in the social studies section of this course listing, they can also be credited as Bible or philosophy electives.

WORLD GEOGRAPHY

Course: Remedial world geography	*Grades:* 9–12	*Prerequisite:* None

MAIN TEXT OR MATERIAL: *World Geography and You, Books 1 and 2*, Steck Vaughn

TEACHER HELPS: Teacher's edition with answers

DESCRIPTION: These geography workbooks are offered for the student who is reading significantly below grade level and needs his program modified. They contain core content for world geography organized regionally.

Course: World geography	*Grades:* 9–12	*Prerequisite:* None

MAIN TEXT OR MATERIAL: *Comprehensive World Reference Guide*, School Specialty Publishing

ADDITIONAL MATERIALS: *Mapping the World by Heart Lite*, David Smith, Tom Snyder Productions or *The Geography Color Book, 3rd ed.*, Wynn Kapit, a world map, *The Continents*, Good Year Books

TEACHER HELPS: None

DESCRIPTION: For students who prefer hands-on activities, this geography course consists of creating a notebook of maps, reports, and puzzles. *Mapping the World by Heart Lite*, the "lite" referring to a nonclassroom-size edition, is the winner of a number of awards. The course guides the student through creating world maps from memory. *The Geography Color Book*, used for upper elementary through adult, provides finely detailed maps for coloring. *The Comprehensive World Reference Guide*, a reference tool with information on every country in the world, provides a starting place for researching a report. *The Continents*, a puzzle book intended for younger children, still has benefit for the older geography novice. This is a good approach for the teen who learns best by doing or for a change of pace from textbooks.

Course: World geography	*Grades:* All ages	*Prerequisite:* None

MAIN TEXT OR MATERIAL: *World Trail Guide Student Notebook CD-ROM*, use Secondary Level, Josh and Cindy Wiggers, Geography Matters

ADDITIONAL MATERIALS: *The Answer Atlas*, Rand McNally

TEACHER HELPS: *Trail Guide to World Geography*, Cindy Wiggers, Geography Matters

DESCRIPTION: The *Trail Guide* books provide a good foundation for creating a geography notebook. Notebook components include map drawing, researching a daily geography question, and a variety of weekly assignment choices. A literature unit on *Around the World in Eighty Days* by Jules Verne is also included. The student CD-ROM includes map forms, geography questions with space to write your answer, notebook pages, templates for creating puzzles, fact sheets, and more. High schoolers will reference *The Answer Atlas* for their geography questions. The *Trail Guide* books are written to accommodate primary through high school age students, making it an excellent choice for a family unit study. For students who enjoy this approach to geography, *Trail Guide* books to Bible and

American geography are also available. (*Eat Your Way through the USA*, Geography Matters, would be a fun addition to an American geography unit!)

Course: World geography	*Grades:* All ages	*Prerequisite:* None

MAIN TEXT OR MATERIAL: **Ultimate Geography and Timeline Guide*, Maggie Hogan & Cindy Wiggers, Geography Matters

TEACHER HELPS: Teacher's guide only, no student book

DESCRIPTION: This is a parent's guide for setting up an individualized geography curriculum. It is more work than other materials, but you can use it to plan your geography for all age levels. It includes geography facts, lesson and activity ideas, ideas for integrating geography into other subjects, and reproducible maps and activity sheets. Figures for a historical time line are also included.

Course: World geography	*Grades:* All ages	*Prerequisite:* None

MAIN TEXT OR MATERIAL: *Around the World in 180 Days*, Sherri Payne, Apologia

TEACHER HELPS: Teacher's guide

DESCRIPTION: *Around the World in 180 Days* is a research-based geography course. Arranged continent by continent, history and geography questions are provided for every major country. Questions vary in difficulty so all ages can participate. The teacher's guide contains answers and suggested resources. Student work sheets are hole punched for creating a study notebook.

Course: World geography	*Grades:* 7–12	*Prerequisite:* None

MAIN TEXT OR MATERIAL: *Geography* Lifepac Select, Alpha Omega

TEACHER HELPS: Teacher's guide

DESCRIPTION: Alpha Omega Select electives are Lifepacs topically chosen to create a one-semester course. Since the course includes both junior-high and high-school level Lifepacs, it will be less challenging than some other choices.

Course: Geography	*Grades:* 6–12	*Prerequisite:* None

MAIN TEXT OR MATERIAL: *Welcome to the Wonderful World of Geography*, Runkle Publishers

ADDITIONAL MATERIALS: *Student Activity Book*

TEACHER HELPS: Teacher's guide

DESCRIPTION: Brenda Runkle, longtime educator, wrote *Welcome to the Wonderful World of Geography* at the encouragement of John Saxon. The book begins with a look at physical geography as a whole, then moves into a study of physical geography by regions. Touted as geography's equivalent to Saxon Math's incremental approach, this full-color hardback offers an enjoyable writing style and attractive visuals. The student workbook is designed for map work and memorization of every country and its capital. The teacher's guide includes teacher instructions, reproducible tests and keys, answers to review questions, and vocabulary definitions. This book can be purchased through Geography Matters.

Course: World geography	*Grades:* 9–12	*Prerequisite:* None

MAIN TEXT OR MATERIAL: *Geography*, Bob Jones University Press

ADDITIONAL MATERIALS: *Student Activities Book, Map Exercises*

TEACHER HELPS: Teacher's edition, tests and key, teacher's edition to student activities, map exercises key, *Testbuilder 2* software

DESCRIPTION: This full-color geography text presents information regionally, looking at land forms, climates, resources, national economies, and governments. Cultural information on the people, lifestyles, sports, arts, culture, and religion is also included. In addition to the text, a student activities book and map exercises are also available. Using all the supplements would make this a challenging college-preparatory class. Questions for this course are included on the *Testbuilder 2* software. This course is available on HomeSat.

WORLD HISTORY

Course: World history	*Grades:* All ages	*Prerequisite:* None

MAIN TEXT OR MATERIAL: *The Story of the . . . Ancient World, Greeks, Romans, Middle Ages, Renaissance and Reformation*, H. A. Guerber, revised by Christine Miller, Nothing New Press

ADDITIONAL MATERIALS: Selected living books

TEACHER HELPS: None needed

DESCRIPTION: Because I am a history lover, I have made the H. A. Guerber books a part of our family homeschool. Christine Miller has done a wonderful job of adapting, revising, meshing, and writing new text to create this series of world history books for us. Although written for a younger audience, they can still make a successful anchor for a living book world history course.

Course: Ancient world history	*Grades:* 9–12	*Prerequisite:* None

MAIN TEXT OR MATERIAL: *Ancient History: A Literature Approach*, Beautiful Feet Books

ADDITIONAL MATERIALS: Selected living books

TEACHER HELPS: Teacher's guide

DESCRIPTION: This teacher's guide, with separate notes for fourth to sixth grade and high school, presents a study of ancient history through the reading of excellent, high interest books. Civilizations covered include ancient Sumeria, Egypt, Greece, and Rome. *Streams of Civilization* by Christian Liberty Press provides a foundation for the course. Literature choices include *Mara, Daughter of the Nile; The Children's Homer; Augustus Caesar's World; Caesar's Gallic Wars;* and more. Necessary literature may be purchased or oftentimes can be borrowed from the library.

Course: Medieval history	*Grades:* 7–12	*Prerequisite:* None

Main text or material: Medieval, Reformation, and Renaissance History: A Literature Approach, Beautiful Feet Books

ADDITIONAL MATERIALS: Selected living books

TEACHER HELPS: Teacher's guide, time line

DESCRIPTION: This independent reading course begins with the Magna Carta in 1215, continues through the Renaissance and Reformation and into early 1600 Elizabethan England. The teacher's guide, for both junior high and high school use, includes one- and two-year study options. Junior-high book selections include *The Door in the Wall, Otto of the Silver Hand, Columbus and Sons, Morning Star of the Reformation*, and more. Among the high school selections are Chaucer, Shakespeare, Sir Walter Scott, and biographies on such notable historical figures as Wycliffe, Tyndale, Joan of Arc, and Luther. Necessary literature may be purchased or borrowed from the library.

Course: World history	*Grades:* 7–12	*Prerequisite:* None

*Main text or material: *TruthQuest History* guides

ADDITIONAL MATERIALS: Selected living books

TEACHER HELPS: Teacher's guide can be used independently by older students

DESCRIPTION: *Truth Quest History* guides offer a chronological and topical look at world history, thorough commentary, living book recommendations, and composition questions. The commentary focuses on God's hand in history and encourages the student to do the same through the "ThinkWrite" activities. A wide variety of book recommendations make this program usable for all ages. If you enjoy this series, the American history guides for younger students, with creativity, might be adapted for older students by using more advanced reading material.

Course: Independent reading in world history   *Grades:* 9–12   *Prerequisite:* None

MAIN TEXT OR MATERIAL: Selected living books

TEACHER HELPS: None

DESCRIPTION: An independent reading course can be used to study a particular historical time period. Using a historical timetable or textbook as a framework, plan an independent reading course using a variety of original documents, nonfiction, and historical fiction books. Use a time record for evaluation. A research paper would be an appropriate requirement. Check the nonfiction and historical fiction lists at the end of this section for suggestions.

Course: World history   *Grades:* 9–12   *Prerequisite:* None

MAIN TEXT OR MATERIAL: *The Fertile Crescent to the American Revolution*, The Teaching Company

TEACHER HELPS: None needed

DESCRIPTION: The Teaching Company offers DVD or audio instruction from well-respected, excellent instructors from across the United States. Course outlines are included with each DVD or CD set. If desired, a complete course transcript can be purchased for an additional fee. Offering more than two hundred college-level courses, their catalog is a feast for learning-addicted homeschoolers. Undoubtedly there are some courses to avoid, but the generous course descriptions make appropriate selections easy. For more information visit www.teach12.com or call the company for a catalog. Sales run regularly, rotating through the different courses. The catalog will alert you to current offers. This particular course is one of the few offered on a high-school level. It would serve as a foundation to a world history course. Other materials need to be added to make a complete course.

Course: World history   *Grade:* 10   *Prerequisite:* None

MAIN TEXT OR MATERIAL: *History and Geography 10* Lifepacs, Switched on Schoolhouse, Alpha Omega

TEACHER HELPS: Teacher's guide for Lifepacs

DESCRIPTION: The tenth-grade program covers world history from the ancient world to modern times. Add to the course some choices from the world history nonfiction and fiction lists that follow this section. For those who prefer a computerized version that streamlines record keeping and provides high-interest add-ons for the student, this course is also available in the Switched on Schoolhouse format. See "Full-Service Publishers" for more information on the Lifepac and SOS program.

Course: World history   *Grades:* 9–12   *Prerequisite:* None

MAIN TEXT OR MATERIAL: *Streams of Civilization, Volumes 1 and 2*, Christian Liberty Press

TEACHER HELPS: Teacher's guide, tests

DESCRIPTION: The first volume presents world history from creation up to the Reformation. Volume 2 begins where volume 1 left off and continues to modern times. These are inexpensive but attractive, black-and-white hardbound books. Teacher helps are reasonably priced. Using one volume a year in a two-year world history course would make this course of average difficulty. Using both texts in one year would create a rigorous college preparatory class. Adding reading selections from the world history reading lists at the end of this section would bring additional interest.

Course: World history   *Grade:* 10   *Prerequisite:* None

MAIN TEXT OR MATERIAL: *World History, 3rd ed.*, Bob Jones University Press

TEACHER HELPS: Teacher's edition, tests and key

DESCRIPTION: Surveys history from creation to modern times including church history. This revised text shares the friendly format of other newer Bob Jones texts: appealing use of color, lots of white space, and student activity pages contained within the text. Replacement activity pages are available.

CHURCH HISTORY

Course: Church history	*Grades:* 9–12	*Prerequisite:* None

MAIN TEXT OR MATERIAL: *Christian History Made Easy*, Rose Publishing

TEACHER HELPS: Leader's guide contained in book

DESCRIPTION: This text provides a thirteen-week beginner's course in church history. Supplementary activities are included. Web sites for further information are also suggested. This book along with supplementary reading, book reports, and research papers could make an interesting independent reading course in church history.

Course: Church history	*Grades:* 9–12	*Prerequisite:* None

MAIN TEXT OR MATERIAL: *History of Christianity*, Vision Video

ADDITIONAL MATERIALS: Student work sheets

TEACHER HELPS: Guide

DESCRIPTION: This excellent video series presents an overview of two thousand years of church history in six half-hour segments. Time periods include the early church, Middle Ages, Reformation, age of reason and piety, New World, and the modern age of uncertainty. A leader's guide and student work sheets are available. See Vision Video's Web site, www.visionvideo.com, for complete information. Now available on DVD.

Course: Church history	*Grades:* 9–12	*Prerequisite:* None

MAIN TEXT OR MATERIAL: *Sketches from Church History*, S. M. Houghton, Banner of Truth

TEACHER HELPS: None required

DESCRIPTION: *Sketches from Church History* brings the reader from Pentecost to the early twentieth-century church. Houghton writes from an evangelical, reformed perspective. This text along with supplementary reading, book reports, and a research paper make an excellent independent reading course in church history.

Course: Church history	*Grades:* 9–12	*Prerequisite:* None

MAIN TEXT OR MATERIAL: *The Church in History*, B. K. Kuiper, Eerdmans

ADDITIONAL MATERIALS: *The Story of Liberty*, Charles Coffman, Maranatha

TEACHER HELPS: End-of-chapter questions but no answer key, study guide available for *The Story of Liberty*

DESCRIPTION: This textbook survey of the Christian church through the ages is often used in secondary schools and Bible institutes. Each chapter ends with review and research questions. Unfortunately, no answer key is available for *The Church in History*. *The Story of Liberty's* storytelling approach offers an interesting read alongside the main text.

WORLD AND CHURCH HISTORY: NONFICTION

Since so much early history is a probable combination of fact and myth, most of the suggested reading for Greece and Rome is in historical fiction. The books are listed with general references first and then follow a chronological progression.

Timetables of History, Simon and Schuster

DESCRIPTION: A timetable with yearly listings on what was happening in history, literature, religion, music, science, etc. A timetable can serve as a framework for a history course using living books.

Timelines of World History, EDC Publishing, Usborne Books

DESCRIPTION: This colorful illustrated time line will not have the thoroughness of the time line above; this may make it easier to concentrate on key events if you are using it as a framework for an independent reading course.

History through the Ages: Creation to Christ, Resurrection to Revolution, and Napoleon to Now time-line packages, Homeschool in the Woods

DESCRIPTION: These time-line packages are a great resource for the hands-on learner. Each figure includes a line drawing of the person or event, date, and key information. Students cut, color, and glue the figures pertinent to their study on the accompanying time line sheets. With many figures to choose from, it is easy to customize the time line to your student's history study. The entire collection of pictures, world and American, is also available on CD.

Kingfisher History Encyclopedia, Kingfisher Publishing

DESCRIPTION: This huge book takes you on an interesting walk through history. The book is heavily illustrated and has an attractive presentation. This could serve as a framework for a history course using living books.

The World's Great Speeches, Copeland, Lamm, and McKenna; Dover

DESCRIPTION: This book contains 292 speeches representing nearly every historical era and nation. A helpful reference of original documents.

The Christian Almanac, George Grant, Cumberland House

DESCRIPTION: A two-page spread for each day of the year includes an essay about a significant occurrence on that day in history, a list of other important events, and an inspiring quotation, all from a Christian perspective.

The Story of Christianity, Matthew A. Price and Michael Collins, Tyndale House

DESCRIPTION: This colorful oversized book offers both an interesting and readable text.

The 100 Most Important Events in Christian History, A. Kenneth Curtis, J. Stephen Lang, and Randy Peterson; Revell

DESCRIPTION: An overview of important events in church history. This is an excellent supplement to a world history course.

Trial and Triumph, Richard Hannula, Canon Press

DESCRIPTION: In forty-six brief biographies Hannula introduces the reader to the trials and triumphs of various well-known and lesser-known Christians of the past. Written in an easy-to-read style the whole family can understand.

Then and Now Bible Maps, Rose Publishing

DESCRIPTION: Seven Bible maps have transparent overlays showing the Holy Lands today. A helpful study aid.

Genesis, Ruth Beechick, available from Mott Media

DESCRIPTION: Ruth Beechick has written a fascinating book suggesting some plausible ideas pertaining to the book of Genesis.

Trial and Testimony of the Early Church, Vision Video

DESCRIPTION: This set of two videos, containing six half-hour segments, presents the history of the early church. This award-winning docudrama also includes a teacher's guide and work sheets. Now available on DVD.

The History of the Church, Eusebius

DESCRIPTION: Eusebius (AD 263–339) is often called "the father of ecclesiastical history." This is the only surviving account of the early Christian church.

Ecclesiastical History of the English People, Bede

DESCRIPTION: The venerable Bede (673–733), a Benedictine monk, relates the spread of the Christian church from Roman times until his day.

What Life Was Like . . ., Time-Life Books

DESCRIPTION: This beautiful series of full-color books has interesting illustrations, photographs, and text. Each book covers a different time period in world history. We have been pleased with the volume, *What Life was Like in the Age of Chivalry*. Although now out of print, a number of Internet sites, such as www.abebooks.com, make finding these volumes possible. I found quite a few *Age of Chivalry* for under ten dollars.

Famous Men of Greece (Rome, Middle Ages, Renaissance and Reformation), Greenleaf Press or Memoria Press

DESCRIPTION: Although targeted for a younger audience, this biographical approach to history makes a good supplement to an independent reading course.

Living History: Pyramids of Ancient Egypt, etc., Gulliver Books, Harcourt Brace Jovanovich

DESCRIPTION: The Living History series offers photographed reenactments of life during various time periods. These are books for the whole family with wonderful full-color photographs and limited text. Not at all difficult, they will be an interesting quick read for your teen. Now out of print, they are available online through used book sites such as www.abebooks.com. Interlibrary loan may also help you find them. Look for the following titles: *Pyramids of Ancient Egypt, Ancient Greece, Classical Rome, The Vikings, The Voyages of Christopher Columbus, Fourteenth Century Towns, Knights in Armor, Italian Renaissance, First World War*, and *Industrial Revolution*.

Augustus Caesar's World, Genevieve Foster, Beautiful Feet Books

DESCRIPTION: Learn all about Augustus Caesar and his world as you read this book. Since Jesus Christ was born during the reign of Augustus Caesar, you will also be learning about the world at the time of Christ. This is an easy, enjoyable read.

The Confessions of St. Augustine, Augustine

DESCRIPTION: Follow Augustine through his life as he embraced various philosophies of the day until his ultimate conversion to Christianity.

Let Me Die in Ireland, David Bercot, Scroll Publishing

DESCRIPTION: A biography of St. Patrick, the early Christian missionary to Ireland. Bercot's sources included the personal letters of St. Patrick.

History of the Kings of Britain, George of Monmouth

DESCRIPTION: Writing in the early 1100s, Monmouth chronicles the history of early British kings. A medieval bestseller, the inclusion of King Arthur in the book propelled the popularity of the legend.

Reformation Overview, Vision Video

DESCRIPTION: This set of two videos, containing six half-hour segments, presents the main figures of the Reformation: Wycliffe, Hus, Luther, Zwingli, Calvin, the Anabaptists, and Tyndale. A teacher's guide and work sheets are included. Now available on DVD.

Morning Star of the Reformation, Andy Thomson

DESCRIPTION: Follow John Wycliffe through his early years at Oxford and his developing dream of a Bible in English. His zeal for God's Word in the common language was the morning star that preceded the Reformation.

Here I Stand: A Life of Martin Luther, Robert Bainton

DESCRIPTION: Martin Luther was the most important figure of the Reformation. Read about Martin Luther's life from prospective law student to monk and then as the figure who drastically influenced the church at great risk to himself.

A Place to Stand, Gene Veith, Cumberland House

DESCRIPTION: Martin Luther, although only a young German monk, succeeded in sending the established church into tumult and beginning what became the Protestant Reformation. Read about his life and beliefs in this excellent volume from the Leaders in Action series.

The Hawk That Dare Not Hunt by Day, Scott O'Dell

DESCRIPTION: Tom and his uncle Jack earn their living smuggling goods across the English Channel. Then an exiled William Tyndale asks them to smuggle an especially dangerous cargo into his native country: the Word of God in English.

Life of John Calvin, Theodore Beza, Back Home Industries

DESCRIPTION: John Calvin was one of the most important figures of the Reformation. He was a reticent man whose desire was to live a quiet life of scholarship. Yet God used him in a way that has borne great influence for centuries. Read history written by Calvin's close friend.

For Kirk and Covenant, Douglas Wilson, Cumberland House

DESCRIPTION: John Knox, the Father of Scottish Presbyterianism, is often remembered for his confrontations with Mary, Queen of Scots, as he called the Scots to righteousness. Learn more about this godly man in this volume from the Leaders in Action series.

Statesman and Saint, David Vaughan, Cumberland House

DESCRIPTION: William Wilberforce, Christian and member of England's Parliament, through much persecution and struggle persuaded England to abolish the slave trade. This is another volume from the Leaders in Action series.

Dr. Jenner and the Speckled Monster: The Discovery of the Smallpox Vaccine, Albert Marrin

DESCRIPTION: A historical look at the smallpox scourge intertwined with the biography of Dr. Edward Jenner, developer of the smallpox vaccine.

Spurgeon: Heir of the Puritans, Ernest W. Bacon, Christian Liberty Press

DESCRIPTION: Spurgeon, known as the "Prince of Preachers," was highly influential in nineteenth-century England. His many printed sermons remain popular today. Read about his life in this Christian Liberty Press volume.

David Livingstone: Man of Prayer and Action, Christian Liberty Press

DESCRIPTION: David Livingstone was both a missionary and an explorer in Africa. Read more about him in this biography for high school students.

The Yanks Are Coming, Albert Marrin, Beautiful Feet Books

DESCRIPTION: Albert Marrin chronicles the American entrance and participation in World War I, from the sinking of the *Lusitania* to Armistice Day.

Never Give In, Stephen Mansfield, Cumberland House

DESCRIPTION: Winston Churchill, a man of principle and courage, brought England through the darkness of World War II. Learn about this hero's life and thoughts from the Leaders in Action series.

Anne Frank: The Diary of a Young Girl, Anne Frank

DESCRIPTION: Almost everyone is familiar with this poignant diary kept by a young German girl during her family's days of hiding from the Nazis during World War II.

Hitler, Albert Marrin, Beautiful Feet Books

DESCRIPTION: A sobering look at the childhood and later life of the man who plunged Europe into darkness. Marrin's matter-of-fact style avoids sensationalism while seeking to discover the source of Hitler's fanaticism and his power over men.

Stalin: Russia's Man of Steel, Albert Marrin, Beautiful Feet Books
DESCRIPTION: A look at Stalin, his early years, revolutionary activities, and dictatorship. His ruthless leadership cost the lives of more than thirty million people.

The Hiding Place, Corrie Ten Boom
DESCRIPTION: The moving autobiography of Corrie Ten Boom, her sister Betsy, and their family as they participate in the Dutch resistance during World War II at the cost of their freedom. It is an inspiring account of God's providential care for His children during the worst of circumstances. Progeny Press has a middle school level guide for this book. Alpha Omega Lifepac 707 also studies this excellent autobiographical account.

Bonhoeffer: The Cost of Freedom, Focus on the Family
DESCRIPTION: This is an audio drama of the life of Dietrich Bonhoeffer. Bonhoeffer, a German minister, was accused of treason and executed by the Nazis shortly before the end of World War II. This is a fine recording from the Focus on the Family Radio Theater.

Bonhoeffer: Agent of Grace, Gateway Films, Vision Video
DESCRIPTION: *Bonhoeffer: Agent of Grace* is a moving film about the life of the German minister Dietrich Bonhoeffer. Safely out of Germany, he feels compelled to return to his fellow believing countrymen. After great personal struggle, he becomes involved in the resistance movement that ultimately costs him his life. (Note: the execution scene contains brief nudity viewed from the back.) Nonrated.

Not a Tame Lion, Terry W. Glaspey, Cumberland House
DESCRIPTION: An examination of the life and unique thoughts of C. S. Lewis, author of *Mere Christianity*, The Chronicles of Narnia series, and other Christian titles. This is part of the excellent Leaders in Action series.

Children of the Storm, Natasha Vins, Bob Jones University Press
DESCRIPTION: Natasha Vins's autobiography allows us a glimpse at an underground pastor's family as they live and minister behind the former Soviet Union's Iron Curtain.

WORLD AND CHURCH HISTORY: FICTION

Books are arranged to flow chronologically through historical time periods. Most books should be easily available at libraries, through interlibrary loan, or by special order from bookstores. We have used the majority of these books in our homeschool. Out-of-print books are usually readily available on the Internet.

Adam and His Kin, Ruth Beechick, available from Mott Media
DESCRIPTION: A fictional but well-researched and believable presentation of Genesis.

The Golden Goblet, Eloise McGraw
DESCRIPTION: Although an easy read for high schoolers, it is still an exciting and well-written book on ancient Egypt. This and *Mara* (mentioned below) are my personal favorites on Egypt.

Mara, Daughter of the Nile, Eloise McGraw
DESCRIPTION: If you read one historical fiction book on ancient Egypt, this should be it.

The Shadow Spinner, Susan Fletcher
DESCRIPTION: Set in ancient Persia, this story is based on the tale of Shahrazad, a young woman in the sultan's harem who must entertain the ruler with a new story every night or lose her life. The main character in *Shadow Spinner* is Marjan, a young girl who seeks out stories for Shahrazad. For one particularly fine story, told in installments to the sultan, Marjan does not know the ending. A fine thread of tension runs through the book as Marjan seeks the story's ending before Shahrazad's life is lost. Although recommended for junior high, I thoroughly enjoyed

this book when I read it a few years ago. I think a high schooler will, too. Progeny Press has a middle school level guide for this book.

Black Ships before Troy, Rosemary Sutcliff

DESCRIPTION: Although you can reach for Robert Fitzgerald's excellent translation of the *Iliad*, an enjoyable introduction to this classic Greek story can be found in this beautifully illustrated retelling of Homer's *The Iliad*. A companion volume, *The Wanderings of Odysseus*, retells *The Odyssey*. Alan Lee does a beautiful job on illustrating both volumes, however, *The Wanderings of Odysseus* does have some minimal nudity. We used these as family read-alouds when studying Greece. Although *Black Ships* is available in inexpensive paperback, a used book search for the illustrated edition is worth the effort.

The Iliad, Homer

DESCRIPTION: *The Iliad* is the ancient tale of the conquering of Troy. It probably represents a combination of actual history and myth. Try the popular Robert Fitzgerald translation.

The Odyssey, Homer

DESCRIPTION: *The Odyssey* describes the adventures of Odysseus on his way back from the Trojan War. It probably represents a combination of actual history and myth. Robert Fitzgerald has translated this work, also.

In Search of a Homeland: The Story of the Aeneid, Penelope Lively

DESCRIPTION: A companion book to *Black Ships before Troy* and *The Wanderings of Odysseus* mentioned above. Aeneas, a Trojan warrior, must find a new home for his young son and father after the devastating destruction of Troy. After numerous dangers he finds a new homeland and becomes the founder of the ancient Roman people. Illustrated by Ian Andrew, the illustrations, while nice, are not as striking as Alan Lee's in the Sutcliff books.

The Aeneid, Virgil

DESCRIPTION: *The Aeneid* is the ancient poetic history of Rome. Look for translator Robert Fitzgerald again.

Pearl Maiden, Sir H. Rider Haggard

DESCRIPTION: The love story of Miriam, a young Christian woman who is courted by Marcus, a Roman officer. Miriam's faith sustains her during the fiery trials of the Roman siege and destruction of Jerusalem and its temple. From Christian Liberty Press.

The Eagle of the Ninth, Rosemary Sutcliff

DESCRIPTION: In AD 119 the Ninth Roman Legion marched north into the wilds of Britain and never returned. This is the exciting tale of the search for clues to their fate and the effort to find their eagle standard. The historical disappearance of the Ninth Legion without a trace and the finding of the lost standard in an archaeological dig are the factual basis for this exciting story.

The Silver Branch, Rosemary Sutcliff

DESCRIPTION: A story of intrigue. A young army surgeon and his soldier cousin discover a plot against the British emperor. Another excellent story of Roman Britain.

The Lantern Bearers, Rosemary Sutcliff

DESCRIPTION: When Rome can no longer maintain its position against the barbaric invaders of Britain, the defenders abandon their posts and return to Rome. Aquila, a young legionnaire stays behind to fight the invaders and try to save the land. If you enjoy Rosemary Sutcliff as much as we have, you will want to read two more of her books on Roman Britain, *The Outcast* and *The Shining Company*.

The Dragonslayer, Rosemary Sutcliff

DESCRIPTION: A retelling of the ancient European tale *Beowulf*.

The Bronze Bow, Elizabeth Speare
DESCRIPTION: Young Jewish Daniel belongs to a group rebelling against Roman rule in Israel. He is confronted with Jesus' followers and stories of the Christ. Daniel must decide how to handle the hatred so imbedded in his heart. Daniel's agony is well-portrayed as he rethinks his hatred. Progeny Press has a middle school level guide for this Newbery Award book.

Beorn the Proud, Madeleine Polland
DESCRIPTION: Set in the 800s. Ness, an Irish chieftain's daughter, is captured by Vikings when her village falls victim to a cruel raid. We join Ness on her voyage to the Viking homeland and watch her relationship with Beorn, a proud Viking youth, slowly turn to friendship. From Bethlehem Book's Living History series.

The Story of King Arthur and His Knights, Howard Pyle
DESCRIPTION: An excellent and thorough presentation of Arthurian legend. As is true of other Howard Pyle books, his storytelling skill and drawing style combine to create an enjoyable book.

The King's Shadow, Dorothy Alder
DESCRIPTION: Evyn, a young Welsh boy, finds his dreams of being a storiawr (traveling storyteller) shattered when his father's murderers cut out his tongue. Through the course of time, Evyn finds himself in the personal service of Harold Godwinson, the last Saxon king of England. The story culminates in the arrival of William the Conqueror, the Battle of Hastings, and the death of Evyn's beloved master.

If All the Swords in England, Barbara Willard
DESCRIPTION: Twin brothers, separated when young, find themselves serving in opposing households. One is in service to Henry II, the other to those who have befriended the exiled Thomas Becket. The book tensely builds to Becket's cathedral murder.

A Proud Taste of Scarlet and Miniver, E. L. Konigsberg
DESCRIPTION: Eleanor of Aquitaine awaits the arrival of Henry II, her second husband, from purgatory. While waiting, Abbott Suger, Henry's mother Empress Matilda, William the Marshal, and Eleanor tell the story of her life. This is a great introduction to the lives of Eleanor, Henry II, and their seven children, most famous of whom are John (of Robin Hood fame) and Richard the Lionhearted. It has been suggested to finish up the book by watching the movie *A Lion in Winter*.

The Merry Adventures of Robin Hood, Howard Pyle
DESCRIPTION: Howard Pyle brings his storytelling and artistic skills to the telling of England's favorite outlaw. As in other Pyle books, his use of archaic language adds to the difficulty of the read but effectively transports the reader to another time and place.

Outlaws of Sherwood, Robin McKinley
DESCRIPTION: A modern retelling of Robin Hood and his merry men. An enjoyable read.

The Brethren: A Tale of the Crusades, Sir H. Rider Haggard
DESCRIPTION: Two English knights, in love with the same woman, find themselves in the midst of the King's Crusade determined to rescue Rosamund from the court of the Muslim leader, Saladin.

The Scottish Chiefs, Jane Porter
DESCRIPTION: A tale of the Scottish fight for independence from England, the book's focus is on William Wallace.

Adam of the Road, Elizabeth Gray
DESCRIPTION: A young boy in medieval England, Adam takes to the road searching for his minstrel father. His travels give a varied and accurate picture of life at that time. An easy and enjoyable Newbery Award book.

Men of Iron, Howard Pyle

DESCRIPTION: Any boy interested in knights will enjoy this book. Myles trains to be a knight, vindicates his father of unjust suspicions, wins a bride, and battles both his own temperament and enemies. This book is considered one of the outstanding books on medieval England.

Otto of the Silver Hand, Howard Pyle

DESCRIPTION: A tale of the son of a valiant robber baron in medieval Germany. Gentle Otto, raised in a monastery, returns home to feuds between his house and a rival baron. If you enjoy this book, you have many more medieval tales by Howard Pyle from which to choose.

Beduin's Gazelle, Francis Temple

DESCRIPTION: Halima falls into the hands of an enemy Beduin tribe. Her beloved Atiyah, with his foreign friend Etienne, set out to rescue her before she becomes the sheikh's youngest wife. An interesting look at nomadic Middle East culture.

The Black Arrow, Robert Louis Stevenson

DESCRIPTION: *The Black Arrow* is set in England during the War of the Roses, clearly demonstrating the suffering that war brings to all sides.

Ivanhoe, Sir Walter Scott

DESCRIPTION: A classic tale of medieval adventure well seasoned with actual historical figures. *Rob Roy* and *The Talisman* have also been read at our home. One of our teens greatly enjoyed Sir Walter Scott.

Lysbeth, A Tale of the Dutch, Sir H. Rider Haggard

DESCRIPTION: Set during the Spanish occupation of Holland. Lysbeth grieves while others fall victim to the Inquisition. She soon finds that same peril surrounds those she loves.

The Foundling, Linda Haynor

DESCRIPTION: Young Willy is abandoned on the parish porch. The plight of foundlings in seventeenth-century England is well portrayed.

A Parcel of Patterns, Jill Paten Walsh

DESCRIPTION: Mall Percival is a teen, soon to be adult, telling the story of the dreadful years when her village was struck by the plague. A powerful and well-written story, based on the true story of how Eyam, England, was devastated by the plague in 1665. I highly recommend it.

Master Cornhill, Eloise Jarvis McGraw

Description: Young Master Cornhill is sent out of London when the plague sweeps the city. Upon returning, he finds all whom he loves dead. Befriended by a young minstrel and a shop girl, he rebuilds his life. The story reaches a tense climax with the Great Fire of London.

The Trumpeter of Krakow, Eric Kelly

DESCRIPTION: Another medieval story, but this one is set in Poland. The hero of an exciting adventure story, young Joseph must protect the Great Tarnov crystal against the plundering Tartars.

The Second Mrs. Giaconda, E. L. Konigsberg

DESCRIPTION: A story of Renaissance Italy, Leonardo da Vinci, and his rapscallion young apprentice. The story closes with the painting of the Mona Lisa.

I, Juan de Pareja, Elizabeth Trevino

DESCRIPTION: Another story of the Renaissance. Juan is the slave of the Spanish court painter, Diego Velasquez. Daily he watches the master paint, learning as he watches. Juan secretly begins to paint, a forbidden activity for a slave. This is a Newbery Award book.

The Scarlet Pimpernel, Baroness Orczy
DESCRIPTION: Set during the French Revolution. The Scarlet Pimpernel, an elusive and daring Englishman, snatches French nobility away from the danger of the guillotine. Chauvelin has sworn to stop him.

A Tale of Two Cities, Charles Dickens
DESCRIPTION: This is a poignant story about the French Revolution. The ending is particularly memorable. *A Tale of Two Cities* has long been my favorite Dicken's book. Progeny Press has a high school level guide for this book.

Things Fall Apart, Chinua Achebe
DESCRIPTION: Set in the late 1800s in Nigeria. The story portrays the life of a respected Ibo tribal man of power, Okonkwo, who must adjust to the British arrival and colonialism. Chinua Achebe is a highly respected Nigerian novelist. A Progeny Press high school level guide is available for this book.

All Quiet on the Western Front, Eric Remarque
DESCRIPTION: This is a popular high school choice for World War I historical fiction.

The Endless Steppe, Esther Hautzig
DESCRIPTION: In this World War II story Esther, her mother, and grandmother struggle for survival as they are transported from Poland to Siberia.

Escape from Warsaw, Ian Serraillier
DESCRIPTION: A World War II story about four children escaping from the Jewish ghetto in Warsaw, Poland.

Life Is Beautiful, Miramax Home Entertainment
DESCRIPTION: This award-winning Italian-made movie is a poignant story of one young couple's happiness threatened by World War II. The ensuing story finds them living separated lives in a concentration camp. The father creates heartwarming (and heart-wrenching) little games to hide the truth of their desperate existence from his little son. I recommend watching the Italian version with the English captions. Losing the beauty of the Italian language in order to get dubbed English is too great a sacrifice. Rated PG-13.

G. A. Henty Books

George Alfred Henty (1832–1902) was a prolific writer of historical adventures well-respected for their historical accuracy. Critics of the day sometimes criticized his characters for being "too Christian," thus making them a great fit for the homeschool market! PrestonSpeed has reprinted the Henty titles below. Check their Web site, www.prestonspeed.com, for descriptions of each book, information on the various editions available, and new titles released. The chronological chart below will help you locate a Henty book for your studies. At least one historical figure appears in most of the books.

Title	Date	Description	Famous Character
The Cat of Bubastes	1250 BC	Egypt during the reign of Thutmose III	Moses
The Young Carthaginian	220 BC	2nd Punic War	Hannibal
For the Temple	70 BC	Fall of Jerusalem	Josephus
Beric the Briton	61 BC	Roman invasion of Britain	
The Dragon and the Raven	AD 870	Viking invasions of England	King Alfred
Wulf the Saxon	1066	Norman Conquest	William the Conqueror

Winning His Spurs	1190	Third Crusade	Richard the Lionhearted
In Freedom's Cause	1314	Scottish Rebellion	Robert the Bruce William Wallace
St. George for England	1340	Hundred Years' War	Edward, the Black Prince of Wales
The Lion of St. Mark	1380	Venice, Italy at her height	
A March on London	1381	Wat Tyler's Insurrection	Wat Tyler
Both Sides of the Border	1400	Battle at Shrewsbury	King Henry
At Agincourt	1413–1415	Battle of Agincourt	King Henry
The Knight of the White Cross	1480	First Siege of Rhodes	Knights of St. John Order
By Pike and Dyke	1579	The Dutch fight for freedom	William the Silent
St. Bartholomew's Eve	1580	Huguenot Wars	Coligny, Queen Elizabeth, etc.
Under Drake's Flag	1580	The Spanish Main	Sir Francis Drake
By England's Aid	1588	Dutch fight for freedom continued	Sir Francis Vere
By Right of Conquest	1595	Spanish conquest of Mexico	Cortez
The Lion of the North	1630	30 Years' War King Gustavus	Adolphus of Sweden
Won by the Sword	1640	30 Years' War	Richelieu
Friends Now Divided	1650	English Civil War	Charles I and II
When London Burned	1665–66	London Plague/Fire	Cromwell, Charles II
Orange and Green	1688–90	Rising of Ireland	James II, William of Orange
Bonnie Prince Charlie	1745	Battle of Culloden	Charles Edward Stuart
With Wolfe in Canada	1759	French and Indian War	George Washington
With Frederick the Great	1760	Prussian Seven Year War	Frederick the Great
True to the Old Flag	1775	American War of Independence	
With Clive in India	1786	Battle of Plassey, India 1st Baron Clive of Plassey	
In the Reign of Terror	1793	French Revolution	
No Surrender	1793	French Revolution	La Vendee resistance
The Tiger of Mysore	1795	Mysore War in India	
At Aboukir and Acre	1798	Napoleonic Wars	Napoleon
Under Wellington's Command	1810	Peninsular War	Wellington
Out on the Pampas	mid-1800s	British colonization of Argentina	
Facing Death	1800s	Welsh coal mines	
With Moore at Corunna	1808	Peninsular War	
Through Russian Snows	1812	Napoleonic Wars	Napoleon

The Treasure of the Incas	1830s	Peru	
To Herat and Kabul	1840	First Afghan War	
With Lee in Virginia	1860s	American Civil War	Robert E. Lee
For Name and Fame	1879	Second Afghan War	Colonel Ripon
By Sheer Pluck	1873	African Ashanti Wars	General Wolseley
The Dash for Khartoum	1885	Siege of Khartoum	
With Kitchener in the Sudan	1898	Battle of Omdurman	General Kitchener
With the Allies in Pekin	1900	Boxer rebellion	

AMERICAN HISTORY

Course: Remedial American history   **Grades:** 9–12   **Prerequisite:** None

MAIN TEXT OR MATERIAL: *America's History: Land of Liberty, Books 1 and 2*, Steck Vaughn

TEACHER HELPS: Teacher's edition with answers

DESCRIPTION: These American history books offer core high-school content for the student reading significantly below grade level. They are most appropriate for the student following a modified high-school program. *Book 1* covers early exploration through the reconstruction. *Book 2* continues with westward expansion through the modern age.

Course: American history   **Grades:** 9–12   **Prerequisite:** None

MAIN TEXT OR MATERIAL: *A History of Us*, Volumes 1–10, Joy Hakim, Oxford University Press

TEACHER HELPS: None

DESCRIPTION: If you have a student who dislikes history, these books may change his mind. These highly interesting history "storybooks" do at times express some of the author's nonconservative views (especially volumes 1 and 10) so be prepared for discussion. Written on a junior-high level, these books may work well as a framework for adding more living books to make the course more challenging. A research paper in an area where the student's opinion differs from the author's wouldn't be a bad idea either.

Course: American history   **Grades:** 9–12   **Prerequisite:** None

MAIN TEXT OR MATERIAL: *The Landmark History of the American People*, Daniel Boorstin, Sonlight Curriculum

TEACHER HELPS: None

DESCRIPTION: This interesting history focuses on how people both great and small came together to form America. Boorstin's easy-to-read approach emphasizes the social and cultural forces that have defined our country's identity. This would make a good foundation for an independent reading course.

Course: American history   **Grades:** 9–12   **Prerequisite:** None

MAIN TEXT OR MATERIAL: *U.S. and World History Study Guide*, Beautiful Feet Books

ADDITIONAL MATERIALS: Selected living books

TEACHER HELPS: Teacher's guide

DESCRIPTION: This one- or two-year study uses literature to examine the 1860s to 1970s (Civil War to the Vietnam War). The teacher's guide, with its scheduling, vocabulary, and comprehension questions, guides you through the reading of *Uncle Tom's Cabin*, *The Red Badge of Courage*, *Around the World in Eighty Days*, *The Hiding Place*, and more. Biographies of Teddy Roosevelt, Stalin, Hitler, and others are also included. Literature books can be purchased separately or sometimes borrowed through interlibrary loan.

| *Course:* Independent reading (American history) | *Grades:* 9–12 | *Prerequisite:* None |

MAIN TEXT OR MATERIAL: Selected living books

TEACHER HELPS: None

DESCRIPTION: An independent reading course can be used to study a particular historical time period. Using a historical timetable or textbook as a framework, plan an independent reading course using a variety of original documents, nonfiction, and historical fiction books. Use a time record for evaluation. A research paper would be an appropriate requirement. Check the following nonfiction and historical fiction listings for suggestions.

| *Course:* American history | *Grades:* 7–12 | *Prerequisite:* None |

MAIN TEXT OR MATERIAL: *A New World in View, Building a City on a Hill, On the Road to Independence*, Gary DeMar, American Vision

TEACHER HELPS: Teacher's packet includes teacher's guide, tests, and key, book 1 and 2 resources also available on CD-ROM, guides for book 3 not available

DESCRIPTION: These first three books in the *To Pledge Allegiance* series begin on an Old World stage and proceed through the revolution. These excellent junior high books could serve as a framework for an independent reading course in American history through the revolution.

| *Course:* American history | *Grade:* 11 | *Prerequisite:* None |

MAIN TEXT OR MATERIAL: *History and Geography 11* Lifepacs, Alpha Omega

TEACHER HELPS: Teacher's guide

DESCRIPTION: The eleventh-grade Alpha Omega Lifepacs cover American history. Like all of Alpha Omega's core subjects third through twelfth grade, this course is also available in Switched on Schoolhouse. See "Full-Service Publishers" for more information on the Lifepac and SOS program.

| *Course:* American history | *Grades:* 9-12 | *Prerequisite:* None |

MAIN TEXT OR MATERIAL: *America: The Last Best Hope, Vols. 1 & 2*, William Bennett

TEACHER HELPS: None

DESCRIPTION: An excellent history by William Bennett, Ronald Reagan's Secretary of Education and author of *The Book of Virtues. America: The Last Best Hope* is both honest *and* patriotic in its look at our country's history. Volume 1 takes the reader from the explorations of Columbus to the brink of World War I. Volume 2 picks up at World War I and brings the reader through the Reagan presidency. A worthwhile read from a man who deeply loves and respects his country.

| *Course:* American history | *Grades:* 9-12 | *Prerequisite:* None |

MAIN TEXT OR MATERIAL: *United States History*, Bob Jones University Press

ADDITIONAL MATERIALS: *Student Activities Book*

TEACHER HELPS: Teacher's edition, teacher's edition for activity book, tests and key, *Testbuilder 2* software

DESCRIPTION: We have found this well-written survey of American history a more interesting read than your typical textbook. *United States History* begins with the discoverers and continues to the present, integrating American church history along the way. Using the text with tests makes this course of average difficulty. Using the activity book and map packet makes this a solid college preparatory course. Adding reading selections from our American history reading lists would add both interest and challenge. These selections are listed at the end of this section.

| *Course:* American history | *Grades:* 9-12 | *Prerequisite:* None |

MAIN TEXT OR MATERIAL: *A Basic History of the United States*, six-volume set, Clarence Carson, American Textbook Committee

TEACHER HELPS: Teacher's guide with questions, well-organized but no answer key

DESCRIPTION: Written by Clarence Carson, this course will provide a conservative approach to the study of American history. We have found Clarence Carson to be readable for history lovers. The teacher's guide was helpful in identifying main ideas, people, etc. for highlighting and study. Adding a research paper or reading selections from the American history reading lists would make this course even more challenging. These selections are listed at the end of this section. An Internet search will turn up several sources for this series. Try www.cumberlandbooks.com for starters.

Course: American Civil War elective	Grades: 9–12	Prerequisite: None

MAIN TEXT OR MATERIAL: *The War between the States: America's Uncivil War*, John J. Dwyer

DESCRIPTION: The author of *Stonewall* and *Robert E. Lee* has received excellent reviews on this nonfiction work. For students with an in-depth interest in the most tragic war in American history, this book is a key resource and a great foundational text.

AMERICAN HISTORY: NONFICTION

History through the Ages: Explorers to 21st Century AD time-line package, Homeschool in the Woods

DESCRIPTION: This is a great resource for the hands-on learner. Each time-line figure includes a line drawing of the person or event, date, and key information. Students cut, color, and glue the figures pertinent to their study on the accompanying time-line sheets. With many figures to choose from, it is easy to customize the time line to your student's history study. The entire collection of pictures, world and American, is also available on CD.

America's God and Country, William Federer

DESCRIPTION: An encyclopedia of quotations that highlights the noble heritage of America.

The Patriot's Handbook, George Grant, Cumberland House

DESCRIPTION: A handbook full of patriotic poems and prose.

Our Country's Founders, William Bennett

DESCRIPTION: The virtues of our founding fathers are presented through poems, letters, speeches, and articles. The adult version of this book, *Our Sacred Honor*, is also available.

To the Best of My Ability, James M. McPherson, Dorling Kindersley

DESCRIPTION: In this excellent reference book, six pages of full-color photographs and biographical information are included for each president. A readable and fascinating book.

Critical Thinking in United States History, Bright Minds, division of Critical Thinking Press

DESCRIPTION: If you like lively discussions, this series will serve as an excellent catalyst. Students are presented with opposing interpretations of controversial historical events often using excerpts from original documents. The challenge is to analyze the data and try to arrive at accurate conclusions. Students will soon see that the "facts" are not as objective as they seem.

America's Christian Heritage, Gary DeMar, American Vision

DESCRIPTION: Gary DeMar's carefully researched book presents compelling documentary evidence for the influence of Christian thought in the founding of our nation.

Never Before in History: America's Inspired Birth, Gary Amos and Richard Gardiner

DESCRIPTION: A well-researched look at Christian influences in colonial and revolutionary America. Can be used as an early American history text.

A Patriot's History of the United States: From Columbus's Great Discovery to the War on Terror, Larry Schweikart and
  Michael Allen
DESCRIPTION: An interesting read for the history-loving student. Its conservative yet balanced approach appreciates
  America's strengths without ignoring its weaknesses.

The Story of Liberty, Charles Coffin, Maranatha or Mantle Ministries
DESCRIPTION: This highly readable story tells the progress of liberty beginning with the signing of the Magna Carta
  up to the discovery of America. This is a worthwhile companion for any study in church or world history. Study
  guide available.

Sweet Land of Liberty (Mantle uses the original title, *Old Times in the Colonies*), Charles Coffin, Maranatha or Mantle
  Ministries
DESCRIPTION: This is a sequel to *The Story of Liberty* ending after the French and Indian War. Charles Coffin's
  storytelling is readable.

America: The First 350 Years, J. Steven Wilkins, Covenant Publications
DESCRIPTION: Listening to this carefully researched Christian presentation will blow the cobwebs out of your mind
  as you develop a new perspective on American history. Full of anecdotal stories and facts you were probably
  never taught in school. Available in MP3 format only. A notebook containing course notes is also included. Our
  family has greatly enjoyed these tapes.

World of Columbus and Sons, Genevieve Foster, Beautiful Feet Books
DESCRIPTION: Genevieve Foster's books study individuals in a way uniquely her own. As you learn of Columbus, you
  will also learn what was happening in the world in which he lived.

Empires Lost and Won: The Spanish Heritage in the Southwest, Albert Marrin, Atheneum
DESCRIPTION: Marrin chronicles the history of the southwest from Cabeza de Vaca's search for the legendary seven
  cities of Antilia in 1528 through the Mexican War. Albert Marrin is a remarkable storyteller, making history
  come alive for his readers. This book makes an excellent addition for a Texas history study. Although out of
  print, Albert Marin books are easily found on the Internet. Check www.abebooks.com.

Sea King: Sir Francis Drake and His Time, Albert Marrin
DESCRIPTION: Albert Marrin is a remarkable storyteller, making history come alive for his readers. Marrin has written more than twenty books for young readers; unfortunately, not all of them are now in print. If you like to
  wander used bookstores, put him on your search list or check www.abebooks.com.

The World of Captain John Smith, Genevieve Foster, Beautiful Feet Books
DESCRIPTION: Learn about Captain John Smith and the world in which he lived.

Of Plymouth Plantation, William Bradford, Mantle Ministries
DESCRIPTION: A readable history of Plymouth written by the godly man who was governor for almost forty years.
  You can't study colonial America thoroughly without at least reading excerpts from this.

Worldly Saints: The Puritans as They Really Were, Leland Ryken
DESCRIPTION: Puritans are frequently mischaracterized among both Christians and non-Christians. Ryken's book
  presents a more accurate picture of our noble ancestors.

Beyond Stateliest Marble, Douglas Wilson, Cumberland House
DESCRIPTION: Anne Bradstreet was an early Puritan poet in Massachusetts Bay Colony. Learn about her Christian
  faith, poetry, and life in the colonies. From the Leaders in Action series.

The Account of Mary Rowlandson and Other Indian Captivity Narratives, Mary Rowlandson, Dover Publications
DESCRIPTION: Captured by the Narragansett Indians in 1676, Mary Rowlandson's story is one of courage and great faith in God. After reading her narrative in BJU's American Literature book, I made it required reading in our high-school program.

Amos Fortune, Free Man, Elizabeth Yates
DESCRIPTION: Although generally considered a junior-high book, this Newbery Award-winning book, provides a fine, if not challenging, read for a high-school student. Amos Fortune is based on the true story of an African tribal prince At-mun, uprooted by slave traders, and brought to America. Purchased by a Quaker family, he embraces a belief in their God. His kind patient character and genuine respect for others is an excellent role model for grace during affliction. At age fifty-nine Amos Fortune received his freedom. Progeny Press has a middle-school-level guide for this book.

George Washington's World, Genevieve Foster, Beautiful Feet Books
DESCRIPTION: Read about George Washington and find out what was happening elsewhere in the world during his lifetime.

The Autobiography of Benjamin Franklin, Benjamin Franklin
DESCRIPTION: The autobiography of one of the most influential men in colonial America.

Forgotten Founding Father, Stephen Mansfield, Cumberland House
DESCRIPTION: George Whitefield, an English preacher, was intimately acquainted with America. Through seven tours of the colonies, he brought the gospel and influenced such men as Benjamin Franklin and George Washington. Patrick Henry was converted under his ministry. Learn about the man, the Great Awakening, and the political effect of his ministry in this fine volume from the Leaders in Action series.

Poor Richard, James Daugherty, Beautiful Feet Books
DESCRIPTION: An older popular biography of Benjamin Franklin republished in recent years.

Daniel Boone: His Own Story, Daniel Boone
DESCRIPTION: The autobiography of the great early American wilderness trailblazer.

Give Me Liberty, David Vaughan, Cumberland House
DESCRIPTION: Learn all about Patrick Henry, his life, and his thoughts in this biography from the Leaders in Action series.

The Boys of '76, Charles Coffin, Mantle Ministries
DESCRIPTION: A third title by Charles Coffin, this one on the Revolutionary War. If you enjoy Coffin's style, Mantle Ministries has one additional Coffin book, *Building the Nation*, which covers American history from 1783 to 1859.

A Young Patriot, Jim Murphy, Clarion
DESCRIPTION: The Revolutionary War as seen through the eyes of a fifteen-year-old American soldier.

Best Little Stories from the American Revolution, C. Brian Kelly, Cumberland House
DESCRIPTION: If you like these little historical vignettes, C. Brian Kelly has other best little books on the Civil War, the White House, and World War II.

The Federalist Papers, Hamilton, Madison, Jay
DESCRIPTION: During the formation period of the United States, these papers were written by ardent defenders of a strong central government.

The Anti-federalist Papers, Ralph Ketcham

DESCRIPTION: The lesser-known Anti-federalist Papers give the views of those opposing a strong centralized government for the new nation.

John Adams, 1776, David McCullough

DESCRIPTION: McCullough's two Pulitzer prizes (*John Adams* and *Truman*) and presence on the *New York Times* Best Seller list attest to both the respect and the popularity awarded his writing. *John Adams* is the engrossing story of our second president and the political scene surrounding the Revolution. *1776* focuses on the military struggle and its leaders. Adult history at its best, McCullough's lengthy, yet engaging narrative style will both challenge the history-loving student and capture his attention.

Jonathan Edwards: A New Biography, Ian Murray

DESCRIPTION: A well-known biography of Jonathan Edwards written for adults but very readable.

Carry On, Mr. Bowditch, Jean Lee Latham, Houghton Mifflin

DESCRIPTION: This winner of the 1956 Newbery Award is an upper elementary or junior high level book but can also provide a quick enjoyable read for a young high schooler. The true story of self-made Nathaniel Bowditch takes place in colonial Salem, Massachusetts, a major seafaring town. When plans to attend Harvard disappear, Nathaniel begins a lifelong pursuit of mathematics and the sea that result in *The American Practical Navigator*, long considered the "Sailor's Bible." Nathaniel Bowditch's rise to excellence through self-education finds a warm place in many homeschoolers' hearts. Progeny Press has a middle-school-level guide for this book.

An American Plague: The True and Terrifying Story of the Yellow Fever Epidemic of 1793, Jim Murphy

DESCRIPTION: Jim Murphy does a masterful job of letting the facts tell a riveting story. Colonial Philadelphia (then our nation's capital) and its terrifying epidemic come to life through newspaper selections, political cartoons, advertisements, and a carefully told history.

The Journals of Lewis and Clark, edited by Frank Bergon, Penguin

DESCRIPTION: The journals of Meriwether Lewis and William Clark's eight-thousand-mile journey (1804–1806) from the Missouri River to the Pacific Ocean.

Of Courage Undaunted, James Daugherty, Beautiful Feet Books

DESCRIPTION: An older, popular narrative of the Lewis and Clark expedition, republished in recent years.

Democracy in America, Alexis de Tocqueville

DESCRIPTION: America as seen through the eyes of a French statesman visiting our country in the 1830s. It is a penetrating view of American society and its character. It may be more practical to read excerpts rather than attempt the whole book.

Old Hickory: Andrew Jackson and the American People, Albert Marrin

DESCRIPTION: Born in a log cabin, Andrew Jackson was a soldier, lawyer, judge, and legislator before becoming our nation's seventh president. Marrin, as always, provides an excellent glimpse at history and the people who made it.

Cowboys, Indians, and Gunfighter: The Story of the Cattle Kingdom, Albert Marrin

DESCRIPTION: Albert Marrin is a remarkable storyteller, making history come alive for his readers. Although this book is out of print, you can find it through used book sources online, such as www.abebooks.com.

The Raven, Marquis James

DESCRIPTION: This excellent biography of Sam Houston gives valuable insight into the settling of the American West. A challenging read, it is most appropriate for the avid history lover.

Davy Crockett: His Own Story, Davy Crockett
DESCRIPTION: Davy Crockett's autobiography was penned in 1834, two years before his death in the Battle of the Alamo.

Inside the Alamo, Jim Murphy
DESCRIPTION: Jim Murphy's careful research gives readers a faithful presentation of the Battle of the Alamo and the events that precipitated it.

The Oregon Trail, Francis Parkman
DESCRIPTION: Harvard graduate, Francis Parkman, writes about his youthful western travels and encounters with the Plains Indians in the 1840s.

Abraham Lincoln's World, Genevieve Foster, Beautiful Feet Books
DESCRIPTION: Genevieve Foster's books study individuals in a way uniquely her own. As you learn of Lincoln, you will also learn what was happening in the world in which he lived.

Abraham Lincoln: A Photobiography, Russell Freedman
DESCRIPTION: Freedman's excellent book won the Newbery Award.

Commander in Chief: Abraham Lincoln and the Civil War, Albert Marrin
DESCRIPTION: Through skillful narration, photos, and quotes, Marrin crafts an enlightening look at our sixteenth president. Marrin has written many worthwhile books which, unfortunately, are not all in print. They are worth frequenting used bookstores and Internet sites to find.

George B. McClellan: The Disposable Patriot, Mike McHugh, Christian Liberty Press
DESCRIPTION: This Northern Civil War general was both a man of honor and a patriot but was largely unappreciated. Learn more about him in this CLP biography for high school students.

To Be a Slave, Julius Lester
DESCRIPTION: Slavery as seen through the eyes of former slaves.

Up from Slavery, Booker T. Washington
DESCRIPTION: The autobiography of Booker T. Washington, former slave, famous black educator, and Christian. It was a privilege meeting this truly great man in the pages of his book. This book is an honored part of our homeschool curriculum.

Then Darkness Fled, Stephen Mansfield, Cumberland House
DESCRIPTION: A biography of Booker T. Washington, the former slave, famous black educator, and Christian. Another excellent choice in the Leaders in Action series.

The Boy's War, Jim Murphy, Clarion Books
DESCRIPTION: The Civil War seen through the eyes of the young men who fought.

The Long Road to Gettysburg, Jim Murphy, Clarion Books
DESCRIPTION: Firsthand accounts of the Battle of Gettysburg seen through the eyes of the war's young soldiers. Jim Murphy's books have won a variety of prestigious awards.

The Civil War, Public Broadcasting System
DESCRIPTION: This excellent nine-volume video series produced by Ken Burns in 1991 can sometimes be rented at video stores, or check your library's video collection. Stores with large video collections will sometimes stock it.

A Call to Duty, J. Steven Wilkins, Cumberland House
DESCRIPTION: This volume from the Leaders in Action series is a combination biography and study of Robert E. Lee's character. *All Things for Good*, a story of Stonewall Jackson, is also available.

Life of JEB Stuart, Mary L. Williamson, Christian Liberty Press

DESCRIPTION: This attractive CLP edition tells the story of General JEB Stuart who was in charge of the cavalry of the Confederate army. Written for junior-high and early high-school readers, Williamson's the *Life of George Washington* and *Life of Stonewall Jackson* are also available through CLP.

Gone A-Whaling: The Lure of the Sea and the Hunt for the Great Whale, Jim Murphy

DESCRIPTION: Jim Murphy once again brings history to life, turning his research and story-telling skills to whaling. Excerpts from letters, diaries, photos, and other original documents add interest and authenticity.

Across America on an Emigrant Train, Jim Murphy

DESCRIPTION: Robert Louis Stevenson's journal entries of his 1879 transcontinental train trip are combined with original photos, lithographs, and careful research to create this interesting look at the American railroad.

The Great Fire, Jim Murphy, Scholastic

DESCRIPTION: A photo biography of the great Chicago fire of 1871. This was a Newbery Honor book.

Blizzard! The Storm That Changed America, Jim Murphy, Scholastic

DESCRIPTION: Another Jim Murphy book, this one about a blizzard that paralyzed New York City on March 12, 1888.

Carry a Big Stick, George Grant, Cumberland House

DESCRIPTION: This is a biography of Theodore Roosevelt, a gifted leader and devoted family man, whose diverse career led him to the presidency of the United States. You will enjoy this volume from the Leaders in Action series.

Citizen Soldiers, Steven Ambrose

DESCRIPTION: With a strong journalistic flavor Ambrose chronicles American involvement in World War II beginning after D-Day until victory. *Citizen Soldiers* tells its tale skillfully by blending firsthand accounts of the common frontline soldiers. Considered a sequel to his best seller, *D-Day*.

Farewell to Manzanar, Jeanne Wakatsuki Houston

DESCRIPTION: The story of a Japanese-American girl and her family's life in an internment camp in California during World War II.

America and Vietnam: The Elephant and the Tiger, Albert Marrin, Beautiful Feet Books

DESCRIPTION: Albert Marrin does an excellent job of portraying the complexity of the Vietnam War. Former POW Everett Alvarez stated, "It portrays the war the way the men who fought remember it."

AMERICAN HISTORY: FICTION

This section contains historical fiction set in America. The table flows chronologically through historical time periods. Most books should be easily available at libraries, through interlibrary loan, or from bookstores by special order. We have used the majority of these books in our homeschool.

The Witch of Blackbird Pond, Elizabeth George Speare

DESCRIPTION: Set in Puritan New England during the witch scare, Kit comes to live with her Puritan cousins. Because of Kit's strong-willed behavior, a woman is imprisoned for witchcraft. This Newbery Award book has a wonderful depth to its characterizations and is not just Puritan bashing (a popular American pastime). Progeny Press has a guide for this book.

The Scarlet Letter, Nathanial Hawthorne

DESCRIPTION: *The Scarlet Letter* is the story of Hester Prynne, condemned by her Puritan community for conceiving her daughter, Pearl, out of wedlock. The story proceeds through Hester's life as an outcast until the public confession of a dying Roger Dimmesdale. Hawthorne's short novel is often studied at the high school level. Progeny Press publishes a guide for this novel.

Calico Captive, Elizabeth George Speare

DESCRIPTION: Young Miriam Willard finds herself an Indian captive and on the way to Montreal during the French and Indian war. Although her books are easy to read, Elizabeth Speare, in my opinion, writes some of the finest children's historical fiction.

Johnny Tremain, Esther Forbes

DESCRIPTION: The abiding tale of Johnny Tremain, an apprentice silversmith, reveals Boston during the days preceding the revolution. You will meet many of the revolutionary heroes in the pages of this book. I have read this book three times, twice out loud. A Progeny Press guide is available for this book.

Traitor: The Case of Benedict Arnold, Jean Fritz

DESCRIPTION: Jean Fritz books always offer a unique look at history. This book for older students is the story of American patriot turned traitor, Benedict Arnold.

Streams to the River, River to the Sea, Scott O'Dell

DESCRIPTION: This is the story of Sacajawea, the young Indian girl who guided Lewis and Clark on their western exploration of America.

Moccasin Trail, Eloise Jarvis McGraw

DESCRIPTION: Jim Keath, long escaped from his pioneer home and living with the Crow Indians, receives an urgent request to return. His mother has died, and his younger siblings need him to help them keep their homestead. Jim returns with misgivings and begins the tumultuous adjustments to a settler's life.

Slave Dancer, Paula Fox

DESCRIPTION: A young boy is kidnapped and taken to sea to be a slave dancer. Read the book to find out what a slave dancer is. It is a cruel picture that you will likely never forget. A Newbery Award winner.

Uncle Tom's Cabin, Harriet Beecher Stowe

DESCRIPTION: Abraham Lincoln, upon receiving Harriet Beecher Stowe at the White House, called her "the little woman who wrote the book that made this great war." Mrs. Stowe's description of the plight of the black slave inflamed Northern sentiments. This book is a testimony to the power of the written word.

The Killer Angels, Michael Shaara

DESCRIPTION: *The Killer Angels*, a story of the Battle of Gettysburg, is considered one of the best Civil War novels ever written. This book has motivated many people to delve deeper into this critical time period in our country's history. (The movie *Gettysburg* was based on this book. Both book and movie are excellent.)

Stonewall, John J. Dwyer

DESCRIPTION: Meet Thomas Jackson, the Confederate lieutenant general whose brilliant battlefield strategies and bravery earned him the name "Stonewall." Jackson, however, was much more than a soldier. His love of God, his devotion to his wife, and his Sunday school classes for African-Americans, slave and free, speak of the honorable character he possessed. The movie *Gods and Generals* would be an appropriate follow-up.

Robert E. Lee, John J. Dwyer

DESCRIPTION: Picking up where Stonewall left off, *Robert E. Lee* traces Lee's life from the death of Stonewall Jackson until his own death in 1870, five years after the War between the States ended. An excellent read for the civil war buff.

The Red Badge of Courage, Stephen Crane

DESCRIPTION: The Civil War seen through the eyes of a young man enamored with the glories of war. We learn about war with him on the battlefield. Progeny Press has a guide for this book.

Across Five Aprils, Irene Hunt

DESCRIPTION: Set in rural southern Illinois, the book's family is divided by the Civil War. Irene Hunt is an excellent writer.

Rifles for Watie, Harold Keith

DESCRIPTION: An excellent book about young Jefferson Davis Bussey who joins the Northern army, later becoming a spy in the Southern army. Your sympathy grows for both sides of the conflict as you read through his experiences. This Civil War book, a Newbery Award winner, is mandatory reading in our home.

My Antonia, Willa Cather

DESCRIPTION: Life on the Nebraska prairie as seen through the life of pioneer immigrant Antonia.

A Lantern in Her Hand and *A White Bird Flying*, Bess Streeter Aldrich

DESCRIPTION: Bess Streeter Aldrich shows life on the prairie as it changes during the course of one woman's lifetime. Girls especially should enjoy these books.

No Promises in the Wind, Irene Hunt

DESCRIPTION: A young boy with his friend set out on their own to ease the financial strain at home during the Depression. Irene Hunt writes an excellent story even when its honest portrayal of family struggle and sudden death is not always comfortable.

Roll of Thunder, Hear My Cry, Mildred Taylor

DESCRIPTION: This Newbery Award book tells the story of Cassie, a young black girl growing up on a farm during the Depression. Her family struggles valiantly to maintain their integrity and independence while facing the prejudices of the day. A Progeny Press middle-school-level guide is available for this book.

To Kill a Mockingbird, Harper Lee

DESCRIPTION: The absorbing story is about a small southern town, the unjust imprisonment of a black man for the rape of a white woman, and the white lawyer who defends him—all seen through the eyes of the lawyer's little girl. An excellent read for mature students. Progeny Press has a guide for this book. After you read the books, rent the old movie starring Gregory Peck. It's good, too!

AMERICAN GOVERNMENT

Course: Remedial American government	Grades: 7–12	Prerequisite: American history

MAIN TEXT OR MATERIAL: *American Government: Freedom, Rights, Responsibilities*, Steck Vaughn
TEACHER HELPS: Teacher's edition with answers
DESCRIPTION: This government book is offered for the student who is reading significantly below grade level. It contains core content in American government for the student requiring a modified program.

Course: American government/economics	Grades: 7–12	Prerequisite: None

MAIN TEXT OR MATERIAL: The *Uncle Eric* books, Richard Maybury, Bluestocking Press
TEACHER HELPS: A separate teacher's guide for each book
DESCRIPTION: Uncle Eric writes his nephew letters explaining all kinds of economic and political ideas from his conservative viewpoint. The books find an easy fit in government, economics, or history courses. Although the books can be read in any order, "Uncle Eric" believes it is most profitable to read them as follows:

1. *Uncle Eric Talks about Personal, Career, and Financial Security*
2. *Whatever Happened to Penny Candy?*
3. *Whatever Happened to Justice?*
4. *Are You Liberal? Conservative? Confused?*
5. *Ancient Rome: How It Affects You Today*
6. *Evaluating Books—What Would Thomas Jefferson Think about This?*
7. *Money Mystery*
8. *Clipper Ship Strategy*
9. *The Thousand Year War in the Middle East: How It Affects You Today*
10. *World War I: The Rest of the Story and How It Affects You Today*
11. *Word War II: The Rest of the Story and How It Affects You Today*

Course: American civics/government	*Grades:* 7–12	*Prerequisite:* U.S. and world history

MAIN TEXT OR MATERIAL: *Land of Fair Play*, Christian Liberty Press

TEACHER HELPS: Teacher's guide, tests and key

ADDITIONAL MATERIALS: *Our Living Constitution*, School Specialty Publishing (Answers in back of book) or *The Story of the Constitution*, Christian Liberty Press (Teacher's manual, tests)

DESCRIPTION: *Land of Fair Play* explains local, state, and federal government. *Our Living Constitution's* helpful two-column format places the original document beside an explanation of the legal language it contains. These junior-high books may be more inviting to a reluctant government student. Using *The Story of the Constitution* would add a bit more challenge. Select a few Uncle Eric books, mentioned above, to round out the course.

Course: American government/economics	*Grade:* 12	*Prerequisite:* None

MAIN TEXT OR MATERIAL: *History and Geography 12* Lifepacs *1201–1210*, Alpha Omega

TEACHER HELPS: Teacher's guide

DESCRIPTION: The twelfth-grade Alpha Omega program covers government and economics. Like all of Alpha Omega's core third- through twelfth-grade subjects, this course is also available in Switched on Schoolhouse.

Course: American government	*Grade:* 12	*Prerequisite:* U.S. history

MAIN TEXT OR MATERIAL: *American Government*, Bob Jones University Press

ADDITIONAL MATERIALS: *Student Activity Manual*

TEACHER HELPS: Teacher's edition, teacher's edition to activities manual, tests and key, *Testbuilder 2* software

DESCRIPTION: This full-color book takes a historical approach to our government. Some of the topics discussed include the form of our government, the Constitution, political parties, elections, and the media. A Christian worldview is applied to all areas studied. *American Government* can be taught as a one- or two-semester course. This course is available on HomeSat.

Course: American government	*Grades:* 11–12	*Prerequisite:* U.S. and world history

MAIN TEXT OR MATERIAL: *God and Government*, Volumes *1–3*, Gary DeMar, American Vision

TEACHER HELPS: *Volumes 1* and *2* tests are available from Christian Liberty Press.

DESCRIPTION: This readable, three-volume set builds a Christian philosophy of government in general and American government in particular. Chapters end with questions, a summarization, and answers to the questions. *Volume 1, A Biblical and Historical Study* considers the role of government in the family, church, and country. The relationship of church and state is discussed. *Volume 2, Issues in Biblical Perspective* includes a study on worldviews and how they relate to economic issues. *Volume 3, The Restoration of the Republic* offers biblical solutions to governmental problems. Each book contains questions, answers, and Bible references for the positions taken.

| *Course:* American government | *Grade:* 12 | *Prerequisite:* American history |

MAIN TEXT OR MATERIAL: *Basic American Government*, Clarence Carson, American Textbook Committee

TEACHER HELPS: None

DESCRIPTION: A conservative presentation of American government. The lack of teacher evaluation tools makes this course most suited for the motivated independent reader. Available from www.cumberlandbooks.com.

| *Course:* Constitutional law | *Grades:* 11–12 | *Prerequisite:* American history |

MAIN TEXT OR MATERIAL: *Constitutional Law for Enlightened Citizens*, Michael Farris, Home School Legal Defense Association (HSLDA)

TEACHER HELPS: Teacher's handbook with answers

DESCRIPTION: Revised and expanded, *Constitutional Law for Enlightened Citizens* begins with a discussion of the Constitutional Convention and the meaning of original intent. The book then provides in-depth analysis on important Supreme Court decisions and their effect on our liberties. Michael Farris offers an online course using this text. See HSLDA's Web site, www.hslda.org, for information.

ECONOMICS

| *Course:* Remedial economics | *Grades:* 11–12 | *Prerequisite:* American history |

MAIN TEXT OR MATERIAL: *Biblical Economics in Comics*, Vic Lockman

TEACHER HELPS: None

ADDITIONAL MATERIALS: *Whatever Happened to Penny Candy?* Bluestocking Press (Study guide)

DESCRIPTION: *Biblical Economics* and *Penny Candy* present some economic basics in an easily understood and entertaining way. These two books will give the struggling student some understanding of economics on a basic level.

| *Course:* Economics | *Grades:* 11–12 | *Prerequisite:* U.S. and world history |

MAIN TEXT OR MATERIAL: *Biblical Economics in Comics*, Vic Lockman, *Whatever Happened to Penny Candy?* Bluestocking Press, *Economics in One Easy Lesson*, Henry Hazlitt)

TEACHER HELPS: Available for *Penny Candy* only

DESCRIPTION: An ease-them-in-gently introduction to economics. *Biblical Economics* and *Penny Candy* present some basics in an easily understood and entertaining way. Once the student understands these basics, begin Hazlitt's book. *Economics in One Easy Lesson*, subtitled *The Shortest and Surest Way to Understand Basic Economics*, was originally written in 1946. It is still going strong due to its approachable explanation of economics. It would be an appropriate book to grade using chapter and book summarizations.

| *Course:* Economics | *Grade:* 12 | *Prerequisite:* American history |

MAIN TEXT OR MATERIAL: *Economics*, Bob Jones University Press

ADDITIONAL MATERIALS: *Student Activities Book*

TEACHER HELPS: Teacher's edition, tests and key, teacher's edition for student activity book, *Testbuilder 2* software

DESCRIPTION: This one-semester course should be one of the last social studies taught in high school because of the more advanced reasoning that economics requires. In addition to covering the basics of economics, it gives case studies of eighteen nations. Biographical sketches of different economists are also included. Scriptural application extends beyond general economics into personal financial considerations. This course is available on HomeSat.

WORLDVIEW AND SOCIAL ISSUES

| *Course:* Modern philosophies | *Grades:* 9–12 | *Prerequisite:* American history |

MAIN TEXT OR MATERIAL: *Thinking Like a Christian*, student textbook, journal, and video, Broadman & Holman

TEACHER HELPS: Leader's guide on CD-ROM, included with textbook

DESCRIPTION: *Thinking like a Christian: Understanding and Living a Biblical Worldview* by founder of Summit Ministries, David Knoebel, is the first part of the Worldviews in Focus series. It encourages students to develop a mind-engaged faith, building their confidence that the Christian perspective makes sense. To accomplish this goal, students examine the Christian worldview as it applies to many areas of life: theology, philosophy, biology, psychology, ethics, sociology, law, politics, economics, and history. Chapter 12, which the guide recommends reviewing at the beginning of the study, presents the worldviews that conflict with Christianity. The journal provides daily exercise pages. The CD-ROM contains outlined lesson plans, handouts, and tests.

| *Course:* Modern philosophies | *Grades:* 9–12 | *Prerequisite:* American history |

MAIN TEXT OR MATERIAL: *Countering Culture: Arming Yourself to Confront Non-Biblical Worldviews*, student textbook and video, Broadman & Holman

TEACHER HELPS: Leader's guide on CD-ROM, included with textbook

DESCRIPTION: *Countering Culture* by founder of Summit Ministries, David Knoebel, is the second part to the Worldviews in Focus series. Whereas the first part, *Thinking like a Christian*, centers on understanding the Christian worldview, *Countering Culture* helps the student understand the conflicting cultures he will encounter in this world and the strength of the Christian view in comparison. Our high school students will soon leave home. College may find them sitting under the questionable teaching of professors who scorn the Christian faith. To be prepared, our students must have hearts *and minds* captive to Christ. *Countering Culture* can help. Program components include a textbook, a video, and a CD-ROM of outlined lesson plans, student handouts, and tests.

| Course: Modern worldviews/College survival | Grade: 11-12 | Prerequisite: None |

MAIN TEXT OR MATERIAL: *How to Stay Christian in College*, J. Budziszewski

DESCRIPTION: This helpful book is a great survival guide for students about to go to college and for those who are already there. Budziszewski covers three main areas: worldviews, including an excellent presentation of the Christian faith; common campus myths pertaining to the existence and pursuit of knowledge, love and sex, and politics; and strategies for coping with the social, religious, and classroom life of the college campus. Use this book to create a meaningful course for a high-school junior or senior about to spread their wings.

| *Course:* Modern philosophies | *Grade:* 12 | *Prerequisite:* American history |

MAIN TEXT OR MATERIAL: *Understanding the Times*, student text and workbook, DVD-ROMs, Summit Ministries

TEACHER HELPS: Teacher's guide with CD-ROM

DESCRIPTION: This upper-level worldview study contrasts the basic worldviews prevalent today with the Christian worldview. Secular humanism, Marxism, New Age, and postmodernism are considered. Social issues, such as abortion, feminism, homosexuality, moral relativism, and euthanasia are also covered. Christian leadership is encouraged. Worldview courses serve as a helpful foundation and an eye-opener for any college-bound student. Designed for homeschoolers, the CD-ROM includes lesson plans, projects resources, quizzes, and more.

| *Course:* Worldview camps | *Grades:* 9–12 | *Prerequisite:* None |

DESCRIPTION: Summit Ministries operates a camp in Colorado (also brought to college campuses in Tennessee and Ohio) where high-school students can go for a two-week study on the major worldviews. All are studied and evaluated in light of the Christian worldview. It is an intense time but good fun also. A similar organization, Worldview Academy, offers a one-week camp. Worldview Academy will accept students a bit younger and is offered at different locations throughout the United States. My three oldest children have had the blessing of attending Worldview Academy. We consider it an essential for a high-school education. Any time spent at Summit or Worldview Academy is time well spent. Check appendix A for address information.

Course: Current events	*Grades:* 6–12	*Prerequisite:* None

MAIN TEXT OR MATERIAL: *Top Story* magazine, God's World Publications

ADDITIONAL MATERIALS: *WORLD* magazine and a local newspaper

TEACHER HELPS: Weekly teaching guide for *Top Story*

DESCRIPTION: A current-events course can be built on reading the local newspaper and a weekly newsmagazine. God's World News offers school-year newsletters (26 issues) for prekindergarten through adult. The sixth- through ninth-grade newsletter is *Top Story*. Tenth graders and above subscribe to the adult newsmagazine *World*. Any level edition can be ordered online at God's World News, www.gwnews.com.

Course: Independent reading (current events)	*Grades:* 9–12	*Prerequisite:* None

MAIN TEXT OR MATERIAL: Selected living books

TEACHER HELPS: None

DESCRIPTION: An independent reading course is well suited to a study of worldviews and how they relate to current issues and events. Plan an independent reading course using a variety of periodicals and books exploring current issues from a Christian perspective. Use a time record for evaluation. An opinion paper on an issue studied would be an appropriate requirement.

ADDITIONAL WORLDVIEW AND SOCIAL ISSUE TITLES

All God's Children and Blue Suede Shoes: Christians and Popular Culture (Turning Point Christian Worldview series), Kenneth A. Myers

DESCRIPTION: Analyzes American popular culture in the light of biblical truth.

Amusing Ourselves to Death: Public Discourse in the Age of Show Business, Neal Postman

DESCRIPTION: Now in a twenty-year anniversary edition, Neal Postman's observations on the negative effects of modern media on literacy and social discourse still ring true.

How Should We Then Live? Francis Schaeffer

DESCRIPTION: Originally written in 1976, this book remains pertinent today. Subtitled *The Rise and Decline of Western Thought and Culture*, Schaeffer's historical survey reveals how we have arrived at modern-day thinking.

How Now Shall We Live? Charles Colson

DESCRIPTION: Colson believes that the struggles of modern life are due to the many conflicting worldviews prevalent today. After a look at various scriptural themes, Colson makes pertinent applications to all areas of life.

In the Shadow of Plenty, George Grant, Christian Liberty Press

DESCRIPTION: Grant looks at the failure of the modern welfare system and shows why true solutions to poverty lie within the Christian church.

The Law, Frederic Bastiat, Foundation for Economic Education

DESCRIPTION: This little booklet was first published in 1850 by the French economist, Frederic Bastiat. His arguments against socialism are as pertinent today as they were when first written.

Lord of All: Developing a Christian World-and-Life View, Dr. D. James Kennedy and Jerry Newcomb

DESCRIPTION: *Lord of All* is a call to Christians to carry their faith into all of life. The necessity of a Christian world-and-life view in six main spheres of life is examined.

Loving God with All Your Mind: Thinking as a Christian in the Postmodern World, Gene Edward Veith
DESCRIPTION: A call to actively engage secular thought with the clarity of the Christian worldview.

Postmodern Times, Gene Edward Veith
DESCRIPTION: If you enjoy reading social issue books, you will enjoy this book that provides an analysis of our world today. We have enjoyed Gene Veith's readable writing style.

The Road to Serfdom, F. A. Hayek
DESCRIPTION: *The Road to Serfdom* deals with the relationship between individual freedom and economic prosperity. It builds a case against government interference and control of the market place.

Seven Men Who Rule the World from the Grave, David Breese
DESCRIPTION: Learn about seven men, Darwin, Freud, Marx, Kierkegaard, Wellhausen, Dewey, and Keynes, whose ideas have had a profound effect on our world.

The Soul of Science: Christian Faith and Natural Philosophy (Turning Point Christian Worldview series), Nancy R. Pearcey, Charles B. Thaxton
DESCRIPTION: Pearcey and Thaxton believe that Christian faith and science are not in opposition. Rather, man's belief in a predictable universe created and governed by a God of order has propelled scientific discovery in Western civilization.

The State of the Arts, Gene Edward Veith
DESCRIPTION: This book examines the arts and sets a standard for Christian evaluation. Parents may want to pre-read, as Veith's straightforward information on the sinfulness of some modern art will be inappropriate for younger students.

Thinking Straight in a Twisted World, Gary DeMar
DESCRIPTION: DeMar defines a Christian worldview and exhorts his readers to acquire and practice it in daily life. An especially helpful read for the college bound.

Unit Studies

Unit studies, sometimes called interdisciplinary studies, are not the province of elementary school only. They can also be successfully used on the high-school level. In unit studies, academic subjects are woven together by a unifying theme. Some studies, especially for younger students, are woven around character qualities. Many unit studies are unified by a historical time period. This makes combining various subjects, such as Bible and character studies, worldview, composition, literature, history, geography, art, music, and sometimes science, work well. With history a major part of many studies, it seemed appropriate to look at some unit study choices before moving on to other subject matter.

The key to using unit studies on the high-school level is keeping records that can be effectively reported on a transcript. Often unit-study authors provide the guidance you need. Some offer record-keeping procedures and/or suggest the number of credits a student can earn following their program.

When designing your own unit study, you can keep separate records for each subject being studied. For example, an in-depth historical study might be divided into three time records or contracts, one each for English (literature and composition), history, and art appreciation.

If you plan to follow a portfolio approach to record keeping, you probably won't feel the need to separate your unit study into separate courses. It also may not be necessary when applying to a smaller college with more individualized admission practices. Always use the approach most helpful to the future of your student.

If unit studies appeal to you, you may want to check into the following programs:

Further Up and Further In, Cadron Creek Christian Curriculum

Designed for grades four through eight, this is an appropriate junior-high study. The program revolves around C. S. Lewis's Chronicles of Narnia series. Each book represents one unit of study with lessons detailed for each chapter. Subjects and activities vary according to chapter content but include history, English, literature, social studies, geography, science, Bible and character studies, art, and cooking. The author recommends supplementing the instruction with history, grammar, spelling, and math.

Konos History of the World is an ambitious two-volume study of world history for high schoolers. Volume 1 covers ancient times. Volume 2 addresses the medieval world. In true unit-study fashion many topics are integrated into the study—in this case history, composition, literature, geography, drama, speech, art, and Bible. Some Latin is recommended in volume 2. Emphases in Konos include college preparatory reading, writing, and research; plenty of hands-on activities to aid retention; independent study; and discussion. Texts and materials include a student book, teacher's guide, maps, and time lines. For a listing of all the literature studied and more detailed information, visit www.konos.com for information.

Literary Lessons from the Lord of the Rings. For Tolkien lovers this program is a real gem. Amelia Harper has written an easy-to-use guide to both the Lord of the Rings series and the ancient literature that inspired it. Student books include fill-in-the-blank chapter reviews while chapter notes provide background information and a study of literary terms. Smaller unit studies within the larger study cover literary concepts and the ancient and Arthurian literature that hold a creative link to Middle Earth. Quizzes, tests, and all answers are provided. This self-directed study couldn't be easier to use. For high school transcript purposes, Ms. Harper suggests entitling the course *An Introduction to Literary Analysis.* This one-year course could appropriately replace one general literature course. She does not recommend using it as a replacement for American or British literature. For more information visit www.homescholar.org.

Sonlight Curriculum is a living book unit study centered around history. Bible is actively incorporated into the program. Sonlight's ministry to expatriates and missionaries has led to a more multicultural feel than many homeschool products. The main component of each year is called the "core" study with a focus on studying history through literature, biographies, and historical fiction. Additional language arts, science, math, and some electives are also available. Core studies are adaptable, but most junior-high students will study world history, and most high schoolers will move through American history (if not tackled in junior high), history of God's kingdom, twentieth-century world history, and civics/American government. British literature is available for the ambitious student who has completed the program or wants to tackle it concurrently. For more information, visit www.sonlightcurriculum.com.

*Tapestry of Grace is a unit-study program that can be used by the entire family. *Tapestry of Grace* is based on a four-year rotation of history from biblical times until the present. Rather than proving redundant, this study encourages students to bring greater skills and abilities to the subject each time it is studied. The teacher's guide provides assignments for students in the three classical learning stages: grammar, dialectic, and rhetoric. Dialectic assignments are appropriate for junior-high students. Rhetoric-level work would be the correct placement for high schoolers. Topics covered include history, fine arts, writing, literature, and church history. A biblical worldview is conscientiously woven throughout. Although the emphasis is on exploring history through reading and literature, this study also includes various activity suggestions. For more information visit www.tapestryofgrace.com.

Where the Brook and River Meet by Margie Gray is a unit study on the Victorian era based on Lucy Maude Montgomery's *Anne of Green Gables.* This full-year high-school study covers literature, history, writing, grammar, fine arts, social studies, Bible, and more. More information on this program can be obtained from www.cadron creek.com.

*Starting Points, Worldviews of the Western World. The Cornerstone Curriculum Project publishes two worldview studies. *Starting Points* is designed for ages twelve and up and is an introduction to worldview studies. Books read include *Know What You Believe,* Chronicles of Narnia, *Frankenstein, Mere Christianity, Never Before in History,* and more. The three-year high-school program, *Worldviews of the Western World,* covers ancient through modern history. The strong Christian worldview is apparent in its yearly titles: *The Emergence of Christianity, The Grandeur of Christianity,* and *The Shift Away from Christianity.* An extensive and ambitious reading program from all time periods is included. The works of Dr. Francis Schaeffer are well represented. Cornerstone Curriculum Project also has math, art, and music courses. See www.cornerstonecurriculum.com for more information.

Foreign Language Courses

Learning a foreign language is achievable at home when the program is chosen carefully. Many programs are directed toward the short-term traveler needing quick exposure to a language. This type of approach will emphasize words and phrases of greatest need while traveling. While helpful for the businessman or student taking a mission's trip, it does not provide the thoroughness of a high-school language program.

High-school language programs follow two basic instructional approaches: immersion or grammatical.

The first priority of an immersion program is learning to converse in the language fluently. Grammar is de-emphasized, with grammatical concepts introduced bit by bit when necessary for further growth in the language. Language immersion is the way we learn our native language as babies and small children. Fluency in our native language did not happen quickly but occurred over many years of childhood. Fluency in a new language won't occur overnight for teens either!

When using an immersion program, be sure that the tapes or CDs present the information with accurate and clear pronunciation. Foreign language studies will also be much more effective if the student has daily opportunities to use the language. For example, homeschoolers living in the Southwest have many opportunities for hearing and speaking Spanish. Short-term missionary service offers both spiritual benefits and the opportunity for instant and complete language immersion. DVDs often allow movies to be played or subtitled in more than one language. (French is particularly prevalent.)

A more traditional approach to language studies begins with an emphasis on the grammatical structure of the language. Grammar is studied as the foundation underlying the language. Students will memorize lists of declensions and conjugations, apply these structures to the vocabulary learned, and translate work from English into the foreign language and vice versa.

Some programs attempt to integrate both immersion and grammar, but generally one approach will predominate. Both will usually contain information on the culture, land, history, and people.

Which way is best? That depends on your goals. If verbal fluency is most important, consider an immersion program (while hopefully not neglecting grammar). If the main goal is learning to read and write in a classical, unspoken language, a traditional approach seems most helpful. If total mastery of the language is the goal, then immersion and grammar are both necessary.

Only four foreign language publishers are suggested in this chapter. All are, or can be adapted for, high-school level work. Yet they are still reasonably doable for home use by parents with little foreign language background.

Why teach Latin?

Teaching Latin is one of the things we did right with our older three students. Unfortunately, it took us three years with three different programs to find the right approach. With that finally settled, we began to see both expected and unexpected benefits.

We expected to see vocabulary improvement. Studies confirm that studying Latin improves SAT scores. However, studying Latin roots may accomplish that without the extra work of studying Latin as a language. The unexpected benefits convinced us of Latin's importance in our homeschool.

We had not expected the study of English grammar to acquire purpose and meaning. Translation work requires an understanding of parts of speech, noun functions, verb tenses, etc. Now there was a reason to remember all those tedious details. We were using them with meaning. They became vital clues to the translation puzzles we were continually solving.

We had not expected Latin to bring order to our thinking. In math, geometry teaches logical thought processes through formal proofs. When studying an inflected language, such as Latin, a similar exercise in careful, methodical thought takes place every time a sentence is translated.

Ideally, it would be nice if every student could study two languages: Latin for its vocabulary, grammar, and logic benefits and a spoken language for real-life practicality. Studying more than one language would be especially helpful for students planning a college program in the liberal arts.

Course: English, Spanish, French, German, Russian, Chinese, Japanese   *Grades:* All ages   *Prerequisite:* None

MAIN TEXT OR MATERIAL: *The Learnables*, CD/picture book set, International Linguistics Corporation

ADDITIONAL MATERIALS: *Basic Structures* CD/picture book set, *Grammar Enhancement* CD/picture book set

TEACHER HELPS: None needed, self-instructional

DESCRIPTION: *The Learnables* focuses on understanding a spoken language. Using only the target language, the course progresses through a series of CDs and picture books (no words included). By mastering the numbers first, students can follow the numbered sequence of pictures. The difficulty and length of spoken words and phrases grows incrementally. The number of *Learnables* levels available varies by language. In addition to the basic course, *Basic Structures* is also available. In this CD-workbook combination written words are included, giving the student the opportunity to see, read, and write the language. A third set, called *Grammar Enhancement*, teaches grammar by repetition of examples rather than direct instruction in the rules. Because Spanish, French, and German are the only courses for which *Grammar Enhancement* is now available, these languages are most usable for high-school credit. Cathy Duffy recommends that a first-year course include *Learnables 1*, *Basic Structures 1*, and *Grammar Enhancements 1* sequentially. You may want to purchase a grammar workbook from another publisher to provide some supplemental, sequential grammar instruction. Bible story sets are also available in Spanish, French, and German. For those who prefer to use the computer, *Learnables 1* in Spanish and French is now available. Check www.learnables.com for additional conversions to software. For students with auditory problems, the emphasis on hearing without seeing the written word will make language acquisition more difficult. Rosetta Stone is a better choice for this type of student.

Course: Spanish, French, German, Mandarin Chinese, Portuguese, Swahili, Farsi, etc.	*Grades:* 9–12 (can be used with students as young as eight)	*Prerequisite:* None

MAIN TEXT OR MATERIAL: Rosetta Stone, CD, user guide, workbook, study guide, tests and quizzes, curriculum guide (a text form of CD content)

TEACHER HELPS: Student management software, keys to workbook, tests, and quizzes

DESCRIPTION: Rosetta Stone is a conversational-style computer program that immerses the student in the target language. Students choose from one of four full-color photos on screen while hearing a word spoken by a native speaker. The length of the spoken phrases grows incrementally as vocabulary is mastered. Students see the photos, hear the word/words spoken, and view the word/words in print, making this a multisensory approach. Students can choose how the material is presented. For example, they can choose to see the photo, hear the phrase spoken, but not see the word written *or* see the photo and the written word, but not hear it spoken. The student chooses between these and other combinations, whichever is most helpful. The student-management system makes it easy to chart progress. Students completing level one receive the equivalent of two years of high-school foreign language. Students completing both level one and level two complete four years of high school foreign language. Level two is not available for every language. Rosetta Stone is widely used by corporations, government agencies, and in university language labs. This means it is available in a wide variety of languages, thirty by last count. A teacher is not necessary to the program, which makes this program a gem for busy homeschoolers.

Course: Spanish I, II, or III	*Grades:* 9–12	*Prerequisite:* None

MAIN TEXT OR MATERIAL: *Spanish I, II, or III*, Bob Jones University Press

ADDITIONAL MATERIALS: *Spanish I, II, or III Student Activities Books*, CD set, Spanish-English dictionary

TEACHER HELPS: Teacher's edition, teacher's edition for student activity books, tests and keys, DVD or video supplements for levels one and two

DESCRIPTION: The Bob Jones University Press Spanish courses emphasize reading, conversational ability, and an understanding of grammar. With Spanish I, II, and III all available on BJUP's HomeSat Linc program, this program becomes usable for homeschoolers. Most quiz and test questions are in a multiple-choice format, but some basic knowledge of the language would be helpful for checking short-answer or sentence responses. A serious language student can use BJU Linc during the school year and Rosetta Stone during the summer to continue strengthening conversational skills.

Course: French I, II, III	*Grades:* 9–12	*Prerequisite:* None

MAIN TEXT OR MATERIAL: *French I & II*, Bob Jones University Press

ADDITIONAL MATERIALS: *French I and II Student Activities Books*, French-English dictionary

TEACHER HELPS FOR FRENCH I AND II: Teacher's edition, teacher editions for student activity books, cassettes, DVD/video supplement, tests and keys

DESCRIPTION: French I, II, and III are all available through the Linc program on BJU HomeSat, making French study accessible for more homeschoolers. Rather than using a text, French III uses a workbook and several novels. Spanish and French are the only foreign languages presently available on the HomeSat program. A serious language student can use BJU Linc during the school year and Rosetta Stone during the summer to continue strengthening conversational skills.

Course: Latin I-II   **Grades:** 7–12   **Prerequisite:** None

MAIN TEXT OR MATERIAL: *The Latin Road to English Grammar I–III* student workbooks, flashcards, Schola Publications

TEACHER HELPS: Includes teacher's manual, pronunciation CD, tests

DESCRIPTION: This is a popular Latin program among homeschoolers. The teacher's manual is well laid out and helpful, offering additional content information and concise daily plans. Parents without a Latin background, but with consistent diligence, can teach this program. English grammar instruction precedes the teaching of new Latin skills, making grammar applications clearer than when learned through workbook pages. Many parents will feel no additional grammar instruction is needed while using this program. Without supplementation the three courses together equal approximately two years of high-school Latin. This makes the program helpful for junior high use also. The parent may wish to supplement with cultural information on early Rome. Training videos are also available for levels I and II.

The Latin Road to English Grammar I is designed for students with no prior Latin experience. Families who have done brief introductions to Latin or studied Latin roots will find it a good fit. If students have systematically completed all levels of a beginner's Latin program such as *Latina Christiana I and II*, a better fit may be the *Henle Latin* recommended by Memoria Press, publishers of *Latina Christiana*.

Fine Arts Courses

Homeschoolers often neglect the fine arts, but that need not happen. Here are a few suggestions.

Having your student home all day makes it easy to expose him to classical music. Consider quietly playing classical music during study time. Watch your local paper for classical or high quality concerts in the area. Sometimes these concerts have no admission charge.

Many students complain about music lessons. Homeschoolers can make piano lessons an expected part of school, no different than English, math, or history. Homeschooling allows practice time to blend into the school day.

Art can often be enjoyed through group art lessons offered in a homeschool support group or local art and craft stores. When traveling, consider adding art museums to your sightseeing plans. Some helpful resources for fine arts appreciation are available through various homeschool catalogs.

Fine art courses can be graded or credited based on the overall direction of the course. For example, evaluation of a music appreciation course, with reading and listening requirements, could be based on time spent. Project courses could be based on the completion of contracted activities, journaled in a time record.

The first course listed is speech. Speech is a good group course so students have an audience for presentations. Consider taking it in eleventh or twelfth grade so the student has learned or is learning the necessary composition skills. Or while keeping a time record, you could spread this course over all four years of high school, beginning with memorized presentations of others' work and progressing to original speeches as composition skills mature.

Speech is a course hard to categorize because it requires both performance skills and writing ability. I have placed it in fine arts, but you can also credit it as an English course, or consider it as a separate discipline all its own. If in doubt, follow your state's lead.

SPEECH

Course: Speech	Grades: 11–12	Prerequisite: None

MAIN TEXT OR MATERIAL: *On Speaking Well*, Peggy Noonan
TEACHER HELPS: None

DESCRIPTION: Peggy Noonan is best remembered as President Reagan's speechwriter. This pithy little book gives excellent help in preparing and delivering winning speeches. Interesting anecdotal information from her career often illustrates her points. While not a course in itself, it could be supplemental reading for a co-op speech class. Written for adults, it would be most appropriate for older high-school students.

Course: Speech	*Grades:* 9–12	*Prerequisite:* None

MAIN TEXT OR MATERIAL: *Speech* Paces, School of Tomorrow
TEACHER HELPS: Answer keys
DESCRIPTION: This half-year course uses six worktexts to teach the basics of effective speech.

Course: Speech	*Grades:* 10–12	*Prerequisite:* None

MAIN TEXT OR MATERIAL: *Sound Speech*, Bob Jones University Press
TEACHER HELPS: Teacher's edition
DESCRIPTION: Speech topics covered include vocal production, preparing and delivering different types of speeches, debate, parliamentary procedure, and oral interpretation of poetry, stories, and plays.

Course: Speech	*Grades:* 10–12	*Prerequisite:* None

MAIN TEXT OR MATERIAL: *Classical Rhetoric with Aristotle*, Martin Cothran, Memoria Press
TEACHER HELPS: Teacher's edition
DESCRIPTION: *Classical Rhetoric with Aristotle* covers more than technique. It guides the student through the first part of *Aristotle's Rhetoric:* a study of basic principles of political philosophy, ethics, and psychology that helps the speaker understand his audience and communicate more effectively. The three branches of classical oratory are taught through the use of model speeches. Designed for use in a homeschool cottage school, *Classical Rhetoric* makes a difficult subject accessible.

Course: Speech	*Grades:* High school through adult	*Prerequisite:* None

MAIN TEXT OR MATERIAL: *Secrets of Great Communicators* workbook and DVD, Jeff Myers, Broadman & Holman
TEACHER HELPS: CD-ROM of teacher's helps
DESCRIPTION: This excellent course by Dr. Jeff Myers is friendly, upbeat, and helpful. Myers, long known in homeschool circles for his work with Summit and his speaking engagements at homeschool conventions is, himself, a great communicator. The program consists of a student workbook and DVD. The study sequence includes watching a segment of the DVD, filling out an accompanying work sheet, reading the chapter, completing personal application work sheets, and preparing a speech. Each chapter begins with a focus on a great communicator. Ronald Reagan, Abraham Lincoln, Teddy Roosevelt, Patrick Henry, and Billy Graham are considered. Side boxes highlight some of their most memorable statements. The appendix, "Speech Outlines for Every Occasion" should also prove helpful. The only drawback to the program is its brevity. Plan on adding other activities to the six chapters to earn a half credit. Most homeschool students should find this course engaging and easy to use.

Course: Leadership elective (or add to speech credit)	*Grades:* High school through adult	*Prerequisite:* None

MAIN TEXT OR MATERIAL: *Secrets of World Changers* workbook and DVD, Jeff Myers, Broadman & Holman
TEACHER HELPS: CD-ROM of teacher's helps
DESCRIPTION: *Secrets of World Changers: How to Achieve Lasting Influence as a Leader* is another course by Dr. Jeff Myers. Following the same format as *Secrets of Great Communicators*, the course is an easy-to-use addition to your homeschool toolbox. The difficulty lies in figuring out how to credit a leadership course. The back cover of the book recommends calling it a life-skills study. My thought would be to piggyback it with the speech course using

additional public speaking to fill it out. Although it may be a bit of a stretch, to my mind leadership and ease in speaking go together.

Course: Leadership elective (or combine with speech credit)	*Grades:* High school through adult	*Prerequisite:* None

MAIN TEXT OR MATERIAL: *Secrets of Everyday Leaders* workbook and DVD, Jeff Myers, Broadman & Holman
TEACHER HELPS: CD-ROM of teacher's helps
DESCRIPTION: *Secrets of Everyday Leaders: Create Positive Change and Inspire Extraordinary Results* is another course by Dr. Jeff Myers. Following the same format as *Secrets of Great Communicators* and *Secrets of World Changers*, the main difference is in length. The other two programs each offer six lessons. This offers twice as many. Combined, all three courses offer twenty-four lessons. With some additional reading or activity they would make an enjoyable half-credit course. Now comes the challenge; what would you call it on a high school transcript? You can follow Dr. Myers's lead and call it a life-skills elective. Or, with some speech plumping, how about calling it Leadership Training with Speech Emphasis and count it as your speech half credit? Plan to center public speaking around leadership activities: teaching in VBS or Sunday school, reporting on a mission trip, campaigning for a politician, docenting at a museum or historical home, etc.

MUSIC

Course: Music	*Grades:* 9–12	*Prerequisite:* None

MAIN TEXT OR MATERIAL: Assigned by teacher
DESCRIPTION: Consider any private lessons or co-op homeschool band or choir as a high-school music course.

Course: Music appreciation	*Grades:* 9–12	*Prerequisite:* None

MAIN TEXT OR MATERIAL: *The Spiritual Lives of the Great Composers*, Patrick Kavanaugh
ADDITIONAL MATERIALS: Selected classical music CDs
TEACHER HELPS: None needed
DESCRIPTION: An introduction to classical music and its composers. Reading *The Spiritual Lives of the Great Composers* on various composers is as spiritually edifying as it is informative. Each vignette concludes with thoughts on a particular godly quality outstanding in that composer. Listening recommendations for each composer are also given. Fortunately, classical music is often reasonably priced, and it is not difficult to build a good listening library. Should your student desire to delve more deeply into each composer's life, *The Gift of Music* by Jane Stuart Smith and Betty Carlson gives additional information. This book is also from a Christian perspective.

Course: Music appreciation	*Grades:* 9–12	*Prerequisite:* None

MAIN TEXT OR MATERIAL: Choose from the following DVDs or audio CDs from The Teaching Company: *How to Listen to and Understand Great Music, The Symphony, The Concerto, How to Listen to and Understand Opera*
TEACHER HELPS: None needed
DESCRIPTION: The Teaching Company offers DVD or audio instruction from well-respected, excellent instructors from across the United States. Course outlines are included with each DVD or CD set. If desired, a complete course transcript can be purchased for an additional fee. The above courses are taught by Professor Robert Greenberg. We have thoroughly enjoyed *How to Listen to and Understand Opera*. Offering more than two hundred college-level courses, their catalog is a feast for learning-addicted homeschoolers. Undoubtedly there are some courses to avoid, but the generous course descriptions make appropriate selections easy. For more information visit www.teach12.com or call the company for a catalog. Sales run regularly, rotating through the different courses. The catalog will alert you to current offers.

ART

Course: Art appreciation	*Grades:* 9–12	*Prerequisite:* None

MAIN TEXT OR MATERIAL: (Choose from) *Annotated Art*, Cumming/Dorling Kindersley, *Annotated Mona Lisa*, Carol Strickland, *The Story of Painting*, Sister Wendy Beckett

TEACHER HELPS: None needed

DESCRIPTION: Full-color pictorial walks through art history with helpful commentary along the way. Sister Wendy's volume is a much larger, more thorough volume. As with any art books, expect some nudity.

Course: Art and crafts	*Grades:* 9–12	*Prerequisite:* None

MAIN TEXT OR MATERIAL: Assigned by teacher

DESCRIPTION: This is a project course using classes or materials offered in your community or local craft store.

Course: Drawing	*Grades:* 9–12	*Prerequisite:* None

MAIN TEXT OR MATERIAL: *Mark Kistler's Draw Squad*, Mark Kistler

TEACHER HELPS: None needed

DESCRIPTION: Skill-sequenced, step-by-step lessons build a student's drawing skills through daily practice. Kistler's "ten key words of drawing" explain how to make drawings appear three-dimensional. Although this book is targeted toward younger children, its drawing instruction makes it helpful for any novice. Mark Kistler has several other books geared for younger children that may be adaptable for older students.

Course: Drawing	*Grades:* 9–12	*Prerequisite:* None

MAIN TEXT OR MATERIAL: *Drawing 1*, *Drawing 2*, Walter T. Foster

TEACHER HELPS: Nothing additional needed

DESCRIPTION: Walter T. Foster art books are widely available in arts and crafts stores. To see the whole catalog of drawing, painting, cartooning, calligraphy, etc. books available visit www.walterfoster.com.

Course: Calligraphy	*Grades:* 9–12	*Prerequisite:* None

MAIN TEXT OR MATERIAL: Check local arts and crafts store

TEACHER HELPS: None needed

DESCRIPTION: Check your local arts and crafts store for possible classes and materials.

Course: Art	*Grades:* 7–12	*Prerequisite:* None

MAIN TEXT OR MATERIAL: *Art* Lifepacs, Alpha Omega

TEACHER HELPS: Teacher's guide

DESCRIPTION: This worktext program covers a wide variety of topics including design, color, perspective, figure drawing, sculpture, comics, printmaking, calligraphy, and art appreciation.

Course: Art	*Grades:* 7–12	*Prerequisite:* None

MAIN TEXT OR MATERIAL: *Artistic Pursuits* 7/8 or 9/12, *Books 1* and 2, Artistic Pursuits

TEACHER HELPS: None needed

DESCRIPTION: *Artistic Pursuits* is a self-instructional art course designed to heighten a student's creativity and observation skills. *Book One* covers six elements of art—space, line, texture, shape, form, value, and composition explored through drawing activities. *Book 2* covers the last element of art—color—and continues composition study with painting assignments. The history of art is also studied. The instruction on art elements and principles of composition deepen a student's understanding.

Physical Education and Health Courses

As Christians, we have a responsibility to take care of the bodies God has given us. The study of health and the pursuit of some type of physical activity help meet that responsibility.

The study of health, because it involves lifestyle choices, can include significant spiritual discussion. It can also contain all kinds of questionable content. Teaching health at home allows you to choose what topics to study and lets you study them in a way that harmonizes with your family values. Three textbook options from a Christian perspective are suggested. Living books on health and nutrition, dating or courtship, and marriage and family living can also be incorporated into a health curriculum.

Physical education is often neglected in homeschooling. Many child development specialists believe that higher level thinking skills are built on well-functioning motor skills. Walking, jogging, playing ball, swimming, tennis, etc., may actually help academic performance.

Course: Physical education	*Grades:* 9-12	*Prerequisite:* None

DESCRIPTION: Activities designed to teach a physical skill or improve physical fitness. Some possibilities for completing this requirement include church or community sport leagues, continuing education courses at the junior college, health club memberships, or individual fitness plans. My fourth student has earned her physical education credits through ballet, tap, and ballroom dance classes.

Course: Health	*Grades:* 7-12	*Prerequisite:* None

MAIN TEXT OR MATERIAL: *Health* Lifepacs, Alpha Omega
TEACHER HELPS: Teacher's guide
DESCRIPTION: This one-semester Lifepac course is appropriate for junior high and high school. Topics discussed include physical health, personal hygiene, fitness, nutrition, and living responsibly. *Health* is also available in the Switched on Schoolhouse format as a high-school elective.

Course: Health	*Grades:* 9–12	*Prerequisite:* None

MAIN TEXT OR MATERIAL: *Health* Paces, School of Tomorrow

TEACHER HELPS: Answer keys

DESCRIPTION: Because of the sensitive and moral nature of many health topics, it is wise to stay with health texts from a Christian perspective. This program meets that requirement with an easy worktext format.

Course: Health	*Grades:* 7–12	*Prerequisite:* None

MAIN TEXT OR MATERIAL: *Total Health: Talking about Life's Changes*, junior high student text, or *Total Health: Choices for a Winning Lifestyle*, high school student text, Purposeful Design

TEACHER HELPS: Teacher's edition, test and quizzes with keys

DESCRIPTION: A biblically and scientifically sound presentation of health issues. Students are encouraged to maintain strong relationships with parents and God and to make wise lifestyle decisions.

Course: Health	*Grades:* 9–12	*Prerequisite:* None

MAIN TEXT OR MATERIAL: *Health*, Bob Jones University Press

TEACHER HELPS: Teacher's edition, tests on two difficulty levels, black-line masters

DESCRIPTION: Because BJUP recommends this text for use in seventh grade and above they have produced two levels of tests. Black-line masters include student work sheets for chapter enrichment. The most sensitive health topics also appear in the black-line masters rather than the text so these topics can be added at the teacher or parent's discretion.

Course: Sex education	*Grade:* When age appropriate	*Prerequisite:* None

MAIN TEXT OR MATERIAL: Learning about Sex series, Concordia Publishing House

   How You Are Changing (ages 8–11)

   Sex and the New You (ages 11–14)

   Love, Sex, and God (ages 14 and up)

or

God's Design for Sex series, NavPress

   What's the Big Idea: Why God Cares about Sex (ages 8–11)

   Facing the Facts: The Truth about Sex and You (ages 11–14)

TEACHER HELPS: *How to Talk Confidently with Your Child about Sex*, Concordia and *How and When to Tell Your Kids about Sex*, NavPress

DESCRIPTION: Both series offer age-appropriate information written directly to the child or teen. Books are also available for younger children.

Home Economics and Auto Mechanics Courses

As the focus of our culture moves away from the home, home economics has fallen out of favor. Yet courses such as these help students learn to build the refuge every person needs from the stresses and strains of the world. Both men and women alike need to know how to create and maintain that refuge from day to day. Many living books, available in Christian bookstores, help in these studies.

Young women have endless study possibilities. Anything that teaches the biblical role of a woman, nurture of a family, and comfort of a home is a fair course topic. When planning, don't forget to teach your own areas of talent to your teen. How about gardening, canning and preserving, housecleaning, home decorating, etc., for additional possibilities? Six to eight week units of study can collectively create a solid home economics course.

Young men also have extensive possibilities for study. Consider courses in personal skills such as basic cooking, cleaning, and sewing; future family life skills such as male leadership, marriage relationships, and parenting; and resource skills such as money management, home maintenance, car repair, and carpentry skills.

Both young men and women would benefit from a study on courtship and dating. Several book suggestions are included in the Bible and character course section earlier in this book.

For course evaluation, a course contract that establishes reading and activity goals is appropriate. This could be combined with a time record, if desired, to ensure that sufficient time is spent to justify the credit awarded.

Course: Cooking and Nutrition	*Grades:* 9–12	*Prerequisite:* None

MAIN TEXT OR MATERIAL: Use cookbooks and nutritional information from home or the library.

TEACHER HELPS: Not needed

DESCRIPTION: Make this a practical hands-on course. Study nutrition, plan nutritionally balanced menus, shop, and prepare meals. You determine the exact goals.

| *Course:* Child care | *Grades:* 9–12 | *Prerequisite:* None |

MAIN TEXT OR MATERIAL: *Shepherding a Child's Heart*, Tedd Tripp

ADDITIONAL MATERIALS: A pediatric CPR course (check with your local Red Cross)

TEACHER HELPS: Application questions at the end of each chapter in *Shepherding*

DESCRIPTION: A course combining Christian childrearing and safety. Evaluation could include some free babysitting for a friend so your teen can practice improving her skills under your supervision.

| *Course:* Family living | *Grades:* 9–12 | *Prerequisite:* None |

MAIN TEXT OR MATERIAL: (Choose from) *Christian Living in the Home*, Jay Adams, *The Shaping of a Christian Home*, Elisabeth Elliot, *Hidden Art*, Edith Schaeffer, *What Is a Family?* Edith Schaeffer

TEACHER HELPS: None available

DESCRIPTION: A course with an emphasis on relationships in the home.

| *Course:* Family living | *Grades:* 9–12 | *Prerequisite:* None |

MAIN TEXT OR MATERIAL: *Family Life Skills*, Bob Jones University Press

ADDITIONAL MATERIALS: *Student Applications Guide*

TEACHER HELPS: Teacher's edition, teacher's edition to student applications guide, tests and key, *Testbuilder 2* software

DESCRIPTION: A course preparing students for their many roles in life: child, friend, spouse, parent, in-law, caregiver.

| *Course:* Handwork | *Grades:* 9–12 | *Prerequisite:* None |

MAIN TEXT OR MATERIAL: Any how-to book from a local craft store.

DESCRIPTION: A practical hands-on course in various types of handwork—you choose. Choices could include counted cross-stitch, quilting, knitting, crocheting, etc. If mom doesn't have the skills to teach this course, grandmother, a friend, or a course at a local sewing or craft store may do nicely.

| *Course:* Garment construction | *Grades:* 9–12 | *Prerequisite:* None |

MAIN TEXT OR MATERIAL: Pattern, fabric, notions, sewing reference book of your choice

TEACHER HELPS: None

DESCRIPTION: A project course. I sewed my first garments with the help of my retired great aunt. It is a wonderful memory.

| *Course:* Economic living | *Grades:* 9–12 | *Prerequisite:* None |

MAIN TEXT OR MATERIAL: (Choose from) *More with Less Cookbook*, Doris Longacre, *The Complete Tightwad Gazette*, Amy Dacyczyn, *Live Your Life for Half the Price: Without Sacrificing the Life You Love*, Mary M. Hunt, *Everyday Cheapskate's Greatest Tips: 500 Simple Strategies for Smart Living*, Mary M. Hunt

DESCRIPTION: A course teaching the student money-saving tips and economical cooking. Implementing some of the money-saving ideas learned in these books into your home could be a course requirement. Other possible resources could be: *Once a Month Cooking*, *Dinner's in the Freezer*, or *Living More with Less*. Check your County Agricultural Extension Service (or similar state organization) for free publications.

| *Course:* Home economics | *Grades:* 9–12 | *Prerequisite:* None |

MAIN TEXT OR MATERIAL: *Home Economics* Lifepacs, Alpha Omega
TEACHER HELPS: Teacher's guide
DESCRIPTION: This is a workbook program covering all the major topics in a home-economics course written from a Christian perspective. It is also available in the Switched on Schoolhouse format.

| *Course:* Home/auto maintenance | *Grades:* 9–12 | *Prerequisite:* None |

MAIN TEXT OR MATERIAL: Anything the parent finds useful.
DESCRIPTION: A practical course where the student works with his mother or father in routine home and car maintenance. Grant credits based on time spent.

Computer Skills Courses

Computers may seem beyond our capability as parents, but they never seem to intimidate children. The best way to learn to use a computer is to use a computer.

Although a computer is a wonderful technological help, use caution, particularly with unrestricted and unsupervised use of the Internet, chat rooms, or blogging. Although many marvelous things exist on the Internet, so do new depths of depravity. Be wise and aware. Help your children guard their hearts and minds.

I am not recommending any particular courses for computer use. Here are just a few suggestions.

Always teach proper use of the keyboard first. By high school your teen already has been taught to use the keyboard properly or has developed his own hunt-and-peck style. Habits are hard to break. It would be to your student's advantage to learn the proper way to type. Mavis Beacon's course is just one of the programs available to teach this skill.

Once they can type properly, teach your students how to use the word-processing program on your computer and any other software frequently used on your home computer (games excluded!). Other possible resources for learning computer skills would be continuing education classes or classes for credit at the junior college and courses offered by computer stores.

If you do not have a computer, you may want to consider making the purchase. Word-processing skills will be vitally important for the college-bound student and for most students who enter the workforce instead of pursuing college.

Thinking and Study Skills, SAT Preparation, and Career Courses

Finally, let's consider the study of thinking skills, study skills, SAT preparation, and career exploration. We will look at each area briefly.

First on the list are materials for sharpening figural and verbal thinking skills. Logic materials from three popular publishers follow these general thinking skill recommendations. We all think, but most of us have not been formally trained to think logically!

Next are materials for developing good study skills. Success at the college level depends as much (or more!) on organizational skills and carefully cultivated study habits as it does on natural ability. Therefore, I have included two video courses for improving general study habits.

A few products for college entrance test preparation follow including the DVD math prep program from Chalk Dust. A thoughtful browse through almost any large bookstore will allow you to compare SAT/ACT prep books.

Finally, I will recommend materials for career exploration. The first suggestion, coming from a Christian perspective, is especially helpful for the Christian young person seeking God's will.

Course: Thinking skills	*Grades:* 10–12	*Prerequisite:* None

MAIN TEXTS OR MATERIAL: *Building Thinking Skills, Book 3: Figural, Building Thinking Skills, Book 3: Verbal,* Critical Thinking Press
TEACHER HELPS: Separate teacher's manual for each
DESCRIPTION: A course geared to developing verbal and nonverbal thinking skills to improve overall academic performance.

Course: Thinking skills/beginning logic	*Grades:* 10–12	*Prerequisite:* None

MAIN TEXTS OR MATERIAL: *The Fallacy Detective, The Thinking Toolbox,* Nathaniel and Hans Bluedorn, Trivium Pursuit

TEACHER HELPS: None, self-study

DESCRIPTION: The Bluedorn brothers have produced informal, fun introductions to logical thought. *The Fallacy Detective* identifies common errors in logic and propaganda techniques. *The Thinking Toolbox* teaches logic and critical thinking skills. Both books contain end of chapter exercises with answers at the end of the book. The books can be used alone, together, or to supplement a more thorough logic program.

Course: Logic I and II, material logic	*Grades:* 9–12	*Prerequisite:* None

MAIN TEXT OR MATERIAL: *Traditional Logic I & II, Material Logic*, Martin Cothran, Memoria Press
TEACHER HELPS: Answer key included
DESCRIPTION: I have reviewed a lot of materials on logic from my nonexpert perspective of a parent who feels totally incompetent to teach the subject. This program gives me hope! Mr. Cothran's writing style is easy to understand. His assignments for mastering the material are easy to follow. To further entice you, the courses are now available on DVD. *Material Logic: A Traditional Approach to Thinking Skills* can be used as a follow-up to *Traditional Logic* or as a stand-alone course. The two courses focus on different areas: traditional considers the process or *how* of reasoning while material considers the content, or *what* to think.

Course: Logic I	*Grades:* 8 and up	*Prerequisite:* None

MAIN TEXT OR MATERIAL: *Introductory Logic*, Douglas Wilson and James Nance, Canon Press
TEACHER HELPS: Tests and key, DVD set
DESCRIPTION: Among the skills taught in this introductory logic course are logical statements, syllogisms, and informal fallacies. The three-DVD course makes this usable for the homeschool parent unschooled in formal logic.

Course: Logic II	*Grades:* 8 and up	*Prerequisite:* None

MAIN TEXT OR MATERIAL: *Intermediate Logic*, Douglas Wilson and James Nance, Canon Press
TEACHER HELPS: Solution key, DVD set
DESCRIPTION: *Intermediate Logic* continues instruction with presentations on propositional logic, formal proofs, and truth trees. The three-DVD course makes this usable for the homeschool parent unschooled in formal logic.

Course: Study skills	*Grades:* 9–12	*Prerequisite:* None

MAIN TEXT OR MATERIAL: *How to be a Superstar Student*, The Teaching Company
TEACHER HELPS: None required
DESCRIPTION: This two-DVD set is a course on how to study with the goal of college success. Watching this course early in the student's high school years will give him four years to practice the techniques taught before beginning college. Tim McGee, the video instructor, is both a coach and an English teacher. This unusual combination results in a lively presentation style with many sports illustrations. This is a plus for male viewers but should not be a problem for unathletic viewers. See appendix A for address information.

Course: Study skills	*Grades:* 7–12	*Prerequisite:* None

MAIN TEXT OR MATERIAL: *Study Skills for Teens* DVD, Lisa Seibert, Bob Jones University Press
TEACHER HELPS: None required
DESCRIPTION: This 97-minute DVD covers listening tips, taking notes, how to read textbooks effectively, time management, and test-taking.

Course: SAT Preparation	*Grades:* 10–12	*Prerequisite:* None

MAIN TEXT OR MATERIAL: *SAT Math Review*, Chalk Dust Company
OPTIONAL TEXT: *The Official SAT Study Guide*, College Board

Teacher helps: None needed

Description: A series of five videos/DVDs brings the student through the algebra and geometry skills necessary for success on the SAT college entrance exam.

Course: SAT/ACT Preparation	Grades: 10–12	Prerequisite: None

Main text or material: Choose from: *The Real ACT Prep Guide*, ACT Publications, *Cracking the ACT*, The Princeton Review, *The Official SAT Study Guide*, College Board, *Cracking the SAT*, The Princeton Review, *SAT Premier Program*, 2008 Edition, Kaplan. *The SAT Writing Workbook*, Kaplan.

Teacher helps: None needed

Description: Choose from one of the test preparation books above to facilitate preparation for college entrance tests.

Course: College planning	Grades: 9–12	Prerequisite: None

Main text or material: *College Planner*, Switched on Schoolhouse, Alpha Omega

Teacher helps: None needed

Description: A one-semester computerized course that helps students with college planning, selection, and application.

Course: Career exploration	Grades: 9–12	Prerequisite: None

Main text or material: *Career Direct Guidance System* Software, Crown Financial Ministries

Teacher helps: Student-directed program

Description: This one-hour computerized test generates an approximately thirty-page report that analyzes the individual's personality, interests, skills, and values. Several audio messages provide career and educational direction. Two references, a PDF electronic book (*The Guide to College Majors and Career Choices*), and a softcover book (*The Pathfinder*), provide additional direction. This course is geared toward adults making career decisions and high-school students determining a college major. When finished, the adult or student should have a realistic picture for formulating future goals.

Course: Career exploration	Grades: 9–12	Prerequisite: None

Main text or material: *What Color Is Your Parachute?* Richard Nelson Bolles, Ten Speed Press

Teacher helps: None required

Description: *What Color Is Your Parachute?*, as its cover proclaims, is the best-selling job-hunting book in the world. While designed for an older audience, discussions on determining an appropriate direction for your skills and presenting yourself well in a resume and interview offer older students wise instruction for their future. A workbook explores personal interests and abilities and their transference to marketable job skills. Blending this information together provides insight into personally fulfilling occupations. Understanding career interests can help a student choose an appropriate college major. Because of its popularity you should be able to find *What Color Is Your Parachute?* at any major bookstore or your public library.

Evaluating Coursework Objectively

The Importance and Difficulty of Objectivity

One of the joys of life I have yet to experience is being a grandparent. My husband and I are looking forward to those days. Parents must be constantly vigilant to nurture the good and weed out the bad in their growing offspring. Grandparents, on the other hand, can delight in the flowering of their grandchildren, kindly overlooking the weeds. They don't have to be balanced or objective.

Homeschooling would be a pleasant job if we could take a similar perspective. Unfortunately we can't. High school students need to receive an *A* when they earn an *A* and a *D* when they earn a *D*. They need to recognize when they have done exceptional, average, or inferior work. Our students need us to be objective, not benevolent.

In all too short a time your student may be arriving on a college campus. Rather than being in a class of one, he may be joined by hundreds or even thousands of classmates. He needs some idea of how he will fare against all the competition. If you have done a good job of being objective, he will be learning a healthy appreciation for his strengths and an understanding of his weaknesses. He will be poised to make realistic decisions concerning college majors and future career directions. The more honestly he can assess his performance, the fewer startling disillusionments he will experience.

Being objective is hard for homeschool parents. We have not had a classroom of twenty or more age mates with whom to compare our student's performance. Our inexperience can lead to grading methods that are too stringent or, just as likely, too lenient.

Our student's transcript especially needs objectivity. Grades and college entrance test scores should complement each other. If there is a significant disparity between the two, with transcript grades high and test scores unimpressive, you may undermine the credibility of your homeschool program in the eyes of the admissions officer.

Before we get too hard on homeschoolers in particular, note that all students have to mentally adjust their placement in the academic pecking order when beginning college. Teachers grade differently. No absolute objective standard exists.

Grades, even when they appear to be straightforward, are still subjective. For example, consider how differently a student would score based on the following situations:

1. The student studies independently and takes quizzes and tests with no specific help from the teacher.
2. The teacher goes over everything to be covered on the test.
3. The textbook is for remedial students.
4. The textbook is college preparatory.

Is the subjectivity described above a problem? Not necessarily. Teachers are individuals trying to achieve different goals and objectives. The teacher of a high-school honors class may challenge and stretch the student academically. The teacher of a less difficult course may do some hand-holding, concerned primarily that the material be grasped and retained. Your student will experience similar grading variations in college. Prepare him.

Let your homeschool student experience a no-nonsense, no-mercy approach to grading. He may have that type of professor in college. He may also have some teachers who grade on a curve. Two of my students have found curving an unwelcome part of college grading that makes the final grade difficult to predict. For one student, scholarship money hung in the balance, making it particularly stressful. Although mercy is good, it's best if it shows itself in a careful teaching style and thorough syllabus rather than in a midnight-hour adjustment of everyone's grade.

Let your student know that curving is sometimes used, but don't use it in computing your homeschool grades. A teacher uses a curve when an entire group of students has not met teacher expectations. It is not equitable for a homeschool group of one. However, I do think it is appropriate to throw out the lowest test or quiz score. Everyone has some academically bad days. This level of mercy is reasonable. It can also be written into your course contracts (discussed shortly) so that students know grading standards in advance and can breathe easier when bad academic days hit.

Besides preparing your student for different grading styles, you might vary your expectations for another reason. Because every course is not equally important to your teen's future, it is not necessary to make every course equally rigorous academically. Set the difficulty of a course according to the purpose of the course. If a course is college preparatory and represents a future career field, the difficulty of your textbook and amount of work required should be challenging. If a course is required but has no significant role in future career plans, use less challenging materials to teach the course.

RECORD KEEPING

It is easy to become overwhelmed with the bookkeeping aspects of homeschooling. To preserve your sanity, remember that any methodology you choose for creating and recording credits or grades needs to serve your needs, not enslave you. An overly elaborate record-keeping or grading system can be time consuming. Time spent in record keeping is time not spent in teaching, interacting with your student, or having a life outside of homeschooling. If you are teaching more than one student (and most of us are), you may not complete complicated crediting and grading systems and feel like a failure.

I felt particularly freed when I observed the grading plans of my older children's college professors. A significant variation existed in the way a student's course work was assessed. Some professors based their final grade on numerous intermediate grades, some on only a few. It left me with a comfortable feeling that as long as the student's work is fairly evaluated, simpler methods are fine. Just be sure to set some expectations, however simple, in advance. Expectations that change too readily without good reason do not prepare a student for the inflexible guidelines that sometimes exist in college-level courses.

To ease the burden of record keeping, share it with your student. After all, since the records are for his future benefit, he needs to take some ownership of the process. Working from goals you have created together, you can give the task of daily record keeping to the student while providing oversight as needed.

Course Contracts

I believe the easiest method for setting course expectations and arriving at objective grades is to set up a contract. A course contract, in many ways, is a precursor to the syllabus a college professor will hand your student on the first day of class. Using contracts in your high-school homeschooling will be advantageous for your student's college preparation.

The next section of this book gives you some suggestions for contracting. Should you find my crediting and grading suggestions too complicated or my forms too unwieldy for your situation, simplify them to meet your needs. I have rarely found that the forms designed by others satisfy the needs of my family and homeschool. Use my ideas and forms as a springboard to create the right guidelines for your situation. If my forms work for you, they are available for your use in appendix B and on the CD-ROM in the back cover of this book.

Course Contracts: Tools for Objectivity

When we design our high-school program, we have the interesting task before us of how to be objective in our crediting and grading while maintaining the flexibility and freedom home education provides. One way is to match our crediting and grading procedures to the approach we use for each course. As discussed in a previous chapter, you can approach coursework in three basic ways: through textbooks, independent reading, or projects. Let's look at some logical ways to credit and grade each type.

TEXTBOOK COURSES

Textbook courses are the easiest for determining credits and grades. They have a well-defined body of knowledge. Their tests and quizzes determine if the material has been mastered.

Crediting Textbook Courses

A student using a textbook that covers a subject in one school year, such as algebra I, would receive one academic credit upon successful completion. A student completing a textbook for a one-semester course, such as economics, would receive ½ credit. Teacher's manuals will sometimes offer scheduling plans for using their books in either a one-semester or full-year course.

Grading Textbook Courses

Grades can be based on completed reading assignments, discussion of material, quiz or test scores, and assigned papers or projects. Field trips, field trip reports, videos (for example, a video on Mount St. Helens during geology), video discussions, and other worthy learning experiences can also be evaluated. You decide what percentage of the final grade to give to each item. One possibility would be:

COURSE REQUIREMENTS	PERCENTAGE OF GRADE	POSSIBLE POINTS
Reading assignments	30%	30
Discussion	10%	10
Field trip report	10%	10
Tests	50%	50
Total	100%	100

Textbook Contracts

As discussed earlier, an easy format for recording your course content and crediting and grading criteria is a contract. The contract terms can be a joint decision reached by the teacher and the student.

The contracts I have created have two pages. The first page records the agreed upon goals and the crediting and grading criteria. Make it as clear and uncomplicated as possible. If desired, it can include the projected date for each goal to be reached. The second page records the accomplished goals. These include the final course description, the individual grades, and the final credits and cumulative grade. This second contract page will help you compile your transcript and course descriptions (if needed) for college entrance. Filling out the second page as soon as the course is completed will make it easy to record information accurately. Save yourself the frustration of working backward, trying to remember what you did two years ago, for the college admissions process. Keep your records as current as possible. Too many of us know this from personal experience!

If you have not kept careful records and your high-school program is midstream, you can still correct the situation. Set your course goals and grading criteria now even though it is harder to be objective when you already know your student's performance. Create a course description. Pull out past assignments, quizzes, and tests. Record all your information on page 2 of the contract form, calculate grades, and sleep better tonight.

The following sample contract is for a physical science course using the paces and videos from the School of Tomorrow. Although the first page contains a list of all the pace titles with their completion dates, a few simple statements, such as, "Read all twelve paces and watch their videos," and, "Complete all written work and lab reports," still contain all the essential information.

The second contract page may look intimidating, but it is easy to compile. A course description can be derived by noting section and chapter headings in the book being studied or by referring to the publisher's scope and sequence* or catalog descriptions. This particular sample was constructed using the titles of the different paces and lab report sheets. In addition to the course description, the second page also gives the completed crediting and grading data to be used to calculate the final grade. Plug the percentage grades earned, along with the points you assigned to the activity, into the chart at the bottom of the page. Do the simple calculations, and you'll have the final grade.

The course on the sample contract is for a lab science. You will probably notice that the lab work was limited to viewing lab demonstrations on a video and filling in reports. It would have been better to include actual hands-on lab work, but for the "science-phobes" at our house, viewing lab work marked success. See suggestions in the science course listing for better ways to handle labs.

When you are finished, store your contract in a large three-ring binder with other course contracts. A two-inch ring is probably a good choice. My three-inch binders can be unwieldy. See the following box for ideas on what else to store in this binder.

---

*A scope and sequence is an overview of a textbook. It lists the content contained in each book (the scope) and the order in which this content is presented (the sequence). A full-line textbook publisher will often have a scope-and-sequence booklet where all their textbooks are listed and described.

A Note on Examples

The various examples you will find throughout this book do not represent the academic work of only one student. Therefore, the contract examples will not necessarily match the data on the GPA or the transcript.

In addition, use the samples as an example of an assessment tool in use, not as an example of the best or only way to structure a course's content. The best course is always the one designed for the needs of the individual student.

What types of school records should I maintain?

First and foremost, be aware of your state's record-keeping requirements. Abide by them. If your state does not have any record-keeping requirements, you will have more flexibility but will still need well-maintained records for college entrance. Plan on keeping any of the paperwork used to determine the student's grade. Among other possibilities this means keeping course contracts, timed reading records, tests, quizzes, and papers. Projects can be photographed to provide a record. Don't make it more complicated than necessary.

The binder recommended for storing contracts can be an excellent place to store other high school information: samples of your student's work, lists of books read, photograph pages full of special activity and project pictures (your child posing with his athletic trophy, 4-H project, Eagle Scout award, etc.), vinyl sleeves containing recital and play programs, state fair ribbons, special achievement or participation certificates, and any other items that highlight your student's unique personality and achievements. When college admissions time comes, the walk down memory lane will be much easier.

For the sentimentalist in the crowd, you are certainly welcome to keep every piece of schoolwork your student has ever scribbled. However, since this cannot all be lugged into a college admissions office, maintain some abbreviated presentation of your student's high school work should you need to produce it.

For planning daily assignments, *The Homeschooler's High School Journal* by FergNus is a product designed specifically for the homeschool market. It has sheets for recording attendance, grades, daily assignments, and other record-keeping sheets helpful to the homeschooler. The daily assignment sheets even include a method for keeping track of timed course work. Many homeschool suppliers carry this product.

As another alternative you can construct a personalized assignment sheet using the tables function of your word-processing system. Better yet, have your student create it as part of a computer science credit. Personalized assignment sheets help you avoid the daily repetition of filling in course titles and other repetitive information.

PRELIMINARY COURSE CONTRACT

NAME: Student		SCHOOL YEAR: 10th, 2003–2004
COURSE: Physical Science		CREDIT ASSIGNED: 1.0

REQUIREMENTS:	DATE COMPLETED
Text: School of Tomorrow paces & videos	
Completion of all twelve paces is required.	
1. Foundations of Physical Science	09/15/2003
2. Composition of Matter	10/06/2003
3. Gas Laws	10/27/2003
4. Chemical Structure of Matter	11/17/2003
5. Metal and Metalloids	12/08/2003
6. Water and Nonmetals	01/12/2004
7. Organic Chemistry	02/02/2004
8. Motion, Gravity, and Energy	02/23/2004
9. Sound	03/16/2004
10. Lights, Optics, and the Electromagnetic Spectrum	04/06/2004
11. Electricity	04/27/2004
12. Modern Physics	05/18/2004

GRADING METHOD	
20 points: video and reading completed	
20 points: completed written work	
50 points: test scores	
10 points: viewed and completed lab reports	
(100 points total)	

COMPLETED COURSE CONTRACT

NAME: Student	SCHOOL YEAR: 10th, 2003–2004
COURSE: Physical Science	CREDIT EARNED: 1.0
PARENT'S SIGNATURE:	GRADE: 86% or B

COURSE DESCRIPTION

Text: *Physical Science* paces, School of Tomorrow

Chemistry topics include: definitions and limitations of science, scientific measurement, the composition of matter, gases and gas laws, the chemical structure of matter, metals and metalloids, elements and properties of water, nonmetals, and organic chemistry.

Chemistry lab topics include: electrolysis of water, distillation of water, Charles' Law, double replacement reactions, acid-based titration, reaction of sodium and chloride, reaction of copper and nitric acid, properties of hydrogen, properties of oxygen, properties of water, and dehydration

Physics topics include: laws of motion and gravity, energy, sound, light, optics, the electromagnetic spectrum, electricity, electronics, and nuclear physics

Physics lab topics include: first and second laws of motion, conservation of momentum and the third law of motion, wave motion: reflection, refraction, diffraction, constructive and destructive interference, electrostatics and the Van de Graaff generator, electrochemical cells, nuclear radiation: half-life

Labs were viewed on video, and a follow-up lab report was required.

CREDITING AND GRADING DATA

Credits earned for course completion: 1

Percentages Earned

100%—Completed all videos and reading

75%—Completed 3/4 of written work (Some math problems were skipped.)

87%—Test scores: 100, 92, 82, 89, 76, 93, 93, 82, 85, 88, 78, 87 = 1045 (1045 divided by 12 tests = 87%)

80%—Viewed and completed lab reports (didn't attempt some application questions)

GRADE

Criteria	% earned (in decimal form)	x	possible points	% of final grade
Videos/Reading	1.00	x	20	20.00
Written Work	0.75	x	20	15.00
Tests	0.87	x	50	43.50
Labs/Reports	0.80	x	10	8.00
			Total %	86.50 or 87%
			Final Grade	86% or B

INDEPENDENT READING COURSES

When using independent reading courses, there are no quizzes or tests to aid in assessment. How do you credit and grade a course like this?

Crediting Independent Reading Courses

Credit can be issued for an independent reading course based on the amount of time spent reading and on any follow-up activities. How do you decide how much time is enough?

In the school system one credit hour is earned in 120 to 150 classroom hours (based on 40–50 minute classes daily for 36 weeks), plus time spent in homework.

If your homeschool is run smoothly with the majority of class time spent on task, you will undoubtedly get more accomplished in less time. A great deal of time in a formal school setting is spent on classroom management: passing out papers, handling discipline problems, and coordinating the efforts of 20–30 students.

So how much time should the student spend? I do not have a definitive answer, but I do know what should be true. First, any state requirements, should they exist, must be met or exceeded. If no requirements exist, your decision should be made thoughtfully with an eye toward preparing your student for a successful future. I do not believe we should base our standards on what is minimally allowable but on what will best help each student achieve his greatest potential. Homeschoolers as a group need to strive for excellence if we desire our students to be a positive force in tomorrow's society.

The following is a chart based on different amounts of time representing one credit hour. Three times—180, 144, and 135 hours—are given so the time required to earn a credit hour can be adapted to different course difficulties. The time requirement for one-half credit is also given. Class time is based on sixty, forty-five, or thirty minutes since all break into fifteen-minute increments. This is much easier to work with than a forty- or fifty-minute time period. The shaded boxes illustrate the schedule of a half-credit course stretched out over a full school year.

The Class Schedule column suggests an easy weekly way to fulfill the time requirements for four- and five-day class schedules. Families that do core classes four times weekly, saving the fifth day for co-ops or special projects, will find the four-day class schedule helpful.

The chart is based on a thirty-six-week school year (except the last row), but with a little calculation you can adjust it to your particular school year. Take a few minutes to study the chart, and then read on for a few pointers.

COURSE CREDIT TIME CHART				
1 CREDIT		**½ CREDIT**		
HOURS	WEEKS	HOURS	WEEKS	CLASS SCHEDULE
180	36	90	18	5x weekly for 1 hour
		90	36	5x weekly for 30 min.
144	36	72	18	4x weekly for 1 hour
		72	36	4x weekly for 30 min.
135	36	68	18	5x weekly for 45 min.
		68	34	4x weekly for 30 min.

On the surface the 180 hours seems ambitious; however, it represents the total hours spent in a subject which is studied daily for one hour, not a particularly difficult attainment in a homeschool setting. Be reassured that when you occasionally miss days, you can still produce a quality college preparatory course. Should your student take all his courses by timed credit, which is highly unlikely, he would be spending approximately six hours daily on his school work following this recommendation. That is reasonable for a rigorous college-preparatory program.

The 144-hour goal requires slightly less time than is spent in a fifty-minute class that meets daily over the course of a year. The 135-hour recommendation may come the closest to a classroom schedule of forty-five-minute classes meeting daily. Both suggestions are also reasonable goals. The greater efficiency of homeschooling should mean more is still accomplished.

It should be pointed out that some knowledgeable homeschoolers feel that 120 hours (40 minutes daily for 36 weeks) is fine for the motivated homeschool student. The previous chart is not a rejection of that viewpoint but rather a preference for a system based on fifteen-minute increments that I find easier to use on a day-to-day basis.

Once you've decided what your time requirement will be, you will need to determine a way of seeing that the guidelines are met. Three suggestions follow.

1. The most ambitious would be for your student to keep a time record. An example of a time record in process follows this section. Blank forms are included in appendix B and on the CD-ROM. The three record sheets go up to 180 hours. Just stop at the number of hours you have predetermined. (*The Homeschoolers High School Journal* by Ferg N'Us can also accommodate timed course work.)

When combining two subjects, such as history and literature, into one interdisciplinary approach, keep two time sheets. Use one sheet for recording the history reading and one for literature. This allows the courses to flow together but maintains separate records for the transcript. Later, the course description can explain how the two courses intertwined. If you are not planning to separate the courses on the transcript, use a single time sheet for both.

2. An easier way to time an independent reading course is to have a reading time established for each day. I used this method with my third child who is an avid reader. Using a timer, he allotted one-hour reading periods for each of three subjects: history, literature, and a combined government-economics course. He chose his reading from a reading list we constructed together at the beginning of the school year. This reading time combined with discussions, book reports, or an occasional longer paper provided both freedom and accountability.

3. What if your child does not enjoy reading and tends to dawdle through reading assignments? It is helpful in this situation to have some idea of his reading speed. This information will help you encourage a timely completion of books without creating a stressful situation. To derive reading speed, time how long it takes the student to read the first ten pages of the book he is beginning. This will give you a fairly accurate average time for one page. It is then an easy mathematical exercise to determine how long it should take your student to read the book. Even this is not foolproof; the student can certainly choose to dawdle over the first ten pages! However, over time and several books it should be easier to know when you have set reasonable expectations.

What is a Carnegie Unit?

A Carnegie Unit is a measure of classroom or instructional time, with one unit equaling 120 hours and earning one credit hour. Broken down into 50-minute class increments, five days a week, it equals approximately 29 weeks of schoolwork. With many high schools operating on a 34- to 36-week calendar, today's high-school student may spend significantly more time in the classroom. In fact, a 36-week school year of 50-minute classes, five days a week could technically clock 150 hours. Practically, however, due to a myriad of reasons ranging from classroom management issues to illness, 150 hours of uninterrupted learning has little chance of occurring. For this reason some homeschoolers are comfortable using the Carnegie Unit as their measure for awarding high-school credit. The times suggested in the Course Credit Time Chart intentionally exceed the Carnegie Unit recommendations. This allows for more in-depth study for the motivated learner or a less intense pace for the laid-back learner. It also provides a little "dawdle time" when needed.

TIME RECORD

NAME: Student		SCHOOL YEAR: 10th		COURSE: American History	
Hours	**15 min. div.**	**Book or Activity**	**Hours**	**15 min. div.**	**Book or Activity**
1.00	☒ ☒ ☒ ☒	History of Amer. People	31.00	☒ ☒ ☒ ☒	Self-edit summary
2.00	☒ ☒ ☒ ☒	by Paul Johnson	32.00	☒ ☒ ☒ ☒	Edit clean copy w/ Mom
3.00	☒ ☒ ☒ ☒	History of Amer. People	33.00	☒ ☒ ☒ ☒	Summary—final draft
4.00	☒ ☒ ☒ ☒	History of Amer. People	34.00	☒ ☒ ☒ ☒	History of Amer. People
5.00	☒ ☒ ☒ ☒	History of Amer. People	35.00	☒ ☒ ☒ ☒	History of Amer. People
6.00	☒ ☒ ☒ ☒	History of Amer. People	36.00	☒ ☒ ☒ ☒	History of Amer. People
7.00	☒ ☒ ☒ ☒	History of Amer. People	37.00	☒ ☒ ☒ ☒	Democracy in America
8.00	☒ ☒ ☒ ☒	History of Amer. People	38.00	☒ ☒ ☒ ☒	(excerpts) de Tocqueville
9.00	☒ ☒ ☒ ☒	History of Amer. People	39.00	☒ ☒ ☒ ☒	Democracy in America
10.00	☒ ☒ ☒ ☒	History of Amer. People	40.00	☒ ☒ ☒ ☒	Democracy in America
11.00	☒ ☒ ☒ ☒	Federalist Papers	41.00	☒ ☒ ☒ ☒	Democracy in America
12.00	☒ ☒ ☒ ☒	Federalist Papers	42.00	☐ ☐ ☐ ☐	
13.00	☒ ☒ ☒ ☒	Federalist Papers	43.00	☐ ☐ ☐ ☐	
14.00	☒ ☒ ☒ ☒	Federalist Papers	44.00	☐ ☐ ☐ ☐	
15.00	☒ ☒ ☒ ☒	Federalist Papers	45.00	☐ ☐ ☐ ☐	
16.00	☒ ☒ ☒ ☒	Federalist Papers	46.00	☐ ☐ ☐ ☐	
17.00	☒ ☒ ☒ ☒	Book summary—outline	47.00	☐ ☐ ☐ ☐	
18.00	☒ ☒ ☒ ☒	Book summary—first draft	48.00	☐ ☐ ☐ ☐	
19.00	☒ ☒ ☒ ☒	Finish first draft	49.00	☐ ☐ ☐ ☐	
20.00	☒ ☒ ☒ ☒	Self-edit summary	50.00	☐ ☐ ☐ ☐	
21.00	☒ ☒ ☒ ☒	Edit clean copy w/ Mom	51.00	☐ ☐ ☐ ☐	
22.00	☒ ☒ ☒ ☒	Summary—final draft	52.00	☐ ☐ ☐ ☐	
23.00	☒ ☒ ☒ ☒	Anti-federalist Papers	53.00	☐ ☐ ☐ ☐	
24.00	☒ ☒ ☒ ☒	Anti-federalist Papers	54.00	☐ ☐ ☐ ☐	
25.00	☒ ☒ ☒ ☒	Anti-federalist Papers	55.00	☐ ☐ ☐ ☐	
26.00	☒ ☒ ☒ ☒	Anti-federalist Papers	56.00	☐ ☐ ☐ ☐	
27.00	☒ ☒ ☒ ☒	Anti-federalist Papers	57.00	☐ ☐ ☐ ☐	
28.00	☒ ☒ ☒ ☒	Book summary—outline	58.00	☐ ☐ ☐ ☐	
29.00	☒ ☒ ☒ ☒	Book summary—first draft	59.00	☐ ☐ ☐ ☐	
30.00	☒ ☒ ☒ ☒	Finish first draft	60.00	☐ ☐ ☐ ☐	

Notes:

Grading Independent Reading Courses

It is not difficult to grade an independent reading course. Below are several suggestions for objective grading.

1. The amount of time spent reading can determine the course's grade. The more hours, the higher the grade. If the course is important for college or career plans, require more hours.

2. Use narration. This popular homeschool technique was developed by a nineteenth-century educator named Charlotte Mason. Have the student narrate (or tell back) to the parent what he has read. Ask questions that require the student to interact with the material and use higher-level thinking skills. *Why does he think this happened? How does this compare to something else? What is his opinion about the information? Does it measure up to God's standards?* Discussions of this nature help develop the ability to formulate thoughts into a logical oral presentation. This may be hard to grade objectively, but you'll certainly be aware of how much your teen is learning. A possible narration grading scale, based on *Bloom's Taxonomy of Educational Objectives* follows.

GRADE LEVEL OF SKILL IN NARRATION	
90–100 (A)	Can do all of below plus relate own ideas to the information by developing alternative or expanded ideas and defending or criticizing the information for its logic, morality, fallacies, consistencies or inconsistencies, etc.
80–89 (B)	Can do skills below and also analyze the reading for assumptions and points of view, find the main idea, identify persuasive techniques.
70–79 (C)	Understands and can relate the factual content of what he has read. Can also summarize information, make predictions, and judge effects.
60–69 (D)	Doesn't recall material or answer factual questions accurately.
50–59 (F)	Doesn't know what was read or answers questions grudgingly.

3. Write book reports. See page 88 for a possible format.

4. Write summarizations of the most important books. Each day the student can write a paragraph summarizing the main points of his reading. We found a spiral notebook helpful for this since it kept all the summaries together. When the book is completed, these daily summaries can form the basis for a final book review or analysis. A parent can judge by the content of these summaries whether the student is absorbing the material he is reading. All the summarization and composition practice will benefit him greatly when he reaches college. *Format Writing* (section on "The Précis" and "Paragraph Condensation") or *Wordsmith Craftsman* (section on writing a summary) are both helpful in teaching these skills. *Format Writing* also gives help in grading these papers objectively.

5. Do follow-up research or opinion papers on interesting topics discovered while reading.

6. Field trips or videos related to the reading can provide high interest additions to your course of study. These can be evaluated, if desired, by discussion or reports. (Or skip the grading and just enjoy them!)

Independent Reading Contracts

As with textbook approaches, contracts will also work well for independent reading classes. Contracts provide an easy means of keeping track of additional requirements such as book reports, research papers, videos or movies, and any field trips. A list of all books read should also be kept. Books can be listed on the contract or a separate sheet if the list is too long. A book list form for your use is included in appendix B and on the CD-ROM.

Although this may seem like a lot to keep up with, it does not have to be intimidating. The record keeping responsibilities can be shared between student and teacher and completed at different stages of the course.

Complete the preliminary contract before the course begins. It is the result of a joint decision between you and your student.

The separate book list and time records, if used, are filled out by the student while the course is in progress. We have sometimes used our proposed reading list, highlighting the books actually read and adding any new titles we discovered. We use this list until we are ready to record it in final form.

The completed course contract pulls all the information together into a neat format and includes a course description for future college records. This can be compiled by either the teacher or the student. Then file it in the binder along with any time records, book lists, and book reports or papers.

Two sample contracts for reading courses follow. The first is a possible church history course where reading is the main focus. It includes an oral report and composition requirements.

The second contract is based on an interdisciplinary approach to history and literature which I used with my third teenager. It began with world history and slowly progressed into American. It's an ambitious program designed for a student who enjoys the subjects.

Consider the contract course a "before and after" situation. The first page describes where you plan to go, along with your crediting and grading criteria. The second page tells where you actually went, what credits and grades were earned, and the final grade derived from that data.

PRELIMINARY COURSE CONTRACT

NAME: Student	SCHOOL YEAR: 10th, 2004–2005
COURSE: Church History	CREDIT ASSIGNED: 0.5

REQUIREMENTS:	DATE COMPLETED
1. Read *Sketches from Church History*.	02/05
2. Upon completing each chapter, in a spiral notebook write one paragraph summarizing the most important point or points of the chapter.	02/05
3. Upon completing the book, write a three- to five-page summarization of the book. Begin with an outline based on your paragraph summaries. Turn in both your outline and your paper.	03/05
4. Read one biography on a historical person mentioned in this book.	10/04
5. Write a two-page book report on this biography. Follow form provided.	10/04
6. Read the *Didache of the Apostles*.	09/04
7. Read pages 238–73 in Foxe's *Book of Martyrs* on the life and martyrdom of Ridley, Latimer, and Cranmer. Be prepared to relate story and discuss.	12/04
8. Spend three hours reading additional excerpts (your choice) from Foxe's *Book of Martyrs*.	12/04
9. Read *The Westminster Confession of Faith* and *Shorter Catechism*.	04/05
10. Research the history of our denomination. Present a three-minute oral report. Must have note cards for oral presentation.	04/05
11. Choose among the following: Augustine's *Confessions*, Luther's *Bondage of the Will*, Calvin's *Golden Booklet*, portions of Calvin's *Institutes*, *The Protestant Reformation: Major Documents*, or other books OKed by me. Read until completing time requirements of sixty hours.	05/05

GRADING METHOD	
50 points: finishing reading assignments	
25 points: book summary & book report	
25 points: oral presentation on history of our denomination	

COMPLETED COURSE CONTRACT

NAME: Student	SCHOOL YEAR: 10th, 2004–2005
COURSE: Church History	CREDIT EARNED: 0.5
PARENT'S SIGNATURE:	GRADE: 93%

COURSE DESCRIPTION

This course provides a historical overview of the Christian church. The course includes reading, composition, and oral report requirements.

Sketches from Church History (S. M. Houghton, Banner of Truth) served as the main text.

Additional reading resources included: *Didache of the Apostles, Westminster Confession of Faith* and *Shorter Catechism,* Augustine's *Confessions,* Martin Luther's *Bondage of the Will,* Calvin's *Golden Booklet,* excerpts from Foxe's *Book of Martyrs,* Calvin's *Institutes of the Christian Religion* and *The Protestant Reformation: Major Documents.*

The biography on Martin Luther, *Here I Stand,* by Roger Bainton was also read.

In addition to reading the main text, sixty hours of independent reading was required.

Composition requirements included a three- to five-page summary of the main text and a book report on the biography.

In addition to discussions over the readings, a three-minute oral report on the history of our denomination was prepared and delivered using note cards.

GRADING AND CREDITING DATA

Credit earned for course completion: 0.5

Percentages earned:

 93%—reading assignments: completed 55 hours (55 divided by 60 = 93%)

100%—book summary and book report (awarded 100% of points)

 85%—preparation and presentation of oral report (B quality, awarded 85% of points)

GRADE

Criteria	% earned	x	possible points	% of final grade
	(in decimal form)			
Reading	0.93	x	50.00	46.50
Written Work	1.00	x	25.00	25.00
Oral Report	0.85	x	25.00	21.25
			Total	92.75 or 93
Credit Earned	½		Final Grade	93% (or A)

PRELIMINARY COURSE CONTRACT		
NAME: Student SCHOOL YEAR: 11th, 2005–2006		
COURSE: Interdisciplinary Study CREDIT ASSIGNED: 2.00		
REQUIREMENTS:		DATE COMPLETED
Note: This is an interdisciplinary approach to two courses, which will appear		
on the transcript as:		
Early American History or American History: Colonial–Reconstruction		
English III		
Reading and Composition Time Requirements:		
100%—360 hours (two hours daily for two semesters)		
89%—270 hours (90 minutes daily for two semesters)		
79%—225 hours (75 minutes daily for two semesters)		
Basic Texts and Materials to Be Completed, with Requirements		
1. *American Literature*, BJUP, through page 335		
one quiz for each subsection, seven in all		04/06
2. *The Basic History of the United States, Volumes 1–3*, by Clarence Carson		05/06
3. *America: The First 350 Years*, audio course by Steve Wilkins		05/06
Additional Reading Requirements		
Choose titles from master book list, including at least one from each		
list division.		05/06
Composition Requirements		
A book report for each book read from the book list—two to three pages long		05/06
Five paragraph essays :		
One cause-and-effect essay (see Format Writing)		09/05
One comparison essay (see Format Writing)		11/05
One opinion paper—three to five pages		04/06
One research paper—three to five pages		05/06
GRADING METHOD		
50 points: Reading and listening requirements completed		
40 points: Quality of compositions		
10 points: Quizzes		

COMPLETED COURSE CONTRACT

NAME: Student	SCHOOL YEAR: 11th, 2005–2006
COURSE: Interdisciplinary Study	CREDIT EARNED: 2.0
PARENT'S SIGNATURE:	GRADE : 97% or A

COURSE DESCRIPTION

This interdisciplinary course covers the courses recorded on the transcript as:

Early American History and English III.

Main materials which formed the framework of the course were the first three volumes

of *A Basic History of the United States* by Clarence Carson;

the tape series, *America: The First 350 Years* by Steve Wilkins; and

American Literature by Bob Jones University Press.

To the Best of My Ability by James M. McPherson served as a reference on the lives

of the presidents.

Additional titles read are listed on the accompanying reading list. These titles included

eyewitness accounts, biographies, and historical fiction.

Composition requirements included a book report for each book, a five-paragraph

comparison of the attitudes of the settlers at Jamestown and Plymouth, a five-paragraph

cause and effect essay on the role of Presbyterian ministers during the Revolutionary War

and the British response (drawn from notes taken while listening to the tape series),

a five-page opinion paper on the factors leading to the Civil War, and a five-page research

paper comparing the views of Booker T. Washington and Frederick Douglass.

GRADING AND CREDITING DATA

Credit earned for course completion: 2.00

Percentages earned:

100%—360 hours of reading time

94%—Composition scores: book reports (90%), 5 paragraph essays (98%),

      opinion paper (92%), and comparison paper (96%).

      (90 + 98 + 92 + 96 divided by 4 = 94%)

90%—Quizzes: 100, 100, 90, 80, 100, 90, 70 (630 divided by 7 = 90%)

GRADE

Criteria	% earned	x	possible points	% of final grade
	(in decimal form)			
Reading/tapes	1.00	x	50.00	50.00
Written Work	0.94	x	40.00	37.60
Quizzes	0.90	x	10.00	9.00
			Total %	96.6 or 97
Credit Earned	2		Final Grade	97% (or A)

READING LIST

TITLE	AUTHOR
Of Plymouth Plantation	William Bradford
The Mary Rowlandson Story: Captured by Indians	Mary Rowlandson
The Scarlet Letter	Nathaniel Hawthorne
The Young Patriot	Jim Murphy
The Journals of Lewis and Clark	edited by Frank Bergon
Abraham Lincoln's World	Genevieve Foster
Uncle Tom's Cabin	Harriet Beecher Stowe
The Slave Dancer	Paula Fox
The Red Badge of Courage	Stephen Crane
The Killer Angels	Michael Shaara
excerpts from *The Illustrated Confederate Reader*	Rodd Gragg
The Boys' War	Jim Murphy
Call of Duty	Steve Wilkins
My Folks Don't Want Me to Talk about Slavery	edited by Belinda Hurmence
Eneas Africanus	Harry Stillwell Edwards
Narrative of the Life of Frederick Douglass	Frederick Douglass
Up from Slavery	Booker T. Washington

PROJECT COURSES

Some courses are more hands-on or project oriented. Numerous examples include practical life-skill courses such as home economics or auto mechanics, technical or business skill courses such as learning to operate a word-processing program, and physical education courses such as participating on a swim team or a church softball league.

Some courses mix reading, skill development, and application of these skills through community service. For example, a child-care section of a home-economics course could include reading assignments, CPR and basic first-aid training, and volunteering in the church nursery.

Evaluating and Crediting Project Courses

As with an independent reading course, the most accurate way to credit a project-based course is by keeping time records. Refer back to "Crediting Independent Reading Courses" (page 184) for the discussion on determining how much time is appropriate.

It is easy to feel overwhelmed with this type of record keeping. Consider ways to simplify the task. A few suggestions follow:

1. If the project course is based on familiar skills, you may feel that you can estimate the time needed to complete the requirements. Thus, time records are unnecessary. Most homeschooling mothers would be able to estimate the time needed for various skills in a home-economics course.

2. Another option would be reserving set blocks of time for project coursework. Then it is easy to determine time spent to justify the credit you are issuing. If you follow your schedule closely, your student should spend enough time on task.

3. You can easily estimate lessons outside the home and regular hours of community service without keeping daily time records.

Grading Project Courses

There's nothing complicated here. Determine goals and point values with your student. The percentage system used with textbook and independent reading also works well when setting criteria for project courses.

Because high student interest often drives project courses, little parental involvement may be required. However, parental involvement beginning with the planning stage can still be helpful. This parent-student interaction can result in a more balanced course. Instead of the student following interests alone, a parent may suggest that he learn more varied skills. For example, a preplanned home-economics course may mean learning to cook foods in all major food groups instead of a wide variety of desserts.

Setting balanced goals legitimizes your student's efforts in your eyes and his. It also means you'll be able to produce a course description for the college application process if needed.

Project Contracts

As with textbook and independent reading courses, the contract can provide a logical assessment tool for a hands-on course. It establishes the activities. It records the amount of progress you are expecting in skill development. It sets the standards by which you will evaluate these skills in advance. It also moves what could be highly subjective into the realm of objectivity.

A sample contract for a garment construction course follows. (This would be part of a larger home-economics course.) Notice that the grading is based on the activities and their final quality. It also includes some incentive for character building.

PRELIMINARY COURSE CONTRACT	
NAME: Student SCHOOL YEAR: 10th, 2004–2005	
COURSE: Garment Construction CREDIT ASSIGNED: 0.5	
REQUIREMENTS:	DATE COMPLETED
1. Watch video: *Fear of Sewing* by Sandra Betzina.	
2. Demonstrate:	
Threading the sewing machine.	
Operating the sewing machine safely.	
3. Projects:	
Sew buttons on dress using special video method.	
Alter a pair of slacks.	
4. Watch video: *Pattern Sizing and Alterations* by Sandra Betzina.	
5. Project:	
Choose a pattern and fabric to make a dress.	
Use information from the video to alter pattern properly before making dress.	
Follow the pattern directions.	
6. Share your knowledge with your younger sister by:	
Teaching her how to sew on buttons.	
Helping her make a drawstring bag on the sewing machine safely.	
GRADING METHOD	
50 points: completing all requirements	
25 points: quality of finished products	
25 points: creating a positive experience teaching your sister	

COMPLETED COURSE CONTRACT

NAME: Student	SCHOOL YEAR: 10th, 2004–2005
COURSE: Garment Construction	CREDIT EARNED: 0.5
PARENT'S SIGNATURE:	GRADE: 98% or A

COURSE DESCRIPTION

Requirements of this course included gaining skill in garment making by watching the instructional videos *Fear of Sewing* and *Pattern Sizing and Alterations* by Sandra Betzina.

The student demonstrated her growth in knowledge by:

Threading and operating the sewing machine safely.

Sewing buttons on using the special method presented in the video.

Altering a pair of slacks.

Choosing a pattern and fabric for a dress.

Altering the pattern using tips learned from the video.

Following the pattern directions.

In addition, the student shared her knowledge by teaching a younger child how to:

Sew on buttons using the video method.

Operate the sewing machine safely.

Make a drawstring bag.

GRADING AND CREDITING DATA

Credit earned for course completion: 0.5

Percentages earned:

100%—completed all requirements

 90%—quality of finished work

100%—teaching a younger child and creating a pleasant learning experience

GRADE

Criteria	% earned	x	possible points	% of final grade
	(in decimal form)			
completed requirements	1.00	x	50.00	50.00
quality of work	0.90	x	25.00	22.50
teaching child	1.00	x	25.00	25.00
			Total %	97.5 or 98
Credit Earned	0.5		Final Grade	98 (or A)

Why should we keep our standards of evaluation high?

1. Accurate evaluation gives your teen a realistic picture of how he will perform in college. An overly easy pattern of evaluation can set a student up for an unhappy surprise and potential failure in college.

2. When parents design a program for their teen with no external authority to verify the work, they must be conscientious about the quality of the work. There will always be homeschool critics; we don't want the criticism to be justified.

3. Society judges homeschooling as a whole by the individual homeschoolers they meet. Your teen's success or failure will effect how other homeschoolers are perceived.

4. Most importantly, as Christian homeschoolers we are not our own; we have been bought with a price. Everything we undertake should be done to the glory of God.

Are there times we should avoid crediting and grading?

There are two situations in which I believe it may be best to avoid crediting and grading.

The first is when a student develops an all-consuming interest in one area. Maybe it's playing the piano or scribbling stories in a notebook for hours on end. Perhaps it's an insatiable thirst for Jane Austen or Charles Dickens's novels. Maybe it shows itself in a constant upgrading and reconfiguring of the family computer or tinkering with anything mechanical.

Areas of high interest or creativity are often personal. Our desire to credit and grade should not interfere with the joy of creative expression. If coursework will be incomplete without including it, then keep grading criteria light and noninterfering. In lieu of listing it as coursework, it may be possible to appropriately include it somewhere else in college paperwork, such as in extracurricular activities, biographical information, or in an entrance essay. Schools like to know what motivates and draws out excellence in a student.

I would also recommend being extra careful when including life experiences as a part of your academic grades. Randomly drawing on experiences to plump a high-school course deprives the student of more directed college preparation he might have received. A good general rule is this: *only include life experiences when they truly contribute to the quality of the course.* If they don't, leave them out of your course considerations.

Documenting Your Student's Achievement: GPAs and Transcripts

LETTER VERSUS NUMERICAL GRADES

One of the decisions you will need to make when designing your high school program is whether to use letter or numerical (percentage) grades.

Percentage grades are the most objective and are easy to calculate on a test or quiz. If you set your criteria for independent reading or project courses on a point basis, you can also use numerical grades in these more subjective areas. All the contract examples given previously will result in a numerical or percentage-based grade.

If for some reason you decide to change to letter grades, it is a simple matter to convert. It is not as easy to work backward from a less precise letter grade to a precise numerical grade. If you choose to use letter grades, you will also have to decide whether to use just the letters (A, B, C, D) or gradate them into smaller units (A+, A, A-).

Either letter or numerical grades can be used on a transcript. Numerical grades are straightforward and don't require an admissions counselor to refer to constantly changing grading scales from one transcript to another. However, you may want to use the grading system most common in your area.

Both letter and numerical grades can be converted into a grade-point average. Whatever your decision, the chart below will help you change numerical grades into letter grades and vice versa and give you grade-point information. Please note that different grading scales exist; this is just one possibility.

Letter Grades with Number Grade Equivalent and Grade Points									
A			B			C			D/F
A +	A	A-	B +	B	B-	C +	C	C-	Failing
98–100	94–97	90–93	88–89	84–87	80–83	78–79	74–77	70–73	0–69
4.0			3.0			2.0			0.0

Should all courses receive a grade, or can physical education and other nonacademic courses receive a pass/fail designation?

First of all, it is possible to grade nonacademic courses. Set them up on a contract that results in a numerical grade. Just keep your grading criteria straightforward and simple. In our area all courses are graded (and included in the grade point average). Find out what is most commonly done in your state, and follow that advice.

I would not recommend using a pass/fail designation on an academic course. An admissions counselor may perceive this as sloppy record keeping or a means of hiding substandard work. It also skews the grade point average calculation. In addition, we help our students when they have a clear picture of how they have performed against objective criteria. With the national debate on the failures of our educational system continuing, there is an ongoing movement toward a greater accountability. This trend in itself could mark the eventual demise of a pass/fail option. For this reason I would recommend grading all courses.

However, as with all record-keeping matters, check to see how your public school routinely handles grading. If your state regularly uses pass/fail or satisfactory/unsatisfactory designations for nonacademic classes, this option is open to you.

CALCULATING A GRADE POINT AVERAGE

A grade point average (GPA) is usually included on a transcript. A GPA is an average of all the grades earned during high school converted most often to a four-point scale.

Calculating a GPA can be a complicated process. One complication is weighting courses. This involves giving bonus points for more difficult work, such as honors or advanced placement courses. Weighting can also involve lowering the points for remedial classes. In our area, weighted courses do not affect grades, credits, or the GPA. Their sole function is tied to class rank, which is of no help to homeschoolers. In other areas successful completion of an honors class will raise the grade by one point on a four-point scale. For example, if a student earns a B for an AP course, rather than getting the normal three grade points, he will receive four. Many systems of weighting grades exist because state laws or school district policies direct these decisions.

Should a homeschool parent weight a course? It's a tricky issue. A survey among homeschoolers would undoubtedly turn up different opinions. Over the years I am growing more cautious on the issue. To avoid questions about parental subjectivity, I would be cautious in weighting course work. Rather I would indicate challenging courses by their title. For example, if your student's biology course resulted in a successful score on an AP exam, then it can be designated as AP biology. If your student successfully passes a college algebra CLEP exam, then the advanced math course that prepared him can be designated as an honors class. Any successfully passed AP or CLEP exams should be noted on the transcript. If your student successfully passes a college level early enrollment course, note that on the transcript. The common factor in all of these examples is that a third party verified the achievement, whether an exam or college teacher.

If weighting is regularly practiced in your area and you decide to weight your student's advanced work, note the weighted grades on the transcript and the weight that was given. If your grades are unweighted, note that also. Now that my fourth student is investigating colleges, we are again collecting college literature. I was interested to note that the homeschool instructions sheet for one school specifically stated they wanted unweighted grades. The moral of the story? If in doubt, don't.

The following pages contain instructions for filling out a GPA work sheet using percentage points and a completed sample. This in turn is followed by instructions for filling out the work sheet using letter grades and another sample. Appendix B includes a blank GPA work sheet, as does the CD-ROM.

The GPA work sheet is a tool for your use. It is not designed to be part of your transcript. To get the correct GPA you must follow the directions in the exact sequence recommended. Like the order of mathematical operations, calculating in an incorrect order will give you an incorrect answer.

When you study the GPA work sheets, please take note of the elective Bible courses. These courses were half-credit courses (only one-half hour was spent daily) taken over the course of the year. Grades for the year were compiled and included *only for the second semester*. Recording the grade both semesters would inaccurately record it as a full-credit course, skewing the GPA.

Notice also that the work sheet compiles grade points by the semester. This makes it easier to accurately calculate the GPA for half-credit courses. In addition, high-school transcripts sent out in late winter for the following fall college enrollment can then include information current through the first semester of twelfth grade.

Notice that all courses, even nonacademic, are included in the GPA. Just as grading nonacademic courses is debated, so is including them in the GPA. In our part of the country, all credited courses including PE are part of a public school GPA. However, some area private schools do not include it. This may be different where you live. A friendly high school guidance counselor can provide accurate information for your area. Admissions departments of the college/colleges in which your student is interested can tell you their preference. Consider noting on the transcript whether all, or only academic courses, are included in the GPA.

INSTRUCTIONS FOR COMPUTING A GPA BASED ON NUMERICAL GRADES

1. Record each course's numerical grade by semester.
2. Convert the numerical grades to a four-point scale.
3. Record the number of semesters spent in each class.
4. Total the number of grade points and the semesters spent in class each year. (Example: 29 and 29 grade points and 16 semesters of class for ninth grade).
5. Add both semesters' grade points together and divide by the total number of semesters spent in class that year. This is the grade point average for the school year (Example: 29 + 29 = 58, divide this by 16 to get 3.63).
6. Repeat this process for each year of high school.
7. Add together the grade point averages from all four years of high school. (Example: 3.63 + 3.65 + 3.38 + 3.50 = 14.16).
8. Divide this grade point sum by four (Example: 14.16 divided by 4 = 3.54). The cumulative grade point average is 3.54. Record this on the transcript.

COMPUTING A GPA FROM NUMERICAL (PERCENTAGE) GRADES

NINTH GRADE

COURSE	1st semester grade/points		2nd semester grade/points		# of semesters
English I	95	4	93	4	2
Algebra I	86	3	86	3	2
World Geography	98	4	93	4	2
Physical Science	81	3	76	2	2
Word Processing	94	4	92	4	2
Latin I	86	3	92	4	2
Piano	90	4	90	4	2
Bible Survey			97	4	1
PE	95	4			1
Total grade points by semester	29		29		16
Total grade points and semesters	58				16
Total grade points for year divided by total semesters of class = GPA	3.63				

TENTH GRADE

COURSE	1st semester grade/points		2nd semester grade/points		# of semesters
English II	98	4	92	4	2
Geometry	88	3	84	3	2
American History	97	4	91	4	2
Biology	85	3	86	3	2
Latin II	84	3	90	4	2
Piano	90	4	90	4	2
Church History			87	3	1
Home Economics	93	4	97	4	2
Physical Education	95	4	93	4	2
Total grade points by semester	29		33		17
Total grade points and semesters	62				17
Total grade points for year divided by total semesters of class = GPA	3.65				

ELEVENTH GRADE

COURSE	1st semester grade/points		2nd semester grade/points		# of semesters
English III	91	4	89	3	2
Creative Writing			96	4	1
Algebra II	79	2	77	2	2
World History	98	4	96	4	2
Latin III	86	3	88	3	2
Piano	90	4	90	4	2
Speech	86	3			1
Bible Doctrines			96	4	1
Total grade points by semester	20		24		13
Total grade points and semesters	44				13
Total grade points for year divided by total semesters of class = GPA	3.38				

TWELFTH GRADE

COURSE	1st semester grade/points		2nd semester grade/points		# of semesters
English 1301 & 1302	95	4	89	3	2
Consumer Math	95	4	96	4	2
Government	87	3			1
Economics			85	3	1
Geology	86	3			1
Astronomy	84	3			1
Piano	90	4	90	4	2
Worldview Study			86	3	1
Health	90	4			1
Total grade points by semester	25		17		12
Total grade points and semesters	42				12
Total grade points for year divided by total semesters of class = GPA	3.50				

Add four yearly grade points together (3.63 + 3.65 + 3.38 + 3.50 = 14.16)

Divide total grade points by four to get final grade point average (14.16 divided by four = 3.54)

FINAL GRADE POINT AVERAGE = 3.54

Is it necessary to include a GPA on the transcript?

The GPA calculation is important and routinely included on a student's transcript. It may also be requested on the college and scholarship applications your student fills out.

Are there other ways to figure a GPA?

Yes. For example, a grade point scale with increments to the hundredths is sometimes used. On this scale an A+ would earn the full 4.0 while an A- might earn a 3.84, or similar amount of points. In addition, some schools use a five-point scale to accommodate the high achievement levels of honors and AP courses. With diverse scales in use, it is not unusual for a college admissions office to recalculate applicant GPAs to create some standardization. Whatever scale you use—an Internet search will give you plenty to choose from—be sure and include it on your student's transcript.

INSTRUCTIONS FOR COMPUTING A GPA BASED ON LETTER GRADES

1. Record each course's letter grade by semester.
2. Convert the letter grades to a four-point scale.
3. Record the number of semesters spent in each class.
4. Total the number of grade points and the semesters spent in class each year. (Example: 29 and 29 grade points and 16 semesters of class).
5. Add both semesters' grade points together and divide by the total number of semesters spent in class that year. This is the grade point average for the school year (Example: 29 + 29 = 58, divide this by 16 to get 3.63).
6. Repeat this process for each year of high school.
7. Add together the grade point averages from all four years of high school. (Example: 3.63 + 3.65 + 3.38 + 3.50 = 14.16).
8. Divide this grade point sum by four (Example: 14.16 divided by 4 = 3.54). The cumulative grade point average is 3.54. Record this on the transcript.

COMPUTING A GPA FROM LETTER GRADES

NINTH GRADE

COURSE	1st semester grade/points		2nd semester grade/points		# of semesters
English I	A	4	A	4	2
Algebra I	B	3	B	3	2
World Geography	A	4	A	4	2
Physical Science	B	3	C	2	2
Word Processing	A	4	A	4	2
Latin I	B	3	A	4	2
Piano	A	4	A	4	2
Bible Survey			A	4	1
PE	A	4			1
Total grade points by semester		29		29	16
Total grade points and semesters			58		16
Total grade points for year divided by total semesters of class = GPA				3.63	

TENTH GRADE

COURSE	1st semester grade/points		2nd semester grade/points		# of semesters
English II	A	4	A	4	2
Geometry	B	3	B	3	2
American History	A	4	A	4	2
Biology	B	3	B	3	2
Latin II	B	3	B	4	2
Piano	A	4	A	4	2
Church History			B	3	1
Home Economics	A	4	A	4	2
Physical Education	A	4	A	4	2
Total grade points by semester		29		33	17
Total grade points and semesters			62		17
Total grade points for year divided by total semesters of class = GPA				3.65	

ELEVENTH GRADE

COURSE	1st semester grade/points		2nd semester grade/points		# of semesters
English III	A	4	B	3	2
Creative Writing			A	4	1
Algebra II	C	2	C	2	2
World History	A	4	A	4	2
Latin III	B	3	B	3	2
Piano	A	4	A	4	2
Speech	B	3			1
Bible Doctrines			A	4	1
Total grade points by semester		20		24	13
Total grade points and semesters			44		13
Total grade points for year divided by total semesters of class = GPA				3.38	

TWELFTH GRADE

COURSE	1st semester grade/points		2nd semester grade/points		# of semesters
English 1301 & 1302	A	4	B	3	2
Consumer Math	A	4	A	4	2
Government	B	3			1
Economics			B	3	1
Geology	B	3			1
Astronomy	B	3			1
Piano	A	4	A	4	2
Worldview Study			B	3	1
Health	A	4			1
Total grade points by semester		25		17	12
Total grade points and semesters			42		12
Total grade points for year divided by total semesters of class = GPA				3.50	

Add four yearly grade points together (3.63 + 3.65 + 3.38 + 3.50 = 14.16)

Divide total grade points by four to get final grade point average (14.16 divided by four = 3.54)

FINAL GRADE POINT AVERAGE = 3.54

COMPILING A TRANSCRIPT

A transcript is a compilation of all the courses your student has taken each year along with the credits and grades he has earned. If you have pursued a home-designed high-school program, it is up to you to use the records you have been keeping to compile the transcript.

A transcript usually includes:

1. Biographical information on the student. Be sure to include the student's full name (first, middle, and last name), address, birth date, sex, and social security number.
2. Date of graduation
3. The number of credits earned cumulatively
4. The student's grade point average
5. Courses listed individually, grouped by academic year
6. Grades and credits earned for each course. Include grades for each semester and a final grade. Do early or mid-January calculations on grades earned thus far to arrive at first semester totals. Use the grades for the rest of the year for second-semester calculations. A second option is to report yearly grades if you know these are acceptable to the college your student is considering.
7. Transcript grades recorded as numbers (78, 89, 95, etc.) or letters (A, B, C, etc.). Use the system most prevalent in your area.
8. The grading scale that was used for assigning letter grades or grade points for the GPA.
9. The date the transcript was issued. Most transcripts will be sent out before the student has completed his senior year. Leave the last semester and final grades for twelfth grade blank. Include a projected date of graduation and the issue date of the transcript. It helps the college admissions department keep up with the newest and most complete transcript. You will need to send a second, final transcript at the end of high school.
10. Something to designate it as official. Different things can make a transcript official in a school's eyes: calling it official in the title, notarizing it, including a parent's signature, or presenting it in a sealed envelope are all possibilities. Find out what the college of interest considers official.
11. An administrator's signature. This will most likely belong to the father of the student or someone who has overseen the course of study.
12. SAT or ACT scores can be included on the transcript. This is optional since they must be officially reported to the college by the College Board or American Testing Service. These organizations automatically report your student's scores to the college/colleges your student requests at the time of test registration.

Transcripts can be constructed in different ways. The key is including the above information in a neat, professional, and understandable format. Two sample transcripts follow—the first based on percentages, the second on letter grades. The first transcript includes a second page for a summary of credits, test scores, and additional pertinent information: classes taken outside the home, awards, extracurricular activities, etc. Space is provided for two sets of college entrance scores. If your student takes more than two tests, include scores in the additional information section of the form. The additional information section is not subdivided in order to accommodate each student's unique mix of outside courses, awards, extracurricular activities, and more. Include a phone, e-mail address, or both in the contact information. Some people may choose not to use the second page since the information will be available on the completed application and the official test scores sent to the college. The second transcript sample is complete through first semester twelfth grade.

Blank transcript forms are included in appendix B and on the CD-ROM that accompanies this book. Should my forms not accommodate your needs, an Internet search will turn up a number of possible transcript formats.

What about the GED?

The General Educational Development test, when passed, certifies that a student has the equivalent of a high-school education. Because it is often used as a "second chance" test for students who have dropped out of high school, it is sometimes viewed as attracting a lower caliber of student. Given this unfortunate perception, you may desire to pursue a method other than the GED to validate your student's education.

As noted earlier, students interested in the military are better served by submitting a transcript.

However, in some circumstances a GED need not be detrimental. Because the standards at a junior or community college are usually not highly competitive, a GED may offer no impediment to your student's enrollment. After students have proven their ability to complete college level work successfully, they can often transfer to a senior university on the basis of their college work alone. It is up to you and your student to collect the necessary information to make wise decisions concerning the GED. If you can determine that it will have no adverse effect on future educational or career plans, a GED may be an option.

My student took the GED. Should this be noted on the transcript?

Because some consider the GED evidence of a substandard education, do not include it on your transcript. Present your student as a high school graduate with a diploma and a transcript. Should the GED ever be needed as back-up documentation, present it separately.

ACADEMIC TRANSCRIPT RECORD

Name: Amy C. Jones
Address: 521 E. School Ave.
Someplace, TX 12345
Date of Birth: 4/17/89   Sex: Female
Social Security Number: 000 00 0000
Parents/Guardian: Mr. and Mrs. Steven Jones

School: Homeschooled
Credits Earned: 29.0   GPA 3.54
Date of Graduation: 5/19/2007
Date Transcript Issued: 06/05/2007
Date of College Entry: Fall 2007
Administrator's Signature: Mr. Steven B. Jones

NINTH GRADE   YEAR: 03/04

COURSE	1ST SEM	2ND SEM	FINAL GRADE	CREDIT
English I	95	93	94	1.00
Algebra I	86	86	86	1.00
World Geography	98	93	96	1.00
Physical Science	81	76	79	1.00
Word Processing	94	92	93	1.00
Latin I	86	92	89	1.00
Piano I	90	90	90	1.00
Bible Survey		97	97	0.50
Physical Education	95		95	0.50

9TH GRADE GPA: 3.63   9TH GRADE CREDITS: 8.00

TENTH GRADE   YEAR: 04/05

COURSE	1ST SEM	2ND SEM	FINAL GRADE	CREDIT
English II	98	92	95	1.00
Geometry	88	84	86	1.00
American History	97	91	94	1.00
Biology	85	86	86	1.00
Latin II	84	90	87	1.00
Piano II	90	90	90	1.00
Church History		87	87	0.50
Home Economics	93	97	95	1.00
Physical Education	95	93	94	1.00

10TH GRADE GPA: 3.65   10TH GRADE CREDITS: 8.50

ELEVENTH GRADE   YEAR: 05/06

COURSE	1ST SEM	2ND SEM	FINAL GRADE	CREDIT
English III	91	89	90	1.00
Creative Writing		96	96	0.50
Algebra II	79	77	78	1.00
World History	98	96	97	1.00
Latin III	86	88	87	1.00
Piano III	90	90	90	1.00
Speech	86		86	0.50
Bible Doctrines		96	96	0.50

11TH GRADE GPA: 3.38   11TH GRADE CREDITS: 6.50

TWELFTH GRADE   YEAR: 06/07

COURSE	1ST SEM	2ND SEM	FINAL GRADE	CREDIT
English 1301 & 1302	95	89	89	1.00
Consumer Math	95	96	96	1.00
Government	87		87	0.50
Economics		85	85	0.50
Geology	86		86	0.50
Astronomy	84		84	0.50
Piano IV	90	90	90	1.00
Worldview Studies		86	86	0.50
Health	90		90	0.50

12TH GRADE GPA: 3.67   12TH GRADE CREDITS: 6.00

GPA Scale: 4 pts: 90–100, 3 pts: 80–89, 2 pts: 70–79, 0 pts: 0–69.

GPA calculated by semester.

1 Credit hour = 135–180 hours.

Academic Transcript (page 2)

Summary of Credits

English	4.5	Computer Science	1.0
Mathematics	4.0	Fine Arts	4.5
Social Science	4.5	P.E./Health	2.0
Natural Science	3.0	Electives	2.5
Foreign Language	3.0		
Total Credits: 29			

Test Scores

1/2007	3/2007
SAT Cumulative: 1690	SAT Cumulative: 1760
Critical Reading: 590	Critical Reading: 630
Writing: 560	Writing: 580
Mathematics: 540	Mathematics: 550

ADDITIONAL INFORMATION

English 1301 and 1302 dual credit earned at East Texas Community College (ETCC transcript attached)

Extracurricular Activities

Evening Pianist at Church: 9/2004–present

11/03 MTNA State Piano, Junior Division—3rd place

11/05 MTNA State Piano, Senior Division—2nd place

Play piano for monthly service at Pine Ridge Retirement Home, 9/2004–present

Piano accompanist for *My Fair Lady*, local civic theatre, Summer 2005

Summer mission trip to Guatamala, 2004

Volunteered with local Red Cross shelter, Hurricane Katrina relief, Fall 2005

Habitat for Humanity, participated in building two local homes, Summer 2006

STUDENT CONTACT INFORMATION

Amy B. Jones

521 E. School Ave.

Someplace, TX 12345

Phone: 555-123-4567

E-mail: amyj@aaa.com

ACADEMIC TRANSCRIPT RECORD

Name: Amy C. Jones

Address: 521 E. School Ave.

Someplace, TX 12345

Date of Birth: 4/17/89   Sex: Female

Social Security Number: 000 00 0000

Parents/Guardian: Mr. and Mrs. Steven Jones

School: Homeschooled

Credits Earned: 26.5   GPA 3.54

Date of Graduation: 05/07

Date Transcript Issued: 01/15/2007

Date of College Entry: Fall 2007

Administrator's Signature: Mr. Steven B. Jones

NINTH GRADE   YEAR: 03/04

COURSE	1ST SEM	2ND SEM	FINAL GRADE	CREDIT
English I	A	A	A	1.00
Algebra I	B	B	B	1.00
World Geography	A	A	A	1.00
Physical Science	B	C	C	1.00
Word Processing	A	A	A	1.00
Latin I	B	A	B	1.00
Piano I	A	A	A	1.00
Bible Survey		A	A	0.50
Physical Education	A		A	0.50

9TH GRADE CREDITS: 8.00

9TH GRADE GPA: 3.63

TENTH GRADE   YEAR: 04/05

COURSE	1ST SEM	2ND SEM	FINAL GRADE	CREDIT
English II	A	A	A	1.00
Geometry	B	B	B	1.00
American History	A	A	A	1.00
Biology	B	B	B	1.00
Latin II	B	A	B	1.00
Piano II	B	A	A	1.00
Church History		B	B	0.50
Home Economics	A	A	A	1.00
Physical Education	A	A	A	1.00

10TH GRADE CREDITS: 8.50

10TH GRADE GPA: 3.65

ELEVENTH GRADE   YEAR: 05/06

COURSE	1ST SEM	2ND SEM	FINAL GRADE	CREDIT
English III	A	B	A	1.00
Creative Writing		A	A	0.50
Algebra II	C	C	C	1.00
World History	A	A	A	1.00
Latin III	B	B	B	1.00
Piano III	A	A	A	1.00
Speech	B		B	0.50
Bible Doctrines		A	A	0.50

11TH GRADE CREDITS: 6.50

11TH GRADE GPA: 3.38

TWELFTH GRADE   YEAR: 06/07

COURSE	1ST SEM	2ND SEM	FINAL GRADE	CREDIT
English 1301 & 1302	A		A	0.50
Consumer Math	A		A	0.50
Government	B		B	0.50
Economics		B	B	0.50
Geology	B		B	0.50
Astronomy				
Piano IV	A		A	0.50
Worldview Studies				
Health	A		A	0.50

1ST SEMESTER GPA: 3.67

12TH GRADE CREDITS: 3.00

11TH GRADE CREDITS: 6.50   1ST SEMESTER GPA: 3.67   12TH GRADE CREDITS: 3.00

1 Credit hour = 135-180 hours   GPA calculated by semester   Grading Scale: A: 90-100 B 80-89 C: 70-79 D: 60-69 F: 0-59

Do high grades make a transcript impressive?

It is not always the highest grades that make a transcript impressive.

Two reasons are:

1. Grades are subjective and may or may not be an accurate reflection of a student's ability. High grades should be backed up by high scores on college entrance tests.

2. Easy classes with straight *A*s are not as impressive as difficult courses with slightly lower grades.

All this talk of credits, grades, transcripts, and grade point averages makes me panic. Can I do all this right?

Try to relax! No national standard exists for any of these concerns, so there is not one right way to do things. Particularly frustrating is recommending guidelines for GPAs; tremendous variations exist in how schools determine them.

Having said that, some general principles do apply. Fairly and accurately portray your student's high school work. The college will be expecting your teen to perform for them at the same academic level shown on his high-school transcript. ACT or SAT scores should also reflect the same student ability. If high-school grades are far higher than SAT scores, the quality of your high school program will surely be placed in question.

Present all information in a clear, consistent, and understandable format. Computers do a great job of accomplishing this!

How important is a diploma?

The diploma is given as a *recognition* of academic achievement, not as *proof* of that achievement. A transcript of courses taken and grades earned and SAT or ACT scores that back up those grades are the real proof that a high school program has merit.

By all means give your hardworking graduate a diploma to show you honor him and his achievement. An attractive diploma is available through Home School Legal Defense Association and some state homeschool organizations. Should your student ever have to produce his diploma as proof of high school completion, it should convey authenticity rather than a produced-at-home-in-a-hurry look. Besides, your student may want to decorate his office wall with it someday.

Can junior-high courses be included on a high-school transcript?

In recent years it has become increasingly common for students to begin high-school courses in the eighth grade. Can these courses be added to the transcript?

The main purpose of doing high school work in junior high is to accommodate a student who is ready for the challenge. This in turn frees up the high-school schedule for additional high-school-level courses. For example, algebra I is a high-school course that is frequently taken in eighth grade. When taken in junior high, it allows the student to go beyond the typical high-school courses of algebra I, geometry, algebra II, and precalculus into calculus. The student's high-school transcript is then full of courses much more impressive than algebra I, and there is no benefit in including it.

What if your student stops his high-school math after algebra II and needs the algebra I on his transcript in order to complete course requirements? In this situation I would follow the precedent set by your local public schools. If high-school work completed in eighth grade is included on high school transcripts, feel free to do likewise. The second transcript page presented in this book can accommodate eighth-grade credits if desired. An alternative transcript, which organizes work completed according to subject matter, rather than by grade level, might be helpful in this situation.

High school courses most often credited in eighth grade are introductory skill-building courses, such as algebra I or Spanish I. The student proves the validity of the credit earned by successfully completing the next level course, algebra II or Spanish II, in high school. Taking eighth-grade credit in other course areas is not recommended.

If area schools do not routinely include high-school work completed in eighth grade on the high-school transcript, I would not recommend including it. If public school students can handle the challenge of taking an additional course to complete their high-school requirements, our homeschool kids can, too.

SECTION SEVEN

Recognizing Your Student's Achievement

Graduation

You thought the day would never come; it seemed so far away. Yet now it is upon you. The child who couldn't answer a neighbor's friendly inquiry without first asking, "Mom, what grade am I in?" now has no doubt where he is in his academic training. It's time to graduate.

What do homeschoolers do for graduation? Homeschool graduation ceremonies are as different from one another as the homeschoolers who plan them. Some are formal. Others are casual. Some ceremonies have many graduates; others honor the accomplishments of one. Whatever your style, send your student off in a manner that communicates your pride. Recognize your student for this major milestone in his life.

Perhaps you aren't sure what to include in a homeschool graduation ceremony. When graduation time arrived for my oldest three students, my two boys had no interest in participating in the formal ceremony planned by our local homeschool group. (To be honest, with my oldest son, I don't even remember if there were enough homeschool graduates to plan a group graduation.) Regardless, my husband and I did not push any elaborate plans on them; life was busy enough as it was. As with many larger families, a dinner in a nice restaurant was a special treat. We decided to mark the occasion that way. My oldest daughter, despite initially feeling she did not want a formal graduation, was cajoled into participating by a friend. I know she has never regretted it.

Although a family dinner out seemed like a good solution to the homeschool graduation dilemma, it did not accomplish something necessary. Although pleasant, there was nothing that set it permanently aside in my sons' memory banks. I called one of my sons last night to ask him what we did for his high-school graduation. His response was, "I'm not sure, but I think we went out to eat." Not quite the warm, fuzzy memory for which I had hoped. My daughter, on the other hand, can tell you exactly what she did for her graduation. It left her with a distinct memory. Contrasting my sons and daughter's experiences, I have but one piece of advice for you. Whatever you do for your student's graduation, simple or elaborate, make it memorable. Plan a celebration of this achievement distinctly set apart from the other pleasant moments of your son or daughter's life.

My fourth child will be graduating soon. I have no doubt this outgoing child will want to participate in graduation ceremonies. Thanks to a couple of go-getter moms, her graduating class has been meeting for group activities since their freshman year, helping them gel as a group. When her graduation day arrives, the time shared with classmates will be a festive occasion for them all.

Now that I've encouraged you to make graduation day memorable, let me give you some ideas. First we'll look at some ideas for a group graduation and then move to individual ceremonies. Hopefully it will give you some helpful ideas for planning a special day for your graduate.

GROUP GRADUATIONS

Most of us have experienced a formal group graduation. Invitations. "Pomp and Circumstance." Columns of black-robed graduates. "The National Anthem." Speeches. Diplomas. Caps thrown triumphantly in the air. These honored traditions are part of many homeschool graduation ceremonies.

Yet other things can be different. Below are just a few of the distinctives that can make a homeschool graduation unique and special.

The graduate's parents award the diplomas. Gone is the ritual of a solemn school official, who may not personally know your child, offering a diploma and a handshake. The proud homeschool graduate will most likely receive his diploma from mom and dad. When our oldest daughter graduated, nine students participated. Parents awarded the diploma with proud words of acknowledgment. Our most recent homeschool graduating class honored twenty-four graduates. In the interest of time, parents silently awarded diplomas with warm hugs and congratulatory pats on the back. This was a relief to the parents who did not enjoy public speaking and kept the ceremony within reasonable time constraints. As homeschool graduation classes continue to get larger, the individual celebration of each student becomes more difficult. A slide show is a wonderful way to retain the warmth of a homeschool graduation.

Slide shows make each graduate special. With all the computer technology available today, a talented mom, dad, or student can make a lovely multimedia presentation for the graduation ceremony. Pictures of group activities in which graduates participated are often shown. Most recently I viewed a wonderful presentation at our local graduation ceremony. Each graduate prepared a one-minute taped, spoken presentation. While music played in the background and pictures progressed from earliest childhood to the present, each teen told about his life and ambitions and expressed thankfulness for those who had molded him along the way. Each graduate's segment concluded with a current picture and an on-screen Bible verse that was meaningful to him. Parents solved the dilemma of honoring each graduate in a poignant and memorable way.

Memory tables further individualize the graduate. Memory tables have become a tradition at our local homeschool graduations. The hallway or reception area resembles a science fair with its plethora of trifold presentation boards. However, the similarity stops there. These tables overflow with treasured pictures, books, awards, and other memorabilia chronicling the life of a special teen. Memory sheets offer guests the opportunity to leave a message to the graduate. It's a meaningful tradition.

Graduates participate in developing the graduation program. This may include choosing a class Bible verse, a class song, and possibly a class motto. Graduates often choose the commencement speaker. Rather than listening to a dignitary unknown to them, homeschool graduates may choose someone special to bring the traditional exhortation.

Parents may offer a parental blessing. At some graduation ceremonies, at the conclusion of the diploma presentations, parents may be given a brief moment to pray for their graduate. A short, meditative piano solo or other quiet music can accommodate this private moment with their teen, without the audience getting restless. It also provides an audible time parameter for the parents and graduates.

Other homeschool families offer their service. It is nice when the parents of graduates are free to visit with guests and bask in their student's achievement rather than tie on an apron and retreat to the kitchen for the concluding reception. It is a much appreciated act of mercy when parents of previous graduates or graduates yet to come manage the refreshments for the celebrating families.

Undoubtedly other special traditions have grown up in homeschool groups in other areas of the country. Yet all ceremonies have a common theme: homeschool graduation is a special achievement.

INDIVIDUAL GRADUATIONS

Some homeschoolers live in areas without large support groups or prefer to recognize their graduate in a private ceremony. How do you make your student's graduation a memorable experience? Through the years I have been to a number of private graduation ceremonies. They are as diverse as the graduates honored.

Whether planning a short or long ceremony, include a formalized presentation of the diploma. Print a graduation program informing guests of what is coming next. This will provide your student with an item for a scrapbook or memory box. A graduation ceremony will often include:

A welcome to guests with a thank-you for sharing in this special event
An opening prayer
Special music
A short parental testimony about the life and accomplishments of the student
A short testimony from someone else who knows and loves your child
A brief exhortation from the father, pastor, or other person meaningful to the student
The presentation of the diploma
A parental or pastoral prayer of blessing
An opportunity for the student to thank those who have helped mold his life
A closing hymn
An invitation to the following reception

Some musically gifted students will perform at their graduation. I watched one accomplished ballet student do a lovely pointe solo. Those talented in other areas may make a memory table where their meaningful experiences and accomplishments are displayed. Some families include slide shows in the graduation ceremony or at the reception following.

Graduation ceremonies often take place in the family's home. If a large number of guests are invited, some families will rent a community center, church hall, or other facility. In our area where homeschool ballroom dance classes are popular, the reception may include refreshments and dancing.

Other Rites of Passage: The Homeschool Way

A homeschool graduation can truly be a memorable experience, but what about the other standard high-school hoopla our students are missing? They may not be missing as much as people sometimes think.

The early days of downplaying our homeschool identity have long since past. We now display it with pride. For example, this year our local homeschoolers had the opportunity to purchase letter jackets. An enterprising homeschool parent or student might also arrange for class rings.

Last year in our homeschool community, a few students with photography and computer talent created a DVD homeschool yearbook. They advertised through our local homeschool newsletter and a DVD display near our local Christian bookstore's homeschool department. Students prepaid orders. The yearbook creators delivered the final product at an end-of-the-school-year party.

Homeschool critics often bemoan the lack of a prom. Can a student have a satisfying high-school experience without one? Given the popularity of ballroom dancing among our local homeschool students, each school year in our area ends with a formal senior banquet to which our homeschooled high schoolers are invited. Formals and tuxes are the dress of the evening. A sit-down dinner is followed by an evening of dancing. Rather than enduring the trauma of securing a date for the evening, most of the students go without a date, enjoying the company of all the guests in attendance. Between high-school banquets and formal music recitals, my present high schooler has had more than one girl's share of Cinderella attire.

Now that jackets, rings, yearbooks, and proms are taken care of, what about sports? While difficulties continue to exist, the growth in the homeschool population is leading to some answers. Many homeschoolers with athletic ability participate on the teams of local private schools and city teams. In some states, state law allows homeschoolers to play on public school teams. National homeschool sports are a growing activity. Large homeschool communities sometimes field their own teams. For more information on homeschool sports visit Homeschool Sportsnet, www.hspn.net. Information on the National Christian Homeschool Basketball Championship is available at www.homeschoolbasketball.com.

A great concern among homeschoolers is providing homeschool athletes the opportunity to play college athletics. The National Association of Intercollegiate Athletics (NCAA), with input from HSLDA, has crafted eligibility guidelines for homeschool athletes who wish to participate in college-level sports. See www.ncaa.org for more information.

With all the bells and whistles of the high-school experience available in some form or fashion to homeschoolers today, what about the day-in and day-out socialization of high schoolers and the friendships that spring from daily contact? While homeschooling parents rejoice that much routine high-school socialization is missed, such as drug, alcohol, and promiscuity pressure, they are eager to provide positive social contacts for their students. This has led to many creative opportunities for students to gather with their peers. As mentioned earlier, some homeschool groups plan activities for the different high-school graduation classes. After four years of various shared activities, students form significant bonds. These activities may be academic co-op classes and field trips taken together. They may be purely social pizza parties and game nights. All in all, home schoolers enjoy the camaraderie of the high-school experience.

In writing this chapter, I have realized anew how blessed my children have been. This is especially true of my younger two who are products of a maturing homeschooling movement and all the advantages that go with it. Rather than missing out on socialization, our families and children have lifted these activities to a higher level. Through these, students can enjoy friendships and fellowship without compromising their walk with God. Homeschool activities will vary tremendously from family to family and from one homeschool organization to another. My student's town experiences may be significantly different from their country homeschooling friends. One thing is true: the socialization experienced by homeschoolers is good.

Special-Needs Students

The High Schooler with Special Needs

Many parents decide to homeschool because of the learning difficulties or physical handicaps of their children. This was the situation in our home. Our three oldest children are hearing impaired. Unlike deaf children they function quite well in a hearing world. For this we are thankful. However, like all people with disabilities of one sort or another, it has added some struggles to their lives. Homeschooling can significantly reduce these struggles.

HOMESCHOOLING BENEFITS FOR SPECIAL-NEEDS STUDENTS

Although we began our oldest son's education in the public school system, it was not long before we saw the advantages of bringing him home to school. Let's take a look at some of the benefits of homeschooling a special needs student.

Your student will have a motivated teacher striving for his success. Yes, that's you! Your desire for your student's success cannot be matched by a classroom teacher. Although a teacher may initially surpass you in her knowledge, serious research of your student's disability will rapidly close the gap. Before long you will be a self-taught expert on your child's disability. You will gain insight on the best ways to help him achieve. The most conscientious teacher cannot approximate the determination of a parent striving for her own child's growth.

Your student will have a teacher with a deep understanding of him. You have known your student longer than anyone else. You have an inside track on his personality, strengths, and weaknesses. When searching for answers to the challenges he faces, you may intuitively discover some of the best ways to help your student. That doesn't mean the first key you try will unlock the door, but you may find you don't have to try as many.

Your student will be surrounded by people who love him. People can be cruel, and teens are no exception. Teenagers' quest to fit in can leave them with little time or kindness for a fellow student they perceive as different. Special-needs kids can be lonely in a crowd, finding it difficult to establish comfortable friendships. Students who sometimes have trouble relating to their peers need a haven of peace where they know they are accepted and loved. A fresh start may lead them to better friends within the homeschool community.

Your student will be encouraged in appropriate behavior. Students who struggle socially sometimes earn peer approval by becoming the class clown. This may entertain the other students, but it rarely earns brownie points with the annoyed teacher. Homeschooling, by removing the peer pressure, may improve the behavior and reinforce proper attitudes toward authority.

You can school in a setting free from distractions. The many distractions of a classroom environment can be difficult for a student with ADHD or sensory integration issues. Staying on task can seem almost impossible. In contrast, with careful attention homeschooling can create an environment with minimal distractions, enhancing the opportunity for effective learning.

You can school when your student is fresh. If early morning is not a productive time of day for your student, you can choose to start school a bit later. Success may come more quickly if you are not working against your student's biological clock.

You can choose your curriculum. If your student is presently mainstreamed with modifications, evenings may find you battling to finish homework that seems inappropriate for the needs of your student. When homeschooling, you can choose curriculum that is more closely aligned to his needs. You can introduce new concepts or goals on a timetable more likely to promote success. If your best laid plans are unproductive, you have the power to make modifications without the input of a committee.

DOES MY STUDENT HAVE A LEARNING DISABILITY?

Diagnosing learning difficulties is not an exact science. While physical impairments like hearing loss can be measured objectively, this is not the case with many learning difficulties. For example, a young boy may be diagnosed with ADHD by matching his behavior to a criterion list of ADHD behaviors. If enough similarities exist, he will be diagnosed with ADHD. This process, by its very nature, is subjective. In fact, the diagnosis is only as good as the experience and skill of the diagnostician. In my work at the bookstore, I have heard many mothers wonder aloud if their sons really have ADHD or are merely active little boys. While learning disabilities are real, it is possible that something else is causing the difficulties your student is experiencing. Let's look at a few possible causes for academic difficulties.

My student is "teaching impaired." It is not unusual for young students to serve as guinea pigs for new methodologies taught in college education classes. This is especially prevalent in reading. The look-say method of the past and the whole-language method of more recent years have invaded schools, much to the detriment of national literacy levels. Although phonics is again regaining acceptance, it may not have come back in vogue in time to benefit your student. Reading weaknesses created in these early years can still haunt students in high school. Sometimes revisiting phonics can help remediate poor reading skills.

Is my student reading enough? Reading, like other skills, improves with practice. If your student is a "read-a-phobic," he will be slow in gaining the comfort that more voracious readers experience with the written word. Comprehension, spelling, and writing ability can all be affected. Look for materials that interest your student and encourage a daily independent reading time. In addition many high schoolers still enjoy a family read-aloud time with high interest books on the appropriate level. Books read aloud by parents can become friends your student will revisit on his own, improving his reading skills in the process.

Am I teaching consistently? Successful homeschooling is a product of successful plodding. It is the daily attention to our student's education that cumulatively yields a fruitful crop. Be willing to examine your diligence. Are you giving your student every opportunity to succeed by conscientiously pursuing your job as his homeschool teacher?

Maintaining consistency in school scheduling can be a real challenge. Classes outside the home, church activities, doctor appointments, shopping, phone calls, and other normal activities of life can intrude into our homeschool schedule with surprising regularity. Protect your school time, especially during the high-school years. There is much to be accomplished at this academic level!

Does my child get enough physical activity? I have fond memories of riding my bicycle all over town, walking to and from school with friends, and performing with our high school's synchronized swimming team. Our world is different now. In many situations our students haven't ridden bikes with a happy freedom, can't meander where they choose with their friends, or, as homeschoolers, can't enjoy the sport activities offered by the local high school. Instead they spend their leisure indoors; video games, TV, and chatting with friends on instant messenger have replaced more active pursuits. Encourage your child to enjoy physical activity. Well-developed motor skills improve mental sharpness. Physical exertion relaxes and improves emotional well-being. All of us tend to sleep better after a day of strenuous activity.

Are there dietary issues? My youngest son told me of a midterm college cramming session where he guzzled a bit too much coffee. He found himself in the testing situation with a racing mind, writing at a furious pace. Normally easygoing, he could see the effect of too much caffeine. Work at providing healthy meals for your family that are low in sugar. Avoid caffeine. Removing these stimulants from the diet of a student with attention problems can sometimes prove helpful and is certainly healthier.

Do I cultivate an atmosphere of mutual respect? A high schooler increasingly needs independence. This is normal, but schooling and the whole family can suffer if the move toward independence is accompanied with furious intensity. Treat your teen respectfully as a young adult rather than as a child. Expect respect in return. Recognize that emotional angst is natural and will blow over more quickly if you extend some understanding and grace. Take a deep breath and stay calm. Don't add your own intense emotions to the moment. Be quick to ask forgiveness when you fail. Save the heart-to-heart discussions for calmer, more reasoned moments. Practicing mutual respect and understanding can keep schoolwork from getting lost in emotional struggles.

DESIGNING A SPECIAL-NEEDS PROGRAM

How do you go about creating a homeschool program for your student? Much as we would like one, there is no magic formula. A one-size-fits-all curriculum would fit as badly as one-size-fits-all clothing. Each child and his needs are too unique for such an easy solution.

In addition special-needs students are a diverse group. Some children face significant struggles and will always live life within the nurturing bounds of their family. Others, while facing challenges, will tackle life more independently, learning a trade or even attending college. Because of this diversity, I will look at designing a homeschool program on two distinct tracks, first for students with greater challenges and then for those who will live a more mainstreamed life.

DESIGNING A PROGRAM FOR OUR MOST CHALLENGED STUDENTS

When planning your homeschool program, you need to consider a number of areas. You may need to teach skills that other students pick up as they live life. You may draw more heavily on domestic and life skills than on academics. In this situation, developing an IEP, or Individual Educational Plan, can be appropriate.

An IEP is a product of the Individuals with Disabilities Education Act, also known as IDEA. This law guarantees that all special-needs children, kindergarten through twelfth grade, have a right to a "free appropriate public education." It requires schools actively to seek out students at risk and provide successful early intervention, such as the Preschool Child Find program. The IEP helps the student at-risk progress in the general curriculum while it addresses the needs created by his disability. The student, parents, and school personnel participate to reach cooperative decisions at ARD (Admission, Review, and Dismissal) meetings. During the teen years an IEP will include a transition plan to ensure the student is equipped for life after school years are completed.

Although our homeschooled students may not be subject to the guidelines in IDEA, an educational plan for your special-needs student is a good idea. The record serves a twofold purpose. It helps you direct your efforts appropriately and, in moments of discouragement, reminds you of what you have accomplished. It can also provide a written record of your student's progress should you ever need to produce documentation. State homeschool laws vary tremendously. It is your responsibility to comply with any regulations governing the education of your special-needs student. Legal information should be available from your local or state homeschool support groups. HSLDA (Home School Legal Defense Association) provides members with information on their rights and, if necessary, the appropriate way to document your homeschooling for your particular state.

The steps toward an IEP for your student include:

1. Set long-range goals for your student, reviewed and developed annually to reflect the current school year. Set academic, character development, domestic, life skills, or other goals that contribute to the growth and development of your student.
2. Determine what steps you will take to help your student reach these goals. These steps should be *realistic* and *attainable* over a shorter time period.
3. Decide what methods, activities, or materials will help you fulfill each step.
4. Periodically evaluate whether you have reached your short- and long-term goals. Provide a space on your IEP to record this evaluation.
5. Set new long- and short-term goals as necessary, especially if your initial ones were unrealistic!
6. If your student is receiving therapy outside the home, include this information.

An IEP does not have to be complicated. In preparation for writing this chapter, I pulled out my oldest son's IEPs from public school. In his situation they were primarily a list of the speech sounds he was currently attempting to master. Your goal list, long or short, varied or specific to one area, should depend on the needs of your student.

A possible *Educational Plan* form is provided on the next page. There is absolutely nothing official about it. It is just one idea for organizing your goals, be they academic, character, domestic, life skills, or something else appropriate for your student. The tables that function on your word-processing program can also help you design a form that suits your needs. If your state has guidelines for documenting a homeschooled student's progress, use their forms.

Can students following a significantly modified program receive a high school diploma?

Yes, award your student a diploma for completing the course of study you have developed for him. His efforts and achievement deserve to be recognized. While the standards may be different from those pursuing a postsecondary education, they are still worthy of noting and celebrating.

DESIGNING A PROGRAM FOR STUDENTS WITH MILDER DISABILITIES

Many of our students with milder disabilities can finish high school with fewer modifications and will transition into the workforce or postsecondary education. In this situation it is important to prepare students for the challenges before them. To poise your student for later success, consider the following:

Modify your student's schoolwork only when necessary. If your student can handle standard academics, encourage him to do so. Use grade-level texts, trying to stay with accommodations your student can expect in a postsecondary situation. These might include additional testing time, reduced course load, and audio textbooks. If at all possible, do not modify course content. A homeschool version of appropriate modifications might include a five (or six!) year high-school program that allows yearly course loads to be reduced and gives difficult courses extra time. In addition, mom or dad may read textbooks aloud, into a tape recorder, or both. Shop for curriculum carefully, looking for presentations that meet your student's needs and reduce wear and tear on the teacher. For example, Apologia science texts are now available in MP3 format. School of Tomorrow videos follow the text of the Paces closely. Teaching Textbooks provides CD-ROM math instruction with a teacher who won't get tired of repeating himself. Classic

Educational Plan	
Name:	
School Year:	
Goal:	
Materials:	

Steps to Accomplishing Goal:	Completed

Evaluation:

literature is often available in audiobook format. For the advanced student with great audio skills, The Teaching Company offers many college-level courses in DVD or audio format. Teach your student to face his learning needs squarely and develop strategies for success.

Document your student's learning disability if your student will need college or workforce modifications. Homeschoolers are able to modify a student's academic load without professional proof of its necessity. However, when your student enters either college or the workforce, he will need professional documentation to obtain any needed accommodations.

Encourage your student's growing independence. Let him learn some things the hard way. Organizing life can be challenging for students with learning disabilities. Punctuality can be a major challenge. After years of instruction and practical tips, parents must step back a little. Mistakes made in junior high and high school will be less costly than mistakes made during employment or college. A teen that develops solid strategies for dealing with his learning disability will enter the workforce or college with more confidence in his ability to succeed.

Teach your student self-advocacy skills. Through high school, parents and even the law advocate for students. This changes at the college level. Postsecondary schools are not required to offer accommodations to at-risk students. The student will now be responsible to be his own advocate, seeking out services of help to him. These self-advocacy skills need time to develop. Help him develop a strong awareness of his learning needs and the accommodations most helpful to him. Encourage your student to practice a proactive approach toward help or accommodations when appropriate. He will need the skill should he pursue postsecondary education.

SEEKING PROFESSIONAL HELP

Sometimes it is necessary to seek outside help in order to effectively meet the needs of your student. Although some homeschoolers seek help through public school special services, this is an area where caution is necessary. Professionals sometimes interpret laws in various ways, causing difficulty for the family. For example, because federal law requires each student to have access to a free appropriate public education, school personnel may put pressure on a family to put their special-needs student in the local public school. They may see the law as mandating a public school education for special-needs students rather than providing an opportunity. The opposite can also happen. If you seek out help for your student's special needs while homeschooling, school personnel may not feel obligated to provide any services for your student because you have rejected the free appropriate public education they have to offer.

Seek council from your local and state homeschool group before seeking public school services. If you are members of a legal defense organization, seek their advice before taking such a step. By accepting school services, you may be inviting public school intrusion into your homeschool. Don't make a decision in haste that you may regret later.

Instead consider seeking help from homeschool friendly professionals. Your local or state homeschool support groups may know of such professionals in your area. Often a therapist can evaluate your student and train you to continue therapy at home. This minimizes the number of visits to the therapist and keeps the cost under some control. You may also find a homeschool mom who has a background in speech therapy, occupational therapy, or another area in which you need help. Homeschoolers tend to be an educated bunch. A reduced price or even a barter arrangement may be possible in such a situation.

If your student's therapist is training you to work with your teen at home, be prepared for some extra strain in your relationship. At a time when students crave independence, you are parent, teacher, and therapist (with all the instruction and correction that comes with each role). This can strain the relationship between parent and teen. The cost of hiring a tutor or therapist to do some of the remediation may be worth it, allowing you to focus on being positive and supportive while the therapist does at least some of the correcting.

THINGS TO REMEMBER ALONG THE WAY

Before closing this chapter, it seemed important to leave you some in-the-trenches tips and encouragement.

Help your teen be comfortable with his special needs. "I will praise You, for I am fearfully and wonderfully made" (Ps. 139:14). Your teen's struggles are not an accident. They are a vital part of God's unique design for him. What your student may view as a curse can become a great blessing. God does not waste our struggles but uses them for His glory, our growth in grace, and the benefit of others. Help your teen recognize his worth.

Love your child. First and foremost, be mom or dad. It can be hard to balance our roles when we are parent, teacher, therapist, social director, etc. In our desire to provide our students with a bright future, we can often spend so much time trying to "fix" that we do not spend enough time accepting and loving. I learned this the hard way. I should have spent more time encouraging and less time correcting. Life is harder for our special-needs students, and they need to know someone is on their side.

Be generous with praise and gentle with correction. Sometimes a warm compliment is the reward most desired by your student. Students that struggle can be exhilarated when they receive honest praise for "getting it right."

Appreciate your student's strengths. It is so easy to focus on what we are laboring to control or overcome that we become blind to our child's strengths. A number of years ago *World* magazine had an article on Down syndrome children. The author, a mother of a Down syndrome child, mourned the little ones who would never see life because a prenatal test had discovered their disability and marked them for an abortionist's services. She saw and appreciated the unique joys her daughter brought to her family and felt the world was much poorer for the loss of such children. She was able to see the blessing in the affliction. We, too, need to recognize that God did not make a mistake when He created our children. They are a blessing and a heritage from the Lord. God is in control, and He is good.

Set reasonable standards. A perfectionist or driven mom will demoralize her student. Have patience with slow progress and expect lots of forgetting along the way. However, don't set standards too low. A teacher who is too "free spirited" will not provide the order LD students need or challenge them to excel as they are able. As always, we must strive to strike the proper balance.

Allow your student to learn at his pace. Don't be discouraged if your student's timetable is different from other students. Academic skills for the special-needs student are often not neatly divided into first-grade skills, second-grade skills, etc. Maturity and social ease often develop slowly. Success in the short haul is meeting the goals you have set, not hitting every developmental stage on time. Long-term success is helping your student arrive at adulthood, functioning as fully as he is able.

Appreciate the virtue of steady plodding. Stay the course. Keep your commitment. Let the joy in small accomplishments sustain you. God will bless your faithfulness.

Maintain appropriate discipline. Pray for wisdom to discern which behavioral issues are caused by the disability and which require correction. Don't rebuke when the behavior you desire is beyond the student's capabilities. Conversely, don't allow the disability to excuse behavior that is controllable. Seek God's wisdom to recognize the difference.

Educate yourself. Seek support and wisdom. Read books, surf the Internet, and talk to other parents. Learn about organizations such as NATHHAN and TX Special Kids (see appendix A) that support parents who are homeschooling children with special needs. Keep learning!

Get your student professional help when necessary. This requires an active decision and hard investigative work to find the right situation for your child. The cares of life always stand ready to smother the search for solutions. Don't procrastinate; many struggles are easier to remediate if they are discovered when the student is young.

Understand legal issues surrounding home educating a special-needs child. Because educational laws occur on both the state and federal level, each homeschool family must familiarize themselves on any laws that would impact their homeschool. A book like this cannot provide the legal information you need. Be aware of any testing, special services, or documentation required to homeschool a special-needs child in your state.

Take care of yourself. Do things that revitalize you. (Reading a lightweight mystery book is still a favorite escape for me.) When we get too weary and worn, all of life suffers.

Seek out sympathetic fellowship. Enjoy the comfort of sharing with someone who understands your struggles. Every January when my oldest three were young, almost like clockwork I could count on being overwhelmed with the homeschool task before me. A good cry and a chat with a friend who taught the deaf would return some steel to my backbone.

Take care of your relationships. Marriages stressed by children with severe struggles often end in divorce. Don't pour all of your emotional resources into your child. Save some emotional energy for building strong relationships with your husband and other children.

Pray for your teen. Ask for God's wisdom in finding the best way to love your teen and help him reach his fullest potential. Rely on God to help you find the right path. Pray for endurance. God in His wisdom has placed this child in your care. Remember that He has called you to the task and will not fail to equip you for it.

How do I report modifications on my student's transcript?

Hopefully, with extra time and careful choice of curriculum, your student will have completed the content of a high-school program. If content was not modified, the courses will appear as normal on the transcript. If content was modified, a course title, such as Remedial Math, or Algebra IA and Algebra IB, will indicate that modifications have been made.

In Closing

Trying to offer direction to homeschool families with such diverse students is a daunting task. Hopefully, some of the information in this chapter has been helpful to you. Some will be more applicable to another reader. Because I am not a special-needs teacher, I may sometimes miss the mark. Please discard what is not helpful and trust your own judgment. My distant advice cannot replace what your experience and love for your child have taught you.

In section 5, "A Comprehensive Homeschool Course Listing," you will find curriculum recommendations for junior-high and high-school students. Most core subjects will include remedial suggestions. Choose materials that will prepare your student for his future academic goals. Look for materials with a clear, well-written presentation that will enhance your student's ability to learn.

In the next chapter we will discuss how to choose an appropriate school for college-bound, special-needs students.

College and Special-Needs Students

How do we choose a college for our students with learning disabilities? Will they fit comfortably into a college scenario?

To have a successful college experience, a student with a learning disability must choose the college with great care. One helpful publication is *The K&W Guide to College for Students with Learning Disabilities or Attention Deficit Disorder* by Marybeth Kravets and Imy F. Wax. The *K&W Guide* provides helpful information on the disability laws and the importance of self-advocacy. A large portion of the book takes a close look at the special services offered on a number of different campuses. Even if the college favored by your student is not listed, the other information contained in the book will teach you and your student how to be informed consumers as you search for a good college fit.

Colleges vary in how they accommodate students with learning disabilities. Some colleges comply with federal mandates and provide no help beyond these mandates. Other colleges provide support that exceeds what is required by law. The services offered by a college can determine whether a student has the optimum chance to succeed.

DISABILITY LAWS AND DOCUMENTATION

IDEA, the law that assures an appropriate education for special needs students in public elementary, junior high, and high school, does not apply to college. The Americans with Disabilities Act of 1990 Title II (ADA) and the Rehabilitation Act of 1973, Section 504, apply to employment and postsecondary education. The student's situation is now significantly different.

Postsecondary schools are not required proactively to seek disabled individuals for enrollment in their schools. The law requires only that they not discriminate against them because of their disability. Disabled students have a right to effective accommodations but do not have a right to receive every service they request. Reasonable accommodations are available to a student who can document his disability. If the student was diagnosed young and has had periodic documented follow-ups, he is more likely to obtain the services he requires. The validity of a learning disability undocumented until adulthood may be questioned.

For documentation to be acceptable, it must be current and from a certified professional who will use various standardized assessment tools to measure aptitude, achievement, and information-processing skills. An information-processing skills test could include an assessment of short- and long-term memory, sequential memory, auditory and visual perception, processing speed, and motor ability. Based on test results, the certified professional will recommend appropriate accommodations.

ACCOMMODATIONS

If your student needs accommodations, it is best to look for them before the first semester of study. Although core course requirements will not change, reasonable accommodations such as extended time on tests or assignments, a note taker, or permission to tape record lectures, can be the difference between success and failure. Don't assume simple requests without documentation will be granted. My daughter was once denied preferential seating for her hearing impairment until she presented the teacher with the appropriate documentation from Disabled Student Services (DSS).

I recognize that self-advocacy is difficult for many students. Students who are tired of being different will sometimes not seek out the help they need when beginning college. This can make a rough transition even rougher. Even if your student has done well without accommodations at home, he may need them in this confusing new environment. Encourage your student to get the help he needs.

The smoothest transition to college will occur when the student investigates the available services before enrolling in the school. A visit to DSS (or a similar office) may help the student judge whether the college will be a good fit. If the student does not believe the offered accommodations will be sufficient, he may want to apply elsewhere.

If he decides to proceed with enrollment, encourage him to fill out any appropriate paperwork at the DSS office. In addition, a visit to his teachers to discuss modifications will give each teacher a greater awareness of the student. This will set him up for success as he begins his college experience.

Other considerations can also contribute to a student's success. Colleges with small classes will prevent a student from getting lost in the crowd. Moderate rather than high academic standards will make passing grades more obtainable. Dorm living may make it easier to get to class on time than living in an off-campus apartment. Conversely, an apartment may offer fewer distractions than the dorm!

Should an individual disclose his learning disability?

In the normal course of events, an employee or student is not required to disclose his disability to his employer or college. To do so is a personal decision. In an academic setting, nondisclosure means accommodations will not be available.

In an employment situation many individuals choose never to disclose a disability. Others, after proving their worth to their employer, will disclose their disability if they feel it will be well received and provide them with accommodations that will make their good job performance even better.

A PARENT'S ROLE

How do parents help their learning-disabled student succeed in college? Here are a few suggestions.

Help your student investigate his options. He may not know where to start if left entirely on his own.

Be patient! Many college students now take five years to finish their degree plan. Expect the same length of time for your student (or more!).

Cultivate an open relationship with your student. In the eyes of the college, he is an adult, and parents have no legal right to student information. Keeping communication strong will help you better understand how he is handling this new challenge.

Educate yourself. You will find some helpful Web sites listed in the appendix.

SECTION NINE

Choosing a College

The College Search Begins!

We have spent a great deal of time planning an appropriate high-school program and documenting it effectively. The zeal behind our careful strategizing was borne of high motives: to develop students' talents and strengthen their weaknesses so they might live lives that glorify God.

Many of our students will develop their talents through a college degree. The college years are profoundly influential. During this time, students grow from teens to adults, determine careers, and meet future spouses. All of these life-changing events may take place on a college campus far from our daily influence. This makes the college choice extremely important.

To help your student clarify his thoughts on college, ask him to compile a list of the characteristics he most desires in a college. Then encourage him to research each school in which he is interested, answering the questions on his list. This information can be effectively used to compare school to school.

If your student is unsure what he is looking for, a visit to the college search area of the College Board's Web site, www.collegeboard.com, may prove helpful. Their excellent college search function includes helpful demographic information on many colleges. Links to college Web sites are also provided.

The following are some questions regarding student preferences and general college information to get your student started.

1. How close do you want to be to home?
2. Do you want a secular or Christian college?
3. Do you prefer a large or small student body?
4. Are you looking for a rural, suburban, or city campus?
5. What academic majors are offered?
6. What is the average SAT score of the other students? (Will you be competing with students of a similar ability, or are they all geniuses operating over your head?)
7. What's the professor to student ratio?
8. Are undergraduate courses taught by professors or teaching assistants?
9. What is the estimated annual cost?

10. On average, how much scholarship money is awarded per student?
11. What's the gender ratio?
12. What is the cultural and ethnic mix of the campus?
13. What extracurricular activities are offered?
14. What types of dormitory accommodations are available?
15. Do most students live on or off campus?
16. Are you allowed a car on campus?
17. What are the crime statistics on campus and in the neighboring area?
18. Is there a study abroad program?
19. How successful are graduates in finding jobs in their chosen field?
20. How many students go on to higher education?

There are many other places to get college information.

The Internet. You could spend days and days on this information source alone. In addition to the College Board site already mentioned, many other sites can also prove helpful. A look at www.campuslifecollegeguide.com, www.usnews.com, and www.petersons.com can keep you busy should you ever exhaust the College Board site. Don't forget to check out the Web sites for the colleges of highest interest to your student. State universities often have well-developed Web sites that offer excellent information, both for their institution and college entrance in general. The appendix of this book offers a number of Web sites worth pursuing, but many more are out there for you to find!

People who have attended the college of interest. This might be a graduate of the school or a present student. Especially helpful is the opinion of a student who was also homeschooled. It is sometimes amazing how readily you find information once you start searching for it.

College fairs. Perhaps your city, like ours, hosts a college fair. Booths are manned by college representatives who provide students with basic information on their institutions. Mail-in request forms are usually available for the student to request additional information. The quality of college fairs varies. The last one we attended was a bit of a disappointment. Several college booths we planned to visit remained empty. However, we were able to visit several booths where the college representatives were informed and helpful.

Magazines. U.S. News & World Report publishes an annual college issue. The attention received by the *U.S. News & World Report* college issue has been a mixed blessing. Colleges feel great pressure to gain and retain favorable ratings. This pressure does not necessarily result in better academics or admission policies. In addition many excellent schools are overlooked each year. If you are interested in the college ratings game, you will find *Harvard Schmaarvard* by Jay Mathews an interesting read.

Advertisements in homeschool magazines. If a college is advertising in a homeschool magazine, you know they are seriously recruiting the homeschool student.

The Homeschool Legal Defense Association rates colleges and universities by the friendliness of their homeschool admissions policies. Look for this information at www.hslda.org.

A campus visit. As your student begins to narrow his college choices, schedule a campus visit. Don't make any final decisions without visiting. Anything can look good on paper and in photographs. Expect all the students pictured to be beautiful, smiling, and having a great time while diligently studying! Only through visiting can you get a feel of that college community and whether it's a comfortable fit for you. Attend classes. Stay in the dorm. The special activities of a get-acquainted event can be helpful for both student and parent. Colleges usually hold parent orientation meetings and often offer helpful information on financing, housing, health care, campus safety, and other issues of parental concern. In addition to a get-acquainted event, it is helpful if your student visits at a quieter time when everyone is following a normal weekday schedule. If at all possible, visit at both times to get the clearest look at the campus.

Sometimes a student will apply and be accepted to several schools. Most schools need to know whether a student will accept or reject their offer by May 1. If the student remains undecided, an April campus visit can sometimes be squeezed in to help the student in his final decision making.

Should our student attend an accredited college?

Two main difficulties can occur when attending a nonaccredited college. First the US Department of Education does not allow the use of federal loans or grants for nonaccredited schools. In addition, students that transfer to another college or plan on attending graduate school may have trouble getting their coursework accepted, regardless of the merit of the program. Although students must be wary of bogus schools that are just diploma mills, some nonaccredited colleges offer an excellent education. Students desirous of attending a nonaccredited college must meet these challenges with eyes wide open and a strategy in place.

Pros and Cons of Various College Options

Determining where your student should begin his college experience is a major decision. So many choices exist. Not only that, but the choices themselves can be mixed and matched to create a personalized college experience. All of my older children have spent college time on more than one campus. Whether it was high school dual credit, a transfer situation, or picking up a course that wasn't offered at their residential college, my first three children have walked down the hallowed halls of five different institutions. This has included work at one community college, two state universities, and two Christian colleges. My fourth student, with different interests from her siblings, has us on an entirely different track of college investigations.

Between our experiences and the varied experiences of my homeschool customers at the bookstore, one thing is clear: there are pros and cons to each educational approach. To aid you in your decision making, we will look at the pros and cons of junior/community colleges, public universities, Christian colleges, and conservatories. The breakdown of college types can be handled differently. For example, I have not considered private four-year colleges separately knowing that some pros and cons from both four-year state universities and Christian colleges would apply. I chose the options below because I felt they would be most helpful to my readers.

JUNIOR/COMMUNITY COLLEGE

Junior/community college is a two-year school usually offering a mixture of college transfer courses and training in various technical fields. Degrees offered by junior colleges include two-year associate's degrees or technical certification. Many students do not earn a degree but transfer their course work to a senior institution. Junior colleges often offer remedial or developmental courses for students not quite ready for college level work.

We are blessed to have an excellent junior college less than ten minutes from our home. All five of our children have been involved in something on the campus. They have taken dual credit, college credit, applied music lessons, and children's theater. We are thankful for all of these opportunities.

Positively, junior/community college can provide:

- *A transition between homeschool and an away-from-home college experience.* When needed, it provides a little more time for the student to mature, particularly if he completed his high-school work at an early age.

233

- *A low-cost method for exploring career options.* It is not unusual for a college freshman to be unsure of the career direction he desires to pursue. It is also not unusual for a student who has known for years what he wants to do suddenly to begin second-guessing. We have experienced both situations. A few exploratory courses may open or close the study area under question. It is much easier for the family or student budget to absorb the cost of these changing plans at the junior-college level then at a four-year university.
- *A pardon for negligent homeschool records.* Junior-college admissions are usually much simpler than admission to a four-year university. With enough credits your student may be able to transfer to a university on the basis of his junior-college transcript alone, giving your record keeping a permanent reprieve!
- *Reasonable student-teacher ratio.* This is different from the freshman lecture hall course taught by a teaching assistant at the four-year university.
- *Excellent teaching.* This observation is subjective and varies with the teacher and department. However, we have found teachers at the junior-college level generally of a high quality. Because of the diversity of the student body, they tend to expect less background knowledge from the student. This often resulted in a careful sequential teaching style and a teacher available for "dumb questions."
- *Availability of affordable remedial classes.* I know it goes against the established homeschool canon, but sometimes homeschool students are not where they need to be academically. Because of our ability to customize our student's education, we sometimes take the easy road and concentrate our academic efforts where our students are interested and receptive. This leaves subjects lurking in dark closets that need to be pulled into the light of day and taught. The developmental classes of the junior college are one way to address the need. Students are often less resistant to learning a disliked subject from someone other than mom. Once their foot hits the college path, they may begin to see the necessity of mastering the subject so they can get on with their future. The junior college is a better place to pick up secondary-level skills than at the higher priced university.
- *An opportunity to earn an associates degree concurrent with high-school graduation.* Well, almost concurrent. Technically you'd probably have to graduate your student first, change his status at the junior college, and then the degree would be awarded. Close enough! However, be sure this strategy doesn't change freshman status. See third negative below.
- *An early completion of general college academic requirements.* This may lighten the college course load enough to allow the student to double major.

Negatively, junior/community college can:

- *Include students academically disinclined.* We found this problem lessened somewhat with the completion of the first round of required courses. The least serious students weeded themselves out.
- *Offer courses that will not transfer to a four-year institution.* The wide range of student abilities requires non-transferable developmental courses. Two-year technological programs also offer courses not required for the academic core of many four-year degrees. We found our local junior college offered biology programs for both science majors and nonmajors. The majors biology was the one recommended to ensure transfer. In addition, there is a limit to the number of freshman- and sophomore-level courses that a senior university will accept. Your student's college advisor can help your student plan a program that transfers well.
- *Mean missing some university scholarship money available only to incoming freshmen.* Sometimes a careful juggle of dual credit and credit earned after high-school graduation can retain your student's freshman status. It is also possible that a student with a high GPA in junior college can earn significant merit-based scholarship money when transferring. Success with either scenario requires a thorough understanding of all the ins and outs of the scholarship-award program of the senior university of choice.
- *Rival universities with their political correctness and anti-Christian thought.* Although I have heard this, it has not been our experience, but we live in the Bible Belt. With both a junior college and a state university in our small city, we have found the junior college more conservative.
- *Be a social continuation of high school.* Local friendships established through years of interaction in public school will continue. If your homeschool student has a quiet nature, he may find it difficult to find his social niche.

- *Have a commuter-campus feel.* Student's lives are lived primarily off campus. This makes it difficult to develop the same unique camaraderie that students at a four-year resident campus experience. Upon transferring, some students will find it difficult to join a social situation that has been forming for two years without them.

PUBLIC STATE UNIVERSITIES

Many college-bound students will ultimately earn their degrees from a state university. State universities are publicly funded by taxpayer dollars. They often have diverse programs with a number of undergraduate colleges and schools offering bachelor's degrees. Graduate and doctoral work may also be available. Prestigious universities often have excellent research facilities. Diverse extracurricular programs may include sports, sororities, fraternities, clubs, and musical events. On-campus housing is usually available. The attendance at a large state university can rival the population of a mid-sized city. This educational situation offers both pros and cons for the homeschooler.

Positively, a state university:

- *Offers numerous majors.* This is a great help to the undecided student. A change in degree plans does not have to mean a change in schools. The four-year student has ample time to investigate options while completing the general requirements of his first one or two years.
- *Offers excellent facilities.* With the state coffers behind them, state schools sometimes offer better facilities than the small private university. Buildings, grounds, and equipment benefit from taxpayers' dollars.
- *Offers research opportunities.* Many professors at large universities are involved in research. Assisting in this work presents some students with a marvelous opportunity that is usually not available on smaller campuses.
- *Has an affordable price tag.* Although no education comes at bargain basement prices, the state university still offers some of the best deals in education. Depending on your state funding regulations, state institution prices may vary.
- *Can be alive with activity.* Some students love the excitement of a large campus environment. Rather than feeling lost, they are invigorated by the crowd.
- *Often have strong Christian student organizations.* A secular campus is an alien world for Christian, home-schooled students. Christian fellowship groups can provide an anchor and solid friendships for their four-year journey. Involvement in a strong church close to campus can also keep a student's feet planted in Christian realities.

Negatively, a state university can:

- *Have an extremely large student body.* The University of Texas in Austin works hard to stay at approximately fifty thousand students. Many of you reading this live in towns and cities much smaller than this! Although most campuses are not that big, a more reticent student can still get lost on a campus of ten to twenty thousand students.
- *Have large classes.* The ratio of student to professor in required undergraduate courses is far from cozy. Students are often taught in large lecture halls by a teaching assistant while the professor is working on his research.
- *Be socially liberal.* The absolute standards of Christianity are seen as intolerant. Learning is sometimes supplanted by indoctrination. The Christian student may sit in classes that mock and denigrate his beliefs.
- *Be hotbeds of sinful behavior.* Colleges no longer view themselves as acting *in loco parentis.* Instead, they view students as young adults capable of making their own decisions. Many students, experiencing their first dose of total freedom, abandon all restraint to the wind. Incoming freshmen who are often required to live on campus may find themselves in co-ed dormitories that turn a blind eye to permissive, indulgent behavior.
- *Have problems with crime.* Given the wild behavior that often accompanies freedom, it is no wonder that colleges often have significant problems with substance abuse. Theft and assault, including sexual, sometimes occur. Campus life is not a trouble-free oasis. It requires students to take reasonable safety precautions.

CHRISTIAN COLLEGES

Two of our three older children have completed a significant amount of their college education on a Christian campus. When the fit is right and the college sincerely upholds the Christian faith, it is a remarkable experience. If your student is interested in attending a Christian college, consider reading *An Educated Choice* by Frank Brock. It will open up many new thoughts for your consideration. Below are some of the pros and cons of a Christian college education.

Positively, a Christian college can:

- *Integrate academics with a Christian worldview.* As Christians, we educate our students so they can effectively serve God through their chosen profession. An education that is conscientiously integrating a Christian worldview into the course work will produce a well-equipped servant for Christ.
- *Have professors who enjoy teaching and like college students.* Because professors are hired to teach, not to research, they are often skilled instructors who love their subject matter. Student-teacher ratio is usually excellent, and it is not unusual for professors to be actively involved in the students' lives outside of the classroom.
- *Provide like-minded friends.* Friendships built on the solid foundation of Christ are eternal. A Christian campus offers many opportunities to build these friendships and, through God's grace, may yield a marriage partner who loves the Lord as well.
- *Have a close-knit campus community.* Our third child recently graduated from a small residential Christian college. Students and professors alike were warm and friendly. Our son flourished in this homelike environment.
- *Encourage godly behavior.* The boundaries of Christian freedom are drawn differently by different believers. This is also true of Christian colleges. A student should be fully aware of and in agreement with the behavioral standards of an institution before enrolling. It is better to uphold the rules with cheerful integrity than with a resentful spirit.
- *Nurture our students in their faith.* All of the positives mentioned above—professors, students, a consistently taught worldview, and godly behavioral standards—cumulatively nurture our students in their faith.
- *Be homeschool friendly.* Christian colleges are aware of the homeschool community and have been for years. Students are often warmly welcomed. Some even offer special homeschool scholarships.

Negatively, a Christian college may:

- *Be very expensive.* However, generous scholarship packages sometimes make up the discrepancy in cost between public and private education. It is only by going through the enrollment process that you will know if a satisfactory financial arrangement can be reached.
- *In some situations, undermine our student's faith.* Many historically Christian schools left their standards of faith long ago. Professors may actively teach positions contrary to the school's traditional standards. Christian students attending such a school are well-served to view it as a secular school. This will help prevent disillusionment.
- *Have students who are lukewarm in their Christian commitment.* A Christian campus is not a total oasis from the world. The level of Christian commitment from student to student will vary. A rebellious heart can still be rebellious on a Christian campus.
- *Not have state-of-the-art facilities.* Private Christian colleges do not operate with a tax-funded budget but depend on generous donors and student tuition for revenue. Sometimes, but certainly not always, this means facilities may be of a more modest nature.
- *Not have a large variety of majors.* Smaller schools mean a smaller program. Be sure the school offers several programs of interest to your student.
- *Have fewer professors.* Once a student is fully involved in his major, he may find himself with the same professor for a number of classes. This can be either good or bad. Positively, the close relationship between student and professor may add a greater depth to the studies. Negatively, if your student and the teacher don't relate, they're both stuck.

- *Avoid accreditation.* Some schools avoid entanglement with secular educational agencies. While accreditation does not guarantee quality, a lack of accreditation can sometimes negatively impact students transferring to a secular institution at a later date or seeking a graduate degree.

CONSERVATORIES

A conservatory can be an independent institution or a music school within a larger university. Conservatory degrees are professional degrees preparing students most often for a career in musical performance. In addition to pursuing performance, conservatory graduates sometimes complete masters or doctoral degrees in order to teach college or graduate level music.

A look at conservatories is new for our family. Our fourth child took us by surprise. With interests in music, music, and more music, we have found ourselves pursuing an educational path different from our older three students. Although most readers of this book will not have students interested in a conservatory education, some of my thoughts may transfer to specialized schools in other areas of the arts.

Positively, a conservatory can:

- *Allow a student to wholeheartedly pursue his love.* Sometimes a student has both the talent and the discipline to pursue his art but limited interest in other areas. When the handwriting is clearly on the wall, a conservatory education may be the right choice.
- *Provide a competitive edge over students pursuing a more well-rounded degree.* Many university music degrees require a full program of generalized studies in addition to music courses. Depending on the institution, a conservatory student usually takes fewer general courses, placing most of his educational energies into the study of music. This may provide a competitive edge for future auditions.
- *Offer exceptional training.* The single most important ingredient to successful music training is the teacher. A conservatory's faculty is usually of excellent quality.

Negatively, a conservatory may:

- *Limit career options.* Unless followed by additional training, a performance degree may offer less career flexibility.
- *Be highly competitive.* The training at conservatories or excellent university music departments may draw talented students both nationally and internationally. Undergraduates may find themselves in competition with graduate students for teachers and performance opportunities.
- *Require auditions for entry.* Auditions are not for the faint of heart. Yet entry into a quality musical program is not possible without one.
- *Espouse a pagan worldview.* Although there are Christian schools with excellent music departments, most options will be secular institutions. Your student will need to be a light not easily snuffed out in a sometimes dark world.

What about Ivy League schools?

We have all read or heard stories of homeschooled students who have been accepted into Ivy League schools. With acceptance rates at our nation's most prestigious schools running as low as 9 percent, can a homeschooler have any hope of admission? The answer is an unequivocal "maybe."

Every serious applicant to an Ivy League school has exceptional credentials. Astronomical test scores, sterling academic records, profound essays, exemplary extracurricular activities, and impressive references are the order of the day. When it comes to learning modalities and styles, everything is a strength. So how does an admissions counselor differentiate between thousands of over-qualified applicants? One way is by seeking campus diversity.

Campuses today are interested in creating a diverse student body. Accepting some homeschooled applicants admirably fulfills that mission. In fact, a homeschooled student who is equally qualified in other respects may hypothetically have a better chance of admission to an Ivy League school than a student from an elite prep school. Why? Because the prep school applicant has a school full of classmates who are pursuing an Ivy League education. The homeschooled student has only himself. The homeschool student will diversify the campus; the prep school student will not.

This reasoning, however, does not consistently predict the admission of homeschoolers to Ivy League schools. *The Stanford Daily* of February 22, 2000, has an article by Amy L. Kovac that received wide coverage in homeschooling circles. That year Stanford University accepted homeschool applicants at a rate of 27 percent, a rate nearly double that of other applicants. Harvard, however, presents a different story. An article entitled, "Homeschoolers a Small but Growing Minority" appeared in the April 17, 2006 issue of *The Harvard Crimson* online edition. In it staff writer Rachel Pollack interviewed director of admissions, Marlyn McGrath Lewis. Although Harvard does not separately track homeschool applicants, between one and two hundred apply each year. McGrath stated that three to eight are accepted annually. With a 2006 general acceptance rate of 9.3 percent, this means homeschoolers were accepted at a lower rate than other students.

Given the situation at Stanford and Harvard, are homeschoolers who pursue an Ivy League education helped or handicapped by their educational choice? The jury is still out. In the meantime, encourage your student to apply to several colleges, including one where admittance can be safely assumed. Then college plans can go forward even if the Ivy League dream does not materialize.

When applying to a highly competitive college, as with all college applications, play by the rules and give information in the form it is requested. Remember, every applicant to an Ivy League school will be a documented superstar. The high achievement of a home-educated student will reflect the norm and may not provide any edge over other applicants. Don't complicate the admissions process, and your student's opportunity for admission, with documentation that is not readily deciphered.

(For an interesting, well-written read on the pros and cons of pursuing an Ivy League education, try *Harvard Schmarvard* by Jay Mathews, a Harvard graduate and education reporter for the *Washington Post*. Mathews's book includes an eye-opening look at the *U.S. News & World Report* ranks, the notorious "wait lists" and what they mean, and a listing of one hundred outstanding but often overlooked schools. Although not written with homeschoolers in mind, Mr. Mathews has much to offer us.)

What a College Is Looking for in Potential Students

Thus far we have considered what we might look for in a college. Perhaps it's time to consider what a college might look for in potential students. It is fairly easy to make a list of criteria that colleges find desirable. It is less easy to predict the amount of weight they will give to each item. Colleges are diverse, with different mission statements and different worldviews. This influences the level of importance given to the various admission considerations. Some of these considerations are:

Grades in college-prep classes. According to college admission counselors, grades in college-prep courses are the single most important admissions factor. However, this is not an invitation to place your student under continual stress for his entire high-school experience. Your high-school program must match the abilities of your student.

College entrance test scores comparable to the rest of their student body. A student who scores as well or better than most other students or applicants to their institution will have a greater likelihood of success. For homeschool applicants, entrance scores may be the most important admissions factor.

A strong academic performance overall. A counselor wants to know that your student can handle the academic challenge they offer in all of his coursework.

Leadership qualities and the ability to work in a group. Many college departments are fond of cooperative learning experiences. Students who work well in groups are an asset to their chosen college and their future workplace.

Involvement in extracurricular activities. Socially involved students help create an active, dynamic campus. A vibrant college community will then draw other students.

A good fit for the school. A school's ability to retain students through college graduation is important. This means every effort will be made to admit students who fit academically and socially into their program.

Diversity in the student body. Although it is impossible to have a campus full of perfectly well-rounded students, a college often strives to create a campus population that is collectively well-rounded. For this reason a homeschooled student's unique educational background may appeal to a college admissions counselor. However, the student's high-school achievement must be well documented so the student is viewed as capable of success and not an academic risk.

A spiritual commitment. This will be a primary concern of a conservative Christian college. Other schools may look for evidence of a community spirit and a desire to contribute to society.

SECTION TEN

Understanding College Entrance

Puzzle Pieces to College Entrance

Completing the college application process is similar to putting together a challenging puzzle. What may seem a hopeless jumble of pieces can be skillfully joined to complete a picture. Below are the pieces most commonly requested by colleges. When thoughtfully assembled, they will give the admissions counselor an accurate picture of your student.

THE MAIN PUZZLE PIECES

An application. Filling out a college admissions application is a tedious process, yet it is important to fill it out thoroughly and carefully. Although it may seem simpler, do *not* substitute your own paperwork for the college's form. What may be simpler for you will make the admission counselor's job harder, a fact that will not be well received. Because of the large number of applicants, the selection of students may of necessity be impersonal. Should a computer (or a person with a checklist) do the initial processing, a nonstandard application may be set aside. This can delay or prevent your student's application from being processed. In addition, an application asks for the student information in which the college is most interested. Provide it!

Have a second person check the application for spelling and grammatical accuracy. An admissions counselor can learn almost as much from the care used in filling out the form as he does from the information it contains. Take care not to exaggerate capabilities.

A transcript. In March 2005 the National Association for College Admission Counseling (NACAC) published the *State of College Admission.* Of the seventeen hundred institutions that responded to their survey, 82.5 percent required a transcript or record of grades from applying homeschoolers, making it second in importance only to SAT/ACT scores. This important document of high-school achievement was discussed in section 4. The CD-ROM included with this book will help you compile a neat, professional transcript for submission with your student's college application. Since the initial admissions paperwork is usually sent before high school is completed, depending on when your student applies, a transcript should be sent with the application, after completion of your student's first semester of senior year, and again upon graduation and the completion of all high-school work.

A list of extracurricular activities and awards. Colleges are busy social environments that desire applicants who will contribute positively to campus life. This means an admissions counselor is interested in how your student presently spends his spare time.

Therefore, be sure to include activities that develop the types of skills a college would find attractive. For example, leadership positions indicate good people skills and an ability to handle responsibility. Community service activities and mission trips show initiative and a servant's heart. Athletic, academic, or music awards illustrate the ability to work hard and stay with a goal. It's possible there may still be an admissions counselor out there who thinks your student does not know how to socialize because of the years spent in homeschool. A listing of your student's interests and any awards earned may help dispel misconceptions.

This does not mean your student should exhaustively list every activity in which he has participated. Depth, rather than breadth, seems to be the current rule of thumb. A commitment to excellence in one or two areas is preferable to a broad but more superficial list of activities. In other words, *doing* is more important than *joining*.

The application will include space for these extracurricular activities. If the space given is not adequate, then include a separate activities and awards list. Beware, however, of presenting the admissions counselor with a tiresome list of self-adulation. An honest presentation that illustrates your student's deep interest and achievement in a few areas may serve the applicant better.

A three-ring binder is helpful for storing both academic and extracurricular records. Plastic sleeves can hold award and activity memorabilia. When it comes time to fill out college applications, these memory joggers will be greatly appreciated.

Scores from college entrance exams (SAT I or ACT). College entrance tests are an important part of the college entrance puzzle. The next chapter will look at them closely.

An essay. This may give the student an opportunity to tell more about himself, setting him apart from other applicants. The essay is an excellent place to let an applicant's personality shine. An appropriate touch of humor or healthy humility can be a welcome addition to a college essay. Life lessons learned or a topic that genuinely interests the student are a more enjoyable read than a litany of achievements. An essay should be the student's work entirely. If authorship is questioned, an admissions counselor has access to an applicant's SAT essay for comparison purposes. It is, however, perfectly acceptable to have a second person proof it for errors. If your student hopes to attend a highly selective college, the college essay takes on great significance. Consider purchasing an essay guide to help your student compose an effective paper. Essay writing can also be easily integrated into your student's high-school English courses.

A personal interview with the student. A neat, respectful student who is confident, articulate, and can look an adult in the eye can excel in the interview process. Practicing an interview at home is a wise idea. The student should be ready to talk about himself by sharing interesting information that would set him apart from other applicants. He should also expect to answer questions. (Example: How has your homeschool experience made you a good prospect for our university? What have you read of interest lately?) The student who comes prepared with questions of his own will communicate his interest in the school. If your student is applying to a college some distance away, he may be interviewed by a college alumnus. Your student should be prepared to ask about and show interest in the interviewer's experience with the school.

Recommendations from teachers, parents, pastors, or employers. Even if optional, a recommendation is a helpful way to highlight your teen's character and abilities. Consider recommendations from an employer, the director of a volunteer organization to which your teen has given time, or a state official in whose campaign your teen has worked. Don't overlook the helpfulness of recommendations from successful college alumni. Encourage your student to request recommendations from people who have an honest regard for him and will convey that with sincerity.

An artistic portfolio. This may be necessary when a student's skill needs to be demonstrated for admission. Enrollment in an art or graphic design school is an obvious example.

An audition. Students interested in applying to a music conservatory or theatrical department will usually be required to prepare an audition. Although a student is sometimes allowed to audition via DVD, a live audition is preferable. These are intense, nerve-racking experiences for any student. A student who has competition or performance experience will be better prepared to withstand the unique challenges of the audition process.

ADDITIONAL PUZZLE PIECES

Because of the uniqueness of the homeschooling choice, additional documentation may sometimes be needed to clarify your student's homeschool experience. Below are a few possibilities.

Documentation of course work taken outside your home. Be prepared to document any group co-op classes, advanced placement tests, CLEP exams, courses from a correspondence school, or early college credits your student has taken. For most of these situations, documentation will be required. Depending on which is most appropriate, provide this documentation yourself or request official records be sent to the college.

Course descriptions. Some colleges may desire brief course descriptions to supplement the condensed information appearing on a transcript. This would include a list of textbooks and materials used, activities, and projects. If you have used the contract format suggested in this book, this will not be a heart-stopping experience.

Book lists. A book list may be compiled separately or be part of a larger course description. If requested, present it in the format the college prefers.

A general portfolio. A portfolio is a selective sampling of your student's finest written work, most significant awards, and pictures of his most impressive projects. A highly competitive school or a school unfamiliar with homeschool students might require a portfolio. Maintain a three-ring binder of test scores, papers, and awards from which the more selective portfolio can be pulled if needed.

Sometimes homeschoolers are advised to use portfolios as a replacement for a transcript. This may work with a small college that provides plenty of individual attention for each applicant. In a large school that handles thousands of applicants it may be difficult to find someone to review thoughtfully your student's work. It is interesting to note that a portfolio was not among the twelve entrance criteria surveyed in the NACAC's *State of College Admission* report. With college admission counselors often reviewing the paperwork of hundreds, and possibly thousands, of applicants, it is not surprising that portfolios are not something they usually request. Therefore, keep a portfolio primarily as back-up proof of the integrity of your homeschool program. Do not include it with college application paperwork unless it is specifically requested. Give the college the information they request in the format requested. Your student's information can then be evaluated with greater accuracy.

RECORDS FOR YOUR STUDENT'S BENEFIT

In addition to information the school may request, there are records worth keeping for you and your student's benefit.

Create an application file. If your student is applying to several different schools, keep a separate file folder for each institution. *Make copies of all application paperwork.* Put it in the folder along with all correspondence to and from the college. Taking the time to organize at the beginning of the application process will prevent a lot of headaches along the way.

Write a student resume. A resume puts all the student information for filling out a college application in one easy-to-find location. This can effectively streamline the completion of paperwork, especially when applying to more than one school. Compiling a resume is a practical assignment for an upper-level English course. If the student thoughtfully reviews and includes the information requested on a college application, he will add to the resume's functionality.

A calendar of deadlines. There are so many things to remember in the application process. Multiply this by the number of schools to which the student applies, and you have a formidable juggling act. One central calendar that holds all deadline information can be helpful.

Should college admissions paperwork identify the student as a homeschooler?

In years past, when homeschooling was largely unknown, some families were reluctant to identify their student as a homeschooler. With the growing awareness of homeschooling among college admissions counselors, this reluctance can be discarded.

The NACAC *State of College Admission* 2004–2005 report stated that of seventeen hundred surveyed colleges, 83 percent had formal policies for the evaluation of homeschool applicants. With policies largely in place, it is important to identify your student as a homeschooler and abide by the college application process requested.

Failure to comply with the established policies does not help the applicant and can lead to several unhelpful perceptions. It can convey a lack of consideration on the student's part for the busy admissions counselor. Expecting special concessions can also have an arrogant appearance that will not enhance a student's application process.

To determine an institution's friendliness toward homeschoolers, don't hesitate to call the school's admissions department and ask for their policy for admitting home-educated students. This information may also be readily available on the school's Web site or in their catalog or admissions packet. It is also helpful to question other homeschoolers who have sought admission at the school under consideration. A visit to the *Issues Library* at HSLDA's Web site, www.hslda.org, (look under College and Universities, then Rating Colleges & Universities by their Home School Admission Policies) or a phone call to the homeschool organization in the state where the college is located may provide valuable information about a school's policies and attitude toward homeschoolers.

In the past decade the first large wave of homeschoolers began arriving at many colleges and universities. Hopefully, their success will result in a growing college recruitment of homeschool students across our nation.

FOR MORE INFORMATION

The *State of College Admission* report is issued annually. To view the most current report, visit the research area of www.nacacnet.org.

College Entrance Tests

College entrance test scores are important for every aspiring college student. A few progressive schools have done away with entrance exams. However, for the vast majority of colleges, test scores remain an important admissions consideration. Standards of evaluation and course content can vary tremendously from one high school to another. For the admissions counselor faced with difficult decisions, college entrance tests provide a standardized method of comparing one applicant to another.

Test scores can be doubly important for students who have been home educated. The NACAC's report, mentioned in the last chapter, found that 89 percent of surveyed colleges required standardized test scores from homeschool applicants. Why are these tests so important? Because homeschooling, by its nature, makes some of the other admission considerations impossible.

Class rank can figure into college admissions. What does this mean for homeschoolers? Does your student rank first or last in his class of one? In some states, automatic admission to public universities is extended to students in the top 10 percent of their graduating class. What possible relevance does this have for your student? In addition, college admission counselors sometimes approach a homeschool transcript with reservation. Can a mother be trusted to evaluate her son or daughter with an impartial detachment? In the eyes of some admission counselors, the college entrance test provides the only objective means of evaluating the academic potential of a homeschool student.

This emphasis on test scores can put tremendous pressure on the homeschooled student. He needs to perform at his best on these tests, especially if he hopes to attend a highly competitive college. How can he maximize his performance? With appropriate preparation and test-taking strategies a student can make considerable gains in his scores.

Before we look at some of the strategies for test-taking, let's look at the tests themselves: the PSAT, SAT, PLAN, and ACT. However, we'll take a look at junior/community college tests first.

Junior /Community College Testing

The admission policy of a junior or community college is often one of open enrollment, allowing anyone with a high-school diploma or a GED to attend. Homeschoolers usually find an easy welcome.

Community colleges also have admissions testing. These tests will vary from state-produced exams to the SAT. If a student's scores are not up to the required standard, rather than deny him admission, they often offer developmental courses that will improve his skills. These developmental classes do not result in college credit, but when successfully passed they position the student to move into credited college courses at a later date.

A vast number of community colleges exist today. Any generalized test information I present will be of limited value to you. The safest plan is to contact the community college your student is considering attending and get information specific for that institution.

PSAT

The PSAT/NMSQT (Preliminary Scholastic Assessment Test/National Merit Scholarship Qualifying Test) is a preliminary test to the SAT. For most students it serves as practice for the SAT testing soon to come. For approximately fifty thousand high-performing students nationwide, it will lead to National Merit Scholarship evaluation and possibly valuable scholarship offers.

The PSAT/NMSQT is offered each October nationally and is normally taken in eleventh grade. Some students take it in tenth grade for practice. (Programs, such as Duke University's, use it to identify academic talent in seventh-grade students.) The PSAT is taken at local public or private high schools. Sometimes public schools resist assisting homeschoolers, even though the College Board has encouraged cooperation. Consider checking with your local homeschool support group for a homeschool-friendly test location or check www.collegeboard.com for a list of sites in your area. Look into your options months in advance; last-minute decisions may make it difficult to find a place that can (or will) accommodate your student.

The PSAT changed in the fall of 2004 to correlate with the new SAT. The PSAT is basically a mini-version of the SAT, with similarities and differences. It is similar to the SAT in its level of difficulty and multiple-choice format. However, taking approximately two hours of testing time, it is significantly shorter than the SAT. You can reassure your student that the dreaded essay feature of the new SAT is *not* on the PSAT.

SAT I AND II

The SAT, or SAT I, is a three-hour and forty-five-minute test. Significantly revised in 2005, it is primarily multiple choice with the exception of some grid-in math problems and the infamous essay. The test is broken into ten sections: three math, three critical reading, three writing, and one experimental section that is used to try out questions for future editions of the SAT. The student will not know which section is experimental. The student will receive scores in three areas: math, critical reading, and writing. A perfect score in each area is eight hundred points, making twenty-four hundred points the highest score attainable on the overall test.

The math section now tests the concepts learned in three years of high-school math: numbers and operations, algebra I and II, geometry, statistics, and probability. The verbal section, now renamed *critical reading*, no longer has analogy questions. The majority of the test is spent responding to questions about long, short, and dual reading selections. It also tests vocabulary through sentence completion. The writing section tests a student's writing ability by having him identify errors and improve the writing in sample sentences and paragraphs. It also includes a twenty-five-minute essay.

The persuasive essay, a new feature for the SAT, has been the source of a lot of anxiety for students. The student is given a quotation (sometimes two) to consider and a related writing prompt to answer. A successful essay will have an opening paragraph expressing a clear point of view, two to three body paragraphs that provide examples or evidence for the viewpoint expressed, and a concluding paragraph that summarizes the argument. It is extremely important that the student stay on topic. A well-written essay that does not address the prompt is given a score of zero. In addition, an essay grader may be spending all of one to two minutes evaluating the student's essay, so legibility is important.

The SAT is offered at numerous college locations a number of times each year. Calling your local college or visiting their admissions or student services office should provide you with a general information packet for the test. You can also check the test sponsor's Web site at www.collegeboard.com. Registration can also be conveniently completed online.

For those desiring to take the test more than once, SAT's Question and Answer Service can be helpful. A student who requests this service when registering will receive a report that includes a copy of the questions from the test, the difficulty level of the questions, the correct answers, and the answers the student chose. This information can help a student pinpoint his errors and perform better on a retest. This service is not available for every testing date.

When registering for the SAT, students can choose which colleges they would like to receive their scores. If the student is unsure, he can request these scores be sent at a later date. If the student takes the SAT more than once, the scores from all tests taken are sent to each college the student designates. He cannot send some test scores and omit others.

SAT II tests are one-hour tests on various subject areas. In fact, the new essay test is the old SAT II writing test revised. The more selective the college, the more likely they will request some SAT II tests.

PLAN

The three-hour PLAN test is a tenth-grade exam given as a precursor to the ACT. Although not a college entrance test itself, it can help a student predict his future success on the ACT. The PLAN is one component of ACT's Educational Planning and Assessment System (EPAS). Other components of the EPAS program include the eighth- and ninth-grade program, EXPLORE, and the ACT college-entrance test.

Like the ACT, PLAN tests academic achievement in English, mathematics, reading, and science. In addition, PLAN also collects information on the student's perceived academic needs and his high-school course of study. Test results also evaluate college readiness. Career options are explored through the UNIACT Interest Inventory.

PLAN results facilitate appropriate eleventh- and twelfth-grade high-school planning with potential college and career goals in mind. This in turn can increase the likelihood of the student's future success in life.

Like the PSAT, it may take some searching to locate a high school that will accommodate your student.

For those desiring to identify academic strengths and career ideas for younger students, EXPLORE is available for eighth- and ninth-grade students. Whereas the goal for PLAN is successful college and workforce preparation, EXPLORE is designed to maximize success in high school. For more information on EPAS visit www.act.org.

ACT

ACT is a two-hour and fifty-five minute test with an optional thirty-minute essay. With the essay included, total testing time is three hours and twenty-five minutes. Unlike the SAT that tests reasoning ability, the ACT is an academic achievement test. Therefore, brushing up on the material learned thus far in high school is an effective test-preparation strategy.

The ACT is a multiple-choice test broken into five sections: English, math, reading, and science reasoning. Taking the optional essay portion is generally recommended because it cannot be taken at a later date without retaking the entire test. The ACT sometimes includes an experimental section. When included, it is much shorter than other ACT subject tests, making the experimental portion easily identifiable.

Scores are reported on a scale of one to thirty-six for each of the four main sections. These four scores are then converted into a single composite score of one to thirty-six. If the optional essay test is taken, its score is reported separately and is not included in the composite score.

Like the SAT, the ACT essay is a new feature. The student is given thirty minutes to respond to a prompt with an essay of appropriately five paragraphs. While introductory and conclusion paragraphs follow the same basic format as the SAT, the student may handle the body paragraphs somewhat differently. Rather than focusing primarily on supporting positions, the ACT seems to favor including a *con* paragraph that acknowledges the opposing argument along with the body paragraphs supporting the student's position.

The ACT is offered four to six times a year depending on your location. Testing dates and sites are available on the Web site, www.actstudent.org. The ACT also offers online registration. Some testing dates offer the Test Information Release program. For an additional fee, the student receives a copy of the test he took, answers, and a photocopy of his completed score sheet. This information can be a great study tool if the student plans to retake the test at a later date. The student requests and pays when he registers for the test. Again, this additional service is not available for every testing date.

The student can have his test scores sent directly to colleges or only to him. If the student takes the test more than once, he can choose (at a later date and for a small fee) which score report he wants sent to the colleges of his choice. Unlike the SAT, the ACT allows the student to choose the test scores to be sent. This can be important depending on how a college uses test scores for scholarship considerations. While many colleges calculate scholarship offers from the highest scores the student earns, it is certainly possible that they could use the first scores submitted.

WHICH TEST SHOULD MY STUDENT TAKE?

To determine which test to take, find out which test is acceptable to the college your student is interested in attending. If both the SAT and ACT are acceptable, consider preparing for both. Some students will do better on one than the other.

It is often wise to take these tests more than once because test scores can usually be improved. If a student has effectively used the SAT's Question and Answer Service or ACT's Test Information Release, he may be able to make significant gains in his score. Additional course work or study in test preparation books may also yield fruit when retesting. Consider taking the test up to three times. After the third time, gains tend to diminish. If the college your student is considering bases scholarship money on test scores, this extra effort may be richly repaid. We found multiple testing to be an excellent strategy for our third child. By retaking the tests, he was able to increase his merit scholarship by $2,500 annually. This increased his scholarship package by $10,000 over the course of four years.

If your student plans to take the test several times, begin testing in the late winter or spring of the eleventh grade. Take a final test in the summer or no later than early fall of twelfth grade (or both). Testing after October of twelfth grade may be too late to make college-enrollment deadlines, which are usually in late winter or early spring. Students applying under early decision programs may need to complete final testing earlier.

TESTING STRATEGIES

In the year or months prior to the test:

I highly recommend adding SAT or ACT preparation to your school curriculum. A visit to a large bookstore should yield a number of test preparation guides for your consideration. In addition to familiarizing you with the test, they also teach helpful test-taking strategies, provide reviews of the content being tested, and include practice tests. The guides that include a CD-ROM of practice tests are particularly helpful because the computer will score them. Test preparation guides are included in the appendix along with a helpful DVD math preparation program, *SAT Math Review*, from Chalk Dust.

When studying an SAT or ACT preparation guide, give special attention to all test directions. A good understanding of directions before the clock starts ticking on test day will provide more time for answering questions.

Register in a timely fashion. Late registrations and standby arrangements add to the cost of the test. In addition, it is not always possible to accommodate standbys.

On the day of the test:

Physical comfort helps a student stay focused. Get a good night's sleep and eat breakfast. Dress in layers to stay comfortable in rooms that are too hot or too cold. Use the restroom before reporting for the test.

Come prepared. Bring your admission ticket, picture identification, number 2 pencils, calculator, and watch. Turn your cell phone off!

Although food may not be eaten in the testing room, a small snack brought in a purse or pants pocket can be quickly consumed at a bathroom break. The additional energy may help you refocus for the remainder of the test.

Students are allowed to write in test booklets. Circle each answer in the test booklet as a decision is made. Should you later get off on your bubbling, you won't waste valuable time revisiting each question but can make corrections quickly.

Educated guessing is helpful on both tests. The ACT does not penalize wrong answers. The SAT penalizes one-fourth point for each wrong answer.

Pray, do your best, and leave the results with God.

What if my student doesn't test well?

Not all students test well on college entrance tests. Other students are not balanced. They shine in one academic area and struggle in another. Fortunately many colleges are comfortable with students who exhibit both strengths and weaknesses. One of my students is strong in English and weak in math. His test scores reflected this. The professor interviewing my son for an English scholarship simply noted, "Don't like math, do you?" This did not prevent my son from getting the English scholarship he sought. The professor recognized that math would be a minor part of the degree program my son planned to pursue and would not impact his likelihood of success at their institution. Smaller colleges considering fewer applicants sometimes have a greater ability to see each student as an individual and evaluate applications accordingly.

Although colleges recognize that entrance tests do not measure a student's initiative, his drive to succeed, or the interpersonal skills integral to the college experience, it is unlikely that test scores will diminish in importance anytime soon. Therefore, it is important that students be as prepared as possible before taking a college-entrance exam. Make use of the many test preparation guides available. For the student plagued by test anxiety, adequate test preparation is doubly important. It is also important that parents not add to a stressful situation by being visibly stressed themselves. Encourage your student as you together commit his performance to God. Send him off with a smile. Your student's future, including his college-entrance tests, are in God's hands.

Unfortunately, college-entrance tests are just the beginning of college performance pressure. When choosing a college, note the average SAT and ACT scores. Don't pursue a college that will make success an overwhelming struggle for your student.

College Financing

So far we have considered college choices, paperwork, and entrance testing. That leaves the all-important topic of college financing. Understanding the college financial process and navigating it successfully may make or break your student's college dream.

The FAFSA

Every college scholarship journey begins with filling out the FAFSA, or Free Application for Federal Student Aid. This government form collects family income information that is used to establish a student's eligibility for grants, loans, scholarships, and work-study programs. Filling out the FAFSA is not the way most parents of college-age students would choose to spend a quiet winter evening. Nevertheless, most parents will find themselves tackling it in February as soon as the last W-2 has arrived and the final computation is completed on the income-tax return. The stress of completing taxes and the FAFSA so early will be somewhat compensated by the calm you will possess while others are rushing to the last postal pickup on April 15. The greatest compensation, however, comes from knowing you have given your student the best opportunity to receive the financial assistance he needs for college. FAFSAs received after March 1 find this money rapidly depleting.

The information you provide for the FAFSA forms the basis of the SAR or Student Aid Report. Your student's SAR reports the EFC, or Expected Family Contribution. The EFC is the amount parents and student are expected to contribute to the student's education for the coming school year. The college's financial aid personnel will use the EFC to determine your student's eligibility for a government Pell Grant and other grant, loan, or scholarship opportunities. Plan on taking a deep calming breath before viewing the EFC. Although others may have a different experience, we have never found the expected contribution to mirror our day-to-day financial realities. Nor have we been asked to contribute the entire EFC for a student's education. (With two more students to go, I may have to revise that statement in the next edition of this book.) Between a variety of scholarships, work-study programs, minimal student loans, part-time or summer jobs, and parental contributions, we have partnered with our three oldest in helping them pursue a college degree. Somehow we have still eaten and paid the mortgage.

The easiest way to file the FAFSA is online at www.fafsa.ed.gov although it can also be filed via US postal mail. Online filing will go most smoothly if you have prefigured the financial information and filled out anything that isn't stored in your memory on a hard copy first. Upon starting a new student account, a PIN (Personal Identification Number) will be assigned to the student. Parents will also receive a PIN for their official online signature. File these numbers in a safe place because they will be needed to access or sign the student account each year or whenever changes are made. Although a forgotten PIN can be retrieved, it can take a few days. If paperwork is filed at the midnight hour, this delay can be problematic.

The FAFSA must be filed annually. Failure to file will result in a reduction of your student's financial aid package or loss of his work study. The first year's filing is the most difficult. When filing for subsequent years, much of the vital information will be retained, leaving you to add the new financial figures.

The FAFSA is used by both government and private colleges. Sometimes a private school will collect financial information on an additional form, such as the College Board's CSS/Profile (College Scholarship Service Financial Aid Profile). This form may be used to award nonfederal student aid. The college will let you know what forms they need to process your student's financial aid package.

The FAFSA results are also used to determine eligibility for the Pell Grant. The Pell Grant is a government educational subsidy awarded to students with significant financial need. A Pell Grant does not have to be paid back.

THE SCHOLARSHIP SEARCH BEGINS

Scholarships and grants are a blessing, sometimes turning an unaffordable academic dream into reality. Unlike loans, they do not have to be paid back. However, obtaining significant scholarship awards, for most students, does not come without hard work. Sometimes that work takes the form of an exemplary high-school career. Sometimes it is the result of hours honing a musical or athletic skill. In addition, applying for scholarships often requires a significant amount of paperwork. Even then the process is not necessarily over. Sometimes a student is required to meet various criteria to continue to receive the money awarded.

Finding Scholarship Money

How does a student go about finding scholarship money? Through old-fashioned hard work and diligence. A good starting point is the Internet. A great place to begin is www.finaid.com. Finaid, which calls itself "the smart student guide to financial aid," is a public service Web site, has won numerous awards, and offers its information free of charge. Use it! The information covers all aspects of financing a college education and provides links to other helpful sites. A general scholarship search can begin long before the college has been selected.

However, the primary source of scholarship money is the college itself. It is usually wise for the student to apply to several schools. If accepted, he will receive information on the financial package each school is willing to offer. With information in hand, the student can determine the feasibility of attending each institution and compare one with another. It is always wise to apply to at least one financially reasonable school. If the financial award from the dream school is not sufficient, the student will be positioned to start his education where he can afford it.

A number of books are available to help you locate scholarship opportunities. *The Scholarship Book* by Daniel Cassidy includes a CD-ROM that offers direct links to the home pages of various scholarship sources and a search function for finding the most applicable scholarships. *The College Board Scholarship Handbook 2007* is another long-standing choice. Both books are widely available and can be purchased online. A visit to a large bookstore may afford you the opportunity to see these books and others before purchasing. It is also possible that your public library's reference section makes these books available.

Sooner or later your student will probably receive information about scholarship search services. These services offer help locating scholarship money for your student. Should you decide to use their services, you will probably pay for information you can find through your own searching. Check www.finaid.com for information on common scholarship scams.

Should we go into debt to finance our student's education?

Whether a student should incur debt for a college education is a matter of debate. Obtaining a college degree, in most cases, will significantly increase lifetime earnings. This may compensate many times over for the debt incurred. Parents must also determine whether they will obtain loans on behalf of their student's education. With fewer years left in the workforce, their long-term earning power is significantly shorter than their student's. The effect that educational loans will have on preparing for the reduced income of the retirement years needs to be seriously considered. In addition, students and parents must wrestle with their personal convictions regarding debt.

If you decide to borrow money, you must consider the amount. How much is reasonable? How much is too much? The college your student will be attending can provide you with average student indebtedness figures. In addition, government loan programs limit the amount of money students and parents can borrow. The indebtedness figures and amount of loan money available may be of some help in making your decision. However, just because the student is able to borrow significant amounts of money does not make it wise. The limit on student borrowing increases with each year of college. Cumulatively it is a very sizable amount. Loan repayment will likely coincide with entry-level jobs, marriage, and establishing a home. Excessive debt will add stress to the next phase of life.

Most students will use the government loan programs when financing their education. The government offers both subsidized (the government pays the interest while the student is in school) and unsubsidized (the student pays all interest but can defer it until after graduation) Stafford student loans. The college's financial aid counselor can offer valuable help on SAR-based options open to your student. Many lenders participate in the government loan program. The college will often have lender recommendations. Interest rates on government student loans are more reasonable than general consumer loans.

Repayment of a student loan begins after a six-month grace period following graduation. Continued deferment is granted if the student pursues a graduate degree upon completion of his undergraduate work. Should the student have trouble obtaining work or meeting his loan obligation during the life of the loan, short-term deferments are often available, and terms can sometimes be renegotiated. Government educational loans, unlike credit cards, are not immediately punitive, but often actively work with the student to help them successfully pay back the loan. Open communication is an important part of making adjustments when necessary.

Should parents want to help finance their student's education through a government loan, the PLUS loan program is available. Terms are different from the student Stafford loans. To obtain additional information on the FAFSA, government grants, loans, and work-study programs visit www.studentaid.ed.gov.

Types of Scholarships

Scholarships are awarded for a number of different reasons and can be found in a number of different places. Below are some scholarship possibilities.

National Merit Finalist and Semi-finalist. For the outstanding student with excellent PSAT scores, impressive, but competitive, scholarship opportunities are available.

Academic excellence. Academic scholarships may be determined using different criteria such as high school grade point average (GPA) or class rank. Colleges often use the SAT and ACT scores as an objective way to compare student performance.

Artistic achievement. Music, dance, and drama awards are often awarded via auditions or competitions. In the field of art, a portfolio will most likely be required.

Athletic skills. Academic eligibility for athletic scholarships is determined by the National Collegiate Athletic Association (NCAA) or National Association of Intercollegiate Athletics (NAIA). Contact the school of interest to find out their organizational affiliation, obtain the appropriate paperwork, and learn the school's athletic requirements for your student's sport. Visit NCAA's Web site, www.ncaa.org, to read Frequently Asked Questions by Home School Student Athletes. A strong academic high-school program will aid the athlete seeking a scholarship.

Parent's workplace. Some large corporations have scholarship funds for which employees' children can apply.

Civic organizations. Community organizations often offer scholarships to students who plan to pursue studies in the area of interest to the organization such as a music coterie funding an annual scholarship to an outstanding music student.

Scouting. Boys who have earned their Eagle award can compete for college scholarships funded by Boy Scouts of America.

Church matching grant programs. In this sort of program, the college matches the amount given by the student's home church for his education. Funds are sent directly to the college. The amount of money colleges will match varies. In our experience with two different Christian institutions, $500 and $1000 could be matched annually. Like other scholarships and grants, the appropriate paperwork must be filed by the designated time to use the program.

Dependent of a_____ (fill in the blank). Some organizations offer scholarships to students with a parent who is or was in a career field it represents or supports. For example, a Christian school may offer a scholarship to missionary or minister's children. Some schools offer aid to children of alumni.

Ethnicity based. Some scholarships are available to minority students who desire a college education. If the student has mixed ethnicity, identify the student as being of the minority race for the greatest advantage.

One-of-a-kind scholarships. Students with specific skills or interests can sometimes find scholarships offered by organizations with similar interests. An Internet search can turn up some interesting and unusual opportunities.

Once you complete the research, the tedium begins. Your teen may need to spend many hours filling out forms. Hopefully, the reward will be worth the effort. When researching scholarships, your student may be tempted to ignore the smaller awards and focus on the largest awards available. However, large awards are especially competitive. Encourage your student to make the effort to apply for smaller scholarships. The scholarship search can be likened to a part-time job. Should even a small scholarship come his way, the student applying for it can sometimes convert his time to an impressive hourly wage.

Additional Thoughts on Scholarships

Go where the student is wanted. If the school is eager to have your student, that desire should be evidenced by an attractive financial aid package. The best scholarship search can be thwarted if the student is considering the wrong school. For example, highly competitive schools are deluged with outstanding applicants. Even excellent students may be offered minimal financial assistant if all applicants share the same exemplary credentials. In contrast, many lesser known schools offer excellent educational opportunities and the financial help to go with it.

Have a thorough understanding of the school's financial aid policies. Policies vary from institution to institution. For example, many institutions give their best financial packages to students entering as freshman. Questions about financial-aid policies that will help you plan effectively include the following:

- Are the best packages offered to incoming freshman?
- What is the definition of an incoming freshman?
- What affects freshman status?
- Do dual enrollment, developmental classes, CLEP exams, or AP courses affect it?
- Do college credits earned during high school affect freshman status? (Some schools allow unlimited college credit prior to high school graduation without affecting freshman status for financial award consideration.)
- How many credits can a student earn after his declared high-school graduation and still be considered a freshman for scholarship evaluation? (This may be highly limited.)

In addition to the all important questions regarding freshman status, a second set of questions revolve around transfer situations.

- Is significant financial help available for transfer students?
- Does the amount of credit transferred change the amount of financial help available?

We found an interesting answer to the second question at one school. Scholarship help was impressive for strong students who retained their freshman status by arriving with fewer than twelve college credits. Scholarship awards dropped for transfer students with twelve to twenty-three credit hours but improved significantly for strong students transferring twenty-four or more credits. This situation, and others like it, require thorough and careful planning to maximize the scholarship award.

Don't look at the price tag first. Being frugal by nature, I initially found this advice difficult to accept. However, many private schools, knowing the sticker shock accompanied by a look at their tuition costs, work hard to make their schools affordable. Often they make efforts to bring the student's final cost more in line with the cost of a public education. You cannot know the final financial picture at any given institution until the student has applied, been accepted, and received his financial award package. Happily, sometimes the financial package makes enrollment feasible. At other times it remains out of reach. The wise student applies to at least one financially safe school should his first-choice school prove unattainable.

Maintaining Merit Scholarships

Many homeschooled students will go to college on merit scholarships. Although helpful, they are not always the pot of gold at the end of the rainbow. Two of our children have received sizable merit awards. Although we were grateful for the financial help, there are sometimes catches to merit-based money.

It is important to understand the rules if obtaining a merit-based scholarship. Sometimes they require maintaining a specific GPA. Some students welcome and thrive on the challenge. A student who lacks confidence or is a perfectionist may find the pressure unbearable. Every grade in every course gains an unreasonable significance. Sometimes the struggle to keep every grade high can take away much of the pleasure of learning.

In contrast, some schools require a student to make "reasonable progress" to retain merit-based money. This allows the student to have strengths and weaknesses instead of requiring near perfection in every academic area. My students have experienced both situations. The first created a great deal of unhealthy stress; the second made the learning process much more enjoyable. When evaluating merit scholarships, keep your student's personality and resiliency to pressure in mind. Consider his academic drive. If he does not drive himself academically and enjoy the process in high school, it will be hard to learn this in college. A good academic fit will make the college experience more enjoyable for the student, and his parents will rest easier at night.

Should your student find himself in a pressurized merit situation, a number of strategies can help.

Balance course loads each semester with a mixture of easy and hard courses. Unfortunately, this advice is more difficult for transfer students to apply. GPAs generally start over at each institution. This means a transfer student starts his junior courses without a high GPA buffer from his easier freshman and sophomore courses. However, if your student finds the courses in his major of great interest, he may do fine with a challenging upper-level course load.

Concentrate on the courses that have the most potential for improvement. A *B* turned into an *A* gains a grade point.

Drop classes that earn less than the needed grade. Stay in the course as long as possible to learn as much as possible, then drop it to retake with a better grade later. If the class is an elective, get out quickly and never return! Caution: don't use this strategy too often, or it can delay graduation! Also, be sure this strategy does not change full-time student status, which can jeopardize scholarships, and for some families, health insurance.

If you despair of ever getting more than an average grade in a course, get approval to take it elsewhere. This strategy only works when courses transferred in are not included in the GPA calculation or the transferred classes are significantly easier than their counterparts at the four-year university. Courses in a student's major may not be approved to take elsewhere.

Be wary of taking advanced courses when a standard-level course is acceptable. A standard-level course will often satisfy the graduation plan without risking the GPA.

Listen to the opinion of other students. This information from the trenches can help you find the best teachers and determine the overall difficulty of a course in advance.

When possible, try to mix courses that base final grades on papers with those that require final exams. Papers can be finished during the semester, thus relieving the finals crunch.

It can be difficult to play this academic game after a homeschool lifestyle of learning for its own sake. Unfortunately, the necessity of keeping merit scholarships is a hard fact of reality for many students. While the adjustment may be uncomfortable, it is important to learn how to play the game. Bear in mind that the keep-the-merit-based-scholarship game is only temporary. Thankfully, learning does not end with a college diploma. It will continue for a lifetime through both the rewards of professional growth and the simple pleasure of pursuing personal interests.

Are honors designations calculated differently than GPAs?

While a number of strategies can be successfully employed to maintain a high GPA and to keep scholarship money intact, it is important to note the rules may differ for earning an honor's designation upon graduation. Summa, magna, and cum laude recognition is often based on the cumulative GPA earned from the student's entire college career, including transfer credit. This makes these designations harder to obtain but certainly adds to the honor of these awards.

College Admissions Terminology

Early action—One of two forms of early admissions. In early action a student applies during the fall (generally by early November) of his senior year to the college of his choice. The school acts on his application early, with students usually knowing by January or February (sometimes December) whether they have been accepted. Early action decisions are termed Non-Restrictive Application Plans and are nonbinding.

Early decision—The other form of early admission. Early decision is much like early action. The student applies during the fall (generally early November) of his senior year to the college of his choice. The school acts upon his application, usually letting students know by December whether they have been accepted. However, a significant difference exists. Early-decision admissions are termed Restrictive Application Plans and are binding. If students are accepted, they are obligated to accept the offer if the family determines the financial award is adequate for the student's needs. Why would students apply under an early-decision program? For many institutions early-decision students are accepted at a higher rate than their regular enrollment students. This would be helpful for the student absolutely sure of his preferred college choice. If there is any hesitation at all, it would be best not to file an early-decision application.

Reach school—A college that is beyond the student's credentials for an assured entry.

Regular admission—Admission that is handled under normal deadlines and timing.

Rolling admission—Reviewing applications and accepting students on a first-come, first-served basis.

Safe school—A school where the student can confidently assume he will be accepted.

Wait list—A secondary list of students who aren't accepted in the first round of admission offers from a college. If students who receive initial acceptance letters choose not to enroll, an applicant from the wait list is offered the spot. Wait-listed students should have a safe school back-up plan.

College Admissions Calendar

College planning and decision time can be overwhelming. To help organize your thoughts, I have included a planning calendar that encompasses all four high-school years. Because every school will have different deadlines and procedures, this calendar can only offer general guidelines. Always read the material for the colleges of particular interest carefully so you miss no deadlines.

GENERAL GUIDELINES FOR EACH YEAR

- [ ] Take challenging courses and keep grades up.
- [ ] Pursue interests outside of school, but keep school at the top of your priority list.
- [ ] Don't vegetate in the summer: attend camps, take classes, do volunteer work, maintain a summer reading list, get a job, etc.
- [ ] Keep a resume or activities file; add to it all four years. Include both activities and awards.
- [ ] Keep a list of school and pleasure reading.
- [ ] Start and add to college information folders. A separate one for each school will make materials easier to find.
- [ ] Develop a college comparison checklist; add information all four years.
- [ ] Visit convenient college campuses. Even if you're not particularly interested in the school, it will give you a feeling for what you like and don't like in the college environment.
- [ ] Incorporate essay skills in schoolwork; this is important for both the SAT and college-entrance essays.

FRESHMAN YEAR

- [ ] Plan your four-year academic program. Keep it challenging. No coasting allowed! Refer to the "High School Course and Credit Guidelines" in this book. Include something in each core area: English, history, math, science. Begin your foreign language; some colleges want three years. Plan to use elective credits to strengthen areas of particular career interest.

☐ If you already have a strong college preference, check the school's Web site to see what high-school courses the admissions department prefers. Find out about specific homeschool requirements.

☐ Investigate and pursue appealing extracurricular activities.

☐ Become an avid reader. You'll need those reading skills for college.

☐ Over the summer familiarize yourself with the PSAT if taking it in the fall.

SOPHOMORE YEAR

Fall

☐ Take the PSAT in October for practice, if desired.

☐ The PLAN is offered between September and December.

Winter/Spring

☐ If planning to take eleventh-grade dual enrollment at the community college, now is the time to look into it. In late winter or early spring begin preparation for the placement testing if one is required. In late spring take the placement test and meet with the admissions officer to enroll and choose fall classes.

☐ AP testing is held in May. Although most sophomores will not be ready, a few hardy individuals who have completed a college prep biology course may want to take the biology AP exam.

Summer

☐ Begin preparation for the PSAT taken in October of your junior year. This is the one that counts.

☐ Make a list of all the things most important to you in a college. "Section 9, Choosing a College" can get you started. The college search on www.collegeboard.com provides information on many colleges including links to their Web sites. Make a list of up to ten schools of interest. Organize the information you accumulate in a spreadsheet or comparison chart.

☐ Start familiarizing yourself with scholarship opportunities via the Internet. Finaid at www.finaid.com is a good starting place. Appendix A includes some other sites of interest.

☐ If you are interested in a career, see if you can spend a day shadowing someone working in the field of interest. Look for summer job opportunities in the field.

☐ Keep reading!

JUNIOR YEAR

Important: College-related planning will accelerate in the eleventh and twelfth grades. Keep a calendar of all important dates: registration and testing dates for SAT and ACT, application and fee deadlines, financial aid deadlines, campus days, auditions, etc. Don't trust the college paperwork juggle to memory!

☐ Actively use your planning calendar!

Fall

- [ ] Take the PSAT in October. This is the test sitting that counts for National Merit Scholarship consideration.
- [ ] Begin an SAT and/or ACT preparation book or take a preparation course.
- [ ] When PSAT scores arrive (approximately December), adjust school courses as necessary to address academic weaknesses.
- [ ] Register for a spring testing of the SAT, ACT, or both.
- [ ] Attend a college fair if available in your area.
- [ ] Continue work on your list of schools. Develop a list of up to ten colleges of interest.
- [ ] Collect and study college literature and applications. Organize all the material in separate college files.
- [ ] Begin visiting schools of interest if traveling in the area. Be sure your high-school program will meet college expectations.
- [ ] Be sure you have a social security number. You will need it for college applications.

Winter/Spring

- [ ] Take the SAT, ACT, or both.
- [ ] AP tests are offered in May.
- [ ] If planning to take twelfth-grade dual enrollment at the community college, now is the time to look into it. In late winter or early spring begin preparation for the placement testing if one is required. In late spring take the placement test and meet with the admissions officer to enroll and choose fall classes.
- [ ] Begin official visits to colleges of interest. Try to go when school is in session. Arrange an interview, if possible. Send a follow-up thank-you note. Attend a specially planned campus day if any are scheduled. Make sure your parents attend any parent orientations offered during your visit. Actively study your college files and comparison list. Make sure you have literature for every school of special interest.
- [ ] Begin looking more actively at scholarship opportunities. Pay special attention to essay requirements.

Summer

- [ ] Repeat SAT or ACT if a higher score is desired.
- [ ] Continue college research to begin narrowing your list of potential schools. Only add a college if it is particularly promising.
- [ ] Summer may afford more time to actively research scholarship opportunities.
- [ ] If considering an art or music school, familiarize yourself with portfolio or audition requirements. Do any appropriate preparation.
- [ ] Read through college applications to get a thorough grasp of the information requested. To save time, collect this information in a personal resume for reference when filling out applications for each college.
- [ ] Pay close attention to entrance essay requirements. If you are applying to several schools it is not too early to get started on them.
- [ ] Students interested in college athletics must register online with the NCAA Clearing House, www.ncaaclearinghouse.net, to determine eligibility. In addition to general academic requirements, look for information specific to homeschoolers. A transcript of six semesters of high-school work is required.

Have everything ready to send as soon as you complete eleventh grade. If any academic deficiencies are found, you can address them in twelfth grade.

☐ Begin considering from whom you will request a recommendation. Consider people who know you well, will portray you positively, and can write well.

☐ Keep reading!

SENIOR YEAR

☐ Actively use your planning calendar!

Fall

☐ College paperwork will begin in earnest. *Important: Make copies of all paperwork before sending!*

☐ Continue to take college prep courses.

☐ You're running out of time to take the SAT or ACT. Allow approximately two months between your last testing date and deadline for the college application.

☐ Narrow your college list to only those of most interest. It's fine to include "reach" schools that are competitive, but also include at least one or two "safe" schools in your list, where acceptance is all but guaranteed.

☐ Attend a college fair. Spend time at the booths of the schools on your short list. Ask specific questions you may still have. You may be able to narrow your list a bit more.

☐ Continue your scholarship search and watch application deadlines closely. Don't miss out on opportunities!

☐ Visit the schools of greatest interest on planned campus days, if you haven't yet done so.

☐ In advance of your visit, request an interview. Prepare a list of questions. If you receive an interview, send a follow-up thank-you note.

☐ Continue work on any required essays.

☐ Update your resume to streamline the completion of college applications.

☐ Complete your applications if you desire an early decision, early action, or rolling admissions (see chapter, "College Definitions"). Don't miss your deadlines.

☐ Request letters of recommendation from people who know you well, will portray you positively, and can write well. Provide the college's form, if applicable, and be sure to supply a stamped envelope.

☐ Begin applications for schools with later deadlines. Send them off by the required date.

☐ Request recommendation letters for these additional schools.

☐ Watch for the deadline on the CSS/Profile if the college requires this for financial aid consideration. The CSS/Profile is due earlier than the FAFSA.

Winter

☐ All applications will most likely be due by January.

☐ Once you have finished applications, refocus on the scholarship search.

☐ Parents should fill out the FAFSA as early as possible. Financial aid disbursement usually begins March 1.

☐ For any schools who received transcripts without first-semester grades, send a second transcript now.

☐ Stay in touch with colleges to be sure all paperwork has been received. This sometimes can be done online.

☐ If you receive an acceptance via early admissions and decide to go to that college, notify other schools that you are withdrawing your application.

Spring

☐ Acceptance or rejection letters should be arriving in March or April. For applicants placed on a waiting list, college should finalize decisions in May.

☐ If you are accepted at more than one school and can't decide, compare financial aid offers.

☐ If still undecided, plan a final campus visit to aid decision making.

☐ Some schools, even after acceptance, will allow you to retake the SAT or ACT to improve your scores for financial aid. If this is the case, watch deadlines and consider retaking one or both.

☐ Notify the school you are accepting and send in required deposits by the deadline. If you fail to do so, the college might give your place to another applicant.

☐ Now that you have been accepted, keep all paperwork from the chosen college carefully filed. A new round of information, some with deadlines (such as housing), will be sent. Use your calendar and stay organized.

☐ Notify the schools whose offers you are not accepting, generally by May 1.

☐ Take any final AP exams in May.

☐ Make plans to attend the selected college's orientation. This can take place in the spring or summer before college entrance.

Summer

☐ Send your final transcript with all grades and graduation date to the selected college. If you are an athlete, send one to the NCAA.

☐ Attend summer orientation, if one is scheduled.

☐ Shop for necessary items for school. The school will let you know what to bring.

☐ Congratulate yourself for a job well done! Because of your careful research and diligent work, your college choice should be an excellent fit for you.

SECTION ELEVEN

College Credit
the Alternative Way

Is your student interested in getting an early start on college? If so, there are a number of ways to accomplish this goal.

A number of tests, such as the DANTES, a test with military roots; the PEP, from the makers of the ACT; and the Graduate Record Exam, a test used for entry into graduate school, are sometimes awarded college credit by colleges with external degree programs (see the discussion below on the CLEP). However, the three most popular ways to earn college credit alternatively are by Advanced Placement exams, CLEP testing, and early enrollment at the local college. In addition to looking at the advantages and disadvantages of these three methods, we will also look briefly at college courses and degrees by correspondence.

Advanced Placement Courses and Exams

A P, Advanced Placement classes, are high school courses with college level content. AP courses are usually taken in eleventh and twelfth grade. (Ninth- and tenth-grade honors courses may be referred to as pre-AP.) Upon completion, students take the AP exam offered for that course. Examples of some of the exams available include biology, English, Spanish, and US history. The number of AP exams exceeds thirty, each two to three hours long. AP exams are scored on a one-to-five scale. A three is considered passing. A score of four or five, at the discretion of the college, may earn college credit. Successful AP exam scores may also earn a student advanced placement in college.

AP exams are offered in May each year, most often at public high schools. In many states, no cooperative arrangement exists that allows homeschoolers to attend either AP classes or take AP tests. The College Board, sponsor of the AP tests, will actively help an interested student find a testing location to accommodate him. Private schools are generally more willing to assist homeschooling students. Thanks to the home business PA Homeschoolers (www.pahomeschoolers.com), AP preparation courses are available to homeschoolers nationwide. Although other online services exist, PA Homeschoolers' prices may fit the homeschool pocketbook better. For general AP information, go to www.collegeboard.com.

A student is not required to take a specified course prior to taking an AP exam. A motivated student, through self-disciplined study, may be successful in passing an AP exam.

ADVANTAGES TO ADVANCED PLACEMENT EXAMS

1. The College Board offers the Scholar Award recognition program for students reaching noteworthy levels of achievement using AP exams. Although not a monetary program, it can sometimes lead to increased financial offerings from the college of interest.
2. Competitive colleges expect applicants to have AP-level course work. Passing some AP exams demonstrates the capabilities of the student.

3. An ambitious student who successfully completes a number of AP exams can begin college with a sopho-more standing.
4. Less ambitious testing plans can still enhance your student's chances of being accepted at more competitive colleges, perhaps with scholarship money included.
5. Your student can experience college level work without leaving home.

DISADVANTAGES TO ADVANCED PLACEMENT EXAMS

1. AP exams do not necessarily replace college credits. Testing out of courses does not automatically mean the student will receive credit for those courses; it may mean he will bypass early level college courses and advance directly into more advanced courses.
2. Colleges make their own decisions about how to handle AP exams. This means you must research carefully to avoid false expectations. Check Web sites or college catalogs for policies.
3. As mentioned above, AP exams are offered on high school campuses. School personnel are not always eager to accommodate homeschoolers in their testing situations.
4. AP exams are offered in May. This means senior-year AP exams will not appear on transcripts until college decisions and financial awards are already made. For this reason, AP work, for capable students, should be started during the junior year.
5. A student who passes several AP exams may not have any light freshman courses his first college year to ease the transition and balance the stress of a difficult course load.

CLEP Exams

The College Level Examination Program, commonly known as the CLEP, helps students earn college credit through successful examination. The CLEP is a product of the College Board. Other well-known tests from the College Board include the AP exam, the PSAT/NMSQT, and the SAT college-entrance test.

In the past the CLEP may have been most widely used by adults returning to college and seeking credit for the learning they acquired through life and in the workforce. College students might choose to "clep" a course or two because of scheduling conflicts that would delay their graduation. With the cost of college skyrocketing and more students taking five years to graduate, a few strategic CLEP tests can be helpful financially. Students can also use the CLEP program to avoid classes having an anti-Christian bias. In recent years homeschoolers have seen the advantages of the CLEP. Books have been written that outline strategies for obtaining a legitimate college degree through testing, via the CLEP and other testing programs, while never setting foot in a college classroom.

CLEP tests are primarily ninety-minute multiple-choice exams. In 2001 the CLEP was moved to computer, making it possible to take the test and receive your scores immediately. (An exception is the optional essays available for some exams. These essays are sent to and graded by the college that will be issuing credit.) A visit to www.college board.com provides practice with the format of the test so the student doesn't go into the testing situation cold.

CLEPs can be taken at many college campuses. Check the College Board Web site for the location closest to you.

CLEP exams take two forms: general and subject. The six general examinations cover core courses normally taken the first two years of college: English composition with essay, English composition without essay, college mathematics, humanities, natural science, and social sciences and history. Satisfactory completion of these tests can result in three to six college-credit hours per course.

Subject area tests correspond to individual college courses with similar titles: American government, introduction to psychology, college algebra, and general biology. More than thirty CLEP tests are presently available.

Study guides are available to help you prepare for both the general and subject matter tests. These guides, in addition to providing sample test questions, usually do a thorough job of explaining all the ins and outs of the CLEP. Textbooks for effective preparation are often recommended.

The college where the student is pursuing a degree awards credit for a successful CLEP exam. If the student is not presently enrolled in an institution, CLEP credit can be "banked" with the College Credit Recommendation

Service (CREDIT) of the American Council of Education (ACE). Credits earned by exam are consolidated on one transcript. This transcript, at your request, will be sent to any college you indicate. ACE CREDIT's fees for these services are reasonable. Appendix A contains contact information.

Students interested in earning their entire college degree nontraditionally via credit-by-exam, life experience, and transfer credit have three external degree options: Charter Oak State College, Excelsior College, and Thomas Edison State College—fully accredited institutions accepting both in-state and out-of-state students. Address information is included in appendix A. Many other colleges and universities have a somewhat modified external degree program that combines nontraditional crediting options and on-site classes. A school's catalog should contain the information you need.

ADVANTAGES TO CLEP EXAMS

1. Homeschool high schoolers can prepare for a CLEP and get a jump start on college credit.
2. General course requirements that the student has already mastered do not need to be repeated, allowing the student to move into his major field of study at an accelerated pace.
3. CLEP exams are reasonably priced, potentially saving the student a substantial amount of money over the course of a four-year college program.
4. Careful clepping can substantially reduce the time spent in college.

Despite the advantages to the CLEP, distinct disadvantages should also be considered. It takes a great deal of care to "clep" wisely. To help you in your decision making some cautions are listed below.

DISADVANTAGES TO CLEP EXAMS

1. Colleges will only award CLEP credit to students enrolled in their academic program.
2. Each college decides which CLEP tests they will accept. Some accept a wide variety; others significantly limit what they will take. "Clepping" without complete knowledge can lead to disappointment and frustration, not to mention wasted time and money. Check individual college Web sites or catalogs for policies.
3. Rather than awarding credit for a successful exam, some colleges allow exemption from the clepped course. The student then replaces the course with an elective or higher-level course. This may or may not fit into your plans.
4. Taking CLEP tests in the student's major area of study can be an inferior learning experience to the interaction of the live classroom.
5. If a student fails a CLEP exam, he must wait six months before retaking it. This can be problematic if the exam served as the prerequisite to another course or the student's graduation date is approaching.
6. If the student plans to pursue a college degree that is a mixture of "clepping" and classroom courses, it is imperative that he understand the effect, if any, early CLEP credit may have on his freshman status. Some of the best scholarship money goes to college freshman. The financial advantages of the CLEP can rapidly disappear if scholarships are lost in the process.

Although I am not opposed to the CLEP and see some real advantages when it is used strategically, I do have one significant misgiving. In some circumstances the CLEP is not a positive choice to do something helpful for a student but rather represents a judgment against the college environment. The truth of the matter is that many college experiences are academically and morally bad and should be avoided. Other college experiences, however, are life expanding and enriching, helping a student become the person God desires him to be.

This has been the case with our third child. He attended a Christian college and double majored in English and philosophy. The school has an excellent worldview curriculum required of all students. This commitment to conscientiously building a Christian worldview in their students made me comfortable with my son's instruction in his philosophy courses. His friendships were the type that will endure far beyond college. His college experience has forged who he is becoming. Wholesale "clepping" would have been a poor substitute for what his college experience has given him.

Early College Enrollment

Early college enrollment is often called dual or concurrent enrollment. A student who is dually enrolled takes college courses while still in high school. Many homeschoolers begin their college studies under a dual/ concurrent enrollment agreement with a local junior or community college. Four-year colleges and universities may also offer dual-enrollment programs. These courses are generally taken at the college campus although colleges may offer Internet or correspondence course options. The college credit may be held and officially awarded after the college receives proof of high school completion. A completed transcript with a date of graduation should be acceptable proof.

Students enrolling in the concurrent credit program may be required to pass a general college placement test before receiving permission to take courses. Course loads are usually limited. However, policies and procedures for taking and crediting dual enrollment courses will change from school to school. To avoid misunderstandings and potential disappointment, research school policies carefully.

ADVANTAGES TO EARLY COLLEGE ENROLLMENT

1. When college admissions counselors are skeptical of a homeschool transcript, successful dual enrollment courses provide additional proof of the student's capabilities.
2. Students can get a taste of college before leaving home, making the college transition easier.
3. Sometimes college credits earned before the high-school graduation date do not affect freshman standing (and scholarship money) regardless of the number of credits earned. This can change from institution to institution.
4. Getting some courses out of the way can bring extra flexibility to the student's schedule at the senior university. This allows him to take additional courses in his major, enjoy more electives, double major, take a lighter load during difficult semesters, or graduate early.
5. Several advantages occur when taking difficult courses such as a lab science or math courses by dual enrollment.

- The student receives good instruction while relieving the parent of a substantial preparation burden.
- The student can complete a difficult course before he has the stress of juggling a full college load.
- Since GPAs generally do not transfer from institution to institution, these courses can be taken without affecting the student's GPA at the senior university. (Negatively, a low GPA in dual-credit courses can affect scholarship awards to the senior university.)

DISADVANTAGES TO EARLY COLLEGE ENROLLMENT

1. Earning college credits can affect a student's freshman standing when applying to four-year institutions. This may disqualify your student for scholarships offered only to four-year students. (Check policies at the senior university carefully.)
2. Many community college courses, such as courses in technical fields, are not part of the academic core transferable to senior universities. Choose dual enrollment courses with care, or they may not transfer.
3. Taking college courses at a younger age may expose homeschool students to issues and situations they are not yet prepared to handle. If this is a concern, check to see if your local junior or community college offers any classes via the Internet.
4. Once college is begun, students can lose zeal for the rest of the schoolwork to be done at home.

FINAL NOTE

Although I have used early, dual, and concurrent enrollment as synonymous terms, they can hold small, but possibly important, differences in meaning. A thorough understanding of any particular college's program can be obtained from an admissions counselor or from the school's catalog.

College Courses and Degrees
by Correspondence

Although it has been possible to earn an advanced degree by correspondence for many years, the distance learning choices are increasing. With the technology now available through the Internet, this trend will continue to grow. However, any time a new field opens, businesses can spring up rapidly. Not all will be reputable. It is no different with distance learning.

Research all schools offering degrees by correspondence carefully. Dr. John Bear has been researching these schools for years. *Bear's Guide to Earning Degrees by Distance Learning* is a large volume with a comprehensive selection of programs. *College Degrees by Mail and Internet*, also by Bear, reviews only the correspondence schools he considers especially praiseworthy. Jason D. Baker's book, *Baker's Guide to Christian Distance Education* may also prove helpful to you. Another option is Peterson's *The Independent Study Catalog*. A visit to a large bookstore may reveal even more choices. Two Web sites, www.geteducated.com and www.petersons.com, are also helpful.

ADVANTAGES TO CORRESPONDENCE

1. Courses are often reasonably priced.
2. You can study at your convenience.
3. Many well-reputed state universities offer correspondence.
4. Scheduling difficulties for nonmajor courses at the student's resident college can be overcome by using correspondence.

DISADVANTAGES TO CORRESPONDENCE

1. There are many illegitimate diploma mills operating. Check the school's credentials carefully. The guides mentioned above will be especially helpful.
2. Be careful if looking for transfer credit. Many colleges limit the amount of correspondence credit they will accept into their degree program.
3. Not all college courses or majors are available via correspondence.

SECTION TWELVE

Reflecting on the Journey

My goal in writing this book has been to equip parents to make clear-sighted, practical schooling choices that help students reach their potential. However, I know your mind may be spinning with all the information we have covered together. Before closing I would like to share my heart with parents who are overwhelmed with their homeschooling task or are experiencing difficulty with their teens.

Homeschooling Imperfection

Even though I have written a how-to book on high school homeschooling, do not assume that my homeschool is always neatly packaged. My academic plans have not unfolded flawlessly. Like the shoeless cobbler's children, my record keeping does not always follow my own best advice. As a person who loves order and predictability, I have certainly tried. But children aren't like furniture that we arrange to our liking and know it will stay put. Children are dynamic, always changing, and I have sometimes been slow in matching my expectations to the young person unfolding before me.

At times it has been a roller-coaster ride. Sometimes a child puts the queasiness in the ride; sometimes it is brought on by my own attitudes. My children have often filled me with joy. They have also filled me with emotions that are not listed under the fruit of the Spirit. As a parent striving to grow them up in the Lord, I am growing up myself.

Our children's college experiences have also developed in unforeseen directions not always in line with my careful planning. You would think we had a household competition to see how many different ways college credit could be accumulated. My two boys have earned their degrees with a mixture of community college, state university, and private Christian college. My oldest daughter completed her undergraduate program with credits earned four ways: community college, two state universities, and correspondence credit. CLEP testing also received serious consideration. I guess since my students are products of what some consider a radical educational choice—homeschooling—I should not have expected them to tackle education in simple, traditional ways. Although chaotic at times, it has added a strong foundation of personal experience to the college portion of this book!

While this book is the product of what I have done right, it is also the product of lessons learned the hard way. Hopefully, it will help you avoid some errors in your homeschool experience. My prayer is that my writing will not overwhelm you. Please take my advice and adjust it to your situation, fully aware that I didn't get it all right either.

OUR BIBLICAL COMFORT

It is easy for homeschool parents to feel overwhelmed. Many success stories float around homeschool circles. At times it seems that every homeschool family except ours has students who love learning, are behaviorally flawless, run successful home businesses, are National Merit Scholar finalists, and defer to mom and dad for every important decision in life. Without stepping into another homeschooler's home, I can assure you on the best authority, the Word of God, that perfect homeschool households do not exist.

First, the Bible makes clear that we are all sinners. Rather than being a demoralizing reminder, it's a guilt-relieving doctrine. This truth makes us realize that homeschooling does not create perfect homes, perfect parents, or perfect children. That is the life work of Jesus Christ. And while homeschooling can contribute greatly to nurturing our children in the Lord, it doesn't cause the problem of sin to disappear. In fact, as we live closely with each other, sometimes it seems that our sin abounds! Despite our great desire, we cannot homeschool the sin nature out of our children. Our sin struggles, both child and parent alike, are daily reminders of how greatly we need the Lord Jesus and His sacrifice.

Keep your homeschooling in perspective. A God-honoring homeschooled upbringing is a wonderful gift to any child, but don't tarnish your efforts by placing expectations on your homeschooling that only God can fulfill.

Second, all problems are not handled easily. Sometimes I nostalgically remember earlier years when problems could be solved with a kiss and a rock in the rocking chair. A teen's life is not so simple. Helping him solve problems often means a willingness to listen, and listen for a long time, when you would rather be doing something else. God will bless you for pausing in your activities to make eye contact and listen with both ears.

Third, when we hand our high schoolers their diploma, they are not finished products. Yet, as homeschool parents, we sometimes expect them to be. We may find our emotions defining our daily existence. The right decisions our children make can leave us in triumph, justified in our labor of love. Unfortunately, every wrong decision can leave us wondering how they could forget the lessons we worked so hard to put in them.

Sometimes it comes as a shock to realize our teens are autonomous individuals. Surprise! All of those years of homeschooling may not have produced a mom or dad clone. Our teen's thoughts and actions are his own. Sometimes those thoughts and actions will carry a clear stamp of his upbringing; sometimes they will not. Just as we learned some of life's lessons the hard way to the dismay of our parents, so will our teens.

Remember, God's work of sanctification unfolds in a Christian over a lifetime, and a newly graduated homeschooler is continuing in that process, not completing it. We must give our children the same opportunity to grow in grace that God gives us. Every decision they make will not be wise, any more than all of our decisions as parents are seasoned with wisdom. Let a realization of this truth sow patience as we view the imperfections of our shared humanity.

Finally, it is hard letting go. As homeschoolers, we have kept our children more closely by our side than most parents. The growth in independence that begins gradually when most children are dropped off at the kindergarten door can hit us almost overnight as our high schooler finishes his homeschool program. Despite after-school jobs, summer camps, and other wing-testing opportunities, the break can be more sudden for homeschool parents.

As our children become adults, in a real sense we return our caregiver responsibilities to God. If our teen is a Christian, we have confidence that God loves him perfectly and completely. We know He watches over him more diligently than we ever could and that His powers of influence have unsurpassed strength. We don't know what the future holds for our teen, nor has God chosen to reveal all the details to us. Part of our growth in grace is trusting Him just the same.

Appendix A

Resources

B oth secular and Christian resources are included, so discretion may be needed to sift out some occasional chaff. On the whole, however, you will find a wealth of helpful information.

COLLEGE INFORMATION

Advanced Placement Classes

www.pahomeschoolers.com

College—general help/college search

www.collegeboard.com
www.campuslifecollegeguide.com
www.ecampustours.com
www.petersons.com
www.usnews.com

College Search—distance learning

www.geteducated.com
www.petersons.com

College Search—homeschool-friendly schools

www.hslda.org (go to the issues library)

College Testing

ACT: www.actstudent.org
PSAT, SAT, AP, CLEP: www.collegeboard.com

College Financial Aid

FastWeb: www.fastweb.com
Finaid: www.finaid.com

EXTERNAL COLLEGE DEGREE PROGRAMS

ACE CREDIT
One Dupont Circle, NW
Washington, DC 20036
202-939-9300
www.acenet.edu

Charter Oak State College
55 Paul Manafort Drive
New Britain, CT 06053-2150
860-832-3800
www.charteroak.edu

Excelsior College
7 Columbia Circle
Albany, NY 12203-5159
888-647-2388
www.excelsior.edu

Thomas Edison State College
101 West State Street
Trenton, NJ 08608-1176
888-442-8372
www.tesc.edu

SPECIAL NEEDS WEB SITES

For Homeschoolers

www.NATHHAN.com. The National Challenged Homeschoolers Associated Network is a support Web site for parents who are homeschooling a special-needs child. Archived articles, resources, and classifieds are included. A discussion board and additional resources are available for members.

www.TXSpecialKids.org. Begun in Texas, but expanding nationwide, Texas Special Kids offers individual family support to those raising special-needs children. The Arnolds frequently speak at homeschool conventions. Check their Web site for upcoming seminars.

General Sites

www.schwablearning.org. Founded by Helen and Charles Schwab of the large investment firm to give parents information on disabilities. Both Mr. Schwab and his son are dyslexic. This is a great informational Web site.
www.ldonline.org (parents informational section)
www.collegeboard.com/ssd/student (procedure for accommodations on PSAT, SAT, and AP exams)
www.act.org/aap/disab (for ACT accommodations)

NATIONAL ORGANIZATIONS

Home School Legal Defense Association
(National Center for Home Education)
P.O. Box 3000
Purcellville, VA 20134
540-338-5600
www.hslda.org

NATHHAN
(National Challenged Homeschoolers Associated Network)
P.O. Box 310
Moyie Springs, ID 83845
208-267-6246
www.NATHHAN.com

Summit Ministries
P.O. Box 207
Manitou Springs, CO 80829
719-685-9103
www.summit.org

Texas's Special Kids
P.O. Box 151335
Arlington, TX 76015
www.TXSpecialKids.org
(will help outside TX)

Worldview Academy
P.O. Box 2918
Midland, TX 79702
800-241-1123
www.worldview.org

RETAIL AVAILABILITY OF HOMESCHOOL MATERIALS

Homeschool Headquarters
www.homeschoolheadquarters.com

CORRESPONDENCE SCHOOLS AND PUBLISHERS

This list contains address information for major correspondence schools and smaller publishers whose materials are not always widely available through bookstores or home-school catalogs. It is not meant to be exhaustive. With address information in continual flux, the Internet is usually your best source for updated information.

A Beka Book, Inc.
Box 19100
Pensacola, FL 32523-9100
877-223-5226
www.abeka.com

A Beka Academy (distance learning)
P.O. Box 17600
Pensacola, FL 32522-7600
800-874-3592
www.abekaacademy.org

Academy of Home Education
See Bob Jones University Press

Alpha Omega
804 N 2nd Avenue East
Rock Rapids, IA 51246
800-622-3070

Alpha Omega Academy: 800-682-7396
(offers both Lifepac and Switched on Schoolhouse options)
www.aop.com

American School
2200 E. 170th St.
Lansing, IL 60438
www.americanschoolofcorr.com

American Textbook Committee
(check Internet sources, such as
www.cumberlandbooks.com)

American Vision
P.O. Box 220
Powder Springs, GA 30127
770-222-7266
800-628-9460 (orders)
www.americanvision.org

Beginnings Publishing House, Inc.
328 Shady Lane
Alvaton, KY 42122
800-831-3570
www.beginningspublishing.com

Bob Jones University Press, also:
Academy of Home Education
HomeSat
Testing and Evaluation
1700 Wade Hampton Blvd.
Greenville, SC 29614
800-845-5731
www.bjupress.com

Cadron Creek Christian Curriculum
4329 Pinos Altos Road
Silver City, NM 88061
505-534-1496
www.cadroncreek.com

Canon Press
P.O. Box 8729
Moscow, ID 83843
800-488-2034
www.canonpress.org

Castlemoyle Books
P.O. Box 520
Pomeroy, WA 99347
509-843-5009
www.castlemoyle.com

Chalk Dust Company
PMB 375
3506 Hwy 6 South
Sugar Land, TX 77478-4401
800-588-7564
www.chalkdust.com

Christian Liberty Academy/Press
502 W. Euclid Ave.
Arlington Heights, IL 60004-5495
Catalog: 800-832-2741
Academy: 800-348-0899
www.homeschools.org

Cornerstone Curriculum Project
2006 Flat Creek
Richardson, TX 75080
972-235-5149
www.cornerstonecurriculum.com

Covenant Home Curriculum
N63 W23421 Main Street
Sussex, WI 53089
800-578-2421
www.covenanthome.com

Covenant Publications
224 Auburn Avenue
Monroe, LA 71201
318-323-3061
e-mail: swilkins@auburnavenue.org

Crown Financial Ministries
Gainesville, GA 30503
800-722-1976
www.crown.org

Cumberland Books
P.O. Box 558
Russell Springs KY 42642
877-244-5184
www.cumberlandbooks.com

Design a Study
408 Victoria Avenue
Wilmington, DE 19804-2124
www.designastudy.com
800-965-2719

D.I.V.E. into Math
26484 El Indio Rd.
Waller, TX 77484
936-372-9216
www.diveintomath.com

Eagle Christian High School
2526 Sunset Lane
Missoula, MT 59804
406-322-2722
www.eaglechristian.org

Edcon Publishing Group
30 Montauk Boulevard
Oakdale, NY 11769-1399
888-553-3266
www.edconpublishing.com

Escondido Tutorial Service
Escondido, CA
www.gbt.org

Geography Matters
P.O. Box 92
Nancy, KY 42544
606-636-4678
www.geomatters.com

God's World News
P.O. Box 20001
Asheville, NC 28802
800-951-5437
www.gwnews.com

Great Books Academy
P.O. Box 10726
Bainbridge Island, WA 98110
800-521-4004
www.greatbooksacademy.org

Harcourt Achieve
(Publishers of Saxon Math)
Attn: Cust. Service 5th floor
6277 Sea Harbor Drive
Orlando, FL 32887
800-284-7019
www.harcourtachieve.com

Heart of Dakota Publishing
1004 Westview Drive
Dell Rapids, SD 57022
605-428-4068
www.heartofdakota.com

HomeScholar Books
2311 Harrison Road
Nashville, NC 27856
252-459-9279
www.homescholar.org

Home School in the Woods
3997 Roosevelt Highway
Holley, NY 14470
585-964-8188
www.homeschoolinthewoods.com

Institute for Excellence in Writing
P.O. Box 6065
Atascadero, CA 93423
800-856-5815
www.writing-edu.com

Key Curriculum Press
1150 65th Street
Emeryville, CA 94608
800-995-MATH
www.keycurriculumpress.com

Keystone National High School
420 West 5th St.
Bloomsburg, PA 17815-1564
800-255-4937
www.keystonehighschool.com

Konos, Inc.
P.O. Box 250
Anna, TX 75409
972-924-2712
www.konos.com

Lighthouse Christian Academy
P.O. Box 7300
Seminole, FL 33775-7300
866-746-6534
www.schooloftomorrow.com

Mapping the World by Heart
P.O. Box 253
Belmont, MA 02478
617-868-8575
www.mapping.com

Math U See
www.mathusee.com
(The Web site will connect you to a distributor in
your area.)

Paradigm Company
P.O. Box 45161
Boise, ID 83711
208-322-4440
www.howtotutor.com

Phonics Tutor
P.O. Box 421027
Minneapolis, MN 55442-0027
888-420-READ
www.phonicstutor.com

The Potter's School
8279 Raindrop Way
Springfield, VA 22153
703-690-3516
www.pottersschool.org

Providence Project
14566 NW 110th Street
Whitewater, KS 67154
888-776-8776
www.providenceproject.com

Rod and Staff Publishers, Inc.
P.O. Box 3 Hwy 172
Crockett, KY 41413-0003
606-522-4348

Rose Publishing, Inc.
4733 Torrance Blvd. #259
Torrance, CA 90503
800-532-4278
www.rose-publishing.com

Runkle Publishers
(Orders fulfilled by Geography Matters)
4018 Briarcrest
Norman, OK 73072
405-329-6750
www.runklepub.com

Sandra Betzina
Power Sewing/Nancy Schwab
1390 Pine St. 302
San Francisco, CA 94109
415-359-0440
www.sandrabetzinaonline.com

Schola Publications
1698 Market Street #162
Redding, CA 96001
530-275-064
www.thelatinroad.com

Scholar's Online
P.O. Box 6039
Bellevue, WA 98008
541-490-9353
www.scholarsonline.org

School of Tomorrow/ACE Ministries
P.O. Box 299000
Lewisville, TX 75029-9000
800-925-7777
www.schooloftomorrow.com

School Specialty Publishing
P.O. Box 141487
Grand Rapids, MI 49514-1487
800-417-3261
www.schoolspecialtypublishing.com

Soli Deo Gloria Publications
A Division of Ligonier Ministries
P.O. Box 54700
Orlando, FL 32854-7500
800-435-4343
www.ligonier.org

Sonlight Curriculum Ltd.
8042 South Grant Way

Littleton, CO 80122-2705
303-730-6292
www.sonlight.com

Summit Ministries
P.O. Box 207
Manitou Springs, CO 80829
719-685-9103
www.summit.org

Sycamore Tree
(book or computer-based correspondence)
2179 Meyer Place
Costa Mesa, CA 92627
714-668-1343
www.sycamoretree.com

The Teaching Company
4151 Lafayette Center Drive, Suite 100
Chantilly, VA 20151-1232
800-832-2412
www.teach12.com

Teaching Tape Technology
9975 Chemstrand Road
Pensacola, FL 32514
850-475-7860
www.teachingtape.com

Teaching Textbooks Distribution
P.O. Box 60529
Oklahoma City, OK 73146-0529
866-867-6284
www.teachingtextbooks.com

Texas Tech University
Outreach and Extended Studies
6901 Quaker Avenue
Lubbock, TX 79413
800-692-6877
www.dce.ttu.edu

Tom Snyder Productions
100 Talcott Avenue
Watertown, MA 02472-5703
800-342-0236
www.tomsnyder.com

Total Language Plus
www.totallanguageplus.com
(See Web site for sales rep in your area.)

Truth Quest History
P.O. Box 2128
Traverse City, MI 49685-2128
www.truthquesthistory.com

University of Nebraska-Lincoln
Independent Study High School
Customer Service P.O. Box 888400
Lincoln, NE 68588-8400
866-700-4747
www.nebraskahs.unl.edu

Vic Lockman
233 Rogue River Hwy, #360
Grants Pass, OR 97527
www.viclockman.com

VideoText Interactive
800-254-3272
www.videotext.com

Vision Video
P.O. Box 540
Worcester, PA 19490
800-523-0226
www.visionvideo.com

Wordsmith
1355 Ferry Road
Grants Pass, OR 97526
541-476-3080
www.jsgrammar.com

BOOKS ON HIGH SCHOOL AND COLLEGE

Adams-Gordon, Beverly. *Home School, High School, and Beyond*. Pomeroy, Wash.: Castlemoyle Books, 1999. A nine-week course that involves a teen in planning his high school course of study.

The following three books by Cafi Cohen contain much helpful information. Published by secular publishers, you will find a heavier inclusion of unschooling ideology than is found in publications widely available on the Christian homeschool market.

Cohen, Cafi. *And What about College? 2nd ed.* Cambridge, Mass.: Holt Associates, 2000. A helpful biographical presentation of one family's successful road to college admission.

Cohen, Cafi. *Homeschoolers' College Admissions Handbook.* Roseville, Calif.: Prima Publishing, 2000. More advice on college admissions from Cafi Cohen with suggestions from other home schoolers sprinkled liberally throughout.

Cohen, Cafi. *Homeschooling the Teen Years.* Roseville, Calif.: Prima Publishing, 2000. Another book full of anecdotal information from many homeschool families.

College Board. *The College Board Book of Majors, 2nd ed.* New York: College Board, 2006. Want to find out which colleges offer which majors, along with the requirements, courses, and accompanying career opportunities? This is the book!

Dennis, Jeanne Gowen. *Homeschooling High School.* Lynnwood, Wash.: Emerald Books, 2004. The results of Dennis's extensive college survey on attitudes toward homeschoolers, admissions policies, etc., are a unique and helpful feature of this book.

Duffy, Cathy. *100 Top Pick for Homeschool Curriculum: Choosing the Right Curriculum and Approach for Your Child's Learning Style.* Nashville, Tenn.: Broadman & Holman, 2005. Although not limited to high school, Cathy Duffy's book includes and reviews a number of junior-high and high-school curriculum choices. In addition, her information on learning styles is helpful and thorough.

Kravets, Marybeth, Imy F. Wax and The Princeton Review. *The K&W Guide to College for Students with Learning Disabilities or Attention Deficit Disorder, 8th ed.* New York: Random House, 2005.

Matthews, Arlene. *Getting in without Freaking Out: The Official College Admissions Guide for Overwhelmed Parents.* New York: Three Rivers Press, 2006. This helpful little book is filled with wise advice presented in short, humorous chapters. After you have worked yourself into a lather over college details, read this book as an antidote.

Mathews, Jay. *Harvard Schmarvard: Getting Beyond the Ivy League to the College That Is Best for You.* New York: Three Rivers Press, 2003. Any student or parent who dreams big about college entrance will learn a great deal from this book. Mr. Mathews has a pleasing, easy-to-read writing style.

BOOKS FOR PARENTS

Priolo, Lou. *The Heart of Anger.* New York: Calvary Press, 1997. Excellent biblical advice on dealing with a child with an angry heart. In the process of seeking help for the child, you'll also find help for the parent!

Tripp, Paul David. *Age of Opportunity.* Phillipsburg, N. J.: P&R Publishing, 1997. Tripp encourages us to see the teen years as a time of opportunity for spiritual growth in both teen and parent.

Tripp, Paul David. *War of Words: Getting to the Heart of Your Communication Struggles.* Phillipsburg, N. J.: P&R Publishing, 1997. This excellent book encourages us to examine the heart from which our words spring and our relationship with God and others.

RESOURCES FOR TEST PREPARATION

Resources for test preparation are updated regularly. Always purchase the most current edition.

ACT Publications. *The Real ACT Prep Guide.* Iowa City, Iowa: Peterson, 2005.
By the makers of the ACT test, this guide includes test-taking tips, information on the new ACT writing test, and three real ACT tests.

The Princeton Review. *Cracking the ACT.* New York: The Princeton Review, 2007. Test-taking tips and study help. The book includes two full-length practice tests. Available with or without a DVD. The DVD contains extra tests, video tutorials, and other helps.

Barron's *CLEP 2007-2008.* Hauppauge, N. Y.: Barron's Educational Services, 2007. This guide presents study help for the CLEP general examinations. Available with or without a DVD. The DVD contains the same tests as the book but with the convenience of automatic scoring.

College Board. *CLEP Official Study Guide.* New York: College Board, 2006. This is the only CLEP book that has sample questions for all thirty-five CLEP tests.

Barron's. *How to Prepare for the PSAT/NMSQT.* Hauppauge, N. Y.: Barron's Educational Services, 2006. This guide presents study help for the PSAT/NMSQT, no CD-ROM of additional testing.

College Board. *The Official SAT Study Guide.* New York: College Board, 2004. This study book from the makers of the test includes eight full-length practice tests. The essay portion is covered with suggested writing prompts, sample essays, and the essay scoring guide.

Kaplan. *SAT Premier Program 2008 Edition.* New York: Simon & Schuster, 2007. Test-taking tips and study help. Includes nine full-length practice tests, four in the book and five on the CD-ROM. Word roots and families, a vocabulary list, and "SAT Math and English in a Nutshell" are included in the resources. Book purchasers are offered additional online services at www.kaptest.com/SATbooksonline.

Kaplan. *SAT Writing Workbook.* New York: Simon & Schuster, 2006. Provides additional practice for the new writing test. Spends fifty pages on the essay instead of the approximately twenty pages in the larger general prep books. The writers actually employ some humor in their writing. Does not stress using literature and historical references to the same extent as Princeton Review.

Chalk Dust Company. *SAT Math Review.* Sugar Land, Tex.: Chalk Dust Company. Over fourteen hours of DVD instruction for the math skills tested on the SAT.

The Princeton Review. *Cracking the SAT, 2008 ed.* New York: The Princeton Review: 2007. Test-taking tips and study help includes three full-length practice tests. Book purchasers are offered additional online services available at www.princetonreview.com including access to four additional tests.

Appendix B

Forms

The forms in Appendix B are to help you plan and organize your high school course of study. Feel free to photocopy any of these forms for your personal homeschool. They are also included on the CD-ROM.

FOUR-YEAR STUDY PLAN FOR _____

9TH-GRADE COURSES	CREDIT	10TH-GRADE COURSES	CREDIT
Total		Total	

11TH-GRADE COURSES	CREDIT	12TH-GRADE COURSES	CREDIT
Total		Total	

TOTAL CREDITS BY SUBJECT AREA

Bible		Computers	
English		Foreign Language	
Math		Fine Arts	
Science		Health and P.E.	
Social Studies		Misc. Electives	
FOUR-YEAR TOTAL _____			

ONE-YEAR STUDY PLAN

Name: _____ Grade: _____ Year: _____

COURSE TITLE	TEXTS OR MATERIALS

Notes:

Educational Plan

Name:

School Year:

Goal:

Materials:

Steps to Accomplishing Goal:	Completed

Evaluation:

PRELIMINARY COURSE CONTRACT	
NAME:	SCHOOL YEAR:
COURSE:	CREDIT ASSIGNED:

REQUIREMENTS:	DATE COMPLETED
GRADING METHOD	

COMPLETED COURSE CONTRACT

NAME:	SCHOOL YEAR:
COURSE:	CREDIT EARNED:
PARENT'S SIGNATURE:	GRADE:

COURSE DESCRIPTION

CREDITING AND GRADING DATA

GRADE

Criteria	% earned	x	possible points	% of final grade
			Total %	
			Final Grade	

TIME RECORD #1

NAME: SCHOOL YEAR: COURSE:

Hours	15 min. div.	Book or Activity	Hours	15 min. div.	Book or Activity
1	☐☐☐☐		31	☐☐☐☐	
2	☐☐☐☐		32	☐☐☐☐	
3	☐☐☐☐		33	☐☐☐☐	
4	☐☐☐☐		34	☐☐☐☐	
5	☐☐☐☐		35	☐☐☐☐	
6	☐☐☐☐		36	☐☐☐☐	
7	☐☐☐☐		37	☐☐☐☐	
8	☐☐☐☐		38	☐☐☐☐	
9	☐☐☐☐		39	☐☐☐☐	
10	☐☐☐☐		40	☐☐☐☐	
11	☐☐☐☐		41	☐☐☐☐	
12	☐☐☐☐		42	☐☐☐☐	
13	☐☐☐☐		43	☐☐☐☐	
14	☐☐☐☐		44	☐☐☐☐	
15	☐☐☐☐		45	☐☐☐☐	
16	☐☐☐☐		46	☐☐☐☐	
17	☐☐☐☐		47	☐☐☐☐	
18	☐☐☐☐		48	☐☐☐☐	
19	☐☐☐☐		49	☐☐☐☐	
20	☐☐☐☐		50	☐☐☐☐	
21	☐☐☐☐		51	☐☐☐☐	
22	☐☐☐☐		52	☐☐☐☐	
23	☐☐☐☐		53	☐☐☐☐	
24	☐☐☐☐		54	☐☐☐☐	
25	☐☐☐☐		55	☐☐☐☐	
26	☐☐☐☐		56	☐☐☐☐	
27	☐☐☐☐		57	☐☐☐☐	
28	☐☐☐☐		58	☐☐☐☐	
29	☐☐☐☐		59	☐☐☐☐	
30	☐☐☐☐		60	☐☐☐☐	

Notes

TIME RECORD #2

NAME: SCHOOL YEAR: COURSE:

Hours	15 min. div.	Book or Activity	Hours	15 min. div.	Book or Activity
61	☐☐☐☐		91	☐☐☐☐	
62	☐☐☐☐		92	☐☐☐☐	
63	☐☐☐☐		93	☐☐☐☐	
64	☐☐☐☐		94	☐☐☐☐	
65	☐☐☐☐		95	☐☐☐☐	
66	☐☐☐☐		96	☐☐☐☐	
67	☐☐☐☐		97	☐☐☐☐	
68	☐☐☐☐		98	☐☐☐☐	
69	☐☐☐☐		99	☐☐☐☐	
70	☐☐☐☐		100	☐☐☐☐	
71	☐☐☐☐		101	☐☐☐☐	
72	☐☐☐☐		102	☐☐☐☐	
73	☐☐☐☐		103	☐☐☐☐	
74	☐☐☐☐		104	☐☐☐☐	
75	☐☐☐☐		105	☐☐☐☐	
76	☐☐☐☐		106	☐☐☐☐	
77	☐☐☐☐		107	☐☐☐☐	
78	☐☐☐☐		108	☐☐☐☐	
79	☐☐☐☐		109	☐☐☐☐	
80	☐☐☐☐		110	☐☐☐☐	
81	☐☐☐☐		111	☐☐☐☐	
82	☐☐☐☐		112	☐☐☐☐	
83	☐☐☐☐		113	☐☐☐☐	
84	☐☐☐☐		114	☐☐☐☐	
85	☐☐☐☐		115	☐☐☐☐	
86	☐☐☐☐		116	☐☐☐☐	
87	☐☐☐☐		117	☐☐☐☐	
88	☐☐☐☐		118	☐☐☐☐	
89	☐☐☐☐		119	☐☐☐☐	
90	☐☐☐☐		120	☐☐☐☐	

Notes

TIME RECORD #3

NAME: SCHOOL YEAR: COURSE:

Hours	15 min. div.	Book or Activity	Hours	15 min. div.	Book or Activity
121	☐☐☐☐		151	☐☐☐☐	
122	☐☐☐☐		152	☐☐☐☐	
123	☐☐☐☐		153	☐☐☐☐	
124	☐☐☐☐		154	☐☐☐☐	
125	☐☐☐☐		155	☐☐☐☐	
126	☐☐☐☐		156	☐☐☐☐	
127	☐☐☐☐		157	☐☐☐☐	
128	☐☐☐☐		158	☐☐☐☐	
129	☐☐☐☐		159	☐☐☐☐	
130	☐☐☐☐		160	☐☐☐☐	
131	☐☐☐☐		161	☐☐☐☐	
132	☐☐☐☐		162	☐☐☐☐	
133	☐☐☐☐		163	☐☐☐☐	
134	☐☐☐☐		164	☐☐☐☐	
135	☐☐☐☐		165	☐☐☐☐	
136	☐☐☐☐		166	☐☐☐☐	
137	☐☐☐☐		167	☐☐☐☐	
138	☐☐☐☐		168	☐☐☐☐	
139	☐☐☐☐		169	☐☐☐☐	
140	☐☐☐☐		170	☐☐☐☐	
141	☐☐☐☐		171	☐☐☐☐	
142	☐☐☐☐		172	☐☐☐☐	
143	☐☐☐☐		173	☐☐☐☐	
144	☐☐☐☐		174	☐☐☐☐	
145	☐☐☐☐		175	☐☐☐☐	
146	☐☐☐☐		176	☐☐☐☐	
147	☐☐☐☐		177	☐☐☐☐	
148	☐☐☐☐		178	☐☐☐☐	
149	☐☐☐☐		179	☐☐☐☐	
150	☐☐☐☐		180	☐☐☐☐	

Notes

COMPUTING A GPA

NINTH GRADE				TENTH GRADE			
COURSE	1st semester grade/points	2nd semester grade/points	# of semesters	COURSE	1st semester grade/points	2nd semester grade/points	# of semesters
Total grade points by semester				Total grade points by semester			
Total grade points and semesters				Total grade points and semesters			
Total grade points for year divided by total semesters of class = GPA				Total grade points for year divided by total semesters of class = GPA			

ELEVENTH GRADE				TWELFTH GRADE			
COURSE	1st semester grade/points	2nd semester grade/points	# of semesters	COURSE	1st semester grade/points	2nd semester grade/points	# of semesters
Total grade points by semester				Total grade points by semester			
Total grade points and semesters				Total grade points and semesters			
Total grade points for year divided by total semesters of class = GPA				Total grade points for year divided by total semesters of class = GPA			

Add four yearly grade points together:
Divide total grade points by four to get final grade point average:

FINAL GRADE POINT AVERAGE =

READING LIST	
TITLE	**AUTHOR**

ACADEMIC TRANSCRIPT RECORD

Name:

Address:

Date of Birth: Sex:

Social Security Number:

Parents/Guardian:

School:

Credits Earned: GPA:

Date of Graduation:

Date Transcript Issued:

Date of College Entry:

Administrator's Signature:

NINTH GRADE   YEAR:

COURSE	1ST SEM	2ND SEM	FINAL GRADE	CREDIT

9TH GRADE GPA: 9TH GRADE CREDITS:

TENTH GRADE   YEAR:

COURSE	1ST SEM	2ND SEM	FINAL GRADE	CREDIT

10TH GRADE GPA: 10TH GRADE CREDITS:

ELEVENTH GRADE   YEAR:

11TH GRADE GPA: 11TH GRADE CREDITS:

TWELFTH GRADE   YEAR:

12TH GRADE GPA: 12TH GRADE CREDITS:

Academic Transcript (page 2)

Summary of Credits

Test Scores

Total Credits:

ADDITIONAL INFORMATION

STUDENT CONTACT INFORMATION